FROM INDIANS TO CHICANOS

THIRD EDITION

FROM INDIANS TO CHICANOS

The Dynamics of Mexican-American Culture

THIRD EDITION

James Diego Vigil

University of California, Irvine

WAVELAND

PRESS, INC.

Long Grove, Illinois

For information about this book, contact:
Waveland Press, Inc.
4180 IL Route 83, Suite 101
Long Grove, IL 60047-9580
(847) 634-0081
info@waveland.com
www.waveland.com

Cover mural:
Title: "Nuestra Vida." (Our Life). Painted by Creative Solutions, S.T.E.P.
Jesus Julian Estrada, Karla, Shyrel, Lilian, Yionara, Oscar, Robert, Mario, and Sandra.
Funded by Los Angeles Conservation Corps. Rodriguez & Sons Market, Fourth St.
and Euclid in East Los Angeles.

To Polly,
my friendly critic and lifelong companion

CONTENTS

STAGE 1

Pre-Columbian Period
30,000 BC–AD 1519

STAGE II

Spanish Colonial Era
1521–1821

STAGE III

Mexican Independence and Nationalism
1821–1846

x   Contents

STAGE IV
Anglo-American and Mexicanization Period
1846–Present

FOREWORD

To understand the history of the Chicanos is to understand the Chicano movement. It is this complex, multi-layered history that Diego Vigil has chosen to record. Chicano history is still being written, since the movement has not fully matured.

There is, of course, no typical Chicano; they are an amazingly diverse group even though they have certain common interests and associations. This text is of special importance, not merely for its scholarship and research, but because it reflects the intellectual evolution and maturing point of view of a representative Chicano, Diego Vigil, who first became interested in the Chicano movement in the middle-1960s. His interest has grown and deepened in the years since then.

The Chicano experience differs in significant respects from that of other ethnic minority groups. It has been affected by many influences that have changed with time and in different geographical and socioeconomic settings. It is an experience that must be patiently unfolded, making allowances for regional and historical differences. Not surprisingly, it has created identity problems for those who have been caught up in it, for it involves racial, class, cultural, and national conflicts in the Southwest, a rapidly developing region of different interests and economies. The Chicano experience has accordingly been marginal and exceptional and has been given a variety of interpretations and definitions. To some extent, it reflects the same syncretic experience that occurred in Mexico but with different causes and results.

The diversity of the experience has spawned the so-called Chicano rebellion, which has altered the consciousness of Mexican Americans in ways that set them apart from their parents and the older generation of Spanish-speaking people, as well as the dominant Anglo majority. The movement seems to be guided less by ideologies and theories than by the Chicanos' determination to forge their own identity and to reject outside influences and imported schemes and ideas. The legacy of the Chicano movement has not yet been worked out; it changes and is constantly being analyzed and restated. The fact that Diego Vigil reflects this experience, in addition to reciting its history and causes, makes this text an important contribution to Chicano studies.

Carey McWilliams

PREFACE

$\mathcal{T}$his text has a dual purpose: provide a historical account, tracing the formation of modern-day Chicano culture and lifeways, and, to help effect this, examine key culture-change dynamics of the Chicano past and present. Being subjected to two major wars of conquest and undergoing at least four cultural imprints made for quite a journey that entailed a passage of five hundred years of conflict and change built on repeated controversies and confrontations.

To clarify and order this long and deep account, two conceptual frameworks are utilized to identify key trends and developments. The first one, the Six C's, shows how class, cultural, and color (racial) attitudes and practices were transformed under intense contact, conflict, and change sequences. The other framework specifies how and why macrostructural identities were formed and perpetuated over time. The latter framework provides insights on how indigenous lifeways were interrupted, turning Indians into peasants and still later into migrants and immigrants, as they lost control of land, labor, and wealth at the hands of "others." Further, the increasingly intense globalization of economic ties and networks has made Mexican labor mobile, adding complexity to the immigrant macro identity.

The text is divided into four major historical stages. Stage I, "Pre-Columbian Period," describes the life of Mesoamerican Indians before European contact and ends with the initial phases of the Spanish conquest. Stage II, "Spanish Colonial Era," summarizes three hundred years of rule, documenting the dynamics of class inequality and intense cultural and racial discrimination leading to the early phase of peasantry. Stage III, "Mexican Independence and Nationalism," begins with the promise and fervor of social movements and independence with an autonomous Mexico struggling to achieve nationhood in the later period of peasantry, including activities in its northern reaches (now the U.S. Southwest), and ends with the Mexican–American War of 1846, which began the years of closer Mexican and American ties. Stage IV, "Anglo-American and Mexicanization Period," examines the rise of the Mexican-American people, the effects of large-scale continuing immigration in the twentieth century, the mobilization of the people culminating in the 1960s Chicano movement, and how that event has played out to the present. A post-Anglo Three C's charts developments in the twenty-first century. The text concludes with some comparative observations on the importance of understanding the culture change sequences that indigenous populations undergo and how natives of a land become labeled illegal.

Being remade by "others," into macrostructural categories, was an especially strained process for native Mexicans. The long, drawn-out macrohistorical account considerably altered their cultural (tribal and regional) identities by transforming their economic bases. The latter takes on more significance because indigenous populations presently number in the hundreds of thousands in the United States (immigrants) and along the Mexican/U.S. border (migrants); peasant movements and unrest, such as the Zapatistas in 1994, have periodically erupted along the rural Mexican landscape.

As with all works of such a broad and encompassing nature, so many people and events contributed to the formulation of the first edition, the reformulation of the second edition, and the present third edition that brings us into the twenty-first century. There is not enough space to express my gratitude to all of the students and colleagues who assisted me. First of all are the students who took my class, Culture Change and the Mexican People: North and South of the Border. Those from Chaffey College helped with the initial, innovative formulations, and students from the University of Southern California (USC), the University of California, Los Angeles (UCLA), and the University of California, Irvine built on these ideas, adding many more facts and refinements. I owe these students a lot, for their receptive manner and enthusiasm as well as their critical feedback. Particular recognition is given to Jose Zamora, Bao Lauren Vinh, and Jessica Perez for assisting me on the third edition.

Over the years, several scholars have offered stimulating conversation and keen advice on some of the main issues of the text. Among them are Henry Pontell, Gil Conchas, Rudy Torres, Tom Weaver, Margarita Melville, Robert Alvarez, Steve Arvizu, Sam Rios, Ed Escobar, Juan Gomez-Quinones, Luis Arroyo, and Leo Chavez. The artwork was contributed by Jeffrey Huereque and Mary Nunez, and the maps by Charles Roseman. My son, Nick Vigil, is responsible for the graphics and final illustration of the Six C's model. My former research assistant, Professor Gisella Hanley, helped with the conceptualization of the Six C's illustration and aided immensely on several chapters with new references and ideas to sharpen the focus. Special appreciation is offered to John M. Long, my longtime friend and research associate, who characteristically took the time to edit and refine major themes of the text. Since so much of my thinking and writing has been influenced by the works of Carey McWilliams, his foreword still resonates and brings warm feelings of appreciation for the time and energy he took to write it over thirty years ago.

Over the decades, my wife, Polly, has been invaluable in her support and freely contributed ideas that have improved and sharpened the major objectives of the book. Tireless and critical in her suggestions and guidance, I have never ceased to be amazed by her insights and inventiveness. Although all of the aforementioned people are credited with helping me in this work, I readily accept the responsibility for all errors of fact, judgment, and interpretation.

INTRODUCTION

*W*ith large-scale immigration in the last 20 years and a high birth rate, the Chicano people now comprise the largest ethnic minority in the United States, having surpassed blacks in the early 2000s. At present the population is anywhere from 30 to 40 million, if one includes undocumented immigrant workers. When combined with other Latinos, primarily Puerto Ricans and Cubans, the total is 50.3 million. By 2050, all Latinos will represent 133 million of the U.S. population. In several areas of the American Southwest, which some activists call Aztlan after the legendary Aztec name for the region, Chicanos are in the majority. Indeed, some of these people's ancestors inhabited the Southwest long before its incorporation into the United States; many more Chicanos, because of the changes noted above, are offspring of recent immigrants from Mexico and often maintain close ties with relatives in that country. In fact, the majority of Chicanos in the U.S. are either Mexican-born or second generation. Although the ethnic label "Mexican American" is still used by some people who take pride in being American, the recent trend appears to favor emphasizing the Mexican background and thus using either the label "Mexican" or the label "Chicano."[1]

Why a Dynamic History?

An ethnohistorical interpretation of Chicanos is needed because there are many unique aspects to their background (Koch 2006; Adelman 1999). First, there are the multiple heritages and influences covering several centuries that need to be examined and assessed. What cultural and linguistic blending occurred? What new customs and traits were introduced, and why did some

1

people adjust smoothly and others resist? Significantly, major upheavals and wars have abruptly and radically transformed their lives, causing repercussions that are still with them today. There are books on Mexico proper and works on northern Mexico (now the American Southwest), but few books attempt to grapple with and unravel the complex strands of Chicanos, as the "in-between" people (the people left behind), who straddle both nations, which are separated by a thin but porous borderline. As we shall see, the Chicanos' experience is so complex and marked with the stigma of lower socioeconomic status that it has tended to blur their sociocultural traditions and lifeways. Further, the Chicanos' experience is rapidly changing back to its Mexican roots.

It is in the last five centuries that the most radical and significant changes have taken place, but the movements, settlements, and revampments that have molded Chicanos actually began thousands of years ago. Their early ancestors, the indigenous people, provided them with a rich cultural foundation. (The ethnic label "Chicano" is a derivative of the Aztec tribal name *Mexica*, with the *x* pronounced like *ch*.) The last of these people, the Aztecs, reached a grand plateau of civilization and in some ways were more advanced than other peoples in the world of that time. The process of their displacement by first the Spanish, and later as Mexicans by the Anglo, has had serious effects on their historical evolution. Most of the facts concerning these historical influences are readily available and easily understood.

However, describing the outcome of the merging of Old and New World cultural styles presents a perplexing problem. What was the result of this merging? Were Chicanos forged from that experience? To what degree can one determine the contributions of each culture to the mixture? These questions continue to engage students and researchers alike, as they probe to uncover the complex issues shaping the Chicano people (Flores and Benmayor 1997). Indeed, many of the contrasts, strains, and mergings rooted in these beginnings are still being played out.

This ethnohistorical account attempts to resolve some of these issues. Taking a dynamic approach that charts various time periods and peoples will help the assessment (Mirande 1985). The narrative begins with pre-Columbian Mexico and focuses on over five centuries of problems arising from the struggle for resources. Key to this engagement is how Europeans and their successors repeatedly battled with the indigenous majority population over land, labor, and wealth: who owned it, who worked it, and who benefitted from it (Wolf 1982; Frazier 1957). Not the least of the problems to be illuminated will be the psychological consequences of the suppression suffered by the Chicano people over many centuries. The text will examine how indigenous peoples adapted to new social systems and how social systems also changed.

Macrohistorical Evolution and the Six C's Model of Culture Change

To aid comprehension of such a long, complex epic, this text will look at the evolution of the Chicano people by focusing on questions of land, labor, and wealth, especially as they involved Europeans and their descendants and transformed indigenous people into peasants. As people's relationship to the land changed and control over their labor shifted, the peasants were further displaced and became migrants and immigrants (Kearney 1996). In short order, people working their land were made to work the land for others; in time, their labor also became expendable and mobile—such that they worked in other places and occupations to benefit the wealth of still others.

It is helpful to look at these changes macrohistorically and macrostructurally as a process of "energy capture" with the aid of tools and technology (White 1949). The early evolution of Indian hunting-and-gathering cultures to dependence on agriculture paralleled changes elsewhere in the world, and with the growth of towns and cities, human energy was captured in new ways to aid expansion. Radical shifts in this independent processual evolution began to take place when Europeans entered the picture and captured most of the energy, relegating most natives to a life of peasantry. In time, as larger social and economic networks arose, the Europeans' strivings for land and other resources needed for economic expansion and exchange, as well as their political control, increased (Robinson 2004). In many areas, peasants were uprooted and forced to immigrate to cities to find work. Both peasant and immigrant experiences amounted to a "supraclass" reality of people collected into a larger generic category.

The establishment of "macro-identities" followed with the generation of the abrupt expansion of ways to capture ever more energy in resources and human labor. Ironically, after so many centuries of such machinations the end result is that many of the immigrants still labor as farmworkers. A macrohistorical progression of the additive and cumulative change provides a clear picture of the process. It is a way of looking at land, human labor, and the control of productive energy in a grand conceptual way to understand, for example, why so much wealth today is in the hands of a small, elite segment of the population. It is useful to divide this progression into a series of historical stages or periods. The historical periods show the introduction of new cultural ways of relating to the resources, noting contests and accommodations where necessary, and suggesting future directions. Today, the situations and conditions have changed so radically that the place we call Aztlan is in fact being reconquered by the modern descendants of Chichimecas, the early founders of Mexico; that is, a people bombarded by so many changes

Historical Periods and Macrostructural Identities

Nobility supported by land- holding calpulli (clan) members	**Class**		**Contact**	Cortes and conquerors seek riches
Complex pantheon; rich literary tradition	**Culture**	**PRE-COLUMBIAN** **PRE-1519**	**Conflict**	Tenochtitlan falls; Spanish introduce new tradition
Race of minimal importance	**Color**		**Change**	Early colonial practices, especially land and religion

INDIANS

Haciendas; native majority debt peons	**Class**		**Contact**	Enlightenment; colonial dissolution
Hispanicization and rise of mestizaje or blending	**Culture**	**SPANISH COLONIAL** **1521–1821**	**Conflict**	Independence; New World Spaniards victors
Racial barriers create problems for those subjugated	**Color**		**Change**	Era of experimentation and budding nationalism

PEASANTS

Criollos take over, some mestizos included	**Class**		**Contact**	Anglo-American land expansionism
Some signs of emerging Mexican style, still mostly imitating Europe	**Culture**	**MEXICAN INDEPENDENCE AND NATIONALISM** **1821–1846 (1910)**	**Conflict**	Mexican-American War of 1846
Some mestizos more accepted, Indians not	**Color**		**Change**	Anglo occupation of Mexican land, sociocultural struggles

IMMIGRANTS

  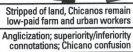

Stripped of land, Chicanos remain low-paid farm and urban workers	**Class**		**Contact**	Drawn-out human rights struggle peaks again in 1960s
Anglicization; superiority/inferiority connotations; Chicano confusion	**Culture**	**ANGLO-AMERICAN AND MEXICANIZATION** **1846–PRESENT**	**Conflict**	Chicanos confront system at all levels
New dimension to racism, internal and external forces	**Color**		**Change**	Ethnic consciousness and pride bring advancement

AND THE PROCESS CONTINUES. . .

over so many centuries has responded with the tools of human reproduction and immigration.

As we proceed, it will be made clear how different aspects of each historical stage interrelate and why a particular type of practice and attitude is found in one stage and not another. While successive stages often are not qualitatively better, each is more complex than the last, if only from the incorporation of what has been learned in previous stages. Of course, there are instances where stages overlap or one takes priority over another, or when development is blocked or uneven. Nevertheless, the implicit goal here is the establishment of a conceptual framework to draw parallels and make comparisons. Looking at larger forces and developments will facilitate discussion of whether progressive evolutionary changes marked each stage or whether each stage brought further devolution from what existed before European contact. The broader categories in these developments show the indigenous to peasant to immigrant transformations (Kearney 1996). The expansion in energy capture required a tremendous reordering of human labor.

For the purpose of this text, Chicano macrohistory is divided into four major historical periods:

1. *Pre-Columbian, pre-1519.* For biological and cultural reasons, Chicanos are, in an evolutionary sense, tied to the Indians of Mexico and the Southwest. Aztecs, especially, impressed their culture on surrounding natives and for their time reached the highest level of indigenous civilization. In addition, they became the first large native group to be defeated militarily by the Europeans and to experience a life of subjugation and a radical change in status.

2. *Spanish colonial, 1521–1821.* This period is one of the most influential in the formation of the Chicano people. Although Chicanos received most of their genetic makeup from Indians, the Spanish were profoundly instrumental in shaping Chicano cultural life, for example, with Spanish surnames and language and the establishment of peasant lifeways. Their 300-year reign was the longest and perhaps the most significant of all the postcontact stages, and one that started Chicanos on a low-status path that is still being worked out.

3. *Mexican independence and nationalism, 1821–1846 for Mexicans in the United States, but up to 1910 for those in Mexico.* The experiences of Mexicans on both sides of the border differed markedly. However, there are important features that bind them together. On the whole, peasant cultural patterns remained similar, and there was some reciprocal immigration that tended to maintain that connection. Often the events in either nation affected affairs in the other. Thus, the awakening of an ethnic and national consciousness must include an awareness of

activities in both regions—witness the present economic and political instability of Mexico and its effects on immigration to the U.S. in addition to the rise of narco-commerce and violence that has marred the country's international image.

4. *Anglo-American and Mexicanization, 1846–present.* By accident or design, the Anglo "assimilation" policy for foreigners began at the time Chicanos entered the United States. This was the government's predominant cultural adjustment strategy until a massive, concerted effort to change matters was implemented in the 1960s. Meanwhile, immigration increased substantially in the late twentieth to early twenty-first centuries to the point where the subject of undocumented Mexican residents has become a national issue as East Coast, Midwest, and Southeast regions now have large Mexican populations. Further, this increase in the critical mass brought large-scale protests and demonstrations against anti-immigration legislation in 2006, heretofore unheard of among newcomers of any background. This change required a new Three C's assessment.

In each of these historical stages, the Chicano people were confronted with new realities and problems, but always there was a developing awareness and growth.

It should be noted that dividing dynamic historical changes into periods characterized by related structural changes is a technique for depicting the growth of a people. The technique could easily be applied to any one of the stages designated above; for example, number 2, the Spanish colonial stage, could be segmented further into an assessment of Indian and Spanish experiences. Every sociocultural beginning is also in some sense an end or a middle, depending on the perspective one takes. Surely the Aztecs and colonial Spanish attained growth pinnacles in their respective eras. The purpose here is not to designate any of the earlier cultural patterns as complete, but to give emphasis to their role in the blossoming of the Chicano variant: to show how a preindustrial, localized people became integrated into an industrial, transnational entity—now commonly recognized as a result of modern globalization (Stark and Chance 2008).

A second method used in the text to clarify Chicano history is a model of sociocultural change, the Six C's: Class, Culture, Color, Contact, Conflict, and Change (see the box). This model provides a framework for understanding both the structure and the process of a social system. Anthropologists might say that the model aids synchronic and diachronic analysis and interpretation. A synchronic assessment refers to the functional approach to the study of culture in a given time, such as what occurs daily, seasonally, or annually. This can be likened to a photograph. A diachronic focus emphasizes the historical

Six C's Model of Sociocultural Change

Functionally Intact and Stable Social Order

1. CLASS—land, income, occupation, home, neighborhood, prestige, and esteem; also includes factors from other sectors of the social system

2. CULTURE—language, religion, philosophy, values, beliefs, customs, and general worldview of the people

3. COLOR—emphasis, or lack of it, on physiognomic or racial traits in the social system in terms of racist ideology, prejudice, discrimination, segregation

Breakup and Evolutionary Transformation of Social Order

4. CONTACT—often military force, but also involves the spread of ideas, such as religious or revolutionary principles; often is guided by economic concerns

5. CONFLICT—a multiple experience, including military confrontation and resistance and rebellion efforts, as well as a host of religious, sociocultural, and psychological ramifications

6. CHANGE—all abrupt and preliminary transformations that take place after contact and conflict and before a new class-culture-color system is firmly rooted

or developmental approach to the study of culture, such as the interpretation of an evolutionary or macrolevel cumulative change (Vancina 1970). The analogy here would be a series of photos that make up a bigger picture, a cinematic rendering.

The application of the Six C's model to each historical period provides a clearer understanding of the sociocultural change that occurred. It simultaneously provides a framework for a synchronic perspective, or what is functionally operative at any given time, and a diachronic assessment of transformations over time (Kasinec and Polushin 2002). Issues and conditions of *class* (sociological or socioeconomic conditions and practices), *culture* (anthropological or sociocultural change and innovation), and *color* (sociopsychological problems caused by oppression on the basis of class, culture, and racial issues) are discussed first. To simplify the presentation, other subjects are included under the major weighted headings listed above. The sequence in which they are presented is also important and emphasizes the mechanism of energy capture. Generally, the class factor is the foundation for developing an examination of the other sectors (Knight 2002; Wolf 1982; Harris 1979), especially in light of the macrohistory and macrostructural developments that reflect major changes. However, there are times when the discussion includes all of the features simultaneously, either because of similar time placement or because they are inextricably interwoven. The categories of class, culture, and color provide a vehicle to highlight the continuous social order and the way in which several major social features intertwine to make a people's history (Marger 1994). The overarching macrostructural identities serve further to underscore the placing of people into large generic categories based on energy capture (White 1949).

The second three categories of contact, conflict, and change aid in explaining the quality and nature of social evolution—the series of events and forces that kick-start macrolevel revampments. *Contact* refers to intrusions that upset an ongoing social system; *conflict* designates the nature of the subsequent struggle; and *change* denotes the reorganization of society in the aftermath, in both a short- and long-term view (Spindler 1984; Spicer 1962). A contact-conflict-change analysis enables one to determine how and why a stable social system is disrupted, transformed, and reintegrated. It does this by graphically showing how a people evolve from one historical period to another. The result in each stage is the establishment of a new social order, by which Chicanos are progressively shaped and molded according to the dictates of that period as well as the cumulative, incremental innovations that mark a changing people.

To summarize, each historical era begins with a relatively intact, stable, class-culture-color system, which in time is altered. A contact-conflict-change explanatory sequence clarifies the transformations that a fully functional social system undergoes and pinpoints specific aspects of the upheaval. Thus, culture change, conflict and continuity, acculturation, and marginality can be viewed in specific moments of history and charted as they move through history. At another level, macrohistorical developments concurrently shape macrostructural identities.

Theoretical Implications for the Present Day

Application of the Six C's model to each historical period yields a categorical framework within which to describe and discuss similar social-system sectors. More importantly, it focuses on social, cultural, and psychological patterns on which to base a comparison for all the time periods. Another purpose the model fulfills is to document specifically the beginnings of certain modern traits and customs of Chicanos. The model has several dimensions that offer insight into different types of issues in a holistic fashion (Stark and Chance 2008; Pitt 1972; Hodgen 1974).

With the use of the macrohistorical evolution framework and the Six C's model of sociocultural change, this sociocultural history should provide an appreciation of the depth and complexity of all these transformations. It is complex because there were so many facets in several time periods, and deep because abrupt and profound changes tumbled one upon one another. Such a diverse contact and change trajectory of necessity generated a legacy of variation—in class status, cultural repertoire and worldview, and color orientation based on variation and hybridization. Could it be that this complex, convoluted culture-change scenario left fissures and cracks on a people's development and evolution, or is it a "subject in process," where so many changes have accrued and need to be sorted out before a new entity appears? An understanding of the broader and deeper developments of these features will aid in identifying and underscoring the weak points as well as the accomplishments of a people.

While it is important to base assessments and understandings on history, especially appreciating the depth and breadth of each epoch, the central point of this work is to look deeper for the macrostructural identity. Uprooting Indian culture and lifeways to create a peasant society (with many varieties within this lifestyle) was a major shift for indigenous peoples. With the passage of time, new tools and technologies emerged to carry peasants to another era. In the last 100 years, under the onslaught of industrialization, urbanization, and globalization, this change has again uprooted the peoples in this time of migration. Thus, an assessment of the Indian to peasant to immigrant sequence is warranted.

As situations of time and place dictate, Chicanos have been affected by many influences (Mirande 1985). In adapting and adjusting to a multitude of circumstances, they have had to change and rechange customs, values, and beliefs. Their experience is different historically from that of most other national minority groups because they were made to feel culturally and racially inferior by more than one dominant group. Hence, a "layered-on" type of oppression occurred.

Clearly, negative material conditions of land, labor, and wealth are germane to this history (Wolf 1982, 1969). Nevertheless, there are also positive inheritances. As one possible reason for their survival, Chicanos epitomize the ability of modern colonized people to fashion multiple-pronged strategies of adaptation. They have learned to integrate and synthesize past racial and cultural mixture experiences. This, in turn, has led to the development of a flexible and comprehensive approach to life, in which first one avenue and then another has assisted their perseverance. Jose Vasconcelos's reference to Mexicans as "La Raza Cosmica" (the Cosmic People) was an early assessment of how cultural diversity makes for strength and vitality. This description also pertains to the even more culturally diverse Chicano people, a legacy of Indian, Spanish, Mexican, and Anglo antecedents; what has been referred to as *personas mexicanas* (Vigil 1997).

Note

[1] The ethnic label Chicano has many definitions (Munoz 1989:61–63). A strict colloquial usage suggests that it is a shortened form of Mexicano, which gained renewed popularity during the

1960s Chicano movement. In this text it is used to represent the multiple-heritage experience of Mexicans in the United States, traced from Indian, Spanish, Mexican, and Anglo backgrounds. The political consciousness-raising events of the 1960s helped develop an appreciation of Chicanos' multicultural heritage. The term Chicano will be used throughout most of the text because the text is a look backward to trace the historical development of a contemporary people.

References

Adelman, J., ed. 1999. *Colonial legacies: The problem of persistence in Latin American History.* New York: Routledge.

Flores, W. V., and R. Benmayor. 1997. *Latino cultural citizenship: Claiming identity, space, and rights.* Boston: Beacon Press.

Frazier, E. F. 1957. *Race and culture contacts in the modern world.* New York: Alfred A. Knopf.

Harris, M. 1979. *Cultural materialism.* New York: Random House.

Hodgen, M. T. 1974. *Anthropology, history, and cultural change.* Tucson: University of Arizona Press.

Kasinec, W. F., and M. A. Polushin. 2002. *Expanding empires: Cultural interaction and exchange in world societies from ancient to early modern times.* Wilmington, DE: A Scholarly Resources.

Kearney, M. 1996. *Reconceptualizing peasantry.* Boulder, CO: Westview Press.

Knight, A. 2002. *Mexico: From the beginning to the Spanish Conquest.* Cambridge: Cambridge University Press.

Koch, P. O. 2006. *The Aztecs, the conquistadors, and the making of Mexican culture.* Jefferson, NC: MacFarland.

Marger, M. N. 1994. *Race and ethnic relations: American and global perspectives.* Belmont, CA: Wadsworth.

Mirande, A. 1985. *The Chicano experience: An alternative perspective.* Notre Dame, IN: University of Notre Dame Press.

Munoz, C. 1989. *Youth, identity, power: The Chicano generation.* London and New York: Verso.

Pitt, H. C. 1972. *Using historical sources in anthropology and sociology.* New York: Holt, Rinehart, & Winston.

Robinson, W. I. 2004. *A Theory of global capitalism: Production, class, and state in a transnational world.* Baltimore: Johns Hopkins University Press.

Spicer, E. 1962. *Cycles of conquest.* Tucson: University of Arizona Press.

Spindler, L. S. 1984. *Culture change and modernization: Mini-models and case studies.* Long Grove, IL: Waveland Press.

Stark, B. L., and J. K. Chance. 2008. Diachronic and multidisciplinary perspectives in Mesoamerican ethnicity. In *Ethnic identity in Nahua Mesoamerica*, ed. F. F. Berdan, J. K. Chance, A. R. Sandstrom, and B. Stark. Salt Lake City: The University of Utah Press.

Vancina, J. 1970. Cultures through time. In *A handbook of method in cultural anthropology*, ed. R. Naroll and E. T. Cohen. New York: Doubleday.

Vigil, J. D. 1997. *Personas mexicanas: Chicano high schoolers in a changing Los Angeles*. Ft. Worth, TX: Harcourt Brace.

White, L. A. 1949. *The science of culture*. New York: Farrar, Straus & Giroux.

Wolf, E. R. 1969. *Peasant wars of the twentieth century*. New York: Harper & Row.

———. 1982. *Europe and the people without history*. Berkeley: University of California Press.

Pre-Columbian Period
30,000 BC–AD 1519

A look at the thousands of years of indigenous prehistory, the successive achievements of one people after another that culminated in the rise to prominence of the people who called themselves Mexica, provides an understanding of how social institutions began and were refined and perpetuated by the Indian forebears of the Chicano people. Experimentation and innovation are at the core of this gradual evolution. Around 7000 BC, seed gatherers settled in the Tehuacan Valley, just southeast of present-day Mexico City. Here occurred a concerted program of plant domestication—or what is termed "evolution directed by the interference" of humans. Around 1500 BC, one group of Indians, the Olmecs—"people from the land of rubber"— reached a refined and sophisticated level of cultural grandeur. Other groups learned from them and prospered. Because of this influence, they have been referred to as the Cultura Madre, or Mother Culture.

Beginning in AD 900 a wave of migrations lasting several centuries swept the valley of Mexico and upset the stability of the area. The Chichimecas (a generic tribal name) came from the far northwestern desert region. Interestingly, the historical and cultural connections between these northern groups and the resident, central valley Mexican indigenous peoples were quite old and deep. Many other Chichimeca subgroups eventually found a niche in the area. Most of them spoke the Nahua language and generally followed a militaristic way of life. Before incorporating the cultural habits of the valley, they filled active roles as mercenaries in the power struggles that were under way.

After Toltecan rule ended in AD 1156, another wave of migration brought a group later to gain power and fame: the Aztecs, named after their homeland, Aztlan. Most of the basic attributes of civilization were firmly established during the Aztec period, laying the foundation for further cultural and intellectual refinement. Thousands of years of ancient developments preceded the Aztecs, who both benefited from the past and built for the future. Aztecs organized a social stratification system, characterized by common land ownership and an agrarian community. Like most peoples, the Aztecs had their positive and negative traits, ranging from a tendency toward military oppression to their cultivation of a very refined, sensitive, and morally based culture. This cultural theme embodies all that the Aztecs represent and their quest to wisen "faces" and strengthen "bodies" through public education. The emphasis on racial features, or racism, as we know it today, did not exist in Aztec society.

European exploration of the Caribbean region had begun with Columbus's voyage in 1492, and his discovery was not so much of a New World but of contact between two worlds that were already very old. There were many sources of conflict. Some caused more friction than others, yet in one way or another all reflect the results of Spanish–Indian contact. The conquistadores sought wealth, in whatever form, and this ambition generally brought problems. The Spanish victory over the Aztecs stemmed from a combination of factors: their technological superiority (weapons), their psychologically astute diplomatic strategy, and their temporary alliances with dissident Indians (Koch 2006). Land and religious practices were serious conflict issues.

In conclusion, sixteenth-century Mexico, and for that matter the New World, was probably among the fastest-moving transitional societies ever, and was the stage for one of the most dramatic cross-fertilizations of cultures then known to humankind. Contact, conflict, and change between the peoples of the Old and New World raised havoc in all sectors of life—often affecting other areas of life.

Chapter 1

HUMAN EVOLUTION IN MESOAMERICA

*B*efore the first Europeans arrived in Mexico, the Aztecs had constructed the most advanced civilization on the continent of North America. It is useful to examine the complex process by which the Aztecs came into being and shaped one of the most sophisticated societies in the Western Hemisphere. A look at the thousands of years of American Indian prehistory, the successive achievements of one people after another that culminated in the rise to prominence of the people who called themselves Mexica, will provide an understanding of how social institutions began and were refined and perpetuated by the Indian forebears of the Chicano (Mexican-American) people.

During this prehistoric period leading up to the Indian civilizations, indigenous people were able to experiment and develop their own way of relating to the land, dividing and allocating labor, and collecting and distributing the wealth in ways that benefit most or all of the participants. Every civilization represents the results of tens of thousands of years of human adaptation. Experimentation and innovation are at the core of this gradual evolution, as the foundation is being laid for later development. In the meantime, human intellectual and cultural powers and networks grow in sophistication and complexity. Later natives benefited from the adaptations of preceding peoples and thereby fashioned a more secure and variable lifestyle. This early development, like the lore and legend of a people, is remembered only in others' telling of it and in the foundations it has provided. Hence, it is illustrative of how past events, however distant or small, operate to shape the present.

Ecological Adaptation

The rise of great Mesoamerican civilizations was preceded by many prehistoric events. Beginning in 30,000 BC (some experts say it was earlier, around 50,000 BC, while others support a more recent period, 12,000–14,000 BC), there were great migrations of people from Asia (Coe and Koontz 2008:18).[1] According to archaeologists, they wandered across the Bering Straits, which during the last Ice Age was a land mass connecting Asia and Alaska, or perhaps arrived here by sea travel at an earlier date. These migrations brought hordes of people whose descendants, over several thousand years, established themselves throughout North and South America. They were the original Americans.

These early pioneers found their way down the streams and valleys of North America, seeking food and water, clothing to keep them warm and protect them from abrupt weather changes, and shelter for rest and protection from predators. These early hunters were forced to follow a nomadic path, restlessly pursuing game wherever it might lead them. This dependence on large herd animals affected other areas of life. Following herds of mammoth or musk ox over the land bridge, taking many routes in this prolonged chase, the hunters learned to fashion tools out of natural objects (Lopez Austin and Lopez Lujan 2001).

Over a period of time, as early humans adapted to their environment, crude flaked stone tools gave way to more refined and useful technology. Techniques to aid in adaptation were consciously fashioned, and tools were invented and perfected to assist in the acquisition of food and the manufacture of clothing.

> We know that man controlled fire. . . . He also knew how to make spears, scrapers and knives. He had the *atlatl* spear thrower, he knew how to cook meat, he had domesticated the dog, wore skins to protect himself, and he probably knew how to make baskets. (Peterson 1962:19)

Initially, this wandering human found temporary shelter in natural caves and ledges. Much of what we know about this time period comes from remains these ancient people left behind in that part of the United States now most densely populated by Chicanos.

The early natives were able to reside in permanent cavelike dwellings only where there was an abundance of natural resources. Otherwise they continued the seasonal nomadic cycle. Over a period of time, however, there occurred a far-reaching change that shifted natives from a nomadic to a sedentary lifestyle.

As the years passed, the Ice Age receded and the climate became warmer and dryer. Groups of natives split off in different directions to find refuge in a variety of regions and climates. Accordingly, they fashioned new relationships to the environment. Some combined the gathering of edible plants with hunting but in time came to rely mostly on the former. Evidence of this relationship to the land, flora, and fauna is supported by the discovery of literally thousands of querns and mullers, grinding platforms, and milling stones left behind by these people. In time, a reliance on plants for meals began to increase chances for survival, making big-game hunters in some areas a thing of the past (Coe and Koontz 2008; Wolf 1959). Other natives, who settled near streams or oceans, learned to subsist on the surrounding plant and animal life. Those who were reluctant to experiment with new food sources eventually were forced to adopt new subsistence patterns through a process of cultural diffusion; that is, culture starting in one place and being spread by humans to other places.

From the earliest times, humans have had the propensity to vacillate between conserving the old and creating or adopting the new. Many individuals are reluctant to test new ways of doing things, even if their own existence is threatened. Clinging to age-old traditions is common because familiar patterns are time-tested and thus verify what has been gained. A conservative orientation is not all bad; many old traits and customs persist because they still fulfill important functions. Eventually, however, ecological pressures may necessitate changes to ensure survival. Individuals and groups who persist in clinging too long to outmoded and worn customs of the past face extinction— that is, they are surpassed by innovative individuals who adapt their lifeways and worldviews to changing conditions, discovering or creating inventive paths that hasten human evolution (Adams 2005).

Available natural resources—flora and fauna—determined for the early native peoples the time, place, and manner of eating, dress, and sleep—the primary needs and drives that motivate humans to control and domesticate the world around them. Consequently, a secure environmental relationship developed as human social and cultural institutions evolved.

Agricultural Revolution

According to some writers, women were in the forefront of the agricultural revolution, for they traditionally gathered fruits, nuts, and seeds near camps while the men were out hunting. It is hypothesized that over time the female seed collectors may have noticed that a grasslike plant with edible seeds at the tip had grown on the previous year's campsite. Where seeds had been haphazardly strewn in the past, there were now plants that could be eaten right on the spot, eliminating the need to go out and search for food. To test their inferences, the gatherers may have scattered seeds in a spot that had similar rich-looking soil but no plants, to find upon their return the following year that the seeds had grown into plants. Thus began the agricultural revolution (Coe and Koontz 2008; McGregor 1982).

Around 7000 BC, seed gatherers settled in the Tehuacan Valley, just southeast of present-day Mexico City. Here occurred a concerted program of plant domestication—or what is termed "evolution directed by the interference" of humans (Coe and Koontz 2008:27). The first seeds produced an edible part the size of a copper penny. After 5,500 years of gradual change, the Indians were able to increase its size and yield until they developed the present form of maize (modern corn).

Once this discovery was made, others followed. Beans and squash joined maize as the primary staples in the diet known as the American trinity. Other crops and products native to the New World are chile, which is high in vitamin C and useful in digesting cellulose products (Chavez 2006; see Andrews 1984, for a fascinating array of illustrations and information on a variety of chilies), pineapples, peanuts, potatoes, avocados, chocolate, tomatoes (which helped change a leavened bread and olive oil dish into pizza!), pumpkins, strawberries, tapioca, quinine, maple syrup, vanilla, cashew nuts, and pepper. These products were the major food sources for both natives and, later, Europeans; in fact, these foods add up to one-half of the modern world's aggregate agricultural wealth (Coe and Koontz 2008; Bellwood 2005; Horna 2001).[2]

Most modern people are unaware of this early cultivation, and Indians have not been given full credit on this account. "Middle America, particularly in the highlands of Mexico and Guatemala, is one of the four or five primary centers of plant domestication in the world. Here . . . an array of other plants was gradually brought under cultivation" (Helms 1975:18). The reliance on these foods, along with small game such as turkeys, decidedly changed the Indians in most of Mesoamerica from meat-eating hunters to settled farmers.

One cannot overstate the importance of agriculture. Fertile valleys and water-filled streams were sought out by former hunters and plant gatherers. As so much in culture change, it was a process of diffusion that spread the techniques and tools to other areas and to many heretofore hunters and gatherers, thus accelerating their cultural growth.

In this way humankind was brought to an important point in historical development. They had time now to expand on and improve other social and cultural practices. Moving from a nomadic life to an established, sedentary, agricultural one allowed for the development of many other artifacts and practices, including pottery and the arts, religious beliefs and rituals, and more elaborate tribal organizations.

By using technology to improve their ability to adapt environmentally, early natives rose to high levels of civilization. Crude tools were replaced by sophisticated ones, and more time was available to pursue other activities. Running and chasing were superseded by sitting, thinking, and creating.

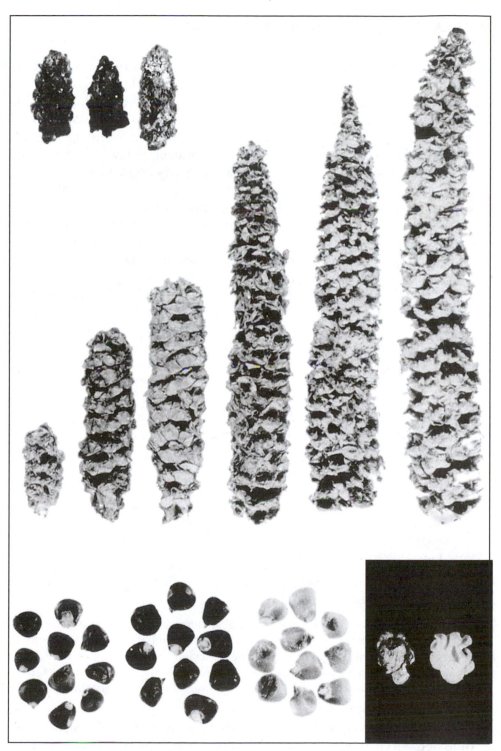

Evolution of maize (corn).

Refinement of Sociocultural Life

At the outset, social and cultural features remained rudimentary, primarily because farming equipment and tasks were simple. Later, as farming practices became more elaborate and cultivation efforts intensified, sociocultural traits grew in complexity. In effect, advanced technology released human labor for other activities, especially the thinking and planning needed to secure these new ways of doing things. Organizing the new, larger community and establishing the different habits and newly needed customs began to dominate human activity.

By at least 2000 BC, among the ongoing transformations, religion and military patterns grew in importance. Nominal leaders among the hunters became warrior chieftains to help expand the territory for farming pursuits. Shaman-priests emerged and invoked the blessings of the heavens for the planting, irrigating, growing, and harvesting of maize. Raised earthen platforms were built for the shaman-priests to conduct rituals and ceremonies. Careful observation and scientific study of celestial movement—stars, sun, and moon—became increasingly important. The movements of the sun and other stars were keys to the development of calendars, the basis of knowledge of when to sow and when to harvest. Warriors and the military complex helped protect and preserve this essential activity as they also worked to expand the land base to support a larger population (Brown and Stanton 2003). Thus, the people of the community soon began to seek direction from both warriors and priests.

Crude earthen pit-houses were built as permanent residences.

> The population grew as the cultivation of corn grew . . . men had time to make life more comfortable. They began to build better shelters, improve their preparations for food, and to accumulate possessions . . . families lived close together near good farming land in order to share in the field work and the protection of the crops, and so the first permanent tiny communities came into existence. (Peterson 1962:31; see also Carrasco, Lopez Lujan, and Moctezuma 2007)

Several other factors were involved in the expansion of social and cultural features. They include, first,

> the appearance of sedentary farming villages; second, the rise of small temples or ceremonial centers; third, the development of civilization with populations clustering around temple centers in true urban zones or living in temple-center-with-outlying-hamlet arrangements; and fourth, the formation of expansionistic civilizations dominating large territorial states. (Willey et al. 1964:488)

This ordering corresponds in general to the sequence in which such events unfolded. To ensure that the accumulated knowledge could be passed on to future generations, record-keeping devices, including written language, were developed. These in turn brought changes to art forms such as pottery, jewelry, and murals. Specialization in various trades and skills became the rule of the day. Religious leaders, warriors, healers, and potters were only the first in a long line of new occupations.

Religion became the most important profession for a number of reasons, not least of which was its effect on other roles and occupations. A large array of gods evolved whose perceived existence helped stabilize the relationship between humans and their environment. Rain gods were the most important among them, for they were needed to balance the forces of nature and ensure that the agricultural system succeeded. Thus, deities constantly had to be nourished, sustained, and worshiped; monumental temples dedicated to them began to grace the land. As will be noted later, religious customs and duties dominated the life of the Aztecs, especially in their artistic expression.

As Eric Wolf (1959:69) has reminded us, after the food quest is secured, human society "raises its sights and strives to transcend its earthbound limitations." The spiritual needs of humans arose to accompany the material needs. While the body finds nourishment in the material world, the soul strives to participate in life's spiritual and intellectual struggles. Spiritual considerations become involved in the everyday affairs of humans—perhaps to ensure that the environment is not abused as a result of selfish motives. The innate human tendency toward self-centeredness needs to be curbed; otherwise, total exploitation of the environment would result.

Olmecs—Mother Culture

Around 1500 BC, one group of Indians, the Olmecs (Olmecas in Spanish)—"people from the land of rubber" (Coe and Koontz 2008:61; see also Knight 2002)—reached a refined and sophisticated level of cultural grandeur. Other groups learned from them and prospered. Because of this influence, the Olmecs have been referred to as the *Cultura Madre*, or Mother Culture. They inhabited the lowland region south of Vera Cruz, along the eastern coast of Mexico, where the modern states of Tabasco, Campeche, and Yucatan converge. Their cultural glory lasted until 300 BC. In subsequent centuries, other Mesoamerican groups inherited the Olmec tradition and readapted it to their own purposes. In different time periods, the Huastecas flourished in northeastern Mexico; the Mayas in the southeast, reaching as far as Central America; the Teotihuacanos in the central Mexican plateau; and the Zapotecs in the southwest. These groups "only represent different cultures within a civilization, just as western Christianity is but one civilization in spite of differences that exist between Spanish, German, or English cultures" (Bernal 1969:187–88; see also Berdan et al. 2008).

The Olmec era is a watershed in the growth of ancient indigenous civilizations. It emerged suddenly as the culmination of all the contributions made by earlier, unnamed peoples, and it blossomed beyond compare (Knight 2002; Weaver 1993). Many of the significant cultural achievements identified with ancient Mexico stem from Olmec innovations, such as the development of the

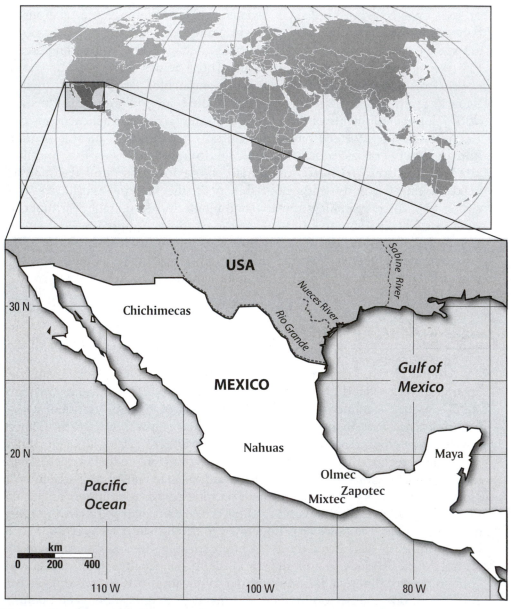

Major cultural groups in Mesoamerica.

calendar, the invention of the zero concept, and the creation of a system of writing. Other features of Olmec life included stone temples and pyramids, ornate personal dress for the budding elite, commercial networks, defensive fortifications, and sea travel. Hence, this early civilization provided the basis on which the following general cultural foundations were laid.

Some of the features shared by native groups were

> hieroglyphic writing . . . books . . . maps . . . a complicated calendar . . . astronomy . . . a team game resembling basketball . . . markets and favored ports of trade; wars for the purpose of securing sacrificial victims; large-scale human sacrifice; private confession and penance . . . tobacco smoking; and a pantheon of extraordinary complexity. (Coe 1962:17–19)

The many basalt stone heads and jaguar art forms found on Olmec sites are a further testimony to the growth of human culture, especially underscoring organizational ability and social structure (Sharer and Grove 1989). The

Olmec basalt head.

gigantic heads, with no necks or bodies, seem to suggest the development of a higher consciousness and awareness and advancement to a more profound level. The jaguar, in contrast, was considered a cult animal, a type of guardian of the spirit that endowed a person with special, mystical powers. Every person had such a *nagual* (spirit) to accompany them through life.

It is relatively unimportant whether religious-philosophical beliefs were imported from Asia or conceived in the New World. What is significant is that natives early developed a mythological basis for spiritual endeavors and that spirituality represented a recognition of the contrasting forces all around them: The external, material reality was joined by the internal spiritual world, and this vision of duality permeated other aspects of life. They assigned "the original foundation of the world to a supreme dual principle, Our Mother— Our Father, which was the origin of everything which exists" (Leon-Portilla 1969:30). The Olmecs believed, for example, that the jaguar's spots symbolized day and night, fire and ice, heaven and hell; the rest of the world was also viewed in this way. Life/death, sun/earth, light/dark, fire/water, male/ female, father/mother are but a few of the dualities of the real and imagined features of life (Knight 2002).

Dual existence was the abiding hallmark, the teaching that ordered their life. One side of any duality could not be embraced or thoroughly understood unless its counterpart was acknowledged. Mother-earth took on more meaning when joined by father-sun. Similarly, an appreciation of water-heaven could occur only when fire-hell was introduced. Generally, those who adhered to this spiritual orientation, accepting and integrating these oppositions into their very being, charted a broadened life path. Religion existed for the group, as "the collective rituals were one of the most significant forces for social cohesion and political action in Mesoamerica" (Lopez Austin and Lopez Lujan 2001:245).

Tens of thousands of Indians over a long period of time participated in the building of Mesoamerica. Like the ocean tide, surging and ebbing, each Indian group took the lead and then lost it to another group through internal decay or foreign encroachment. Of course, progressive changes transpired during these millennia as groups added their particular contributions to the sophistication and complexity that accompanied an agricultural base. However, it is in the nature of human technological and sociocultural evolution to have ups and downs. The periodic moving forward and standing still are universally shared human patterns of evolution. As Will Durant (1983) once stated, human and cultural evolution can be compared to the accelerator and brakes of an automobile: One is for moving forward at any speed and the other is for slowing down and stopping when it is appropriate. In any event, after about AD 500 Mesoamerica remained on the same cultural plane.

Chichimecas—Migration from Aztlan

Beginning in AD 900, about four centuries into this cultural plateau, a wave of migrations lasting several centuries swept the valley of Mexico and upset the stability of the area. The Chichimecas (meaning "lineage of the dog," a proud appellation like the valued "dog soldiers" of the Plains Indians) came from the far northwestern desert region. Interestingly, the historical and cultural connections between these northern groups and the resident, central valley Mexican indigenous peoples were quite old and deep. Many architectural features, cultural habits, language (the Uto-Aztecan family), and trade routes show how geography (or "geopolitical" catchment, where the coterminous northern Mexican desert and southwest American desert join) influences cultural evolution and diffusion (Mathien and McGuire 1986; Suarez 1982).

Chichimecas were from a desert culture in the intermediate area between tillable lands in the modern United States and Mexico. They were forced into a cyclical nomadic pattern that fluctuated with the climate, sometimes farming with limited productivity, but more often gathering food and "communally" hunting rabbits. In time, they began to raid the northern reaches of the central valley of Mexico (Coe and Koontz 2008; Coe 1962). The Chichimecas

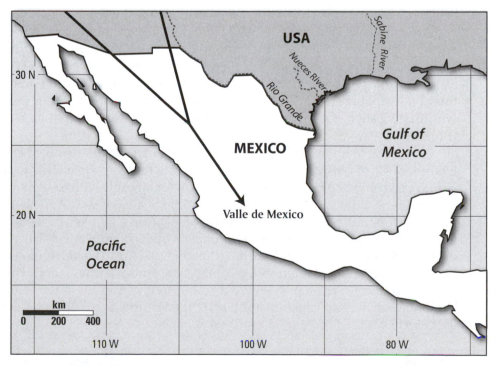

Chichimeca migrations.

either forced their way into the region or simply filled the vacuum left by others, or both. According to legend, they had migrated from Aztlan, their mythological homeland, which is now either northern Mexico or the southwestern United States (Knight 2002).

The Chichimecas later absorbed many of the cultural traits of previous residents of the area, but "warfare and military expansion on the one hand, intensive agriculture and the appropriation of surpluses through tribute payments on the other, are the hallmarks of this new period" (Wolf 1959:117; see also Hassig 1992).

The Toltecas were the first of several subgroups within the generic Chichimeca population to establish hegemony in Central Mexico; they were closely linked to indigenous groups that remained in the Aztlan region (Knight 2002). Borrowing from earlier people, especially the Olmecas, Teotihuacanos, and Mayas, they settled at Tula in AD 968. Here blossomed a cultural epicenter from which Toltec rulers could dominate others in the valley. Borrowing and readapting the culture and lifeways of the settled inhabitants, the Toltecas soon fashioned a grand "high" culture, which subsequent groups remembered with admiration (Riley 1987; Mathien and McGuire 1986).

Many other Chichimeca subgroups eventually found a niche in the area. Most of them spoke the Nahua language and generally followed a militaristic way of life. Before incorporating the cultural habits of the valley, they filled active roles as mercenaries in the power struggles that were under way.

After Toltecan rule ended in AD 1156, another wave of migration brought a group later to gain power and fame: the Aztecs, named after their homeland, Aztlan. With most of the tillable farmland already occupied, the Aztecs at first wandered about, hiring themselves out as mercenaries. Later they found a temporary refuge in Michoacan in western Mexico. Still not satisfied with that location, they finally moved to a most undesirable spot in AD 1325 (Ruiz 1992).

According to myth, the Aztec warrior-god leader Mexitli followed explicit instructions from heaven to find a spot suitable for his people. This location would be visibly apparent. They were to look for an eagle with a serpent in its mouth, stationed on a lone cactus in the middle of a large lake. And so it happened as foretold. "The place was called Tenochtitlan, in token of its miraculous origin, though only known to Europeans by its other name, Mexico City, derived from their war-god, Mexitli" (Prescott 1931:16). This miraculous sign notwithstanding, it was not until AD 1430, after much intrigue and warfare, that the Aztecs were able to secure a stable foothold in the area. With this beginning, they established themselves as the last Indian group to reign over the central plateau.

Opposite page: Toltec ruins of warrior pillars in Tula.

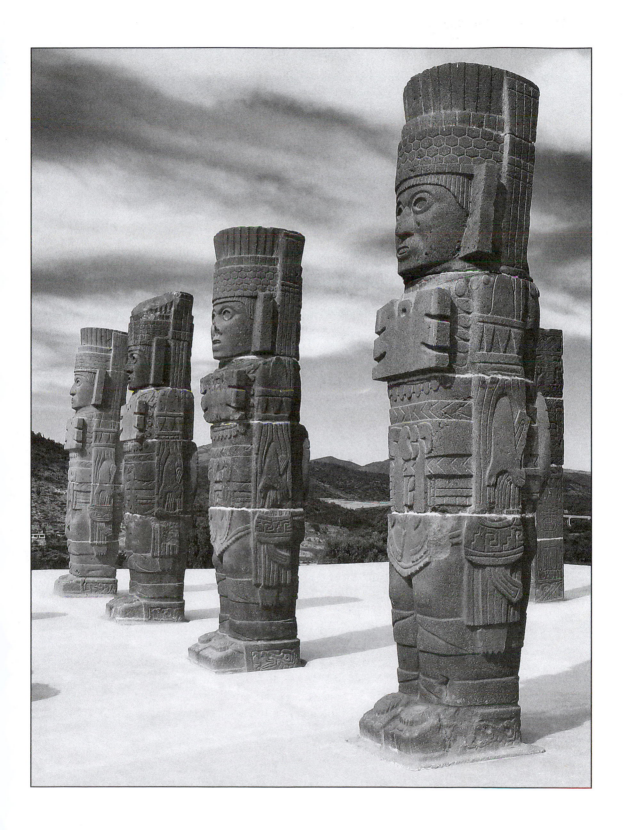

Notes

[1] Mesoamerica refers to a cultural region encompassing an area just north of the central plateau of Mexico City and all the way down to the northern nations of Central America.

[2] Major nonfood agricultural products first domesticated in the Americas include cotton (a similar species was domesticated separately in the Near East), rubber, chicle (chewing gum), tobacco, and cocaine, among others.

Chapter 2

INTACT AND STABLE
SOCIAL ORDER

*M*ost of the basic attributes of civilization were firmly established during the Aztec period, laying the foundation for further cultural and intellectual refinement. Thousands of years of ancient developments preceded the Aztecs, who both benefited from the past and built for the future. As indigenous inhabitants, inheritors of a separate and independent evolution, they followed a communal and agricultural tradition.

It is clear that Aztec society facilitated the satisfaction of human drives such as hunger and thirst, cemented the willpower to satisfy needs, and steered the populace in the preservation of time-honored customs and habits. Further innovation and growth were made possible by the solid grounding of Aztec social and cultural institutions. This period reflects the indigenous stage of social and cultural evolution, and underscores these factors: (1) biological drives were better met; (2) learning through trial and error and emulation of others was becoming increasingly important to societal maintenance; (3) as more and more energy was captured with the aid of larger numbers of humans over a wider expanse of territory, about 25 million in Mesoamerica itself, and over 110 million in the New World (Mann 2005:104–5; see also Coe and Koontz 2008), other difficulties and strains emerged; and (4) in spite of the Aztecs' many accomplishments, a sense of uncertainty still pervaded the scene, as impending flux and ferment filled the air. The comparison of Aztec cultural attainment with this stage of cultural evolution is generally valid for pre-Columbian life.

Class: Nobility Supported by Commoners

Aztecs organized a social stratification system that was a bundle of contradictions. One interpretation is that it was a nonegalitarian aristocracy

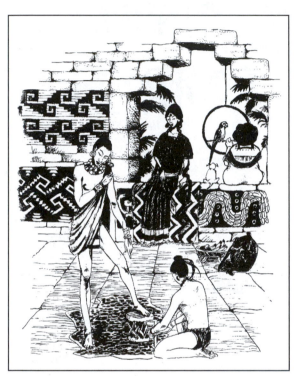

Life of Indian nobility.

(Berdan 1982, 2008; Coe 1962; Coe and Koontz 2008), while another rendition seems to support a basically democratic situation (Morgan 1963). Because the social system was based on past communal traditions that were breaking down under the weight of complex changes, it appears that both views are correct for different times. "One group in particular, the pipiltin, was made by the gods and trained to rule the rest of society. Another group, the macehuattin majority, was made to work for the benefit of society under the control of the pipiltin" (Carrasco 2008:131). The system was initially egalitarian and, over a century, gradually became less so (Berdan 1982, 1989; Berdan et al. 2008). Yet there were moments when older practices prevailed in the midst of the new ones. While this was not exactly democratic in the purest sense, it did seem to incorporate elements of equality (Townsend 1992; Berdan et al. 2008).

Recognizing that role-class assignments were necessary, the Aztecs sought to prevent social conflict and disintegration with a community-oriented ideological framework. This was undertaken at the expense of individuals, who now were taught to integrate their interests and direct their duties to those of the total group. In a sense the Aztecs put much effort into developing a political system that mirrored and indeed supported the unificatory nature of their culture and economy (Coe and Koontz 2008; Carrasco 2008). Thus, as a state-level society, they took on the responsibility of developing a collective ideology and destiny.

Land System

The basis of Aztec society was a land and agrarian community that evolved around the most important natural resource: the people. In general, land belonged to the people in common; their labor built a sophisticated *chinampas* (irrigation agriculture, floating gardens) system and produced basic necessities (Berdan et al. 2008; Berdan 1982; Townsend 1992). Consequently, a large share of the wealth was returned to them. However, as noted earlier, this arrangement had undergone important transformations with the rise of a ruling elite, and with the gradual erosion of a people-oriented land system there arose a new practice, perhaps an incipient form of *latifundia* (large landed estates).

The backbone of the earlier arrangement was the *calpulli*, a socioeconomic unit based on kinship (blood and social relations) and territoriality (ownership of the land required for subsistence) (Coe and Koontz 2008; Berdan 1982). Some even say that it was a "big house" of families with a common ancestor (Leon-Portilla 1988, 1992). Each calpulli possessed a set amount of territory for its own use "rooted according to battlefield achievements" (Carrasco 2008:137; Brown and Stanton 2003). Rights of land tenure and ownership were carefully outlined, as were water and irrigation rights, timberland rights, hunting privileges, and farming for household consumption and for market bartering. Each calpulli set boundaries with maguey plants, stone walls, and worn footpaths. Trespassers from other calpullis were subject to prosecution and punishment (Berdan 1989; Coe and Koontz 2008).

Social Classes and Life

The members within each calpulli were known as *macequales* (commoners, or citizens of the confederacy), who comprised about 85 percent of the population. Most macequale household heads, working on about a ten-acre plot, had enough food to support themselves and their families. Ambitious individuals who labored harder and longer each day were granted the right to farm untilled calpulli land. This added incentive, and the investment allowed them to use surplus earnings for bartering in the marketplace. The macequales also were periodically called upon to provide labor service to ruling elites or for public works.

Family life was well ordered, with each member learning about and carrying out his or her responsibilities. Children were taught to respect their parents, grandparents, and aunts and uncles. Living arrangements followed a pattern. The entire family occupied one rectangular room built on a stone foundation, with adobe walls; the kitchen, granary, and bathhouse were separate, located in the garden, which surrounded the house. Their primary staple was maize, and fields of small hillocks planted with maize dotted the surrounding countryside. When it came time to harvest, the women would gather the maize and grind it into flour, which would then be used to make tamales, or else they pounded the maize dough into flat tortillas and baked them over slow-burning fires. Beans, fruits, and vegetables were also grown in abundance, as well as various types of tasty chiles (Foster and Cordell 1992; Andrews 1984). "The Aztec diet was basically vegetarian, supplemented by fish, wild fowl and game; they raised no domesticated animals as significant food resources" (Townsend 1992:172). Most of the food and cooking techniques were native creations and were named with Nahuatl words: *metate* (grinding stone), *mano* (stone hand grinder), and so on.

"The traveler through the city would pass through the chinampas, visit the great marketplace, and get a protected glimpse of the nobles' homes and the palaces of the rulers. In a real sense, all roads led into the city of Tenochtitlan" (Carrasco 2008:76). "Remembering that the Aztecs constructed an urban society, it is important to give attention to the many ranks, diverse classes of people, numerous social slots, jobs, laborers who held up the social pyramid on their hands, backs, skills, and abilities" (Carrasco 2008:156). In addition to the macequales in social class status, there were two other groups: the

The Great City of Tenochtitlan, Mexico.

mayeques and the *tlacotin*. The mayeques, never more than 2 or 3 percent of the population, were like marginal persons, that is, without certain rights held by the macequales. They worked the fields for the rulers on a permanent basis. Similar to serfs, they received only enough payment to maintain their households. Another slave-type class, the tlacotin, consisted of those who sold themselves to the rulers for a set amount of time and lived on their land as permanent laborers, some of whom improved their lot by gambling or criminal activity. Their tenure could last a few years or a lifetime, but their offspring could not be born into slavery. They comprised 3 or 4 percent of the people, and when coupled with the mayeques never rose above 10 percent of the total population.

It is important to note that the growth in numbers of these two groups increased in direct proportion to the steady expansion of a ruling elite—the latter being former calpulli members who had left agricultural work for positions of political and cultural leadership. Thus, it was a status system based on both ascription and achievement, combining caste (or birthright) and class (mobility) elements (Berdan 1982).

Each calpulli was composed of a group of families related by kin and residing together (Leon-Portilla 1988, 1992). Some observers question the importance of "blood" in the kinship network; in other words, kin ties may have been fictive (Wolf 1959), but it is nevertheless clear that the emphasis on "social" kin relations functioned to make the calpulli a cohesive unit. Often the members of a single calpulli would number into the thousands.

> A localized, land holding corporation, . . . it also had ritual functions in that it had its own temple and gods, and even an association. . . . There were more than 80 calpoltin [plural of calpulli] in Tencochtitlan, some of which have actually persisted as traditional barrios near the center of modern Mexico City. (Coe and Koontz 2002:195)

Several local *tlatoques* (speakers) would be elected to serve as a "natural" calpulli high council, and from their ranks one person would be designated the calpulli "speaker" (Townsend 1992). All the supreme calpulli leaders met as a council to advise the head of government (Berdan 1989). However, this egalitarian practice of calpulli leaders having access to the higher echelons of government was increasingly being phased out.

Rise of the State

Since the Aztecs profited from earlier technologies and thus were able to support a larger population, it similarly followed that social relations would also become more complex. In early Aztec society, tlatoques were selected from the ranks of the people. These leaders knew the people well, for they were of the people and made decisions with their consent; thus, the tlatoques were "natural" leaders. The gradual replacement of this grassroots democracy with an aristocracy was one of Aztec society's major social transformations. This did not mean, however, that the achievements of individuals from the lower classes were no longer recognized and duly rewarded. Although the aristocracy was protective of its exalted position in society, class boundaries were permeable enough to allow worthy lower-born men to ascend into and invigorate the elite (Carrasco 2008; Coe and Koontz 2008).

It can be postulated that a particular calpulli eventually became entrenched as the leading group. Perhaps it became all-powerful because of its military prowess. At first its actions benefited the total community, but before long it had become a hereditary ruling body and no longer took the interests of the community to heart. Michael Coe states that

> a society evolved from a primitive organization in which all lands were originally held by the clans . . . [and] there was no higher authority than clan chiefs, into a fully fledged state with the appearance of a privileged class . . . . Given time, the clans would have certainly declined to total insignificance. (1962:165)

Hence, having initially been seen as merely the extension of the tribe, the city-state had become a force for the acquisition of neighboring territories and resources. The consequences of this development were unfortunate, as class differences grew more pronounced, and animosities between the aristocracy and the lower classes began to surface. Natural leaders, tlatoques, gradually gained control over their own private lands and had the tribute and labor of mayeques at their disposal (Berdan et al. 2008; Berdan 1982).

The members of this ruling group became known as the *pipiltin* (rule by the elite, nobles), presumably descended from Toltec lineage and thus, because of that lineage, superior to other natural leaders. Never more than 2 to 10 percent of the populace, they directed religious and political concerns from the center of the city. Although power was concentrated in their hands, they still were charged with the duties of administration, government, and religion. Because these responsibilities were typically handled fairly and efficiently, the people generally supported their rule. As a matter of fact, the rule of Texcoco, one of the neighboring city allies, was very democratic. Here, the bureaucracy consisted of a number of neatly organized tribunals of varying degrees of influence. The most significant governing event occurred in the capital, where a general meeting or convention was held every 80 days (Prescott 1931; Suchlicki 2001).

The primary support for the pipiltin came from the tribute of the macequales. This was provided in two ways: (1) the contribution of a set amount of produce and (2) labor service for a certain number of days on pipiltin land. Thus, it would have behooved the pipiltin to keep an open ear to macequale demands so long as the latter remained dutiful and productive. After all, it

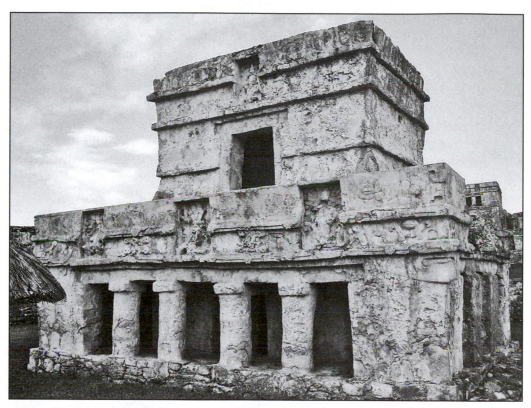

Temple ruins in Tulum, Quintana Roo, Mexico.

was the macequales' extra efforts that released the pipiltin from working the land, allowing them to devote their energy to civic and religious chores.

Priestly duties were closely linked to the pipiltin rule. For example, the emperor Montezuma (Coe and Koontz 2008) ruled over a very complex and multifaceted society. His powers were immense and absolute, and his word was the law. Since he also was technically the high priest of the state religion, his person was seen as being divinely derived and not of this earth. The early chronicler Fray Bernardino de Sahagun describes the great array of deities and the priests who served them, but especially noteworthy in his account was how priests were selected.

> These two pontiffs were equal in standing and honor, even if they should be of very low birth and of very lowly and poor parents; the only reason why they were elected to be the high pontiffs was their having faithfully complied with and followed all the customs, rules, exercises and teachings. (Sahagun 1932:202)

Occupations other than those based on agrarian life also were held by the macequales. Their organization of society was based on social status, and depending on a person's occupation, they lived either in the town or in the adjoining settlements (Carrasco 2008). Those who dwelt in the city were the warriors who made up the standing army (*tectecuhtin*), those who sold and traded goods (*pochteca*), and skilled artisans such as goldsmiths and feather-workers. The merchants and artisans were organized into hereditary guilds located in the residential sections of the town. In short, the pipiltin held the leadership positions in the city and the macequales filled the agrarian roles in the country and skilled occupations in the city.

The class of merchants known as pochteca came into being as trade with other Indian groups throughout Mesoamerica developed. They provided a dual service when away on trading expeditions: They gathered foreign information as spies and they represented Aztec commercial interests. However, because Aztec leaders feared the potential power of the pochtecas, they were watched very closely (Carrasco 2008). Some pochtecas harbored entrepreneurial ambitions and desired to build a separate business dynasty. Eric Wolf (1959:140) suggests that if the pochteca were discovered to be independently accruing wealth, they were put to death and their wealth was redistributed; as a result, they "made a special effort to appear humble and poor." In contrast, recent interpretations appear to show that the pochteca also participated in "potlatch feasts" as a way to redistribute resources and wealth (Berdan 1982). Nevertheless, "Their labors were heroic, and when successful they brought riches and honor to their ruler, the city, and themselves" (Carrasco 2008:156).

Caution should be taken here to avoid perceiving the pochteca and pipiltin as bourgeois and aristocratic classes comparable to those of Europe. Although there are some similarities between the two, the feudal system of Europe had its own characteristics that simply did not exist here. William Prescott (1931:22) chided Spanish historians for being too "fond of tracing analogies to European models" and argued that the Aztecs should be evaluated on their own terms. Still, one cannot resist the temptation to compare the macrohistorical and evolutionary paths characteristic of the two continents.

Every civilization that has grouped over one-half million citizens in one location, as the Aztecs did, has had to establish and maintain a system of law and order. The people of Tenochtitlan were guided by a code of laws ordering behavior, and if they deviated or were remiss, well-defined methods of enforcement ensued. One supreme judge, chosen for life with veto powers over the king, interpreted the law and meted out decisions for all the people. Lesser judicial officials were appointed for each calpulli district and for the remaining outlying provinces of the confederacy, or league of states. A network of higher and lower courts guaranteed that all citizens, no matter where they resided in the central region, would receive a swift and fair legal decision when a law was broken. Social stability was maintained also by a police force (Adams 2005).

Main cities in central valley of Mexico.

Confederacy and Trade

To expand their territory and capture more energy, it was necessary for the Aztecs to establish diplomatic alliances and commercial relations with other groups. Interpretations of the Aztec means of doing this continue to generate controversy. In 1430 they created an alliance that was later to expand into a confederacy, or empire, as some experts have suggested that the Aztecs were military imperialists (Berdan 1982; Suchlicki 2001). Two other Nahuatl-speaking cities, Texcoco and Tlacopan, joined the Aztecs to share obligations and increase their security. During the later expansionist wars, both cities aided in the Aztec military campaigns: Tlacopan provided supply carriers, and Texcoco sent warriors. This triple alliance was able to gain and maintain control over the whole central plateau of Mexico.

In the process of expansion and conquering other tribes, the prevailing type of rule was not that of a single consolidated state but the coexistence of many loosely knit state-like provinces, which retained a modicum of self-rule. Indeed, it was an organization composed of many cultures and languages, with the Nahuatls speaking their own tongue along with the Otomis, Maza-huas, Maya, and many more (Soustelle 1961). "The Triple Alliance did not, however, adopt an attitude of complete *laissez-faire* toward their subjects. Local rulers were expected to spend several months each year at the imperial capitals. . . ."(Carnek 2002:219).

This ruling system benefited the Aztecs, for they could not afford to station a permanent military force in the outlying provinces. Nevertheless, in comparison to most imperial systems, it was rather egalitarian. As in the transition between an egalitarian calpulli and an incipient ruling elite, this confederacy may have been part of an evolutionary phase toward a centralized system in which even more energy was controlled and dominated. Nevertheless, one sixteenth-century observer noted that the native rulers of conquered lands were left in place, as were local languages and cultural practices (Zorita 1963). Berdan (1982:109) maintains that "after a conquest, Aztecs usually refrained from pillaging or destroying the city. The imperial Aztec goal was to add provinces to their empire, to provide them with continuous and assured supplies of goods through tribute, not the spoils of a one-time sacking."

On the whole, in spite of some rivalry among the main allies, the confederacy was able to function fairly smoothly. Under this political unit, far-reaching trade activities were undertaken with other regions north to the modern state of Durango, east and west to the Atlantic and Pacific Oceans, and as far south as Nicaragua. Tenochtitlan, as the leading city of the triple alliance, provided these conquered regions with military protection from other warring tribes and in return received tribute from all 38 provinces that constituted the Aztec empire. This tribute—paid yearly—took on many forms. Usually it was paid with basic foodstuffs such as maize, beans, amaranth, dried chile peppers, and maguey honey, but the giving of other items such as cloth, pottery bowls, and native paper was not unusual (Smith 2008). Groups that were unable to contribute agricultural products gave tribute in the form of labor.

Tenochtitlan reigned supreme over the entire valley. Tlatelolco, its twin marketplace city, served up to 60,000 people daily. There, the shoppers would purchase the innumerable items and services available and pay for them by bartering or with money, the latter being either cacao beans or quetzal bird quills filled with gold.

Generally, then, the socioeconomic and political practices of the Aztecs were shaped to benefit the total community. Interestingly, although the pipil-tin were the elite group, macequales who showed talent and intelligence were given the opportunity to attend their schools. Thus, some egalitarianism yet remained.

Culture: Pantheon of Gods, Moral Order, and Literary Tradition

Like most peoples, the Aztecs had their positive and negative traits, ranging from a tendency toward military oppression to their cultivation of a very refined, sensitive, and morally based culture. This cultural theme embodies all that the Aztecs represent. Learning from the world around them and from the contributions of earlier Indians, they embraced the dual nature of reality. They were similar to the Greeks, who combined the body (materialism) and soul (spirituality) in their paideia: A man should become a speaker of words (soul) and a doer of deeds (body). Here is how the Aztecs phrased their ideal (Leon-Portilla 1963:135):

> The mature man
> is a heart solid as a rock,
> is a wise face,
> possessor of a face,
> possessor of a heart,
> he is able and understanding

To this end, all people from youth onward were taught by their parents and teachers to develop their "heart" (soul) and "face" (body). Always upper-most in their mind as they pursued this goal was how best to serve the community, and religion was the glue for this communal goal (Leon-Portilla 1992). Importantly, females fared relatively well with "an ideology which stressed tribal identity over gender, and the common plight of humankind over tribe, [and] allowed them to escape definition as 'other'" (Clendinnen 1991:206; see also Megged 2010).

Religious principles encompassed this view of humankind and guided the people to be as one with nature. The breadth and scope of their religious beliefs, based on set, formal practices and the internalization of their legends, encompassed and permeated nearly every facet of a person's life. The nation itself was marked by the constancy of its religion, and it governed all levels and aspects of society. It was a major determinant in people's lives from the moment they were born to the time of their passing, dominating even the realms of art and sports. In fact, "the Aztecs looked to these sages [artists], as the lights and guides whose responsibility it was to provide religious, moral, and intellectual leadership" (Boone 2008:182). There was nothing that existed that did not have the heavy imprint of religion on it (Berdan 1982; Soustelle 1961).

Education

The religious goals sought to wisen "faces" and strengthen "bodies" through public education. Accordingly, regardless of socioeconomic background, all male citizens were entitled to participate in a universal system of education. Females were socialized for domestic duties and affairs, which oftentimes included artistic and craft activities, and enjoyed a relatively high status and prestige as wives and mothers. As noted previously, many intelligent children of humble origins were placed in the elite schools, where all the spiritual and intellectual knowledge was found in great books. "The priests were in charge of educating the young people; they were custodians of esoteric knowledge, wisdom, and tradition, of the two calendars, and of the art of writing in painted books and inscriptions" (Leon-Portilla 1969:4). All instruction was conducted in the Nahuatl language.

This constant, daily struggle to balance the dual human drives of environmental adaptation and spiritual betterment caused tension. There were numerous instances when either material or spiritual practices, or both together, failed completely. And yet, in spite of the many failures, there were more successes, and this undoubtedly stemmed from the almost obsessive religious devotion of the Aztecs. It appeared that the philosophical guidance they sought from the heavens enabled them to change and readapt on a continuous basis (Quilter and Miller 2006).

School life was built around two types of learning environments. The *calmecac* (higher college) was devoted to the intellect and spirit, and there the leaders and priests received training. In the *telpochcalli* (arsenal), the crafts of the military warrior were taught. Because military prowess was a highly valued skill, most young men attended the telpochcalli (Hassig 1988). As a military power, the Aztecs had to maintain control of the valley of Mexico, ensuring that the resources and people remained under their domination (Carrasco 2008). Many liberties were granted to those trained at this institution, but a rigorous upbringing under the aegis of religion instilled physical and mental discipline for the production of hardy warriors. In brief, one might say that the calmecac was an intellectual and spiritual school (perhaps analogous to the best of Harvard and Notre Dame), while the telpochcalli was strictly military (like West Point) (Peterson 1962). Although formal education was geared primarily toward the males, females had occasion to attend the *cuicacalli* (house of songs), and some noblewomen were allowed to become priestesses (Berdan 1982).

Official state instruction began at about six years old, when parents would take their sons to school. However, education was initiated much earlier in the home, the father ministering to the sons and the mother to the daughters (Berdan 1989). Such an urgent emphasis was placed on quickly preparing the children for the assumption of adult responsibilities that teaching began as early as three years old, after the child had already been weaned. The case of females in this instance appears to support a somewhat egalitarian role for them, as marriage obligations and domestic duties were accorded high status and importance, especially given that a strong military flavor permeated Aztec society (Clendinnen 1991; Carrasco 2008; Coe and Koontz 2008).

Religious Practices and Moral Code

As noted previously, religion was more than a segment of Aztec life. Accordingly, every day was a holy day and every member of the community was a part of the collective worship. "It was by religion that the city and tribe were one, and by religion that variety was unified" (Soustelle 1961:93; Carrasco 2008). Charged by such a spiritual force, they viewed poetry as a way of gaining an ultimate understanding of reality and as a way of expressing the results of their inspirations (Leon-Portilla 1992). Much of their artistic and creative activity centered on religious beliefs and practices (Carrasco 1990, 1992). Agriculture products and activities were never far from religious ceremonies and rituals, for maize consumption and farming routines were essential to the preservation of the community.

Aztecs believed that beyond mortal life were heaven, hell, and purgatory (these differed in many particulars from the Christian counterparts, however) (Markman and Markman 1992; Quilter and Miller 2006). Warriors who died in battle were rewarded with heaven, a serene place of flowers, birds, clouds, and sunshine. Those who died in sin fell to a dark forbidding hell. A neutral, intermediate purgatory awaited those who had not given service to the community. Forgiveness for one's sins was possible through confession, in which both spiritual and temporal absolution were granted. As Aztec law allowed only one confession for each individual lifetime, not surprisingly, most waited until old age to confess their sins (Carrasco 2008).

There were many other rituals and ceremonies in which citizens actively participated, including baptism with holy water to ward off evil spirits, and dozens of supplicatory prayers—incantations, poems, or songs—directed to one of the many deities were offered on a commemorative holy day or to request a cure for a particular ailment (Berdan 1982; Leon-Portilla 1963). The people's faith in these practices equaled the height of fervor and devotion reached by other world religions.

Worshiping the gods by prayer was not enough, for the community also undertook large-scale projects in building pyramids (and, for lesser deities, smaller buildings). A whole pantheon of deities was honored in this way, each with his or her own temple of a size to reflect the patron god's importance or insignificance and reflective of the syncretic nature of the Aztec religion that borrowed and absorbed from others (Berdan 1982). It was the Aztecs' goal to be all-encompassing. "Thus, architecture, sculpture, and mural painting as a whole represented . . . the worldview that was the fundamental reason for their [the Aztecs'] existence in the universe. . . . " (Olguin 2008:154).

Among the most important of the pantheon figures was Huitzilopochtli, the sun god, who had evolved from a mixture of many deities the Aztecs had incorporated on their journey to central Mexico (Townsend 1992). According to tribal myth, the Aztecs were now in the fifth world of creation—the previous four had been destroyed by wind, water, fire, and the earth. This fifth world was named *El Quinto Sol* (the Fifth Sun). The earlier cycles of rain and drought, feast and famine, and peace and destruction had instilled a fear of the unknown, and as the famous philosopher/poet/king Nezahualcoyotl suggested, the transitory character and absolute ephemerality inherent in all that exists cannot be ignored (Coe and Koontz 2002; Gillespie 1989; Leon-Portilla 1992). According to one source, "Their agricultural world view, emphasizing the cycle of life and death, led their nobles, warriors, and many artists to believe that giving birth and taking power from other human lives were two parts of an intimate process of creativity" (Carrasco 2008:185; see also Florescano 1994). Because of the failure of past worlds through one catastrophe or another, the natives feared the destruction of this one. Thus, they took it upon themselves to conduct ceremonies to keep the sun alive.

Every day, with the rising of the sun, the priests would sacrifice human beings, cutting out their hearts. Offerings of hearts made at the top of the temple dedicated to Huitzilopochtli guaranteed his daily return. This important act of creation, the rising of the sun, kept the people from total darkness and had to be propitiated. Thousands of people were sacrificed in this manner, for their precious blood, *chalchihuatl*, was the only suitable nourishment for the sun (Padden 1967). Mostly a ritualistic rather than a bloodletting affair, the Spanish later overemphasized its barbaric elements to excuse their own behavior (Coe and Koontz 2002; Carrasco 2008). In any event, many of the

Symbol of Aztec
god of death.

intended sacrificial victims faced the affair in a solemn manner, and often they received special treatment. Miguel Leon-Portilla depicts the austere ceremony in this way:

> There were dialogues between different choirs, solemnly recalling myths and religious beliefs. . . . They were all trained to act just once in the cosmic drama of the Aztec perpetual theater. They were messengers from the people, collaborators with the Sun, carefully chosen to begin their journey to the beyond. (1969:98–99)

Many of those chosen for sacrifice received royal attention and were granted special privileges for weeks prior to the event. On the whole, like most people who die for a cause, these sacrificial victims bravely served their community (Gillespie 1989).

Other victims were not so blessed. This was especially true of the many prisoners captured in actual or acted-out "flower wars" (Berdan 1989). Mock battles were organized with neighboring tribes, and the captured prisoners were later sacrificed to each tribe's respective gods. Like contemporary wars, this practice was brutal and savage but can also be seen as adaptive. In keeping with expansionism and military logic:

> The relationship between human beings and the gods were interdependent. Human beings felt they were the beneficiaries of divine favors in their daily lives and at all important moments of their existence; they gratefully received rain, the fertility of the land, health. . . . Therefore, the faithful felt obligated to provide offerings and sacrifices to the gods to repay them for their gifts. (Lopez Austin and Lopez Lujan 2008:145; see also Clendinnen 1991 and Townsend 1992)

According to one writer, from this state of war "arose the strange institution of the war of the flowers, Xochiyaoyotl, which seems to have come into being after the terrible famines which ravaged central Mexico in 1450" (Soustelle 1961:101; see also Carrasco 2008 and Hassig 1992).

This overview of cultural life highlights the most striking customs. Other activities worthy of mention are the arts and music, architecture and stone carving, and the many fine crafts, such as sculpture and gold and silver jewelry making. One can observe that here were the recipients of the traditions of an ancient people, the human cultural repository of all that came before, barely beginning to indigenously form their own brand of civilization. According to the evidence, and despite certain paradoxes, Aztec life was both culturally sophisticated and generally contoured to the requirements of the total population. Among their most lasting accomplishments are their foods and cuisine (Sokolov 1991) and folk medicines and remedies (Ortiz de Montellano 1990).

Chac-Mool stone statue of reclining figure holding a tray over the stomach.

Color: Intragroup Racism

The emphasis on racial features, or racism, as we know it today did not exist in Aztec society. (In a subsequent chapter, it will be noted that "as the Spaniards consolidated power, they introduced a foreign element into Mesoamerica's ethnic mosaic, and that factor was race" (Berdan 2008:215). Of course, there were physiognomic differences between Indian tribes: some were taller than others, higher cheekbones characterized Mayas, broad noses appeared to be an Olmec trait, and so on. These intraracial differences are similar to the heterogeneity found among Caucasian Europeans. Presumably, the French fit the Alpine mold, Swedes are typical Nordics, and Italians are Mediterranean, at least in a general way. In the main, this is also true of pre-Columbian Indians. Racial appearance did not prevent a capable person from rising to the highest position. Generally, cultural cues—dress, gestures, language, and so on—shaped Aztec thinking and behavior regarding opportunities for social mobility and betterment.

The situation was more relaxed within the Aztec group but changed dramatically when outside Indian groups were encountered, with allies faring better than strangers or enemies. The Aztecs oppressed and exploited other groups in Mesoamerica. In some respects their rule was as severe as that found elsewhere in the world, then and now. Nevertheless, it was not purely racial criteria that determined who was to be subjugated and kept that way; indeed it was those who were "enemies" who caught the unmitigated wrath of the Aztecs.

So, in brief, the whole notion of racial superiority and inferiority and the attendant psychological ramifications were not present in the social system, at least not in the same way as we've come to know them today and not on a large scale. This was a system in which the conquering peoples maintained control for as long as possible, dominating the hinterland from an urban center. In the case of the Aztecs, and because they were relative newcomers to the valley, theirs was a trail of conquest that absorbed and integrated what existed before. This was an already established pattern, culture makers replaced by culture seekers, and so on. Myth was then used to legitimize the successors' claims to dominance. Aztec leaders, for example, claimed Toltec heritages.

> Some Toltec were undoubtedly real; but others were Toltec through myth-making, . . . all conceptions of Tollan and Toltec soon passed into the realm of myth. Those who came after [including the Aztecs] regarded these mythical original Toltec as a race of supermen, taller than ordinary men and able to run faster than decadent later breeds. They were the master artificers, the first scientists, the first astronomers. (Wolf 1959:120)

Ruler designation and legitimacy, then, were inconsistent and usually had a cultural basis and, increasingly over time, a class bias.

Chapter 3

BREAKUP AND TRANSFORMATION OF THE SOCIAL ORDER

Contact: Conquerors Seek Riches

After years of scouting various parts of the Caribbean basin, the Spanish accidentally discovered Mexico. Directed by Governor Diego Velasquez of Cuba, early expeditions to that land failed, but they returned with rumors of fabulous wealth and set the stage for an enterprise that succeeded—the expedition of Hernando Cortes. In February 1519, Cortes set out with 11 ships, over 600 Spaniards, 16 horses, 10 brass guns, several large dogs, and over 200 Indian and African slaves of both sexes (Hassig 2006; Diaz del Castillo 1956).

European exploration of the Caribbean region had begun with Columbus's voyage in 1492, and his discovery was not so much of a New World but of contact between two worlds that were already very old (Mann 2005). By 1519 the Spanish had subdued many natives in the Caribbean islands and established a strong colony in Cuba. From there they moved north, west, and south, seeking other territories to incorporate into their expanding empire. Aiding them in this exploration and discovery were the recently vanquished natives and many imported African slaves.

Background to Exploration and Discovery

The background to these events begins in Europe. The European desire for goods from the Orient ignited an age of expansionism. The defeat of the Moors, who controlled Mediterranean Sea commerce, opened the door for further commercial relations. Spain's interests then turned to building an empire. Tardy in the European rush for new lands and access to resources, the Spanish had their own house to set in order. Belatedly unified in 1469, when the kingdoms of Aragon and Castille were joined through the marriage of Ferdinand and Isabella, they then embarked on casting the Moors out of Granada in 1492. Serious expansionist efforts followed these events (Ruiz 1992; Hamnett 2006). In the aftermath, nationalist consolidation was speeded up. Navigational science developed because of the search for riches and commercial ties with the East and made possible the age of discovery and exploration. Adventurous expansionism became fashionable, and many Spaniards were swept away with get-rich-quick schemes (Hassig 2006).

Spanish success can be attributed to several factors:

1. The tension brought about by the establishment of a centralized government under Ferdinand and Isabella, which encouraged Spanish nationalism and expansionism

2. The control of the strategically located continental gateway between the Mediterranean and the Atlantic

3. The evangelical Catholic zeal and nomadic adventurous ambitions born during the Reconquista (expulsion of the Moors)

4. The obsession to become rich, particularly on the part of dispossessed *segundones* (second sons not entitled to a full share of the family estate because of inheritance laws favoring senior sons), who sought to become *hijos de algo* or *hidalgos* (noblemen, "son of something or someone") through military achievements (Koch 2006; Knight 2002)

The last two influences were particularly instrumental. Many segundones were eager for adventure and enterprise. Joined by other commoners and soldiers of fortune, they set out for the New World. One writer says that the messianic missions were a carryover from earlier times: "The idea that they should be received as god-like beings, which initially flattered the pioneers, was later incorporated into a body of imperial myth as further confirmation of Europe's superiority" (Cocker 1998:8). Further, "it was an axiom of Christian thought, propounded in the opening portion of its most sacred text, the Bible, that all organic life on earth was arranged in a hierarchy, at whose apex stood Christian man" (14).

The motivation provided by fellowship and adventure was strongly augmented by personal ambitions. Spanish soldiers of fortune also sought to become landed aristocrats, along the lines of the old Roman principle of *occu-*

patio, or occupancy. This concept was based on a complex set of laws that translated into a natural "possession is nine points of the law" way to expand and control new territory. This acceptable practice of the Reconquista set the ground for the takeover of the Western Hemisphere (Padden 1967; Canizares-Esguerra 2006). Thus, *conquistadores* (conquerors) had reason to expect a prestigious title and landed estate in the Americas. Acquiring wealth for the Crown and themselves, the conquistadores shaped discovery and colonization efforts to exploit new resources and establish new systems of control even as they disseminated Christianity.

Cortes Begins Conquest

Upon setting foot in Mexico, the Spaniards under Cortes immediately established themselves as conquerors. In the first encounter, over 1,500 Yucatan Mayas died, while the victors lost only 37 men. Moving toward the center of Mexico, the Spaniards repeated this bloody pattern. To maintain military superiority, they often wiped out whole Indian groups. Numerous tribes were met and dealt with summarily. Some small disorganized tribes were quickly subjugated. Others, larger and more socially united, required more time and effort. Cortes directed this process with skillful (although unfeeling) military genius.

Cortes and his men were initially ignorant of Indian languages. As a result, most of their early contacts with natives lacked any exchange of information. However, luck was on the Spaniards' side. Early in the expedition the army met Aguilar, a shipwrecked Spaniard who had learned the local Maya dialect (Diaz del Castillo 1956; Prescott 1931; Hassig 2006). This chance meeting enabled Cortes to use Aguilar as an interpreter, or interrogator, of Indians in the area. Later, as Cortes marched closer to the heart of Mexico, he encountered more good fortune. It was an Indian custom to present gifts to any conqueror, and the

Reception of Hernando Cortes by the Emperor Montezuma.

offerings often included young maidens. One such woman, Malinche, known to the Spaniards as Dona Marina, played a crucial role in the conquest (Townsend 2006; Diaz del Castillo 1956). Her life has become a pivotal point in which to examine the conquest (Paz 1961). More recently, attention has been focused on her role as an early "feminist" (Chorba 2007; Candelaria et al. 1980) and even a "shrink" (Chorba 2007:163) in a modern play that extols her virtues as a visionary. Malinche was originally bilingual, speaking the Nahuatl Aztec language and the Maya dialect Aguilar had learned, but she soon learned Spanish. Consequently, although Cortes understood only Spanish at the outset, he quickly utilized the two translators to become totally apprised of Indian thinking and designs. He used this tactical tool to speed up the march and to guard against attack.

Other tactics benefited the Spanish military juggernaut. For example, some dissident Indians welcomed Cortes as a liberator and assisted in the conquest. Having lived under the thumb of Aztec hegemony for many decades, these subjects (or confederates?) were only too eager to support Spanish military maneuvers, ignoring for the moment what their long-term economic and political interests might have been. Tlaxcala was one of these groups; more than 20,000 Tlaxcalans aided campaigns against other Mexican Valley Indians. When numbers alone fell short, Cortes resorted to psychological ploys to prove the power of his Christian God. Once he had cannon sharpshooters blow up an Indian statue of a god gracing the top of a temple. Thus, by exhibiting a technological advantage, in one stroke he demonstrated the superiority of the Spanish deity and the impotence of Indian gods (Townsend 2009; Hassig 2006; Koch 2006).

When all else failed, Cortes turned to the simple and time-proven practice of rhetorical bravado, inspiring his men to extraordinary acts of military prowess. Cortes, his oratory replete with references to Caesar, Pompey, and Hannibal, transformed each military mission into an act of super-human purpose, enhancing the morale of his troops (Wolf 1959).

> Cortes, the exemplar of that racial supremacy was identified by one recent biographer as a Nietzschean Superman. Another British author of a popular work on the conquistadores wrote that Cortes, a man who never faltered, never despaired even when the outlook was utterly hopeless, must rank as one of the greatest military leaders in history. (Cocker 1998:33)

Montezuma and the Legend of Quetzalcoatl

It appeared that the Indian gods had forsaken the defenders. At every turn Cortes undermined native plots and intrigues. Ironically, a most curious legend apparently furthered the Spanish cause and explained to a degree why many Indians openly received the Spaniards. The legend concerned a tall,

Temple of Quetzalcoatl at Teotihuacan, near Mexico City.

bearded, white god, Quetzalcoatl (the Feathered Serpent, or Kukulcan to Mayas). This legendary character had gained prominence several centuries earlier, during Toltec rule. According to the legend, the beneficent Quetzalcoatl left the valley because of troubled times—mainly the downfall of the Toltec empire—with the promise that he would return. The Indians inferred that Cortes was Quetzalcoatl incarnate, returning from the East intent on bringing back the good, moral, and just life (Coe and Koontz 2008; Padden 1967; Leon-Portilla 1962). However, recent writers stress that this explanation came into vogue after the conquest and served as an Aztec *apologia* for the Spanish victory (Levy 2008; Gillespie 1989).

Cortes exploited this legend when he discovered that the Indians connected him with the returning Quetzalcoatl. Like many other Indian groups, the Aztecs had already incorporated this god into their pantheon. As a result, the Aztec ruler Montezuma believed that Cortes was a god-man as well as an ambassador from a foreign land. These beliefs made him waver and vacillate, delaying action, even as he negotiated and tried to bribe Cortes. "The myth of

Quetzalcoatl told that the bearded royal ancestor would one day arrive to 'shake the foundation of heaven' and conquer Tenochtitlan" (Levy 2008:39).

Montezuma had made a fatal mistake in misreading the motives of his opponent (Padden 1967), and he ignored the advice of the royal family. Such men as Cacama and Cuitlahuac early advocated the extermination of foreign interlopers. The legend of Quetzalcoatl notwithstanding, they felt that Cortes's intent was evil. But growing despair weighed heavily on Montezuma as he followed the inexorable advance of the Spanish from his capital at Tenochtitlan. As the leader of his people, he did not have the luxury of contemplating escape into the hinterland. Instead, a malaise of inactivity overwhelmed him (Leon-Portilla 1962). Meanwhile the conquerors moved ahead, tribe by tribe, province by province.

At first gifts of gold and other rare objects were offered to placate the Spanish. These were to no avail, however, and only whetted conquistador appetites. As Cortes himself said, the Spanish suffered from "an affliction of the heart, and gold was its only remedy" (Diaz del Castillo 1956). The more offerings to the Spaniards in return for their retreat, the more they forged forward. Finally, an Aztec retinue escorted them into the great city of Mexico-Tenochtitlan.

Mexico-Tenochtitlan

Cortes's men viewed the central urban area of Mexico-Tenochtitlan with awe, for they had never seen such a splendid place. Spaniards "had seen nothing better during the twenty-five years of exploration of America than the houses of poles and thatch of Indian tribes, none of whom had risen above a state of barbarism" (Diaz del Castillo 1956:202; see also Carrasco 2008).

Although Europeans were skeptical of creations made by "barbarians," they agreed the city was beautiful. In all their previous contacts with regions and cities of the Old World, nothing had impressed them more. All the buildings of the central plaza were plastered a brilliant white, and the streets were lined with trees and flowering shrubs at regular intervals. At night, well-tended braziers in wall brackets illuminated the streets. Canals were filled with canoes carrying passengers to and fro, and after dark the light from crude lighthouses guided them (Berdan 1982; Zorita 1963).

The city was dominated by the main ceremonial precincts, and a huge marketplace was located in the neighboring community of Tlatelolco (Adams 2005). The temple enclosure itself held 25 pyramids, several palaces, two ball courts, and many civic buildings. Activities abounded throughout the city: policemen made the rounds, anxious crowds gathered near medical and dental facilities, teams played on the ball courts, and schools bustled with children. Tlatelolco, the greatest Indian trading center of the Americas, offered a variety of services and goods: tattooers, barbers, leather tanners, jewelers, healers, basket and pottery makers, tailors, storytellers, magicians, wood carvers, cotton, turkeys, bells, slaves, edible dogs, sweets of all kinds, fish, tomatoes, tortillas, rubber, lentils, peanuts, pineapples, iguanas, firewood, perfume, toys, pumpkins, mate, tobacco, vanilla, parrots, pepper, sweet potatoes, strawberries, meal, jade, turtles, and much more (Townsend 2009; Umberger 2008).

Conflict: Destruction of Tenochtitlan

There were many sources of conflict. Some caused more friction than others, yet in one way or another all reflect the results of Spanish–Indian contact. The conquistadores sought wealth, in whatever form, and this ambition generally brought problems. Their motives were very basic, aimed toward accumulation of wealth, acquisition of territory, and enslavement of the indigenous population. Conversion of the Indians to the Christian faith and making a name for themselves were coinciding objectives. After the available supply of mineral wealth dwindled, the Spaniards turned to other sources of support. This caused the escalating conflict between Spaniards and Indians to reach its climax.

Cortes entered Tenochtitlan and was welcomed by many of the inhabitants. Fearing reprisals from the antagonistic Aztecs, and to secure his own tenuous position, he made Montezuma a prisoner in his own land. Cortes believed the Spaniards needed a hostage to prevent their annihilation. What better hostage than the main leader, who was respected and obeyed by all the people—and who, of course, stumbled into their hands? At the outset, relations between the two groups remained steady. Only after Cortes left for the east coast of Vera Cruz did warfare break out in the city. His departure was prompted by an invasion of other Spaniards, sent from Cuba by Governor Velasquez to reassert control over Cortes and to appropriate his gains. Although many Indians were uncomfortable with the Spanish presence in the city, it was the Spanish who initiated the fighting. One of the captains, Alvarado, was charged with maintaining order while Cortes was away. Instead, fearing a plot, he viciously attacked the Aztecs during a dance ceremony. The Indians retaliated mainly to protect themselves from being massacred (Leon-Portilla 1962; Koch 2006). On Cortes's return everything worsened and turned to chaos. There was nothing for the Spanish to do but flee, and so they did, driven from the city by angry warriors. In the words of the eyewitness Bernal Diaz del Castillo: "Had it been in the daytime, it would have been far worse, and we who escaped did so only by the Grace of God. To one who saw the hosts of warriors who fell on us that night and the canoes full of them coming along to carry off our soldiers, it was terrifying" (1956:315).

While the Aztecs celebrated that night, it was *La Noche Triste* (the Sad Night) for the defeated Spaniards. Many of the conquerors tried to escape

Indian portrayals of the Spanish invasion.

with gold but succeeded in saving only their skins. Others, not so fortunate, drowned because of the heavy weight of the gold they carried. Obtaining sanctuary and aid from friendly Indians, the Spanish nursed their wounds and regrouped. Afterward, they returned, laid siege to the city, and eventually subdued the defenders.

Causes of Aztec Defeat

The Spanish victory over the Aztecs stemmed from a combination of factors: their technological superiority (weapons), their psychologically astute diplomatic strategy, and their temporary alliances with dissident Indians (Koch 2006). Many Aztec customs weakened the Indian cause and added to the Spanish advantage. For instance, Cortes was captured by Aztec warriors on several occasions but was not slain. This transpired because the Indian goal in warfare was to capture, not kill, so that the prisoners could later be ceremonially sacrificed to the gods (Hassig 1992, 2006). Spaniards were able to recapture their leader in the heat of a battle. In addition, fighting against mounted men was new to the natives. Since the Aztecs had never seen horses before, the animals naturally terrified them (the prototype of the smaller horse had become extinct in North America earlier).

Most important of all were the eager Indians who helped Cortes, reasoning (incorrectly, as it developed) that they would benefit in the aftermath (Matthews and Oudijk 2007). When the Aztecs realized that certain defeat was ahead, it was already too late to foster alliances with other similarly besieged Indians. Hence, the conquistadores conquered the tribes piecemeal, without facing coordinated resistance—except when the Aztecs mounted a fierce attack that almost won the day, known as La Noche Triste (Cocker 1998; Levy 2008). Perhaps, like so many other peoples who are convinced their way is right, the Indians felt that the gods would not abandon them. The following comment describes the Aztec view of the fall of the city:

> Nothing but flowers and songs of sorrow are left in Mexico and Tlatelolco, where once we saw warriors and wise men. . . . We know it is true that we must perish, for we are mortal men. You, the Giver of Life, you have ordained it. We wander here and there in our desolate poverty. We are mortal men. We have seen bloodshed and pain where once we saw beauty and valor. We are crushed to the ground; we lie in ruins. There is nothing but grief and suffering in Mexico and Tlatelolco, where once we saw beauty and valor. (Leon-Portilla et al. 2006:149)

Following the downfall of Tenochtitlan in 1521, over 20 years passed before most major Mesoamerican tribes were conquered. Spanish expeditions were sent out in all directions to ensure the subjugation of other tribes, as well as to reveal the locations of gold concentrations. As a result, Spanish population centers of various sizes sprang up, some of which were to serve as start-ing points for subsequent military forays (Hamnett 2006; Joseph and Henderson 2002). The Mayas, despite their defeat in a number of earlier skir-mishes, in 1846 were the last important group to be subdued. Some groups such as the Yaquis of the northwest resisted the Spanish much longer and were only subordinated in the twentieth century by the Mexicans (Spicer 1962). The Spaniards usually sought out groups living in heavily populated settlements, with plenty of resources (and energy!) to capitalize on. The Aztecs fit these criteria in two ways: dense groupings and strategic location. This settlement pattern made it possible to bring the area under immediate subjugation with a few heavy battles. Those who fled to the hinterland and mountains were more fortunate, for they escaped the worst excesses of con-tact and conflict.

Friction over Land and Religious Practices

Land and religious practices were serious conflict issues, often affecting other areas of life. With the defeat of the Aztecs, the Spaniards replaced the old elite and became the new collectors of tribute, which directly involved the land system. However, the most serious and intensely observable confronta-tion emerged in the realm of religion (Lockhart 1992). The Spanish earnestly focused attention on the Indians' minds and hearts. They reasoned that con-trol over the natives' laboring bodies would be assured after a new ideology was implanted. Their program of implementation, reminiscent of the heated European holy wars and inquisitions, was calculatedly vicious and effec-tively merciless.

> And attentive to this, the friars agreed to begin destroying the temples, and not to stop until they were all burned to the ground, and the idols like-wise destroyed and eradicated, even though in doing this they would place themselves in mortal danger. They carried out their plan. (Joseph and Henderson 2002:118; see also Ricard 1966)

A well-organized campaign led to the destruction of many religious sites. Native religious roles and activities of all types were banned. All resisters dis-covered secretly upholding the old "pagan" way were punished or extermi-nated. Not surprisingly, many Indians responded to the Spanish campaign pragmatically, interpreting elements of Christianity "as things they might make their own" (Lockhart 1992:443).

Missionaries, beginning with the Franciscans in 1524, followed by the Dominicans and Augustinians, were charged with the Indian Christianization policy. Many ascetic, humanistically inspired clerics undertook the Christian salvation of Indian souls and worked against great odds to convert them. The missionaries' protective intervention softened the cruel impact of military contact. No matter how lofty their goals, though, the church fathers actually further aided the Spanish crown by opening the Indians up—soul as well as body—thus, speeding up the process of transculturation and the integration into the new order. They also placed a wedge between generations, causing intratribal conflict. Church schools taught Aztec children the catechism to combat Indian religious beliefs. Children were instructed to spy on their elders and report parents who continued in the old ways (Brienen and Jackson 2008).

The missionaries initiated a campaign of indoctrination to make Christianity and "paganism" appear incompatible to the neophytes. Some of the frictional contrasts were these: Aztecs believed in multiple creations, and Christians believed in one beginning and one God; Christians spoke of the pains of hell for sinners, whereas such explicit afterworld punishment was unimportant to the Aztecs. In addition, clerical sects competed for Indian souls, each with its own conversion program and all with the intention of rescuing them from damnation. Vine Deloria, an activist Native American, pithily puts it this way for all Indians:

> It has been said of missionaries that when they arrived, they had only the Book and the Natives had the land; now the Natives have the Book and they [missionaries] have the land. An old Indian once told me that when the missionaries arrived, they fell on their knees and prayed. Then they got up, fell on the Indians, and preyed. (Deloria 1988:101)

On the whole, Indians underwent a traumatic period because of these conflicting religious philosophies (Canizares-Esguerra 2006; Chorba 2007). Missionaries constantly preached that individual salvation of the soul resulted from practicing Christianity. Eternal hell awaited those who rejected Christianity. Significantly, one early observer was already laying the groundwork for both their conversion and their subjugation:

> These Indians are free of almost all the impediments to salvation that hinder the Spaniards, for they are content with very little. . . . They are incredibly patient and long suffering, and meek as sheep. I do not once remember having seen one of them nurse a grudge. They, the humble and scorned, live only to serve and work. (Zorita 1963:164; see also Chipman 2005)

As a result, many Indians attempted a balancing act, worshiping both the old and the new religions and symbols simultaneously. Many priests working with the Indians began to notice a laxity—in some an outright refusal—to conform to the impositions of Christian belief and worship. Meanwhile, the continuing practice of old religious customs by the Indians worsened the tensions that existed between them and the priests (Muldoon 2004; Padden 1967).

Religious conversion programs brought superficial native acceptance, sometimes elicited with torture in the name of God. One such example of a common conversion method for that time is the water torture, in which the mouth was fastened open with a stick and water was poured in until the abdomen swelled up, after which the investigator stood on top of the victim until water mixed with blood came out of the mouth, nose, and ears. (Madsen 1967:385)

In giving its blessing to the "higher-purpose" of converting the heathens to the Christian faith, the Catholic Church provided the Spanish with the legitimacy to carry out their policy of conquest.

Change: Colonial Practices Begin

Sixteenth-century Mexico, and for that matter the New World, was probably among the fastest-moving transitional societies ever, and was the stage for one of the most dramatic cross-fertilizations of cultures then known to humankind. Contact, conflict, and change between the peoples of the Old and New Worlds raised havoc in all sectors of life. Centuries passed before any semblance of stability was established. During that time an empire grew. Owing to the Spanish initiatives, the period bore the earmarks of Spain's culture, even though Indians also participated in the events (Lockhart 1992; Wolf 1959).

European dispossession of colonial subjects, the absorption of their most valuable resources and so much of the product of tribal labour, as well as the orientation of colonial economies towards a Eurocentric goal, are major reasons for the Third World status of much of Africa and South America. (Cocker 1998:20)

Adoption of Christianity

At first Christianity was accepted grudgingly; therefore, the Spanish resorted to other ways of teaching religion. These approaches proved more successful, although Spanish leaders no doubt considered such innovations a retreat from the original goal. They were especially unhappy that such a "demonized" religion had to be accommodated in bringing about changes. The Indians had always accepted good and bad, for in their view, life came from death and creation from destruction and all were parts of the complicated human drama (Muldoon 2004; Cervantes 1994). The Spanish disliked this way of looking at existence, for they viewed reality as an either/or choice, good or bad. To speed up the conversion and the accommodation, the conquerors began to learn and adopt native language practices and cultural images, which enabled them to put the new teachings in books for the natives (Ricard 1966; Brienen and Jackson 2008).

Despite such efforts, conversion went slowly. In part, this was due to the conquistadores who had become *encomenderos* (landowners and tribute collectors), for they held responsibility for Catholic conversion of the natives even though clerics actually administered the program (Behar 1987; Chipman 2005). Making it doubly difficult, native religion was highly developed and was an integral part of the sociopolitical system (Muldoon 2004; Lockhart 1992). While the crown sought to mediate here, government officials, far from Spain, often found themselves in competition for the same resources. These recently arrived gentry often took much more interest in the Indians' labor than in their souls.

A unique and far-reaching incident became the turning point of this era. In 1531, Juan Diego, a recent Indian convert, had a vision affecting all of Indian Mexico's future. According to legend, his miraculous experience occurred on a former Indian holy site dedicated to the Aztec mother goddess Tonantzin ("Little Mother of the Earth and Corn") (Burkhart 2001; Smith 1983). Juan Diego reported that he had seen the embodiment of the Virgin Mary in a saintly, brown-skinned apparition (Hamnett 2006; Mosqueda 1986). At first, skeptics dismissed the report as the superstitious preachings of an Indian, but to prove his point, Juan Diego returned to the same place and the vision reappeared. This time he allegedly brought back evidence: roses and the facial imprint of the Virgin on a shawl. Bishop Zumarraga, who at this time played a vital role in the Christianization program, was finally convinced and, recognizing the significance of the event, sanctioned Juan Diego's vision. Thus began the "Virgen de Guadalupe cult" (Ricard 1966:188; see also Johnson 1980; Taylor 1987).

Above: The powerful Aztec god, Tezcatlipoca, and his role in the earth's creation, was a symbol of paganism in the eyes of missionaries. *Right:* The Virgen de Guadalupe and Juan Diego. His vision of her advanced the natives' conversion to Christianity.

This miraculous affair built on native pride and hastened the Indians' acceptance of Christianity (Muldoon 2004; Guerrero 1987). They found it easier to embrace the Catholic faith, if for no other reason than that one of their own kind was accorded a saintly status and God could be reached through this intermediary (Burkhart 2001; Wood 1991; Johnson 1980). One might also infer that this was an Indian way to reclaim and reestablish the importance of the female in their world and bring back old beliefs and practices that placed women at a higher level. In some ways, that reasoning has survived to the present, as Chicanas look to this image for strength and affection (Rodriguez 1994). In time, the effect of the Virgen de Guadalupe spread throughout Mexico, growing in popularity in the sixteenth century and gaining its full momentum in the seventeenth century (Wolf 1982; Taylor 1987). What began as a cult figure was more firmly institutionalized as Queen of Mexico in 1895 and Patroness of Latin America in 1910; in recent years, Juan Diego was made a saint.

During this time the same bishop, Zumarraga, participated in wiping out other vestiges of Indian religion. In a letter of June 12, 1531, he bragged of destroying more than 500 temples and 20,000 idols (Brienen and Jackson 2008; Ricard 1966; Padden 1967).

Altogether, clerics burned over 400,000 manuscripts. The Spaniards considered written words too powerful in supporting the religio-philosophic beliefs of the Aztecs. They reasoned that destroying books would somehow rub out the spiritual ideology in Indian minds and hearts. (Again, book burning also took place among Europeans who were vying for their particular brand of Christianity, mostly Catholics against Protestants.) Unfortunately, almost all the knowledge the Indians had accumulated was lost. Worse yet, human lives were destroyed—several million died in the decade after the conquest.

Many clerics taught the liturgy and catechism in the native Indian languages in order to contribute to a better understanding of the doctrine. "The friars of Mexico, from the moment of their arrival, recognized that the knowledge of Indian languages was the essential prerequisite of serious evangelization" (Ricard 1966:46). Patterning themselves after Jesus Christ, many also gave an excellent example in their daily lives. This further influenced native adoption of Christianity. Some outstanding, humane priests (Bartolome de las Casas, for one) felt that the Indians should learn all that European education could offer. Because this goal did not coincide with Spanish interests, it was unfortunately eliminated (Padden 1967; Ricard 1966). Other reasons, to be discussed shortly, will clarify the reversal of Spanish policy.

Religious Syncretism

An apparently unexpected outcome of the conversion program was the merging of Indian and Spanish religious features—words, symbols, and so on (Chorba 2007; Lockhart 1992). This phenomenon was indeed also part of the

Spanish experience, for there is no such thing as "pure" Catholicism. In the New World case, certain Indian ceremonial dates were retained with Christian symbols being commemorated. In some respects this adaptation eased native adjustment, gaining the Indians' cooperation by showing respect for their culture. Naturally, it also aided the dissemination of Catholicism, although some would argue that the Indians "have not really accepted" Catholicism (Ricard 1966:276). In any case, it is clear that they have mixed both ancient Indian and Catholic rites and cults into something new that they regard as Mexican Catholic ideology.

This kind of religion is known as "syncretic." Syncretism is a process whereby different cultural elements are combined into an entirely new system. In this instance, previous Indian forms and novel Spanish religious conversion techniques made the recombination easier (Ruiz de Alarcon 1984). This occurred in Mexico because: "indigenous and Spanish patterns reinforced each other" (Lockhart 1992:26), and "[since] two complicated societies were intermeshing, opportunities for new combinations continually arose" (Gibson 1964:404). Thus,

> elements of one religious system are fused with those of another to create hybrid gods, practices, and beliefs. . . . The syncretic model of religious assimilation serves as a perfect complement to cultural *mestizaje,* especially in terms of the aforementioned perceptions of racial *mestizaje* as harmonizing and homogenizing. (Chorba 2007:58)

This cultural and biological cross-pollination is sometimes referred to as *mestizaje* (mixing). By blending the Indian and Spanish views of the world, the Spaniards clearly advanced the colonization program. This innovation sparked overall cultural changes and interactions to fuse, in time, a new culture.

Although Mexican culture has been especially known for mestizaje, few have been able to pinpoint with accuracy what portion of the culture was Spanish or Indian, except to state that this was the initial phase of a process to which several other cultural layers were added later (Chorba 2007). Furthermore, the process was dynamic and unfolded differently for different people. Some were able to avoid total immersion into Spanish culture by retaining their own traditions. However, others were assimilated almost overnight, becoming Hispanicized Indians. In short, "the transformation of native society under Spanish rule was neither uniform nor pervasive" (Spores 1993:91; see also Brienen and Jackson 2008).

Initial Changes in Land, Labor, and Wealth

There was a quantum leap into a new system in terms of how social labor was captured and deployed. "Cultural change or cultural evolution does not operate on isolated societies but always on interconnected systems in which societies are variously linked with wider 'social fields'" (Wolf 1982:76). The people's relationship to the land remained essentially the same. What did change was land ownership: who controlled the land, why, and how and for whom resources were extracted. The introduction of large-scale mining enterprises required the relocation of many Indians. Calpulli members once tied to the land were forced to change residences and work in the bowels of the earth (Adelman 1999; Bellwood 2005; Wolf 1982).

As the new "minority" group in the Spanish colony, the Indians became a source of cheap labor (Wagley and Harris 1958). Thus, the early decades of the colonial period began with a series of changes in the labor and landholding system, each change having a new name—*encomienda, repartimiento,* or *hacienda* (a change from one overseer, to payment for labor, to a plantation system). The name might change and so might the social relations, but the result was always the same: the natives remained oppressed as they were securely rooted in this new social system. In short,

> the encomienda was a political-economic system in which rights to the labor of the Indians residing in a granted area were allocated to designated Spanish *encomenderos.* Their labor was managed through the cooperation of the local *caciques* [local chieftains, an Arawak word brought from the West Indies by the Spanish (Gruzinski 1988); italics mine] but enforced by the Spanish. (Hassig 2006:15)

According to James Lockhart (1992), this was the first stage (1519–1545 or 1550) of the three stages that took place in the colonial period.

A new socioeconomic system was introduced and gradually transformed Indian society. Aztec society was built on local tribes and political units and became progressively more complex with larger and higher networks and strands of control, but the conquest eliminated the bigger units and allowed the local and less comprehensive ones to survive (Gibson 1964; Bellwood 2005). The basis of it was the *altepetl* (an organization of people controlling a set territory) (Lockhart 1992). The calpulli kin- and territory-based system was no longer the primary land-ownership unit, though. Colonial authorities ignored kin networks and all the symbolic and social relations that kept people working together for a common cause and purpose (Wolf 1982). In doing so, they broke up and separated families, calpullis, and even whole villages and effectively forced their members to far-flung regions to labor in new occupations for the ever-expanding colonial empire.

However, Spaniards preserved many calpulli land boundary lines, creating encomiendas or haciendas (landed estates) from them. The Spaniards reasoned that the calpulli kin system was in the way; it made for a united Indian group socially and thus had to be reformed into a new social labor group. Therefore, they broke up the calpulli to better exploit workers. The motto of the new overseers was, "Just give us some hands and backs." The important fact is that Indians no longer controlled or owned their land. The Spaniards had appropriated it, making the natives subjects in their own land. According to Wolf (1982:86), "The European merchants engaged in overseas operations brought surpluses into mercantile exchange in a number of different ways. . . . They grew directly out of the operations of the tributary mode and long remained intertwined with it."

Missionary Program

To offset these abuses, the missionaries entreated the crown to establish separate Indian and Spanish towns. These efforts shielded many Indians from ambitious colonists who aggressively pursued lucrative careers on landed estates, and protected and preserved some Indian land rights and cultural traditions. This plan was not altogether successful, for later colonists were still able to partition Indian lands, a process that continued in a different form until just before the 1910 Revolution. Furthermore, during this period the colonists' struggle over the control of Indian subjects reached tremendous proportions. First the encomenderos gained the upper hand, followed by the clerics, then the crown, and the cycle was repeated in a continual dynamic battle. This rivalry over natives consumed the energies of each competing group in New Spain: Should they emphasize that Indian souls be Christianized (church)? That their labor be exploited (encomenderos)? That they be made into good Spanish subjects (crown)? The three factions agreed, however, that it was all for the natives' benefit to become Christianized laboring subjects (Hamnett 2006; Villegas et al. 1974; Gibson 1966).

To achieve this objective, many Indian leaders (former pipiltin and local *caciques*, or chieftains) who collaborated with the Spanish were absorbed as minor colonial administrators—about one-tenth of the Indian population. This indigenous aristocracy initially helped the Spanish gain and maintain power through traditional practices and tribute networks. They were feared and hated by the indigenous majority and considered traitors. But as the Spanish stabilized and particularly as they grew in numbers through immigration and their new mixed offspring, these native elites were gradually phased out (Gruzinski 1988; Wagley and Harris 1958; Wolf 1982). By assisting in the subjugation of their fellow Indians they became *endonado* (Hispanicized, entitled to use the gentlemanly "Don" before their names), but this conciliatory treatment was short-lived and by the eve of independence these "dons" had lost their minor influence.

Beginnings of Instability

There were several stages to the unfolding colonial system, and Lockhart (1992:428) has suggested three historical periods: (1) 1519 to 1545/50, (2) 1545/ 50 to 1640/50, and (3) 1640/50 to 1800 and after. Clearly, the postconquest period was chaotic, especially when contrasted with the relatively more stable indigenous system that had existed previously, although as Wolf (1982:71) notes, "conquest, incorporation, recombination, and commerce were also characteristic of the pre-Columbian New World" (also see Gutierrez 1991). As will be noted, the colonial period introduced a host of phenomena that radically altered society. These include: (1) Spanish, Indian, and African racial intermixture (known as miscegenation, or mestizaje in Spanish); (2) incipient racist practices, a peculiarly Mesoamerican type affecting both social class and mobility; (3) a program of Spanish racial and cultural superiority, which made the native and darker-hued people feel inferior; (4) the beginnings of a new syncretic culture, part of a wide-ranging mestizaje that still defies a simple definition; and (5) racial and cultural marginality, in which the masses found themselves torn between Old World and New World cultural patterns and racial appearance. The Aztecs called this mental state *nepantilism* (marginality). These conditions brought economic and sociocultural problems and generally a native pattern of thought and action best termed a "psychology of colonization."

> European meanings and practices became mixed with Aztec meanings and practices. . . . The best way to understand the mixing is in terms of transculturation. There are two parts to this definition of transculturation: the space where the process takes place, and the action that takes place. (Carrasco 2005:232)

Thus ended the indigenous period in Mesoamerica. Although the Indians suffered from the human imperfections that pertained to all groups, they had established a great tradition, one in which they took pride. To them it was a time when a closer rapport with nature prevailed, when their decisions, right or wrong, determined their common destiny. Now that came to an end. Previously they had been the captors of energy. Now they became captured in a new system that was bigger and just taking off (Robinson 2004; Sanderson 1995; Wallerstein 1974; Frank 1969). In the metaphor of Wolf, Indians, like so many other peoples in other continents, are a part of the larger picture: "We are back in a world of sociocultural billiard balls, coursing on a global billiard table" (1982:17).

The original humans in Mexico no longer had control of society. Their autonomous, indigenous years were interrupted by the arrival of the Spaniards and the subsequent contact, conflict, and change. Now a stern socialization of rigidly enforced conformity to new Spanish-based social rules awaited them, as they were transformed into a new peasantry and changing way of life. Without the Spanish, the Indians would presumably have fought wars to capture more energy, fashioned new technologies to improve and broaden their lives, and generally reordered and remade the lives of other indigenous peoples like themselves. But the usurpation of this stage of development by the Spanish made the process and outcome quite different from what would have otherwise occurred.

STAGE 1 REFERENCES

Adams, R. E. W. 2005. *Prehistoric Mesoamerica*. Norman: University of Oklahoma Press.

Adelman, J. 1999. *Colonial legacies: The problem of persistence in Latin American history*. New York: Routledge.

Andrews, J. 1984. *Peppers: The domesticated capsicums*. Austin: University of Texas Press.

Behar, R. 1987. Sex and sin, witchcraft and the devil in late-colonial Mexico. *American Ethnologist, Special Edition, "Frontiers of Christian Evangelism"* 14(1)(February): 34–54.

Bellwood, P. 2005. *First farmers: The origins of agricultural societies*. Malden, MA: Blackwell.

Berdan, F. F. 1982. *The Aztecs of Central Mexico: An imperial society*. New York: Holt, Rinehart & Winston.

———. 1989. *Indians of North America: The Aztecs*. New York: Chelsea House.

Berdan, F. F. et al. 2008. *Ethnic identity in Nahua Mesoamerica: The view from archaeology, art history, ethnohistory, and contemporary ethnography*. Salt Lake City: University of Utah Press.

Bernal, I. 1969. *The Olmec world*. Berkeley: University of California Press.

Boone, E. H. 2008. Aztec writing and history. In *The Aztec world*, ed. E. M. Brumfiel and G. M. Feinman. New York: Abrams.

Brienen, R. P., and M. Jackson. 2008. *Invasion and transformation: Interdisciplinary perspectives on the conquest of Mexico*. Boulder: University Press of Colorado.

Brown, M. K., and T. W. Stanton, eds. 2003. *Ancient Mesoamerican warfare*. Walnut Creek, CA: AltaMira Press.

Burkhart, L. M. 2001. *Before Guadalupe: The Virgin Mary in early colonial Nahuatl literature*. Albany, NY: Institute for Mesoamerican Studies, University at Albany.

Candelaria, C. et al. 1980. *Chicanas en el ambiente nacional*. Boulder, CO: Frontiers Editorial Collective.

Canizares-Esguerra, J. 2006. *Puritan conquistadores: Iberianizing the Atlantic, 1550–1700*. Stanford: Stanford University Press.

Carnek, E. E. 2002. Aztecs and the Valley of Mexico. In *Expanding empires*, ed. W. F. Kasinec and M. Polushin, pp. 211–224. Wilmington, DE: Scholarly Resources.

Carrasco, D. 1990. *Religions of Mesoamerica: Cosmovision and ceremonial centers*. San Francisco: Harper and Row. Reissued: Long Grove, IL: Waveland Press, 1998.

———. 1992. *Quetzalcoatl and the irony of empire: Myth and prophecies in the Aztec tradition*. Chicago: University of Chicago Press.

———. 2008. *Daily life of the Aztecs*. Indianapolis/Cambridge: Hackett.

Carrasco, D., L. Lopez Lujan, and E. M. Moctezuma. 2007. *Breaking through Mexico's past: Digging the Aztecs with Eduardo M. Moctezuma*. Albuquerque: University of New Mexico Press.

Cervantes, F. 1994. *The devil in the New World: The impact of diabolism in New Spain*. New Haven, CT: Yale University Press.

Chavez, A. H. 2006. *Mexico: A brief history*. Berkeley: University of California Press.

Chipman, D. E. 2005. *Moctezuma's children: Aztec royalty under Spanish rule, 1520–1700.* Austin: University of Texas Press.

Chorba, C. 2007. *Mexico, from Mestizo to multicultural: National identity and recent representations of the conquest.* Nashville, TN: Vanderbilt University Press.

Clendinnen, I. 1991. *Aztecs: An interpretation.* Cambridge, UK: Cambridge University Press.

Cocker, M. 1998. *Rivers of blood, rivers of gold: Europe's conquest of indigenous peoples.* New York: Grove Press.

Coe, M. 1962. *Mexico.* New York: Praeger Publishers.

Coe, M., and R. Koontz. 2002. *Mexico: From the Olmecs to the Aztecs*, 5th ed. New York: Thames and Hudson.

———. 2008. *Mexico: From the Olmecs to the Aztecs*, 6th ed. New York: Thames and Hudson.

Deloria, V. 1988. *Custer died for your sins: An Indian manifesto.* Norman: University of Oklahoma Press.

Diaz del Castillo, B. 1956. *The discovery and conquest of Mexico: 1517–1521.* New York: Farrar, Straus & Giroux.

Durant, W. 1983. *The story of philosophy: The lives and opinions of the great philosophers of the Western world.* New York: Simon and Schuster (originally published c. 1933).

Florescano, E. 1994. *Memory, myth, and time in Mexico: From the Aztecs to independence.* Austin: University of Texas Press.

Foster, N., and L. S. Cordell, eds. 1992. *Chilies to chocolate: Food the Americas gave the world.* Tucson: University of Arizona Press.

Frank, A. G. 1969. *Capitalism and underdevelopment in Latin America.* New York: Monthly Review Press.

Gibson, C. 1964. *Aztecs under Spanish rule.* Stanford: Stanford University Press.

———. 1966. *Spain in America.* New York: Harper & Row.

Gillespie, S. D. 1989. *The Aztec kings: The construction of rulership in Mexico history.* Tucson: University of Arizona Press.

Gruzinski, S. 1988. The net torn apart: Ethnic identities and Westernization in colonial Mexico, sixteenth–nineteenth century. In *Ethnicities and nations*, ed. R. Guidieri et al. Rothko Chapel Book. Austin: University of Texas Press.

Guerrero, A. G. 1987. *A Chicano theology.* Maryknoll, NY: Orbis Books.

Gutierrez, R. 1991. *When Jesus came, the Corn Mothers went away.* Stanford, CA: Stanford University Press.

Hamnett, B. 2006. *A concise history of Mexico.* Cambridge, MA: Cambridge University Press.

Hassig, R. 1988. *Aztec warfare: Imperial expansion and political control.* Norman: University of Oklahoma Press.

———. 2006. *Mexico and the Spanish conquest.* Norman: University of Oklahoma Press.

Helms, M. W. 1975. *Middle America: A culture history of heartland and frontiers.* Englewood Cliffs, NJ: Prentice-Hall.

Horna, H. 2001. *La indianidad: The indigenous world before Latin Americans.* Princeton, NJ: Markus Wiener.

Johnson, H. L. 1980. The Virgin of Guadalupe in Mexican culture. In *Religion in Latin American life and literature*, ed. L. C. Brown and W. F. Cooper. Waco, TX: Markham Press Fund.

Joseph, G., and T. Henderson, eds. 2002. *The Mexico reader: History, culture, politics*. Durham, NC: Duke University Press.

Knight, A. 2002. *Mexico: From the beginning to the Spanish conquest*. Cambridge, UK: Cambridge University Press.

Koch, P. O. 2006. *The Aztecs, the Conquistadores, and the making of Mexican culture*. Jefferson, NC: McFarland.

Leon-Portilla, M. 1962. *Broken spears: The Aztec account of the conquest of Mexico*. Boston: Beacon Press.

———. 1963. *Aztec thought and culture*. Norman: University of Oklahoma Press.

———. 1969. *Pre-Columbian literatures of Mexico*. Norman: University of Oklahoma Press.

———. 1988. *Time and reality in the thought of the Maya*. Norman: University of Oklahoma Press.

———, ed. 1992. *The Aztec image of self and society: An introduction to the Nahua culture*. Salt Lake City: University of Utah Press.

Leon-Portilla, M., J. Klor de Alva, K. A. Garibay, L. Kemp, and A. Beltran. 2006. *The broken spears: The Aztec account of the conquest of Mexico*. Boston: Beacon Press.

Levy, B. 2008. *Conquistador: Hernan Cortes, King Montezuma, and the last stand of the Aztecs*. New York: Bantam Books.

Lockhart, J. 1992. *The Nahuas after the conquest: A social and cultural history of the Indians of central Mexico, sixteenth through eighteenth centuries*. Stanford, CA: Stanford University Press.

Lopez Austin, A., and L. Lopez Lujan. 2001. *Mexico's indigenous past*. Norman: University of Oklahoma Press.

———. 2008. Aztec human sacrifice. In *The Aztec world*, ed. E. M. Brumfiel and G. M. Feinman. New York: Abrams.

Madsen, W. 1967. Religious syncretism. In *Handbook of Middle American Indians, Vol. 6*, ed. R. Wauchope. Austin: University of Texas Press.

Mann, C. C. 2005. *1491: New revelations of the Americas before Columbus*. New York: Vintage.

Markman, R. H., and P. T. Markman. 1989. *Masks of the spirit: Image and metaphor in Mesoamerica*. Berkeley: University of California Press.

———. 1992. *The flayed god: The Mesoamerican mythological tradition: Sacred text and images from Pre-Columbian Mexico and Central America*. San Francisco: Harper.

Mathien, F. J., and R. H. McGuire. 1986. *Ripples in the Chichimec Sea: New considerations of Southwestern-Mesoamerican interactions*. Carbondale and Edwardsville: Southern Illinois University Press.

Matthews, L., and M. Oudijk. 2007. *Indian conquistadors: Indigenous allies in the conquest of Mesoamerica*. Norman: University of Oklahoma Press.

McGregor, J. C. 1982. *Southwestern archaeology*. Urbana: University of Illinois Press.

Megged, A. 2010. *Social memory in ancient and colonial Mesoamerica*. New York: Cambridge University Press.

Morgan, L. H. 1963. *Ancient society*. New York: Meridian Books.

Mosqueda, L. J. 1986. *Chicanos, Catholicism, and political ideology*. Lanham, MD: University Press of America.

Muldoon, J. 2004. *The spiritual conversion of the Americas*. Gainesville: University Press of Florida.

Olguin, F. S. 2008. The art of the Aztec era. In *The Aztec world*, ed. E. M. Brumfiel and G. M. Feinman. New York: Abrams.

Ortiz de Montellano, B. 1990. *Aztec medicine, health, and nutrition*. New Brunswick, NJ: Rutgers University Press.

Padden, R. C. 1967. *The hummingbird and the hawk: Conquest and sovereignty in the Valley of Mexico: 1503–1541*. Columbus: Ohio State University Press.

Paz, O. 1961. *The labyrinth of solitude*. New York: Grove Press.

Peterson, F. A. 1962. *Ancient Mexico*. New York: G. P. Putnam's Sons.

Prescott, W. H. 1931. *History of the conquest of Mexico*. New York: Random House (originally published in 1842).

Quilter, J., and M. Miller. 2006. *A pre-Columbian world*. Cambridge, MA: Harvard University Press.

Ricard, R. 1966. *The spiritual conquest of Mexico*. Berkeley: University of California Press.

Riley, C. L. 1987. *The frontier people: The greater Southwest in the protohistoric period*. Albuquerque: University of New Mexico Press.

Robinson, W. I. 2004. *A theory of global capitalism: Production, class, and state in a transnational world*. Baltimore: Johns Hopkins University Press.

Rodriguez, J. 1994. *Our Lady of Guadalupe*. Austin: University of Texas Press.

Ruiz, R. E. 1992. *Triumphs and tragedy: A history of the Mexican people*. New York: W. W. Norton.

Ruiz de Alarcon, H. 1984. *Treatise on the heathen superstitions that today live among the Indians native to this New Spain, 1629*, trans. and ed. J. R. Andrews and R. Hassig. Norman: University of Oklahoma Press.

Sahagun, B. 1932. *A history of ancient Mexico*. Glorieta, NM: The Rio Grande Press.

Sanderson, S. K. 1995. *Civilizations and world systems: Studying world-historical change*. Thousand Oaks, CA: AltaMira Press.

Sharer, R. J., and D. C. Grove, eds. 1989. *Regional perspectives on the Olmec*. Cambridge, England: Cambridge University Press.

Smith, J. B. 1983. *The image of Guadalupe: Myth or miracle*. New York: Doubleday.

Smith, M. E. 2008. The Aztec empire. In *The Aztec world*, ed. E. M. Brumfiel and G. M. Feinman. New York: Abrams.

Sokolov, R. 1991. *Why we eat what we eat: How Columbus changed the way the world eats*. New York: Simon & Schuster.

Soustelle, J. 1961. *Daily life of the Aztecs*. Stanford, CA: Stanford University Press.

Spicer, E. 1962. *Cycles of conquest*. Tucson: University of Arizona Press.

Spores, R. 1993. Spanish penetration and cultural change in early colonial Mexico. In *The Indian in Latin American history: Resistance, resilience, and acculturation*, ed. J. E. Kicza. Wilmington, DE: A Scholarly Resources.

Suarez, J. A. 1982. *The Mesoamerican Indian languages*. Cambridge, England: Cambridge University Press.

Suchlicki, J. 2001. *Mexico: From Montezuma to the fall of PRI*. Washington, DC: Brassey's.

Taylor, W. B. 1987. The Virgin of Guadalupe in New Spain: An inquiry into the social history of Marian devotion. *American Ethnologist, Special edition "Frontiers of Christian Evangelism"* 14(1) (February): 9–33.

Townsend, R. F. 1992. *The Aztecs*. London: Thames and Hudson.

———. 2006. *Malintzin's choices: An Indian woman in the conquest of Mexico*. Albuquerque: University of New Mexico Press.

———. 2009. *Aztecs*. New York: Thames and Hudson.

Umberger, E. 2008. Ethnicity and other identities in the sculptures of Tenochtitlan. In *Ethnic identity in Nahua Mesoamerica: The view from archaeology, art history, ethnohistory, and contemporary ethnography,* ed. F. F. Berdan et al. Salt Lake City: University of Utah Press.

Villegas, D. C. et al. 1974. *A compact history of Mexico.* Los Angeles: University of California, Latin American Center.

Wagley, C., and M. Harris. 1958. *Minorities in the New World: Six case studies.* New York: Columbia University Press.

Wallerstein, I. 1974. *The modern world-system: Capitalist agriculture and the origins of the European world-economy in the sixteenth century.* New York: Academic Press.

Weaver, M. P. 1993. *The Aztecs, Maya, and their predecessors: Archaeology of MesoAmerica.* San Diego: Academic Press.

Willey, G. R. et al. 1964. The patterns of farming: Life and civilization. In *Natural environment and early cultures: Handbook of Middle American Indians, Vol. 1,* ed. R. C. West. Austin: University of Texas Press.

Wolf, E. 1959. *Sons of the shaking earth.* Chicago: University of Chicago Press.

———. 1982. *Europe and the people without history.* Berkeley: University of California Press.

Wood, S. 1991. Adopted saints: Christian images in Nahua testament of late Colonial Toluca. *The Americas* 47(3): 259–293.

Zorita, A. 1963. *Life and labor in ancient Mexico.* New Brunswick, NJ: Rutgers University Press.

Spanish Colonial Era
1521–1821

As the indigenous way of life gave way to a new one forged in part from their old customs and in part from newly learned patterns, what would later be referred to as a peasant society, there were many unhappy and harsh experiences. The Indians of Mexico were ill-prepared for what they had to undergo, an experience that was repeated in other parts of the world as Europeans incorporated more and more territory and people into their ever expanding empires. The peasant society that resulted from such major upheavals was a strange yet interesting amalgamation, and as noted, there were several stages to it (Lockhart 1992). In Mexico, particularly, it was a fascinating agglomeration of bits and pieces that coalesced from culture contact and change reverberations. One way to look at peasant ways of life is as fragments from the past—taken from societies and taken from cultures—that remain integrated into the present. In many ways, peasant life shows how indigenous peoples clung to the past to preserve some aspects of their identity. A cultural lag thus was always present in the resounding transformation of tribal societies and indigenous states into a subordinate system that became connected with larger political economic systems. In time, the Mexican peasants grew to be an insulated, protective society; perhaps because they were denied significant economic power in the new order, peasant groups were concerned more with social power and prestige.

Not all of the experiences of the colonial period were negative. The sequence and degree of contact and change were not the same for everyone nor were the outcomes entirely predictable. Many natives benefited during the transition phases, sometimes well into the colonial era. Nevertheless, colonial directives were forceful enough to restrict the range of behavior; the majority of Indians were subjected to a cruel pattern. "The colonial relationship . . . chained the colonizer and the colonized into an implacable dependence, molded their respective characters and dictated their conduct" (Stein and Stein 1970:vii). In the end, indigenous society broke down because of an experience that was largely damaging and unrewarding, especially since matters (i.e., independent cultural evolution, innovation, and so on) were taken out of their hands. In some ways, the natives became subservient to cruel, overbearing, and demanding masters; duties and accomplishments dictated by others now ruled the day. A new type of evolution emerged, as reaction to these intrusions eventually called for social movement and radical revolution to bring about change.

Since the Spaniards were the masters of the environment, they largely determined the extent of autonomy and coercion—who would do what, when, where, and why. This arrangement decisively affected the character and health of each person in the social system. Learning experiences and therefore all lives were effectively shaped by Spaniards.

As a tribute to the human character, many native peoples strove to liberate themselves from such harsh and inhumane conditions, if only temporarily. Moreover, Spanish cultural lifeways were not entirely embraced by natives. Still, the Indians were taught how to respond to events (beliefs), to know the difference between good and bad events (values), to integrate the details of proper or improper performance (rules), and finally, to understand that their behavior would be rewarded by positive or negative treatment (sanctions). These directives and regulations were unevenly impressed upon the indigenous population, causing many maladaptations. With all its vicissitudes, the colonial period was extremely significant because it was a macrohistorical imprint that lingered in the people's minds and guided their actions long after it officially fell apart.

Chapter 4

INTACT AND STABLE SOCIAL ORDER

Class: Haciendas and Debt Peons

The Spanish utilized indigenous socioeconomic practices to make quick changes and also introduced piecemeal alterations over several centuries, all in their favor. With variations reflecting the respective time periods, modern problems involving the relationship between developed and underdeveloped societies often echo those generated by the Spanish colonial system in Mexico (Robinson 2004). One country develops by exploiting another country, leaving it underdeveloped; thus, development and underdevelopment can often be viewed as two sides of the same coin. Political and social actions support this system. This is the story of Spain's colonization policies—mercantilism and imperialism—and of how Indian society became underdeveloped (Frank 1969).

Spanish Motives

The motives behind the socioeconomic class structure that emerged can be briefly summarized. Conditions in Spain, even before contact with the New World, had led to the establishment of a centralized, crown-controlled economy. Ferdinand and Isabella sought to establish a monopoly on gold and silver resources. This led to maintaining a favorable trade balance and control of the colonial economy in order for the crown to retain strict control of American metal exports. These monopolistic ventures follow the principles of mercantilism, that is, merchant wealth and the exchange of commodities under the centralized direction of the state (Wolf 1982).

> Two things stand out . . . : specialized production became possible only in the context of increasing commerce, and mining was the stimulus that accelerated all the other factors in the process. Finally, the centrality of these production areas was not only economic but also social and political. (Chavez 2006:85)

At the outset of the occupation of the New World, the Spanish seized and sent to Spain the most readily available sources of liquid wealth. Indian jewelry, often including fine works of art, was smelted into bullion. After the available supply of Indian gold and silver was depleted, the Spaniards forced the natives to work the mines. Since the Indians had only begun to labor in a few mines, the Spaniards strove to locate new ones. The exploration for new mines was an integral part of each step of the conquest and the gradual occupation of Mexico's territory, and it was silver mining that drove the engine of economic growth (Schwartz 2000; MacLachlan and Rodriguez O. 1980; Raat 1992).

Indigenous labor was always the crucial resource for mining, but additionally, new techniques for extraction, production, and shipment evolved. More than 185,000 kilograms of gold and silver were transported from the New World (including Mexico as well as other areas) to the Old World during the period from 1503 to 1660. Calculated at twentieth-century prices, the value of the gold alone amounted to billions of dollars. Silver would bring the total worth close to five billion dollars in mineral resources (Chavez 2006; Wolf 1982). This economic activity was an important feature of mercantilism, the precursor to capitalism in which merchant wealth is developed and regulated in a more or less tributary system.

> The mineral and human wealth found in New Spain shaped Spanish economic policy for the next three centuries. Spain believed, as did other European powers, that colonies existed for the benefit of the mother country. The objective of this policy of mercantilism was to strengthen Spain and to protect Spanish industry and manufacturing. The colonies were to supply minerals and raw materials that could be converted into manufactured products and sold back to the colonists. Local manufacturing and industry were discouraged. (Suchlicki 2001:42)

One would assume that Spain's future was secure with all these riches. However, the Spaniards were concerned with establishing a nonlaboring, genteel, aristocratic life as *gente de razon*—people of reason (Boyer and Spurling 2000; Wolf 1982); they sought to continue a feudal tradition from the middle ages in which prodigality and extravagance were considered lofty human qualities (Elliott 1963). To maintain this lifestyle, they generally used their liquid wealth to purchase manufactured products from others. Spain actually aided the rise of manufacturing in other European nation-states while unevenly developing her own industries (Elliott 1963; Stein and Stein 1970). Nevertheless, since Spain still had an abundance of colonial land and labor to exploit, its decline as a world power was gradual.

Many Dark Age customs flourished in the New World, and the hacienda itself was an offshoot of the medieval feudal system. In the readaptation to the new setting, however, there was a flexibility and resilience that allowed the hacienda to be the production unit for mining, livestock, farming, and other craft and specialty trades. Nevertheless, the 1500 to 1700 era marked the formation of the landed estate, and while local units and networks were important, it was the macrolevel, world developments that generated a peasant class. While they differed somewhat in central and eastern Europe, in Mexico these regional transformations took the forms of encomienda, repartimiento, and gradually debt peonage and outright slavery (Hamnett 2006; Wolf 1982; Stein and Stein 1970; Israel 1975).

Encomienda.   After the proximate wealth of minerals was attained, Indian labor turned to working the land (Ruiz Medrano 2006). Private property and large feudal landholding units were European practices that guided how the Indians fit into the new colonial social organization. Since mere land

A sixteenth-century depiction of Indians suffering from smallpox.

ownership does not produce a commodity, there had to be means whereby Indians could work the land to benefit those who controlled it. Thus, land and laboring natives were immediately brought under Spanish control. In the first decades, Indian slave labor worked the mines and performed other arduous tasks, and Indians became rapidly integrated into the tribute system of the *encomienda* (Hassig 2001; Wood 2003; Zavala 1943).

The encomienda grew out of another Spanish custom during the Reconquista; this custom was the granting of land to reward a faithful conquistador. It only made sense to continue this practice in the Americas, and the encomienda system additionally added Indian tribute practices (or labor) to the arrangement. This trusteeship of land, together with the granting of Indian subjects to military leaders (known as encomenderos), was the basis of the encomienda system (Hassig 2001; Himmerich y Valencia 1991). Since the encomenderos only replaced Indian overlords, accepting tribute from native labor, at first the transition was relatively easy (Chavez 2006; Gibson 1984; Simpson 1966). Arriving late but eager to exploit just like encomenderos, other Spaniards accelerated the acquisition of land and labor, which generated additional difficulties. The encomenderos abused Indians by forcing them to work harder and longer, and many were uprooted and sent to northern mining and southern lowland plantation regions. In addition to these pressures, there were a great many Indian lives lost due to exposure to European diseases for which the native populations had no inherited protection (Hassig 2001; Mann 2005; Himmerich y Valencia 1991).

Many humanitarian clerics influenced the crown in limiting the worst excesses of encomienda. It became obvious to them and others that there would be few Indians left under the present overexploitation practice and thus hardly any souls to convert (Muldoon 2004; Knight 2002). Royal authorities mostly agreed, but they, too, were motivated by self-interest, as the crown must receive its *quinto* (one-fifth) of the take (Chavez 2006). So that they would share in the profitable arrangements themselves, their representatives undermined growing encomendero power, which was increasingly dominating Indian land and labor, and thus wealth. Many encomenderos were challenged for this reason. For example, Cortes, now the Marquis de Oaxaca, was the biggest landowner in Mexico, controlling an Indian population of over 20,000. "His tremendous riches—it is likely that he was at one time the wealthiest person in the entire Spanish world—depended chiefly on encomienda, which furnished him a large annual tribute income and labor for his various enterprises" (Gibson 1966:55; see also Hamnett 2006), including distributing *peonias* (smaller tracts of land that became ranches) to his foot soldiers to help cultivate interest in agriculture (Florescano 1984). He was recalled to Spain to answer charges of treason, for the crown feared his growing power (Chevalier 1966).

Repartimiento.   The crown sought to prevent the decimation of the natives, as occurred in the Caribbean, and initiated a twofold policy: (1) save the natives from total exploitation, and (2) restructure the colony to provide a broader Spanish ruling elite in place of a few enterprising individuals. This new program was called *repartimiento* (distribution or allotment of workers). It was intended to provide wages for Indian labor—but due to the human drive to maintain power and control of resources, it did something else (Gibson 1966).

Under this policy, laborers were to work for wages a limited number of days per year and thus have time for their own needs and plans. Not surprisingly, the results were otherwise. Self-interest guided the adoption of repartimiento, for extraction of Mexico's resources would stop if native labor disappeared. Consequently, the crown's acceptance of pagan Indians as worthy of Christian salvation (as urged by the missionaries) was something of a subterfuge for ensuring that labor services continued. However, it was not very successful in this: the indigenous population fell from 25 million in 1519 to a little over a million by 1650 (Mann 2005; Borah and Cook 1960; Schwartz 2000; Stein and Stein 1970; Gibson 1966). One writer stated that for every 16 Indians in 1519 there was only one left in the next century (Sanchez-Albornoz 1988).

The Mexican hacienda, still standing in twenty-first-century Mexico.

From the beginning, repartimiento was almost totally ignored by the colonists, and the Indians were unhappy because it was obligatory labor. In just a few decades, the conquistadores were joined by lawyers, merchants, doctors, government officials, and some enterprising missionaries in a continuing program of native exploitation (Chevalier 1966; Hamnett 2006). As a general practice, colonists either casually avoided the repartimiento policy or tactfully manipulated it to their advantage. By controlling large parcels of good fertile land, land required for the necessities of life, the landowners held the Indians at their mercy. The latter, in turn, accepted any wages the Spaniards deemed fair. Usually the wages were low, for the Spaniards were interested in high profits. The practice of buying cheap and selling high took precedence over human need. Moreover, as the Spanish dictated the time and wages of work, they also began to introduce specialized craft and occupation sectors (Florescano 1984).

Debt Peonage. Most natives wound up working more days than the number specified by repartimiento. These specified days were a safeguard to allow them time to work their own land, but generally they had little land and were rapidly losing what remained. Instead, laborers sought more work on Spanish-held land for subsistence, and especially to acquire the new medium of exchange to pay the tribute—money (Chavez 2006; Florescano 1984). Because of this need and the landowner's demand for low-paid laborers, the owner– worker relationship turned sharply in favor of the former. The landowners enthusiastically participated, for their enterprise would quickly crumble if labor demands went unmet. Denied the right to leave the farm, the laborers were bound to the land in a very duplicitous way. Goods and money were advanced to them and they became obligated to work off this debt. This was a legal tactic that led to another more solidly institutionalized system known as the Mexican hacienda (Hamnett 2006; Israel 1975; Zavala 1943). Oddly, the initial push was to allow them the right to participate in a "free market" system, but it ended up being the opposite (Florescano 1984), leading to a practice that fit neatly into a mercantilist system, which was closed and bound by Spanish interests. Wolf's words adeptly summarize the process of colonization and imperialism:

> The conquering Spaniard became a mining entrepreneur, a producer of commercial crops, a rancher, a merchant . . . he wanted to organize and press the human resources under his command, to enlarge his estate, to take his place among the other men grown rich and powerful in the new utopia. (Wolf 1959:176; see also Wolf 1982; Robinson 2004)

Haciendas and Debt Peonage

Undoubtedly, the mechanism that established a bonded landowner– laborer network leading to the hacienda system was the practice of advancing Indians money or credit for future work (Wolf 1982; Chevalier 1966). Offering advancements, landowners or their emissaries scoured the countryside for prospective workers, even infringing on mission domains and free Indian communities. The temptation was too great for Indians who lacked resources, for they still had to survive. If the contract was accepted, the worker fulfilled his part by working for a set period. Indians who defaulted were sought by the authorities and punished. In this way, they were bonded to the land as debt peons, and the landowners became their overseers and creditors.

With the available labor pool thus anchored to the land, the hacienda system burgeoned. Its evolution and the gradual consolidation of the native workforce became the socioeconomic features that marked the colonial epoch. Peonage, and specifically debt peonage, was the trademark of the hacienda system. It grew slowly but strongly and lasted until the twentieth century. At first Indians were given money or credit to work a specified time, but later, with meager wages and *hacendado* (landowner) demands for a permanent workforce, the relationship changed. For example, workers frequently extended their stay on a job by accepting more credit or money. A vicious circle resulted in which they seldom completed the contract without asking for more credit ahead of time. They found themselves as poor at the end of the contract as at the beginning and signed on again for more credit. Whenever a family need or crisis required extra money, they might mortgage away a year or two of the future. If the household head died before fulfilling the contract, the sons would inherit the debt. In effect, "heritable debt" (Wolf 1982) weighed heirs down even before they could start their own families.

> Under the pretext of "civilizing" the *castas* [half-breeds] by requiring them to stay in one place and work, landowners would advance them their pay in the form of goods, almost never in money, and hold them against their will to work at *haciendas, estancias* [ranches], mines, or workshops. (Chavez 2006:84)

Other hacienda practices besides debt peonage affected the Indians. Bound to the land, the peons were also required to benefit the hacendados by buying on credit from *tiendas de raya* (hacienda stores). Also, they had to live in dwellings provided by landowners that were poor in quality, since good homes cost money and might lower the hacendado's profits (Chevalier 1966; Schwartz 2000; Whetten 1969).

Still, there were many instances when natives escaped the worst effects of a hacienda-type system. This was especially true in mission, communal towns (called *republicas de indios*) in southern Mexico (Ruiz 1992; Chance 1978), where natives were either in complete control or assisted the church fathers; in these cases they avoided debt peonage.

> Each Indian republic was organized around a principal town, the seat of the main town council or cabildo; secondary towns were known as pueblos sujetos (subject, or secondary, pueblos). The republics operated in the classical framework of direct self-government. Their self-sufficiency was

ensured, as they were granted rights to natural resources such as farmland and water, and forest or pasture. (Chavez 2006:52)

Research has also shown that many peons willingly moved from villages to haciendas when times were hard (Gibson 1984). Despite these exceptions, the native majority, and especially the growing mestizo population, came under the hacienda system in the other regions.

Social Role of Hacendados.   The quasi-medieval manor complex of the hacienda became the cornerstone of colonial society, although with significant variations from region to region (Curtin 2000; Wolf 1982). In an almost knightly fashion, the hacendado patron protected and cared for the native peons, a patronage/peonage social world efficiently and obediently structured to serve the interests of the empire.

Key to Spanish rule was the role of individual and personal initiative. Each of the strong-willed hacendados—whether conquistadors, late-arrival civilians, lawyers, or merchants—established a mini-empire based on a strong hand and an indomitable patron will. A patronage system of social relations prevailed, in which the hacendado opted for the parent role and forced the peons to play children (Suchlicki 2001). If they misbehaved, he sternly upbraided them; if they were hard working and respectful, he solemnly patted their heads in a gesture of assurance. The patron hacendado was a god-figure on the landed estate, regardless of how well or badly Indians conducted themselves (Paz 1961; Gonzalez and Premo 2007).

Much of this paternal quality stemmed from the strong assertive manner of the conquistadores. From the start they used the vanquished race and depressed their spirit to take advantage of the new possessions. Being soldiers rather than workers, they fashioned unjust privileges to acquire wealth (Hamnett 2006; Ramos 1962).

Colonists who followed adhered to this type of manly behavior. Spanish tradition supported this strong, lordly male image that was readapted to New World conditions. *Caudillismo* (charismatic leadership) was the offshoot of this masculinity. Beginning on a small scale on haciendas or in minor military engagements, many *caudillos* rose to high positions of national leadership. Caudillismo is associated with the drive to acquire an economic empire and, later, political leverage. The Indian population served as the backdrop for this scenario.

The Spaniards continued to use Indian labor for farming, now turning to cash crop commerce. Sugar, coffee, maize, rice, bananas, wheat, tobacco, chocolate, and other crops were the mainstays of a growing economic empire. In most instances each of these crops and related enterprises constituted a monopoly (cf., tobacco, Deans-Smith 1992). Much of the harvest was processed for export to the Old World (Curtin 2000; Stein and Stein 1970), and some became sources of immense wealth. Cochineal (a red dye from an insect that feeds on cactuses), for example, became second only to silver in importance (Wolf 1982). Although there was a gain for the natives in having pigs, sheep, goats, and so on incorporated into their subsistence system, on balance they actually lost with these changes in their environment (Florescano 1984).

Specializing in sugar and pulque in the central region and cattle hides in the north, the haciendas supported the colony. Moreover, as self-sufficient estates, the haciendas provided the landowner and peons with all the necessities of life. On some of these estates, particularly the *mestas* (cattle or livestock ranches), the hacendados ruled on horseback. Accompanying the conquest, occupation, and settlement by Europeans was the introduction of livestock and the various related enterprises associated with it: cattle, sheep, *vaqueros* (cowboys), sheepherding, processing and distribution of products, and so on. Such activities speeded up culture change among the population and accelerated Spanish imperialism. In short, the long workdays and exploitation of families and peasant communities were foundational to the economic success of the hacienda (Chavez 2006; Florescano 1984).

Hacendados who controlled the largest parcels of land sought additional rewards, such as prestige and esteem from their fellow citizens. Consequently, social life revolved around the *gentil* (genteel) population, who maintained city residences along with their landed estates—the city for living and the country estate for supporting that lifestyle (Florescano 1984; 1989). Many enjoyed leisure and recreation in both urban and rural settings. Colonial society was based on hacendado–peon relationships, which included a complex of feelings, attitudes, and activities that demonstrated and reinforced superordinate/subordinate and superior/inferior relations and behaviors. Today, even though the hacienda system has presumably ended, this psychocultural construct persists in a large part of Latin America (Kicza 1993; Wagley and Harris 1958).

Life of the Debt Peons: Mechicanos.   As previously noted, the ethnic label "Chicano" was probably derived from the word "Mechicano," a sixteenth-century pronunciation of Mex(ch)icano. After the conquest and subjugation of central Mexican natives, the Spaniards generally referred to them as Mechicanos and later used the term for other similarly vanquished Indians; certain impoverished neighborhoods in cities and towns even became named "mexicanos." The word finally became synonymous with the dispossessed lower-class peons. It is interesting and somehow symbolic that the Aztec tribal name, Mexica, became fixed in this way. Because of the social class relationships of the colonial period, an ethnic label for the lower class became cemented in the minds of a people to remind them of their station, presumably so that they would remain there.

All of the pre-Columbian Indian classes—pipiltin, macequales, and so on—were compressed into one: peons. Limited exceptions were members of the Indian nobility who cooperated during the early sixteenth century and whose families, in some instances, maintained their cacique (local chieftain) role near the end of the colonial period (Gruzinski 1988). Although some remained in leadership positions, most eventually found themselves in the lowest class. According to the thinking of that time, the "doctrine of natural slavery was entirely applicable to the Indians on the grounds of their inferiority" (Elliott 1963:71–72; see also Knight 2002). Noble collaborators assisted in the maintenance of an empire and often mixed with the Spanish racially, but over time, social class barriers hardened and most caciques were eased out of their higher status.

As the natives acculturated (learned about and adjusted to) Spanish culture, they also realized that moving up socially came with it. Of course, upward mobility was an opportunity reserved for the Spanish and was not an option for most natives, especially if they joined in the system that kept most of them in their places (both low status and poor environments). In other words, they became cogs and springs in the wheels that ran the colonial enterprise, aiding and abiding in keeping matters that way.

Socioeconomic Class Rankings

Spanish colonial authorities defined socioeconomic class rankings simply. Usually, "color-class became . . . to a certain extent entangled with labor-class" (de Madariaga 1947). In addition to race, place of birth and occupation determined social status. Spaniards born in Spain were at the top. Known as *gachupines* ("those who wear spurs"), they occupied the highest positions of religious, political, economic, and social life. Gachupines were primarily responsible for curbing overexploitation of Indians by *criollos* (Spaniards born in the New World) and securing and maintaining control of the colony for Spain.

Below gachupines in the social order were criollos, some of whom carried a slight amount of Indian or African blood, a fact they preferred to conceal (Knight 2002; Restall 2005). The criollos adopted the attitudes and behavior of gachupines, but most were artisans, mine owners, parish priests, merchants, and landowners. They were barred from attaining the higher-status businesses or occupations and came to resent the Spaniards. There were close to one million of them by the end of the eighteenth century, and by then, British expansionist threats had opened opportunities for them in the military. Before this military calling (which also opened up and offered social advancement for many *mestizos* [racially mixed individuals] and Hispanicized Indians) criollos were kept from the highest church and state offices.

An interesting group of this period, almost as unfortunate as the Indians, were the mestizos, whose fortunes waxed and waned by virtue of how closely their color matched that of the Europeans (Bennett 2009; Hamnett 2006; Knight 2002). Many racial and social-class subdivisions, based on various combinations of Spanish, Indian, and African descent, existed within this category. Birthright (parentage of a higher status) and racial appearance were the

Commoners in the city of Puebla.

determining factors of group membership. The mestizos' rise was unevenly checkered, and generally they filled occupations in the new colonial enterprises as "rootless" men (Florescano 1984:168). In this period they were mineworkers, vaqueros, craftsmen, soldiers, hacienda peons, and small-store owners. A few could be found in the lower clerical ranks.

Then as today, Indians and Africans were at the bottom of the socioeconomic ladder in Mexico (Vinson and Restall 2009). According to colonial law, Indians were given a high legal status, but social practice placed them below almost everybody else (Morner 1967; Kicza 1993). In some respects their treatment was similar to that of Africans, who were without legal rights and remained peons/slaves throughout this time (Restall 2005; Bennett 2009). A small proportion were able to rise in their status by "raising color" through intermarriage with criollos or mestizos. To escape the grasp of land-hungry Spaniards, and aided by protective clerics, a sizable minority of Indians established communal villages, or republicas de indios (Chavez 2006). However, the majority worked on estates or in enterprises owned by others. High positions in any realm of society were outside their command, with the exception of those individuals who migrated to the cities and became part of the craft and *obraje* (woolen cloth workshops) system (Gibson 1984).

Modern peasants. *Top left:* girls carrying water; *top right:* boy hauling wood in Guatemalan highlands; *bottom left:* man weeding maize field; *bottom right:* men playing native flute and drum.

An additional explanation based on hegemony (nested and interrelated levels and processes of power) may clarify this social-class system (Mallon 1995). At the apex were people living in urban areas (mostly gachupines, criollos, and some mestizo workers) as the beneficiaries of the hegemonic socioeconomic network, especially the merchant class, who sat above all and controlled the capital and credit (Florescano 1984). The Indians, mestizos, and Africans, making up the population of the satellite rural enterprises (agrarian or livestock haciendas, mines, small Indian communal farms, or towns specializing in particular crafts), increasingly fell behind economically because they functioned primarily to provide urban areas with the products of their labor, which under a mercantilist system they had little power to control. This arrangement deprived them of a fair share of production and forced them to live a hand-to-mouth existence. Esteem, prestige, and power were reserved for the Spaniards. This invidious social structure, which developed one group by underdeveloping another, lasted for 300 years. Even today, Indians, as well as other indigenous groups worldwide, have good reason to feel that they are the victims of uneven capitalist development (also known as "structural violence" [Galtung 1969]) and have been so for centuries (Frank 1969).

Culture: Hispanicization and Mestizaje

Cultural life during this period was complex, full of contrasts and loaded with strains. Imagine the earth-shattering effect of the initial conquest, followed by a systematic and pressured expansion into other territories and encounters with new indigenous groups. The natives varied in their reactions and responses, in part depending on the intensity and duration of their exposure to the Spanish presence. Many natives quickly absorbed the dominant culture; however, even to this day others remain Indian. Escape from Spanish jurisdiction usually meant moving to the hinterland or hidden mountain valleys (Gibson 1984). A few refused to leave and somehow retained strong elements of Indian culture. Spanish efforts to impart their culture, whether to assimilate or acculturate Indians, were also very uneven and incomplete. In large part this stemmed from the conflicting goals of different groups and interests that set upon the natives, often working at cross-purposes. This variance also stems from the diverse roots of Spanish culture, especially the Iberian regional differences (Adelman 1999).

Shift in Cultural Orientation

Colonial life was such a hodgepodge of cultural themes and activities that it is impossible to cover all aspects of it. Certain phenomena should be mentioned, however, especially in regard to the larger Indian entities or states that changed in a more uniform way (Boyer and Spurling 2000; Gibson 1984). Such a time of cultural replacement involved the Spanish elites reserving the high culture for themselves. Spanish language and some technology—whatever was essential as well as bits and pieces of culture—were imparted to Indians and later, mestizos. Contributing to a shifting cultural orientation, this lack of a stable cultural adaptation ensured the Indians' and mestizos' permanent placement in the lower classes. In addition, many cultural maladaptations—drinking, fighting, suspicion and distrust, and so forth—eventually became norms for a colonial-shaped lifestyle, further guaranteeing low-class status. A discussion of Spanish colonial culture necessarily involves the process by which the dominant group made the learning of their culture the gateway to success, and conversely, the way in which the subordinate majority was relegated to cultural disorientation, instability, and confusion. These impedi-

Spanish soldier exploring the northern regions (southwestern U.S.).

ments to learning "high" culture thus reinforced the almost castelike system designed to curb social mobility.

Ironically, early in the colonial period, Indians and mestizos became the carriers of either Spanish culture or a hybrid version, what is referred to as a "Hispanicized, institutionalized Indian" way (Gibson 1984:394). For example, Spanish conquistadores and settlers moved north after the pacification of most Mesoamerican people. Many Hispanicized Indian and mestizo settlers accompanied them to the legendary Aztlan, home of the Chichimeca tribes. This area, known as the Spanish borderlands by writers focusing on the colonial period, is now the United States Southwest (Gonzalez 2009; Gerhard 1993). As noted, it is an area with ancient Mesoamerican connections (Ericson and Baugh 1993; Wills and Leonard 1994). There, as early as 1539, the Spaniards searched for gold and silver (Weber and Rausch 1994). The earlier contact-conflict-change scheme was repeated, but with substantial modifications, as the newcomers initiated other enterprises. In 1598, the "silver king" Juan D'Onate moved north from the mines of Zacatecas and founded the first permanent colony in New Mexico (Gutierrez 1991). Thus, Indians and mestizos came to play a cultural role in the further expansion of the colonial empire. Many of them oppressed and exploited the Indians in the new territories. Others became settlers, often merging with the natives as had been the practice in Mexico, thus remingling bloodlines based on ancient traditions. Thus went the expansion and incorporation of new northern territories, New Mexico followed by Texas and eventually California and Arizona, all mostly occupied by the "new" Mexicans. Reflecting early diversity, the pueblo of Los Angeles, known then as the Indian community of Yang-na, was settled in 1776 by two Spaniards, one mestizo, two Africans, eight mulattoes, and nine Indians from Mexico (McWilliams 1990[1968]; Bennett 2003).

During the territorial expansion, both Spanish and native cultures changed. Many new patterns emerged, but three basic types stand out: (1) a culture taken directly from Spain, but reconfigured and altered under New World demands and pressures; (2) a culture primarily native to the New World with slight, mostly technological, influences from Europe; and (3) a wide, variable cultural spectrum derived from the merging of Old World and New World traits. As noted, the Spanish utilized selected Indian political and economic practices in imposing their rule in the New World. The merging of late Spanish medieval hierarchies with indigenous structures brought about a peasant society that affected the bulk of the indigenous population. This society, as previously noted, was an amalgamation of bits and fragments of both cultures that had undergone revisions with the new realities.

Mestizaje: Cultural Blending

Two distinct kinds of cultural matrix had come into existence. One was Ladino, Spanish-speaking but with many features borrowed from the Indians. On the other hand, there were a variety of different mixtures in which the Indian tradition was still dominant. . . . It was almost as though the Indians had borrowed what they wanted, and the Europeans had done the same. (Curtin 2000:76; see also Gillin 1957:158–60)

While this mestizaje process affected each group differently, depending on how close and familiar they were with Spanish culture, it was most clearly reflected in the emergence of a peasant social and cultural life in the Indian communities as well as the new casta or *cholo* (racially and culturally marginal; from the Spanish *solo*, alone, but generalized to mean marginality in different ways) populations rapidly becoming a part of Mexico.

Neither totally Indian nor Spanish, Mexican culture today is largely the result of this merging (Schwartz 2000). With the clash of civilizations, recounted by participants then and by ethnographers today, Spanish elements and Indian traits have been fused, blended, or simply juxtaposed and have evolved to the present cultural ethos of the Mexican people (Gruzinski 1988). "It is precisely this success [of cultural blending] which sets Mexico apart . . . in Latin America" (Madsen 1967:370; see also Vasconcelos and Gamio 1926). Saying this, it is still an "inadequately studied" and poorly understood phenomenon (Gibson 1984:414).

Even the Spanish language underwent a syncretic change. Indian words aided the transmission of European concepts. Some words were integrated into the Spanish language because they represented a feature of Indian reality that was totally alien to the Spaniards. Language borrowing, creating, and synthesizing developed a linguistic spectrum of native and Spanish patterns (Hill and Hill 1986).

Some 5,000 Nahuatl words—like *metate* (from Nahuatl metlatl, "quern"), *chiquihuite* (from Nahuatl chiquihuitl, "basket"), *tepescuingle* (from Nahuatl escuintli, "little dog", in Mexican Spanish, "little boy")—came into everyday use among speakers of Mexican Spanish. (Wolf 1959:46; see also Chavez 2006)

Moreover, many Indians who learned Spanish fashioned a new sound and style. This resulted in the many regional patterns and intonations found today. Some Indians became well versed in Spanish and shed their Indian idioms. Others even today speak mostly the Indian dialect. Either through design or accident, these tribes avoided heavy Spanish influence and remained isolated (Berdan 2008; Horna 2001; Ricard 1966). Unfortunately, this linguistic diversity has led to critical adjustment problems for many people.

One of the most fascinating and creative examples of syncretic development is in the area of diet, medicine, and health practices (Bellwood 2005; McNeil 2006; Ortiz de Montellano 1990). Indian food, basically the American trinity of corn (maize), beans, and squash, with a dash of chile, was revamped and embellished with wheat, rice, and various other ingredients (Sokolov

1991). With a reliance on domesticated animals imported from Europe, many new dishes and flavors emerged. In short, Indian and Spanish food evolved into Mexican food, and when corn was unavailable for tortillas in the northern mining regions, wheat flour (*harina*) substituted and became a new favorite for many. Even the evolution of liquor is traced from pulque to mezcal to tequila, each increasingly a refinement of juices from the maguey plant. This syncretism is evident in many medical practices and cures, with ancient ailments (*susto, mal de ojo*) and cures mixed in with modern knowledge and treatments, and even the persistence today of *curanderos* (folk curers) (Foster 1988).

A syncretic style also pertained to art and architecture, although perhaps these were more dominated by Spanish traits. "Hispanic American arts and crafts, while owing much to Indian developments, reveal profound and far-reaching European influences" (Foster 1960:4; see also Miller 2001). The European culture of that time, including Moorish elements (which go back to the early Middle East), was reflected in official buildings, churches, and domestic dwellings. Indians made their biggest contribution in their labor and construction materials. Adobe materials and designs are both indigenous and Spanish, but the red tile roof has obvious Moorish influences. Conversely, many traditional Spanish customs began to be altered by native forms and practices as in, for example, poetry and ballads. In particular, religious syncretisms generated a diverse and interesting host of developments to make the new Mexican rituals and ceremonies festive and colorful—what is referred to as Mexican Catholic ideology. This mixing process also occurred in other creative activities: philosophy, jewelry, pottery, and music.

Numerous social customs and cultural perspectives evolved through syncretism. Equally important, though, is that many of these traits were adaptive reactions, fashioned for survival reasons, or "defensive reactions" (Gibson 1984:415). For instance, the Indian emphasis on kinship, family, and neighbor relationships persisted for several reasons. For one, kin ties became valuable social "capital" in time of need. Furthermore, Catholic tradition maintained that a baptized person must have godparents, who would assume child-rearing duties if anything happened to the parents. Indians used *compadrazgo* (coparenthood) to establish social ties with nonfamily members, replacing in part the traditional calpulli networks that the Spaniards were breaking up; with the "great dying" in the post-conquest period, this was an adaptive mechanism to ensure that children had surrogate parents.

Close ties between brothers and sisters continued long after they married and established separate households. They actively participated as uncles and aunts in raising each other's children. Grandparents represented the top level of the authority hierarchy in extended families. Children were taught to respect and honor their elders at all times. In the absence of an adult, supervision fell on the shoulders of the eldest child. (With adulthood, however, the male members, even those who were younger than female siblings, usually assumed a higher status [Chinas 1983].) The civil-religious hierarchy and associated ceremonial patterns, so prominent in Mexican village life today, also began as a syncretic sociopolitical practice (Foster 1988), especially in the republicas de indios (Chavez 2006). Gathering together on a small town's patron saint day with fanfare and celebration, and with high social status and religious significance accorded the participants, these *cofradias* (social and religious groups) played a strong role in keeping natives on task. They helped cement a peasant society and gave the natives the form of power without the substance, thus fitting in very well with the new hacienda and ruling network.

Introduction of Catholicism

Religion provides an example of cultural merging. Church leaders attempted to integrate Indian elements—especially from larger, more influential groups' cultures—into the Catechism, finding success especially with saints and saint worship that paralleled icons and spiritual imageries already well developed by natives (Lockhart 1992). Cults centered on natural forces were particularly utilized to effect this end. Acceptance of external signs of Catholicism also became common even as many now unlawful Indian practices continued to be conducted in secret.

> By "baptizing" pagan sites and converting them to Christian use, missionaries could also be said to have brought the pagan spirits that inhabited these spaces into the fold. . . . Shrines honoring the Virgin Mary throughout the countryside made her "an ideal successor to the pre-Christian mother goddesses in the countryside." In this way, not only did the physical sites of paganism become Christian, but even the spirits who inhabited the spaces were converted. (Muldoon 2004:4; see also Schroeder and Poole 2007)

Religion and Spanish language instruction influenced the shaping of a new Indian view of life. At least one author traces the beginning of Indian bilingualism to early religious rites: "It was baptism that started the process of change in the indigenous naming system" (Lockhart 1992:119). Clerics admonished neophytes who failed to serve their hacendados faithfully. While teaching the Indians religion, the missionaries taught respect for authority (Schroeder and Poole 2007; Simpson 1966). Natives were continually reminded that, no matter how bad the conditions or difficult the times, they would surely go to heaven if they remained obedient and dutiful; however, hell was the certain destination if they disobeyed and rebelled (Burkhart 1989). Furthermore, they were told that the Christian God favored especially those who suffered and remained strong in the faith. According to the teaching, earthly experience was merely a testing ground to determine where one would go after death. Missionary success stemmed from the power held by conquistadores who helped make sure that Indian children learned Catholic dogma.

Because the Indians were deeply religious anyway, they followed many Christian teachings perfectly (Muldoon 2004; Lockhart 1992). Further, it made sense to the colonial powers to substitute a new thinking process in the minds of the new workers. Thus, religious worship was the most accessible area of colonial life to Indians. If they were not devoting time to church-related activities, as in the civil-religious hierarchy, they were consciously attempting to follow new teachings and practices in their daily lives. In addition, many Indians built and maintained missions and churches and established permanent residence there. They were very devout subjects indeed, just as they had been when they controlled the world. For example, the civil-religious hierarchy practiced by Indians allowed for official social and political duties for the peasant villagers, which also included religious goals and rituals.

Only one God was placed before them, but the many Christian saints, and especially the Virgen de Guadalupe, found ready acceptance by a people accustomed to a pantheon. Baptism, rituals, ceremonies, prayers, fasting, confessions, heaven, hell, and purgatory were not new concepts to the Indians and were thus easily adopted (Schroeder and Poole 2007; Lockhart 1992; Burkhart 1989). Oddly, the symbolic sacrifice of the Catholic mass, with bread and wine representing the body and blood of Jesus Christ, was also reminiscent of Indian rituals. According to some writers, the sacrifice in the Catholic mass is a legacy of pre-Christian ceremonies when a lamb was slain and offered to the gods. Such similarities simplified the enforced transition to a new spiritual reality.

When possible, missionaries incorporated Indian practices to teach Catholic dogma (Gibson 1966). For example, in pre-Columbian times, towns honored a patron deity with a processional, a tradition that continued in modern peasant villages. The clerics staged the affair on the already established day but replaced Indian idols with Christian saints; thus, a mixed Indian-Spanish ceremony evolved (Muldoon 2004; Ricard 1966). As noted, Catholicism was embraced in a new Indian way. This is most obvious in how peasant religion has evolved, become institutionalized, and lasted, in some places, even to the present (Kearney 1986, 1996; Foster 1988; Chinas 1983; Ingham 1986; Gossen and Leon-Portilla 1993). This syncretism, the combination of two distinct cultural styles into a wide-ranging new one, also occurred in other areas of life.

Cultural Resistance and Marginality

It was during the Spanish colonial era that the word "cholo" (solo) came into use. Initially applied to persons of "mixed" race, but later also to cultural marginality, choloismo became a mainstay in a land of conflicting, competing, and changing cultures. As pressure for Indian assimilation to Spanish ways intensified, forcing Indians into a mold, many rejected Spanish culture entirely at the same time their own was being destroyed. As a result, they were without solid roots in any culture. In contrast to those who had undergone a cultural syncretism—that is, adopted Mexican or mestizo culture in a new bilingual-bicultural way—there were many who remained culturally isolated. This led to widespread anomie—cultural marginality and normlessness, or the equivalent of the Aztec nepantilism, that is, mental and emotional conflict.

Rigid class biases limit movement between two cultural worlds in an effort to freeze members of the subordinate cultural group in their places. Furthermore, the merging of cultures is never a smooth or even amalgamation and sometimes takes rough turns and twists in the mind of an individual. In Mexico, racial intermixture contributed to this dilemma (Ramos 1962), because mixed parentage created a mental confusion, with one parent representing the rulers and the other, the ruled. Significantly, "what the colonial society feared was not the creation of mixed offspring but the growth of a large mass of unattached, disinherited, rootless people in its centers and along its margins" (Wolf 1959:237). Moreover, the gender scheme figured prominently in this dynamic because Spanish males forced themselves on Indian females. Thus, the mestizo offspring were assured of Spanish fathers and Indian mothers (Kellogg 2005).

For people in this quandary, certain problems arise when selecting one cultural world or another. One kind of problem comes when members of the dominant culture reject members of the subordinate culture who seek to join them (i.e., Indian males seeking Spanish females). Another occurs when subordinate members remain in their original cultural milieu but are totally dissatisfied with its offerings. Thus, the group to which they aspire rejects them, and they despise the group to which they belong. Furthermore, such individuals are often members of groups that are themselves set apart on the periphery of social and political institutions and relations, and notably separate from the primary elites and other racial or cultural groups that have attained more favor.

It is precisely in this class and cultural setting that revolutions and revolutionaries are made (Friedrich 1968). Outside the mainstream of economic and political power, bereft of their original cultural moorings, and forced into changing cultural cues and forms, many people are quickly galvanized to push for "greater change or transformation" (Mallon 1995:6). Many Indians, and especially mestizos and cholos, reacted to Spanish contact, conflict, and change in this fashion; even today one could say that this dynamic prevails in Mexico.

Problems of Adaptation

The colonial period reflected a number of sociocultural problems. One that seriously affected demographic conditions stemmed from the diseases brought to Mexico by Europeans. Smallpox, typhus, measles, typhoid fever, and diphtheria epidemics wiped out whole towns (Mann 2005). This was referred to as "the Great Dying" by Eric Wolf (1982:133). Because they were "isolated from the rest of the world . . . Amerindians had developed no resistance at all against these diseases" (Morner 1967:32). As noted previously, the native population suffered radical losses, particularly near the middle of the sixteenth century (1540s) (Lockhart 1992; Gibson 1966). Yet this was only the immediately observable part of the destruction—the aftermath had similarly dire effects.

For example, certain calpullis lost 80 percent of their people through disease, but those who remained were still held to the same tribute quota. "Of more importance is the fact that the recounts and reassessments consistently lagged behind the rapid shrinkage in the number of tribute payers, with the result that the survivors had to bear the tribute burdens of those who had died or fled" (Zorita 1963:12). How were these tribute quotas met? Simply by having survivors work harder and longer to fulfill the tribute goal, with little time for anything else (Gibson 1964).

The colonial social structure was established to benefit the Spanish materially. It is important to stress, though, how the inclusion of new cultural habits complemented new social relations. Programs for Indian cultural awareness were designed to help them take their place in the new social order: ideas about life fitted in with one's position in the social structure.

Even with much resistance and the preservation of Indian lifeways, such as speaking their native language, the long colonial period wore down the population and took its toll. When peasantization took hold, the bulk of the Indians became Catholic (albeit with a Mexican Catholic ideology), joined community organizations (such as the cofradias), and generally adopted many Spanish beliefs and habits (Hamnett 2006; Kearney 1996). Indian acceptance of Spanish authority also meant alteration of their attitudes and behavior toward leaders, and the introduction of the patron–peon complex (Foster 1988). To help natives in acting the "right way," their value system was revised to include highly formal rules of etiquette—all, of course, denoting a superordinate/subordinate relationship. Since Indians were already instilled with a respectful demeanor, they learned the new terms and actions quickly. The preexisting Indian humility was part of their philosophical view, which stressed the immensity of the world and de-emphasized egoism or self-importance. Humans were only a small part of the vast universe; they must coexist with other elements in it. Spaniards recognized how this humility would benefit their rule, pushing them to the apex of the social system.

According to one expert, there were many factors that affected Indian *acculturation* (a broad process that begins upon initial contact between two cultures in which change takes place in one or both cultures).

> Apart from agriculture, the accelerated migration to the cities, the further penetration of Spaniards into the hinterland, the unrelieved expansion of *mestizaje*, the many Spanish goods that found their way into Indian markets, were all factors inducing a progressive Indian acculturation. (Gibson 1984:416)

Of course, in some places these alterations also included new reactions to the imposed and profound changes underway, such as the defensive strategies of (1) repression; (2) symbolic creation of an ideal environment; (3) self-disparagement; and (4) individualism (Kearney 1986). Most of these show the flip side of this type of rapid, intense culture change and its aftermaths.

While Indians fulfilled their part of the bargain, remaining honorable and dutiful, the Spanish skirted theirs. In the words of an early colonial Indian:

> "You have deprived us of our good order and way of government....
> Now all is confusion and without order and harmony. The Indians have
> given themselves to fighting because you have brought it upon them ...
> those who are not in contact with you do not fight; they live in peace."
> (Leon-Portilla 1963:151)

The native people are still patiently waiting for the successors of the Spanish to lead in a way beneficial to all. The 1994 Zapatista revolt in southern Mexico was just another episode of resistance in a long history of fighting oppression and exploitation.

Political Structure

The Spaniards dominated the political institutions, which were linked to economic practices; strangely, with the fragmentation of the Indian state, they reestablished the small political units that existed in pre-Columbian times (Gibson 1984). This was not a simple, routine arrangement, but rather one of "factionalism, infighting, and often complicated alliances of political and economic power" (Altman 1991:417). Conquistadores-turned-encomenderos initially dominated all aspects of the situation, although political power was supposedly concentrated in the hands of the Spanish king. Beginning with the introduction of the encomienda system, 20 percent of all production extracted by a colonist was paid to the king—the crown's fifth. Thus, the king was at the top of the political hierarchy. Situated in Spain, and directly under the king in authority, was the Council of Indies. They approved subordinate leaders and groups, made general policy decisions, and curbed the power and influence of ambitious colonists (Hamnett 2006; Skidmore and Smith 1992; Gibson 1966, Elliott 1963).

The various *audiencias* (advisory and judicial bodies) in the New World were next in importance, particularly the first *cabildo* (town government) organized by Cortes and others. It was from this center that authority spread out into the countryside (Raat 1992). Each of these was composed of *oidores* (justices), whose number varied depending on audiencia land size. Each audiencia controlled its separate domain, serving as the supreme court, council, and executive and legislative bodies; at first these were notoriously corrupt and acquisitive (Chavez 2006; Altman 1991). Depending on the time period and individual personalities, the audiencias were often more powerful than the Council of Indies. Since an ocean separated the council from the colony, it was easy for the audiencia to control affairs. The viceroy was the only barrier to audiencia dominance; he was appointed by the king to protect royal interests in the New World. Although the audiencia legally had the final word in checking the viceroy's actions, the viceroy had the imprimatur of the king, so political power often was determined by the personal strength or weakness of the viceroy (i.e., the caudillo).

Corregidores (governors) and *alcaldes mayores* (mayors) were in charge of smaller administrative units. By collecting tribute, they also could assign Indians to public works. In keeping with the innovative way the Spanish ruled, many local Indian ranking tlatoque were integrated into this network and referred to as cacique or *gobernador* (governor) (Lockhart 1992), apparently maintaining some semblance of this role until near the end of the colonial era (Gruzinski 1988).

Local town government followed a Spanish pattern that was a legacy of Roman times. New World natives filled positions in this framework, however, under the aforementioned cofradia or civil-religious hierarchy (Kearney 1986) system that utilized indigenous ruling models but sharply limited the range of their powers. The town leader, usually a criollo, was the municipal secretary. His authority was paramount. Indians served under the secretary as a council of elders (*principales*), or one was selected by the elders as the alcalde mayor. Others filled lower positions as *aguaciles* (constables). The Indians provided administrative and judicial services under the secretary's continual supervision. The secretary dictated policy and could veto native political decisions (Cancian 1967; Foster 1988).

The Spaniards' use of Indian cultural tradition to govern town members was very effective. This innovative strategy was based on the Indian practice in which leaders carried out duties in both the political and religious sectors (Carrasco 1965). For example, if a man became an aguacile, later rising to the higher rank of principale, he would have a dual role; he would perform civic duties and also lead group participation in religious ceremonies, especially during yearly patron-day celebrations. Different roles made up the civil-religious hierarchy, almost like a stepladder. This tradition was continued because colonial administrators realized that it would serve their purposes. Real political power remained in Spanish hands, and native-turned-peasant roles were mostly for show. This format strengthened the double-pronged strategy the Spanish favored: the crown (civil) and the church (religious) would guide natives, the latter actively; "the kinship ideology of the calpulli, itself largely fictitious, gave way to a conception of solidarity based on spiritual kinship" (Ingham 1986:189).

Education: A Double Standard

For those who were firmly integrated into the Spanish system, the education and training required for important colonial occupations relegated Indians and mestizos to menial, manual labor. Treated as children, the natives were tutored in ways that were demeaning, and even learning the Spanish language was a guarded process that proceeded slowly, lest it encourage thoughts of freedom (Schroeder and Poole 2007; Ricard 1966).

At first, concerned missionaries provided a sound education, especially in mission schools. Frequently, some bright Indian students were given special attention. For these Indians, education meant becoming priests to instruct others in the new faith and doctrine (Muldoon 2004). However, this approach soon ran counter to the overall Spanish policy, which demanded an unlimited number of illiterate manual workers; class and racial barriers prevented total assimilation in any way. For the priests and teachers that were turned out with this education and became Hispanicized, the experience only whetted their appetites for more knowledge and freedom. These select few thus were marginalized in a different way. As part of their striving toward liberation, they often led fellow natives against the Spanish (Schroeder and Poole 2007; Padden 1967).

In the late sixteenth century the Indian education experiment was abandoned (Hamnett 2006). Clerics had unwittingly undermined grander colonial designs and precipitated a clash between church and civil authority. Consequently, around 1570, Jesuit priests and secular clergy more responsive to the crown were brought in to reverse the practice of fair treatment given to some Indians. The new clerics developed programs that catered to criollos.

Too much education was considered dangerous, so only

Education catered to the criollos.

a select few were allowed this privilege. Thus, the educational reversal had two purposes: to de-emphasize native intellectual development, focusing instead on craft training, and to concentrate on criollo instruction in order to enhance their leadership skills. Even a moderate assimilationist policy was aborted, as basic understanding of the Spanish language and reading and writing were kept from most Indians. Few Indians mastered the Spanish language without formal training, a practice that still prevails in many Latin American countries today. Likewise, except for a few humanist missionaries, the Spaniards made no effort to teach and preserve the many Indian languages. Consequently, an Indian education was eliminated, and Spanish policy kept them from a European education. However, this action had some benefits. Isolated communal Indian villages and dozens of Indian mission towns were left alone and thus were able to preserve aspects of native culture—in many cases even to the present day. In the last 20 years or so there has been a tremendous groundswell of Indian language preservation.

The initial successes of clerics wishing to help and convert the native population had a short history. Many socioeconomic benefits resulted from clerical intervention, such as preservation of village landholdings, even though self-interest is what drove the church fathers. Ostensibly, the clerics intended to shield Indians from exploitative and oppressive encomenderos. However, as mentioned previously, these benefits were nullified before the end of the sixteenth century.

Instead of higher education—poetry, rhetoric, history, science, mathematics, and the many calendars—Indians were instructed in elementary, vocational subjects. Already mentioned were the many occupational roles Indians filled and the blending of styles into what was increasingly becoming a Mexican culture. In addition, missionaries taught the Indians masonry, carpentry, blacksmithing, horticulture, pastoralism, and the domestic chores necessary to operate colonial society optimally (Haring 1963). Thus, Indian cultural life was limited because their occupations were basic. High culture was reserved for the Spaniards and their offspring, and all that remained for Indians and mestizos was what George Foster (1960) has called the "part-society" of peasant life.

Native Reactions and Resultant Problems

The Indians and mestizos reacted in a variety of ways to the patterns by which Spaniards shaped conditions to their own benefit (Gibson 1964). One generalized type of reaction that arose intermittently was nativist resistance, which stressed self-determination and the survival of Indian culture (Chavez 2006). This often took the form of a messianic revitalization response, such as the Caste Wars of Yucatan in the nineteenth century (Farriss 1993; Gruzinski 1988). It can easily be generalized that most indigenous peoples, at one time or another, fought and struggled to maintain their independence (Kicza 1993; Spicer 1962). Some chose not to risk failure, inasmuch as the Spaniards maintained military superiority, and instead retreated into wild, unsettled regions (Schroeder and Poole 2007); the Tarahumara and Yaqui of the northwestern Mexico region are most notable in this regard.

On numerous occasions, sporadic, unorganized resistance escalated into large-scale rebellions. One example was the Pueblo Revolt of 1680, which occurred in the northern outposts of the Spanish empire, now the United States Southwest (Weber and Rausch 1994; Bolton 1921). In this case, 13 years passed before the Spaniards returned, and then only after the Indian coalition had dissolved. Likewise, tribes such as the Apaches and Comanches, and many others, successfully resisted for the duration of the Spanish presence. More recent events indicate that this attitude of resistance has prevailed in some areas, as evidenced by the 1994 New Year's Day insurrection of the Zapatista Liberation Army in Chiapas (Collier and Quaratiello 1994). Nativist resistance became a cultural characteristic of many Indians and, later, mestizos; one might say that they had a permanent chip on their shoulders (Schwartz 2000). Although resistance was seen by the Spaniards as deviant because it undermined their social order, it could also be interpreted as a highly adaptive human mechanism to correct injustices and deprivations. In other words, deviant behavior may become a norm when it fulfills some socially useful function (Haslip-Viera 1999; Ricard 1966).

The Spaniards, of course, attempted to suppress native resistance:

> The colonists developed new techniques anticipating . . . similar methods to be employed two and a half centuries later on the expanding United States frontier [such as the] covered wagon . . . ; soldiery . . . organized itself into flying detachments for purposes of patrols and escort. The fort or presidio made its appearance alongside the mission . . . and Spaniards established colonies of armed Indian peasants from the urban area as strategic outposts in the hostile countryside. (Wolf 1959:193; see also Gerhard 1993 and Smolenski and Humphrey 2005)

An emphasis on male physical strength and prowess was closely associated with native reaction. With roots in Spain and the Mediterranean area, Mexican male dominance evolved into an institutionalized behavior. A *macho* (masculine, virile person) equates physical with social power (Hewes 1954; Ramos 1962); he is a fighter and a hard-working protector of home and family in the mold of a traditional patriarch. Because of the misfortunes that befell the natives at this time, there was a need for this male attitude and behavior, especially to defend the honor of females, many of whom were victims of Spaniards. The jury is out on this issue, that the Spanish conquest was also a sexual one (Kellogg 2005; Jaffary 2007). Here is what one account says about the matter:

> While it might be going too far to say that rape was a consciously used strategic tool in conquest and colonial rule, that sexual coercion was part of the process of Iberian exploration and conquest cannot be denied. Yet the frequency of sexual violence and the willingness of military leaders such as Cortés and Pizarro to distribute indigenous women among their close lieutenants suggest that conquerors indeed used "the phallus as an extension of the sword." Seeing women as objects whose bodies could be conquered and who could be given as material reward was linked to another use of indigenous women, women as domestic servants. (Kellogg 2005:60)

On the other hand, the macho syndrome includes some negative traits, such as a close-minded, masculine tyranny in the home and locality. Both aspects of "macho" were shaped by political and social oppression and the aura of aggression and dominance that prevailed in that context.

Another legacy linked to machismo was an increase in drinking and fighting. Before Spanish contact,

> the use of *pulque* [liquor from the maguey cactus] had ordinarily been confined to the sick and aged . . . for public ceremonies and religious celebrations. Consistent popular drunkenness had been unknown. But following the conquest the native population rapidly took to drink. (Gibson 1964:150)

Although this has been disputed (Lockhart 1992), the Spaniards encouraged drinking by expanding maguey plantations and opening more *pulquerias* (bars and stores). While the Spaniards benefited from this enterprise, the Indians used drinking as an escape from the reality of oppression and as an escape valve to allow for the venting of violent and aggressive behavior (Kearney 1986).

As a result, along with the drinking habit, intragroup fighting became the norm. The Indian "chip on the shoulder" became a cumbersome burden that dared any man, usually the closest one and preferably one without the power to retaliate, to knock it off on any pretext (Romanucci-Ross 1986). Fearlessness in the face of death, a positive Indian trait accepting the inevitable end of life, made matters worse, for now machos accelerated a confrontation with death by being overly sensitive to imagined insults and quick to fight. Indians released pent-up frustrations on fellow Indians or mestizos who experienced similar conditions of oppression (Wolf 1959).

Social mobility was adversely affected by jealousy. Many foremen of haciendas and owners of small Indian stores, who had become part of the colonial social order, were considered traitors by their people. Mestizos and *Ladinos* (Hispanicized Indians) were particularly targeted. This early atmosphere of competition for the few relatively higher-class positions open to Indians (even though low by Spanish standards) gave rise to an attitude of *envidia* (hate and envy) rather than support and admiration for those who succeeded (Foster 1988; Wolf 1959). It kept Indians competing against each other for the few available positions, instead of cooperating to create more opportunities. Another consequence, closely related to envidia, is the way in which peons censured those who attempted to become assimilated into the Spanish mainstream. Within the emerging peasant way of life, the juxtaposition of these contradictory and paradoxical attitudes and habits definitely drained human energies and resources. It turned a once proud people into a segmented and diffused society unable to fully reach its potential.

The days of calmecac were gone; no longer were Indians intellectually and spiritually in control under the new social order. Advanced military training, received in the telpochcalli, was obviated as Indians were forced to assume lower positions as supply carriers and unskilled foot soldiers. Although Indians and mestizos were the backbone of the military, they did not receive the credit for victories or the opportunities to rise to hero status. Except for the tribes that allied themselves with the Spaniards, it was a long time before natives were allowed to participate actively in military affairs. And this reality in the throes of cultural change, exchange, and syncretic acculturation made the world even more difficult.

Color: Roots of Racism and Racial Barriers

Human interactions are always tainted by biases and prejudices that make one person or group feel superior to another. Indigenous groups before European arrival certainly showed this by mistreating one another on the basis of cultural or regional differences. However, all of this changed in the European encounter with the New World and other territories worldwide. Race and racism took a new form because of the scale, magnitude, and intensity of the contact experience (Banton 1987). It was a prolonged and deep-rooted affair that soon became permanent. In its permanency, it institutionalized certain practices, among them the self-righteous belief that the European races were better than Indians. To compound matters, the Europeans mixed with the native populations (and later, African slaves) to create shades of races and a "race" problem for many hybrids. Thus,

> color of skin and phenotypic traits of the white ruling elites set the standard to which all others had to measure up, and this generated a new strategy among the mestizo population who now attempted to pass if they were lighter of skin or European in appearance. Known as "socioracial" passing in Mexico, as well as the United States, many utilized this strategy as a means of upward mobility. (Vigil and Lopez 2004:4; see also Restall 2005; Vinson and Restall 2009)

Indians especially experienced these problems in Mexico, and social relations were structured to keep natives and mestizos socially immobile. For this purpose, Spaniards made race, and a host of conditions associated with it, a crucial feature of the social system that became fixed and perpetuated (Morner 1967; Jaffary 2007). Anthropologists today refute the utility of the biological concept of race as applied to humans, but it is clear that as a social construct, it has been and remains very important (Restall 2005; Bennett 2009).

Much of the thinking behind these developments revolves around ethnocentrism, the prevalent mind-set of each ethnic group to see the world through its own cultural lens. In doing this, it is common to be blind or insensitive to other groups' ways of doing things. In other words, ethnocentrism is a way of feeling superior to others. Practically all human groups succumb to an ethnocentric attitude, including Indians (Restall 2005). In this case, however, the Spaniards (and Europeans generally during the age of expansion and conquest) were responsible for the introduction of a different variant of it. It is one thing to follow a benign type of ethnocentrism, where one feels proud and confident of his or her way of life. It is quite another matter to negatively intensify this attitude, infringing upon and denigrating the rights and privileges of others. This is a malignant ethnocentrism, better termed "racism."

Ethnocentrism and Development

The Spaniards used racial criteria to consolidate their ethnocentric program. Racial prejudice and discrimination cemented the economic relationships underway—this was the introduction of an incipient brand of racism (Bennett 2009). Race joined with other barriers to perpetuate inequalities and inequities. Since the age of exploration and discovery, racial prejudice has often been an integral aspect of the formation of a class system based on inequality. The designation of social race worked to advance one racial group at the expense of another and neatly meshed with and solidified socioeconomic development/underdevelopment arrangements. Individual differences based on innate intelligence could not make this system work, for the Indians had at least an equal percentage of potentially intelligent members as the Spanish (Brues 1990). Therefore, a simple device was introduced to act as a hindrance to upward mobility: one group was credited with superior qualities to become and remain dominant, while the other was assigned inferior traits to keep them subordinate (Jaffary 2007; Graham 1990; Wolf 1959; Kicza 1993).

Indians were considered dreary, reticent, lazy, and backward by the Spaniards, who generally looked down upon them (Vinson and Restall 2007; Gibson 1966). Cultural habits and customs are often the criteria for a superior/inferior relationship. The Spanish cultural imperialism program, as noted previously, made natives feel culturally inadequate; for example, speaking the wrong language or worshipping a different god can hamstring a people. But what happens when the subordinate group assimilates the dominant culture? This possibility was foiled by introducing racial barriers. Changing one's culture is far easier than changing one's race or face. Simply stated, racial dogma is adopted to prevent the so-called inferior races from attaining their political right and status as equal competitors.

In establishing the colonial class system, the Spaniards viewed dark-complexioned natives as biologically and physically inferior (Zavala 1943). There was no real basis for this thinking, but the actual social realities dictated that a new belief system was needed. Thus, one's physical appearance determined how high a person would climb on the social-class scale. This attitude, together with the elimination of educational programs for Indians, locked the natives into menial status. Being paternalistic and treating the Indians as children made it easier for the Spaniards (Zavala 1943). "In spite of the Indigenous peoples' presence in Mexican life in murals, museums, sculptures and archaeological zones, they do not have an equal social position in Mexican society" (Vigil and Lopez 2004:28).

Mestizaje: Racial Mixture

Coming to the New World without Spanish wives or companions, the conquistadores had to work out other arrangements (Jaffary 2007; van den Berghe 1967; Morner 1967). When Indian nobles presented young women to the Spanish victors, the Spaniards soon recognized a benefit besides satisfaction of their sexual appetites. By accepting this overture, they gained legitimate entrance into Indian society. In future years their sons could claim dual leadership status: by right of conquest and through the line of native aristocratic descent (Kellogg 2005; Gibson 1964). Soon after, they were part of the criollo group and competed against their Spanish parents.

More often, Spanish males consummated sexual unions by force, adding sexual conquest to the spoils of war (Muldoon 2004; Kellogg 2005). Many of the first mestizo offspring resulted from incidents of forcible rape (van den Berghe 1967; Padden 1967). "Because formal marriages between Indians and non-Indians were rare, it is safe to say that the great majority of first generation mestizos were the bastard offspring of Spanish men and Indian women" (Gibson 1964:144), and as noted, seldom the other way around. With the exception of the offspring of Indian elites, it was rare indeed to find a mestizo who could claim an Indian father and Spanish mother (Cope 1994).

Years later this continued to be true. Bands of mestizo children, 50 or more in number, wandered the countryside seeking sustenance and security, rejected by both Spaniards and Indians. Mestizos were shunned by their Spanish fathers because of their native features and non-Christian, illegitimate birth. Similarly, because they represented a living physical memory of the rape of Indian women and Indian civilization, they were turned out from indigenous communities (Wolf 1959). Illicit unions involving Africans added to the mixed and dispossessed population (Vinson and Restall 2009). With the

5. De Eſpañol, y Mula-
ta, nace Moriſco.

A Spaniard and an Indian, with their mestizo offspring.

sharp decline of the Indian population, more Africans were brought in to maintain the size of the labor force, especially in the tropical lowlands (Bennett 2009). Blacks joined the mestizaje phenomenon to further diversify the racial heritage of Mexico. Coastal regions today, particularly Vera Cruz, Guerrero, and Oaxaca, strongly reflect this influence in both the physical appearance of the people as well as the culture, food, and music (Aguirre Beltran 1946; Carroll 1991; see Vaughn 2009). As the in-between-people, "solos" (alone, abandoned), cholos, and castas were often found in the interstices of society—the back alleys, the taverns, mining camps, and so on, and were limited to these social settings where they effected unions with similarly dispossessed outcasts. The larger number of offspring produced from these unions comprised an almost infinite variety of hybrids (Wolf 1959). There was a gradual increase of the mestizo population, and by the end of the colonial period they constituted a large portion of the people in Mexico.

In a strange way the mestizo population suffered more than the Indian peoples, especially since many of them were clearly stigmatized as illegitimate offspring of Spanish men and Indian women. The unjust rejection by the original (parental) participants in the New World left the mestizo abandoned and unaccepted by nearly everyone. Thus, it is not surprising that the mestizos learned to see themselves as alone in the world. Included in their exclusion and isolation was an awareness that social privileges and political influences were outside their orbit. As opposed to Indians, who viewed power as an attribute of office, the mestizo sought power as a source of personal energy that subjugated and dominated people (Wolf 1959). This gave rise to the mestizo mentality, an approach to life that was unconventional and sometimes deviant. As survivors, they had to readapt anew each day, improvise on the spot, and accept the shifting nature of their social condition. Through the use of "smoke and mirrors," such a person navigated the hidden passageways of society (Wolf 1959). "Undoubtedly, much of the aggressive, boisterous, and untrusting nature of the early mestizo mentality grew from this experience" (Ramos 1962:57–63). In the mestizo philosophical framework, fearlessness and a sense of vulnerability shifted according to the situation, both real and imagined. One could easily affix a mental state based on the racial variety of the mestizos.

Coming from Spanish-Indian or Indian-African racial backgrounds, and an amalgamation thereof, they were a hybrid race representing a color spectrum from white to black, from European to native or African features (Menchaca 2001). There were also new, heretofore unseen variations of color and physiognomic qualities. Mestizos played a significant role in the operation of the socioeconomic class system. Although mestizos were legally ranked below Indians, many appeared European and moved up in the social scale simply because of their white appearance. Furthermore, hybrid bloods, a new breed neither totally Spanish nor Indian, also in time found themselves a niche above the peon Indians. Nevertheless, many mestizos resembled natives or Africans and therefore probably remained peons throughout their lives.

Mestizos were referred to as Ladinos, a term that originally meant Hispanicized Indian. Later, Ladino became synonymous with those (usually mestizos, but often Indians) who had acculturated and risen above the Indian masses (Vigil and Lopez 2004; de la Fuente 1967). Within peasant communities, primarily of native origin but gradually including some darker hued mestizos, the residents often claimed Ladino heritage if they wanted to "pass" socioracially and be accepted as mestizos. This was a calculated social mobility attempt to rid themselves of the stigma of race, even though there was no intermarriage or union with a mestizo or criollo to warrant it. This process was even more pronounced among Afromestizos.

Race and Social Class

Throughout the period, races were kept as separate as possible, in what were essentially castes with different types and degrees of power and privilege (Knight 1990). To ensure one's station in life, detailed baptismal records listed racial heritage: pure blood mixed once, mixed twice, and so on. Here is an example of how they were recorded:

1. Spaniard and Indian beget mestizo.

2. Mestizo and Spanish woman beget *castizo* (pure blood).

3. Castizo woman and Spaniard beget Spaniard. [Some liken this to cleaning one's blood! The opposite, a castizo and Indian woman union would be cholo, and would thus be tarnishing one's blood!]

4. Spanish woman and African slave beget mulatto.

5. Spaniard and mulatto woman beget *morisco* (Moorish).

6. Morisco woman and Spaniard beget *albino* (brownish color).

7. Spaniard and albino woman beget *torna atras* (restore to original), and so on (Morner 1967:58).

A complicated racial mixture—a little of this, a little of that—earned the names of *ahi te estas* (there you stay) or *sal si puedes* (get out if you can)! Hybrid racial types were placed on the colonial socioeconomic ladder in this manner (van den Berghe 1967). "This organizing mechanism of colonial social life was enacted through legislation that imposed distinctive restrictions, rights, and obligations on each racial group as it interacted with the others throughout the colonial period" (Restall 2005:115).

Effects of Racism

Aside from its role in class relations, the mestizo phenomenon also produced sociopsychological difficulties. Thus, "the mestizo offers a richer opportunity for psychological interpretation than the phlegmatic, subordinated Indian" (Gibson 1966). Cultural marginality was now joined by racial marginality, a mixture of the Old and New Worlds, and often a strange and exotic combination at that (Vinson and Restall 2009). In addition to valuing assimilation into Spanish culture, subordinate members of colonial society got ahead by honoring the color and appearance of Spaniards. Indians and mestizos became traitors to themselves (Wagley and Harris 1958). Paradoxically, female mestizos were considered excellent mistresses. As the colonial elite used to say, white women for marriage and home, black women for work, and brown women for amorous adventures.

In addition to these psychological burdens, feelings of racial inferiority further oppressed the majority. Many became ashamed of their racial countenance, thinking it disgusting and unworthy. This inferiority complex hindered the advancement of both natives and mestizos. They were taught to dislike their faces so that their minds would remain troubled and uncertain about their self-identity. Meanwhile, those responsible for this attitude went unchallenged. Although this method of rule is unjust, vicious, and unscientific, it assured dominance over the majority population (Bennett 2009; Vinson and Restall 2009). Unfortunately, native action to remove that burden was generally disorganized and sporadic, and because of this, efforts to unite with others who suffered a similar condition failed. This proves how crippling its effect really was (Wolf 1959; Ramos 1962; Paz 1961).

Racism and Group Conflicts

In their efforts to identify with the powerful "superior" race, Indians, mestizos, and Afromestizos competed with each other, even though they shared many problems. Mestizos especially copied Spanish ways to get an edge on the Indians. As a result, whenever the opportunity arose, these mestizos harassed and exploited Indians (Zorita 1963). Prodded by protective clerics, colonial administrators shielded Indian communities. Thus, mestizos were harmed by being excluded from both Spanish and Indian towns (Helms 1975). This maneuvering taught them to survive in a relentlessly stubborn way. Nevertheless, Indians were still worse off because they were regarded by both Spaniards and mestizos as a despicable, inferior race. "They ascribe to Indians inferior traits and scorn many of their customs and beliefs as backward, infantile or gross, befitting primitive or rude people" (de la Fuente 1967). Further,

> the church too encouraged racist and ethnocentric mechanisms of control over persons of color and non-Hispanic ethnicity for the same reasons. Such strategies were reflected in the records public officials and clerics kept. As a result, state and church documents popularized negative perceptions of subaltern peoples and overemphasized instances of antagonistic interactions between them in order to keep these groups divided and more easily controlled. (Restall 2005:249)

Race and racism worked to sociopsychologically constrain a people's thoughts and actions. Once a sense of inferiority followed and replaced more physical subjugation practices, self-rejection and repression assisted in the dominance of the people. Whenever the lid on this defeated attitude was lifted, any area that rebelled against racist practices and conditions was quelled by harsh military force. If resistance intensified, stronger coercive measures were taken, such as punishment or death for the instigators. Native backwardness and underdevelopment were necessary for the success of the colonial empire, and racism, with the emphasis on color and facial features, supported this arrangement.

Chapter 5

BREAKUP AND TRANSFORMATION OF THE SOCIAL ORDER

Contact: Enlightenment

While military contact is often the physical means that forces change, it must be remembered that human thoughts shape and move those physical actions. The colonial period that destroyed indigenous Mesoamerican lifeways began with pressure from the Spanish sword, an externally derived force. Yet there were get-rich-quick schemes and other motives behind the sword. In the breakup of the colonial social order, actions and thoughts again intertwined (Hamnett 2006; Romanell 1967), but it was ideas that dominated because the most crucial forces of change come from within. One writer stated this period was a mix of historical memories (i.e., Indian, Spanish, and Mexican) that made for an incompleteness, fragmentation, and strains and stresses that had to be dealt with someday (Florescano 1994; see also Cheng 2009). That some-day came in several phases, each step in the direction of the resolution of the strains and contradictions (Israel 2010; MacLachlan and Rodriquez O. 1980).

Social action is usually based on conditions that require some type of adjustment. Often the necessary changes bring improvements; in the case of Mexico, change was another step toward incorporation into a "worldwide trading network" (MacLachlan and Rodriquez O. 1980:292), in effect a larger energy system. Incipient peasants, some still in control of their land and labor, were now subjected to a major macrostructural transformation: "The economy underwent a gradual dissolution of the mercantilist capitalist mode of accumulation and its replacement by more capitalist ones" (Cockcroft 1990:45). Peasant life became even more tied to the regional and world economy.

Europeans who were unhappy with existing social conditions gained inspiration from Enlightenment thought, which emphasized that human reason could overcome ignorance and oppressive power to improve the world. In some European countries, this thinking led to challenging the top-heavy aristocratic elite—landed gentry, nobility, and clergy. They could no longer rule absolutely as they had for centuries, and a new society emerged. European upheavals toppled regimes and stimulated the breakup of colonial territories. The ideas that sparked and drove the processes of change in Europe were slow to unfold in the New World, but they eventually caught the imagination of every disenchanted person as progress and reform came to mark this transitional historical period, furthering the development of the modern peasant lifestyle (Robinson 2004; Wolf 1966, 1982).

Revolutionary Beginnings

There were many ways that Enlightenment thinking reached and permeated beyond the shores of the New World: through word of mouth or from books and pamphlets brought by travelers, merchants, and government officials. Throughout the New World people participated in philosophical discussions inspired by Enlightenment ideas (Meyer and Beezley 2000; Haring 1963). An idea born in one time and place usually undergoes a process of revision in a new setting, and this happened in the New World. Latin American criollo intellectuals and dissidents rapidly learned from the revolutionary thinking in the Old World and applied the knowledge to their conditions—thus developing finer nuances to the theories (Israel 2010; MacLachlan and Rodriguez O. 1980). The rise and spread of literary clubs carried these new doctrines far and wide, and the pen surpassed the sword in its ability to subvert the political regime (Van Young 2001; Gongora 1975).

This assertive program took time to gain momentum, since ideas are never enough—humans must always implement them. Generally speaking, the revolutionary movements in the United States and France were the catalysts that accelerated the revolutionary ideas that eventually touched and spread all over Mexico and Latin America. The United States Revolution in 1776, especially as the first successful one in the New World, and the French Revolution in 1789 greatly influenced the Spanish colonial social structure. While also strongly affecting Europe, the American experience served as an example and had a significant impact on Latin American independence. The effect of the French Revolution was more indirect. Napoleon's armies spread the doctrine of "liberty, equality, and fraternity" throughout Europe, eventually loosening the hold the aristocratic elite had on their subjects. Almost immediately, the Spanish people felt the impact of the French slogans, especially after Napoleon took control of Spain. The political debate and struggle around socioeconomic issues that began in the mother country necessarily involved the colonies and led to the dissolution of the empire (Van Young 2001; Gongora 1975). "They [Spaniards] had imbibed many of the concepts of the French Revolution and British liberalism, and planned a new and liberal Spain" (Simpson 1967:233; Israel 2010). Eager participants began proposing social theories to correct unjust and unequal conditions (Servin, Reina, and Tutino 2007).

> Liberals began to think about society in unprecedented ways, inventing the individual and new behaviors and authorities to serve the individual. Modern sociability came with the invention of the individual, with the appreciation of contractual links and the ideal of equality. (Guerra 2007)

In the end, Spanish bureaucrats were unable to hold back what they feared most: the collapse of central authority, rebellion, and the fragmentation of the colonial empire into competing regions, each with its own economic and political agendas (Stein and Stein 1970). In large part, the mercantile economic system became a liability as criollos reacted to the colonial machine that unevenly spread power and influence (Gongora 1975; Holloway 2008; Kellogg 2005).

Enlightenment Legacy

These years of Enlightenment ferment set the tone for subsequent world history. For example, the question of left against right (the terms originated in the French National Assembly, where change-oriented representatives were seated to the left and the status quo elements to the right), or Jacobins vs. reactionary conservatives, was formalized by the French. In the New World the process of taking sides—whether to create a new political system or to retain and strengthen the old one—was repeated, though the ideological lines were less sharp. The struggle reached some of the most isolated regions and affected many oppressed Mexican people. Criollo intellectuals and writers, lay and cleric alike, began to look at Spain as a province, and "condemnation of the atrocities committed by the conquistadors became a frequent topic in writings, and praise was reserved for the Indian cultures" (Gongora 1975:184), as the center of their universe shifted to the New World. To accelerate and cement this trend, the Pope declared the "universal sponsorship" (meaning recognition) of the Virgin of Guadalupe over New Spain (1757) and archaeological expeditions, discoveries, and writings began to uncover and promote the grand style and refinement of what once was Indian civilization (Florescano 1994; Reina 2007).

Other issues increased the revolutionary momentum of the Enlightenment period. Among them: (1) European nations, particularly England, were interested in breaking the Spanish colonial commercial stranglehold and advocated a freer trade policy; and (2) much like North American colonists, the criollos were tired of oppressive colonial rule and sought independence and home rule. Economic issues in combination with ideas of social justice and examples of revolutionary activity heavily impacted the New World (Sierra 1969). Time had run out on Spain and its colonial stranglehold that shackled the majority of the population, as the Spanish elite could no longer rest on its laurels (Servin, Reina, and Tutino 2007).

The first centuries of the growth of a Mexican peasantry were altered by the Enlightenment, open-door trade, and home rule. Ideas stimulated the movement toward dissolving the colonies. But this was only the first interval. In a gestation period that lasted 300 years, it took a great deal of reflection, discussion, and action to move people into a new era and overcome firmly entrenched practices and beliefs. Many years passed before the ideas took hold and eventually flourished. It took a long time to erase the colonial thumbprint even as new impressions were made. As might be expected, confusion reigned after this contact period, as everything and everyone was in flux. Native and, later, peasant resistance was always part of the colonial experience, but with the end of this era, even more eruptions and disturbances in different provinces marked the nineteenth century, lasting until the 1910 Revolution (Knight 2007; Cockcroft 1990). One can even argue that the peasant inspired Zapatista revolt in 1994 is a blip on the radar of the old struggle to erase the colonial thumbprint (Collier and Quaratiello 1994).

Conflict: Independence

It never sat well with the criollos that the Spaniards had leverage over them by virtue of birthplace. Criollos considered themselves the true rulers of the New World, for they were of the New World, while newcomers such as the Spanish immigrants were the usurpers (Sierra 1969). Thus, the criollo challenge to gachupine rule ignited a full-scale conflict and brought other smoldering issues out into the open. To help in this effort, a new type of nonelite, hard-working, thrifty immigrant, arriving in large numbers in the late colonial period, joined the resident criollos to push for change (Gongora 1975). Because of disastrous financial conditions in Spain, a result of costly European wars, the colonists were pressured into paying high tributes to the mother country (Cockcroft 1990). This excessive burden further drove criollos to seek home rule. During the first years of the struggle, active participation and dialogue centered on nationalism, because political parties were ill-defined and loosely organized (Van Young 2001). Later, after the Spanish expulsion, political definitions and distinctions were made, sides chosen, and political and military battles fought.

Before ideological conflicts take root, there must be a receptive soil to nourish them. Hence, "the colonial elite found natural allies in the mestizos, mulattoes, and castas in general; the Indians they handled gingerly . . . if mobilized intelligently, [Indians] could be controlled to aid in the elimination of the handful of Spanish bureaucrats and merchants" (Stein and Stein 1970:114–15). Mestizo discontent resulted from the Spanish policy that disdained mixed bloods. Consequently, the persisting socioeconomic and racial problems of the mestizos and Indians provided fertile ground for colonial unrest, even though these problems were ignored after liberation. Undoubtedly, the discontent of the majority mestizos and Indians contributed heavily to the mounting revolutionary dissent (Reina 2007).

Liberals vs. Conservatives

The independence movement in Mexico was particularly divisive and rending. Two opposite sectors worked toward different objectives. With the separation from Spain, one side wanted to continue the same system apart from the motherland and the other side desired to wipe out the colonial order and establish an entirely new one (Burns and Charlip 2007). Those criollos who wanted separation and a home-rule type of monarchy were known as conservatives. Liberal criollos followed a more humanist orientation and demanded a more extensive program of political reform. To a degree, they desired to improve socioeconomic conditions, basing their program on a constitutional parliamentary model. Initially, the conservatives were stronger; they held powerful positions in the Catholic Church and the military, groups that were highly supportive of their goals. The criollo liberals, a smaller group, championed reform issues, which included minor concessions to mestizos and Indians. Their objectives, however, also included changes that more directly affected their class interests, such as free labor and private property, all leading Mexico on a path to agrarian capitalism (Cockcroft 1990). This in turn would promote more rapid conversion of the Indian and mestizo population into a peasantry.

A further clarification of this political split must be made. Conservatives were usually members of the urban upper class who had developed a centralist political strategy. They believed that power should remain in the cities, the center of sociocultural life. In contrast, liberals favored a federalist plan that catered to provincial chieftains and the nascent middle class (Servin, Reina, and Tutino 2007; Cockcroft 1990). Their plan emphasized regional input in decision-making processes (Bazant 1977). The liberals' numbers were swelled by many mestizos, especially those with middle-class positions or aspirations.

During the first years of the independence struggle, both the conservative and liberal ideologies were recast under various proponents. Opportunism characterized the political philosophy of many of these self-serving leaders. Nevertheless, political wrangling over the nation's future direction generally found liberals addressing mestizo and Indian issues. It was necessary to include these groups in the political process, for they constituted the majority of the population whose oppressive conditions commanded attention. With tacit support from mestizos and Indians, the liberals more strongly argued for reform, if only giving it lip service, and sometimes doing so to disguise other, more personal goals (Israel 2010).

A split in liberal ranks resulted. "Some wanted to 'go quickly,' to fulfill the aspirations of Liberalism at all cost and as soon as possible; others wanted to 'go slowly,' to achieve the same ideals at less cost and without haste. The former were called 'puros' or 'reds' [purists] and the latter 'moderados' [moderates]" (Villegas et al. 1974:104). Although lines were not clearly drawn, the *moderados* were usually criollos and the *puros* mostly mestizos. One example of a criollo puro was Lorenzo de Zavala, who advocated a vast program of social revolution to promote Mexican nationalism. However, he is the exception to the majority of upper- and middle-class criollos and mestizos who protected their own interests with less concern for the condition of the bulk of the population.

In any event, the Mexican nation-state dates from this period and, even today, reflects the recurring conservative/liberal encounter to redefine and direct the people's future (Cockcroft 1990).

1810: El Grito de Dolores

By 1810, there were four million people in Mexico, and increasingly, more were found in urban areas (Gongora 1975).They were divided into three groups: 10 percent of Spanish lineage, 30 percent of mestizo and mulatto background, and the remaining 60 percent of Indian descent (Kellogg 2005; Alba 1967; Rodriguez O. 1989). Dissident activity was already a pattern throughout Mexico, but the cause celebre of independence was El Grito de Dolores (The Cry of Pain), a proclamation made by Miguel Hidalgo, a parish priest, on September 16, 1810 (Meyer and Beezley 2000). Although a criollo, a Jesuit, and fairly well-off, Father Hidalgo felt concern for less-fortunate members of society. He could be characterized as an activist puro. His goal was the liberation of Mexico, even if gachupines must be slaughtered. When the opportunity arose, he led the first large military forces against the gachupines. Shortly thereafter, he was captured and executed by a firing squad. In the aftermath, however, the gates of revolution remained open.

Following in the footsteps of Hidalgo was another small-village priest, the poor mestizo Jose Maria Morelos. Interestingly, both based their actions on the teachings of Jesus Christ and repudiated the reactionary position of the

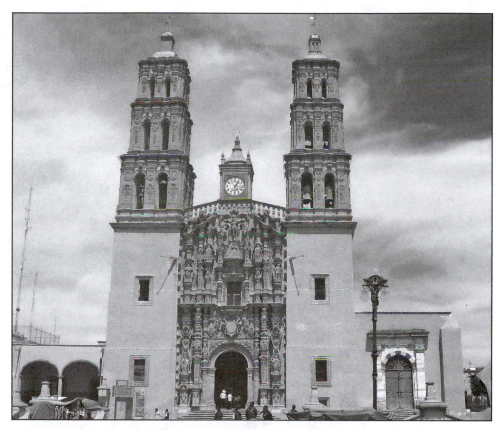

Every town had its Catholic church. In 1810, on the steps of this historic church, Father Hidalgo uttered his famous cry for the independence of Mexico.

church. A farseeing political and military genius, barely five feet tall, Morelos rallied the revolutionary forces until his execution in 1815. He outlined radical propositions aimed toward a true social revolution.

> The revolution was justified, Morelos insisted, because the perfidious gach- upines were enemies of mankind, who for three centuries had enslaved and subjugated the native population, stifled the natural developments of the kingdom, squandered its wealth and resources, and violated the sacred cult. (Simpson 1967:218–19; see also Meyer and Beezley 2000)

Some of his goals were the nullification of internal tariffs, the division of the land, the burning of official archives, the elimination of slavery, and the con- vocation of a congress (Alba 1967).

By 1820, the people had tired of the struggle, as much of the agricultural and mining enterprises of central Mexico had been devastated (Rodriguez O. 1989). The time was ripe for a compromise, despite the fact that both Hidalgo

Miguel Hidalgo.

Jose Maria Morelos.

and Morelos had lost their lives for the radical cause. Augustin de Iturbide, a moderate leader, mediated the ideological conflicts between conservatives and liberals. He made a pact with the liberal rebel Vicente Guerrero. As the inheritor of the Hidalgo-Morelos tradition, Guerrero, along with other liberals, had eventually grown weary of the prolonged anarchy. The agreement between Iturbide and Guerrero was called the Plan of Iguala. Its provisions included setting up Mexico as an independent monarchy, ruled by a king or European prince, in which the Catholic Church would maintain its privileges, and criollos and gachupines would be considered equals; these agreements were known as the three guarantees (Skidmore and Smith 1992). The guarantees are symbolized by the colors of the modern Mexican flag: green for the monarchy, white for the Catholic Church, and red for the union of gachupines and criollos. Religion was the unifying feature of the plan.

> It was necessary to defend the Catholic faith. With this issue, the author of the manifesto—whoever he was—found the common denominator for Spaniards and Mexicans, for landowners and landless, for whites, Mestizos, and Indians, for higher and lower clergy. (Bazant 1977:27)

1821: Peace

Liberal/conservative ideological rivalries were temporarily put aside when the compromise was reached in 1821. However, they resurfaced after Iturbide named himself president of the provisional governing junta, which selected the five-person regency that would temporarily govern the newly independent Mexico. Members of the republican insurgent movement were left out of this government. In 1822, Iturbide became the constitutional monarch, and opposition groups soon began to form against him, causing him to leave Mexico in exile in 1823. Upon his return in 1824, the local legislator held a trial and sentenced him to death. Iturbide was executed shortly thereafter. In the wake of this event, Guadalupe Victoria, a liberal afro-mestizo, became the first elected president of the Republic of Mexico. However, the liberal/conservative battle continued throughout the first half of the nineteenth century. "From 1821 to 1850, Mexico was in a state of constant turmoil. In thirty years there were fifty governments, almost all the result of military coups and eleven of them presided over by General Santa Ana" (Villegas et al. 1974:97).

Change: Experimentation and Nationalism

Age of the Caudillo

"It is not easy to follow the thread of reason through the generation following the Independence of Mexico. The loosely cemented strata of colonial society had split apart in the cataclysm of 1810–1821, and their mending is still an uncertain and remote aspiration" (Simpson 1967:230; see also Van Young 2001). In the wake of this earth-shattering upheaval, economic and political systems and practices were shaken and remained unsettled for over 60 years (Rodriguez O. 1989). This time is best summarized as the age of the caudillo (strong, charismatic leader).

The setting for the rise of military and political strongmen was provided by the liberal/conservative conflict and by dissension among the liberals. There were so many coups, countercoups, intrigues, and palace-guard incidents that political goals became secondary to personal motives. Regional forces began to dominate, usually in the hands of caudillos, who aggressively sought local control and even national power positions to amass personal prestige and status (Wasserman 2000). General Antonio Lopez de Santa Ana, labeled by Cockcroft (1990:72) as an "unprincipled ideological chameleon," was a fine practitioner of this art. Beginning as a supporter of liberal causes, he repeatedly switched sides to advance his own career. For over 30 years, this comic pattern of usurpation and exile continued, while Mexico suffered under the vogue of personal aggrandizement. When institutions were weakened and lost their influence, strong individuals seized the leadership and the personal privileges that came with it.

Early Difficulties

Despite this instability, liberals made some sincere efforts to challenge church influence, a power amassed over a 300-year time span (Meyer and Beezley 2000). Anticlericalism rose during this time, and when Benito Juarez, the culturally assimilated Indian, took office in 1857, laws were implemented to curtail vested church power and land ownership. Contrary to some interpretations and perhaps as an unintended outcome, these Juarez-inspired laws also infringed on Indian land tenure practices (Cockcroft 1990; Bazant 1977).

The ingredients for Mexican nationalist aspirations could never quite coalesce prior to independence, despite occasional, spontaneous strivings, but after independence an incipient type of nationalism gradually took shape. At first, efforts revolved around construction of an entirely new governmental model. In time, nationalist sentiment produced a hybrid strategy derived from Spanish and Indian traditions (Van Young 2001). Furthermore, foreign nations coveted Mexican territory, recently won but poorly protected because of the political turmoil, and this also ultimately helped the growth of nationalism (Sierra 1969). Such threats from outsiders helped bring Mexicans together, for xenophobic fears often make bedfellows out of enemies (Wasserman 2000). However, a cohesive nationalist ideology was still not fully formulated by the end of the nineteenth century. Another revolution in 1910 partially fulfilled this goal of clarifying a nationalist path.

Within liberal ranks, puros, pushing harder than moderados, became frustrated with the slowness of change. Their activity was a prelude to the 1910 Revolution. One of them, Lorenzo de Zavala, migrated north to the borderlands, hoping to institute social experiments unwanted by central Mexican authorities (Alba 1967). He later predicted that this northern region (now the United States Southwest) would separate from the increasingly despotic conservative government. This prophecy would later come true, although under different circumstances than he imagined (Kessell 2002; Bazant 1977).

Borderland settlement appeared imperative because the sparsely populated region required a more permanent body of residents to fend off foreign landgrabs, a threat that mounted after independence (Gongora 1975).

> For three centuries, the northern frontier was a dynamic periphery of the Spanish empire. Even in 1821, when independent Mexico emerged out of New Spain, all the governors in the far north were still Spaniards born in the mother country. . . . Each had warned the higher authorities that the United States coveted New Mexico, Arizona, Texas, and California. And none would have been surprised by the redefinition of their provinces—in a scant twenty-five years—as the American Southwest. (Kessell 2002:xvi)

However, Indians controlled most of the area, making settlement difficult, if not impossible. To counter foreign intervention, some Mexican leaders sought to establish a colony in the borderlands, inviting non-Mexicans (usually United States frontiersmen) to join them in an outpost of the new nation. Reasons for this varied: some Mexicans simply wanted more whites there to offset Indian influence; others, politically idealistic, wished to have the new society modeled after United States democratic traditions. This goal was only partially attained but nevertheless highlights the discontent and frustration of radical Mexican liberals toward conservative policies. One such liberal Mexican invited the well-known British utopian socialist, Robert Owen, to found a new Mexican social order (Alba 1967). Instead, Owen brought the experiment to the United States, where it failed. These and other episodes reflect the Mexican unhappiness with a government unwilling to chart a new political course. Some, in short, refused to wait for change.

Conflict over the Indian Program

On several issues, political ideologies were mixed. For example, a goal of the nationalist program was the granting of citizenship and other rights to "all residents of Mexican territory," primarily the Indian population that had been kept outside the mainstream of social and political life. The conservatives supported Indian national integration because Indians still were closely allied with the church, one of the conservatives' interest groups. The liberals also agreed with the integration policy, hoping to improve opportunities for mestizos as well, but they alienated the natives through lack of an effective liaison with them. Most significantly, the natives showed lukewarm acceptance of the program. Their well-founded wariness was based on history, because further integration was often associated with more complete native exploitation and oppression; the history of transformation from encomienda to repartimiento to hacienda is one of the most obvious examples of change that brought devolution rather than evolution.

Behaving like their Spanish forefathers, the Mexican nationalists refused to acknowledge the basis of native distrust. In fact, the leaders shaping policy ignored the overriding issue of that time: members from the privileged classes and the masses of the people had always struggled historically, and it was this problem source that was central to the Mexican experience. Using force and punishment, all with "for the good of the natives" in mind, Mexican leaders rushed headlong into accommodation programs without assuring the people of their good intentions. For example, liberals broke up Indian communal lands and villages with the idea of helping them. Instead, as noted previously, it created more problems for the Indians, who were made unhappy "for their own good."

"In the first twelve years of independence, Mexico had experimented with monarchy, moderate constitutional republic, radical populist regime, conservative government, and liberal government; each in turn failed to produce stability" (Bazant 1977:61). Lacking this foundation, or perhaps because of its tenuousness, the native and mestizo populations remained powerless. It did not matter whether the social planners were gachupines, criollos, mestizos, or culturally assimilated Indians; the majority of the people, mostly Indian in this period, continued as before—on the receiving end. Eventually change took place, but not before much bloodshed had occurred and many years had passed.

STAGE II REFERENCES

Adelman, J., ed. 1999. *Colonial legacies: The problem of persistence in Latin-American history*. New York: Routledge.

Aguirre Beltran, G. 1946. *La población negra en México, 1519–1810*. México: Ediciones Fuente Cultural.

Alba, V. 1967. *The Mexicans: The making of a nation*. New York: Praeger.

Altman, I. 1991. Spanish society in Mexico City after the conquest. *Hispanic American Historical Review* 71(3): 413–445.

Archer, C. I. 1989. Where did all the royalists go? New light on the military collapse of New Spain, 1810–1822. In *The Mexican and Mexican American experience in the 19th century*, ed. J. E. Rodriguez O. Tempe, AZ: Bilingual Press/Editorial Bilingue.

Banton, M. 1987. *Racial theories*. Cambridge, England: Cambridge University Press.

Bazant, J. 1977. *A concise history of Mexico: From Hidalgo to Cardenas, 1805–1940*. New York: Cambridge University Press.

Bellwood, P. 2005. *First farmers: The origins of agricultural societies*. Malden, MA: Blackwell.

Bennett, H. L. 2003. *Africans in colonial Mexico: Absolutism, Christianity, and Afro-Creole consciousness, 1570–1640*. Bloomington: Indiana University Press.

———. 2009. *Colonial blackness: A history of Afro-Mexico*. Bloomington: Indiana University Press.

Berdan, F. F. 2008. *Ethnic identity in Nahua Mesoamerica: The view from archaeology, art history, ethnohistory, and contemporary ethnography*. Salt Lake City: University of Utah Press.

Bolton, H. 1921. *The Spanish borderlands*. New Haven, CT: Yale University Press.

Borah, W., and S. F. Cook. 1960. *The population of central Mexico in 1548*. Berkeley: University of California Press.

Boyer, R., and G. Spurling. 2000. *Colonial lives: Documents on Latin American history, 1550–1850*. New York: Oxford University Press.

Brues, A. 1990. *People and races*. Long Grove, IL: Waveland Press.

Burkhart, L. M. 1989. *The slippery earth: Nahua-Christian moral dialogue in sixteenth-century Mexico*. Tucson: University of Arizona Press.

Burns, E. B., and J. A. Charlip. 2007. *Latin America: An interpretive history*. Upper Saddle River, NJ: Pearson-Prentice-Hall.

Cancian, F. 1967. Political and religious organization. In *Handbook of Middle American Indians*, vol. 6, ed. R. Wauehope. Austin: University of Texas Press.

Carrasco, P. 1965. The Mesoamerican Indian during the colonial period. In *Indian Mexico: Past and present*, ed. B. Bell. Los Angeles: University of California, Latin American Center.

Carroll, P. J. 1991. *Blacks in colonial Veracruz: Race, ethnicity, and regional development.* Austin: University of Texas Press.

Chance, J. K. 1978. *Race and class in colonial Oaxaca.* Stanford, CA: Stanford University Press.

Chavez, A. H. 2006. *Mexico: A brief history.* Berkeley: University of California Press.

Cheng, Y. 2009. *Creating the "new man": From enlightenment ideals to socialist realities.* Honolulu: University of Hawaii Press.

Chevalier, F. 1966. *Land and society in colonial Mexico.* Berkeley: University of California Press.

Chinas, B. 1983. *The Isthmus Zapotecs: Women's roles in cultural context.* Long Grove, IL: Waveland Press.

Cockcroft, J. D. 1990. *Mexico: Class formation, capital accumulation, and the state.* New York: Monthly Review Press.

Collier, G., and E. L. Quaratiello. 1994. *Basta!: Land and the Zapatista rebellion in Chiapas.* Oakland, CA: Institute for Food and Development Policy.

Cope, R. D. 1994. *The limits of racial domination: Plebeian society in colonial Mexico City, 1660–1720.* Madison: University of Wisconsin Press.

Curtin, P. 2000. *The world and the West: The European challenge and the overseas response in the age of empire.* Cambridge: Cambridge University Press.

Deans-Smith, S. 1992. *Bureaucrats, planters and workers: The making of the tobacco monopoly in Bourbon Mexico.* Austin: University of Texas Press.

de la Fuente, J. 1967. Ethnic relationships. In *Handbook of Middle American Indians*, vol. 6, ed. R. Wauehope. Austin: University of Texas Press.

de Madariaga, S. 1947. *The rise of the Spanish American empire.* New York: Macmillan.

Elliott, J. H. 1963. *Imperial Spain 1469–1716.* New York: The New American Library.

Ericson, J. E., and T. G. Baugh. 1993. *The American Southwest and Mesoamerica: Systems of prehistoric exchange.* New York: Plenum Press.

Farriss, N. M. 1993. Persistent Maya resistance and cultural retention in Yucatan. In *The Indian in Latin American history: Resistance, resilience and acculturation*, ed. J. E. Kicza. Wilmington, DE: Scholarly Resources.

Florescano, E. 1984. The formation and economic structure of the hacienda in New Spain. In *The Cambridge history of Latin America, Vol. 2: Colonial Latin America*, ed. L. Bethell. Cambridge: Cambridge University Press.

———. 1994. *Memory, myth, and time in Mexico: From the Aztecs to independence.* Austin: University of Texas Press.

Foster, G. 1960. *Culture and conquest.* New York: Quadrangle Books.

———. 1988. *Tzintzuntzan: Mexican peasants in a changing world.* Long Grove, IL: Waveland Press.

Frank, A. G. 1969. *Capitalism and underdevelopment in Latin America.* New York: Monthly Review Press.

Friedrich, P. 1968. *Agrarian revolt in a Mexican village.* Englewood Cliffs, NJ: Prentice-Hall.

Galtung, J. 1969. Violence, peace, and peace research. *Journal of Peace Research* 6(3): 167–169.

Gerhard, P. 1993. *The Southwest frontier of New Spain.* Norman: University of Oklahoma Press.

Gibson, C. 1964. *Aztecs under Spanish rule.* Stanford, CA: Stanford University Press.

———. 1966. *Spain in America.* New York: Harper & Row.

———. 1984. Indian societies under Spanish rule. In *The Cambridge history of Latin America, Vol. 2: Colonial Latin America,* ed. L. Bethell. Cambridge: Cambridge University Press.

Gillin, J. 1957. Mestizo America. In *Most of the world: The peoples of Africa, Latin America and the East today,* ed. R. Linton. New York: Columbia University Press.

Gongora, M. 1975. *Studies in the colonial history of Spanish America.* Cambridge: Cambridge University Press.

Gonzalez, M. 2009. *Mexicanos: A history of Mexicans in the United States.* Bloomington: Indiana University Press.

Gonzalez, O. E., and B. Premo, eds. 2007. *Raising an empire: Children in early modern Iberia and colonial Latin America.* Albuquerque: University of New Mexico Press.

Gossen, G. H., and M. Leon-Portilla, eds. 1993. *South and Meso-American native spirituality: From the cult of the feathered serpent to the theology of liberation.* New York: Crossroad.

Graham, R., ed. 1990. *The idea of race in Latin America, 1870–1940.* Austin: University of Texas Press.

Gruzinski, S. 1988. The net torn apart: Ethnic identities and Westernization in colonial Mexico, 1600–1900 centuries. In *Ethnicities and nations,* ed. R. Guidieri et al. Austin: University of Texas Press.

Guerra, F-X. 2007. Mexico from independence to revolution: The mutations of liberalism. In *Cycles of conflict, centuries of change, crisis, reform, and revolution in Mexico,* ed. E. Servin, L. Reina, and J. Tutino, pp. 129–152. Durham, NC: Duke University Press.

Gutierrez, R. 1991. *When Jesus came, the Corn Mothers went away.* Stanford, CA: Stanford University Press.

Hamnett, B. 2006. *A concise history of Mexico.* Cambridge: Cambridge University Press.

Haring, C. H. 1963. *The Spanish empire in America.* New York: Harcourt Brace Jovanovich.

Haslip-Viera, G. 1999. *Crime and punishment in late colonial Mexico City, 1692–1810.* Albuquerque: University of New Mexico Press.

Hassig, R. 2001. *Time, history, and belief in Aztec and colonial Mexico.* Austin: University of Texas Press.

Helms, M. W. 1975. *Middle America: A culture history of heartland and frontiers.* Englewood Cliffs, NJ: Prentice-Hall.

Hewes, G. W. 1954. Mexicans in search of the Mexican: Notes on Mexican national character studies. *American Journal of Economics and Sociology* 13: 209.

Hill, J. H., and K. C. Hill. 1986. *Speaking Mexicano: Dynamics of syncretic language in central Mexico.* Tucson: University of Arizona Press.

Himmerich y Valencia, R. 1991. *The encomenderos of New Spain, 1521–1555.* Austin: University of Texas Press.

Holloway, T. H. 2008. *A companion to Latin American history.* Malden, MA: Blackwell.

Horna, H. 2001. *La Indianidad: The indigenous world before Latin Americans.* Princeton, NJ: Markus Wiener.

Ingham, J. M. 1986. *Mary, Michael and Lucifer: Folk Catholicism in Central Mexico*. Austin: University of Texas Press.

Israel, J. I. 1975. *Race, class, and politics in colonial Mexico*. London: Oxford University Press.

———. 2010. *A revolution of the mind: Radical enlightenment and the intellectual origins of modern democracy*. Princeton, NJ: Princeton University Press.

Jaffary, N. E., ed. 2007. *Gender, race, and religion in the colonization of the Americas*. Aldershot, England: Ashgate.

Joseph, G., and T. Henderson, eds. 2002. *The Mexico reader: History, culture, politics*. Durham, NC: Duke University Press.

Kearney, M. 1986. *The winds of Ixtepeji: World view and society in a Zapotec town*. Long Grove, IL: Waveland Press.

———. 1996. *Reconceptualizing the peasantry: Anthropology in global perspective*. Boulder, CO: Westview Press.

Kellogg, S. 2005. *Weaving the past: A history of Latin America's indigenous women from the Prehispanic period to the present*. New York: Oxford University Press.

Kessell, J. L. 2002. *Spain in the Southwest*. Norman: University of Oklahoma Press.

Kicza, J. E., ed. 1993. *The Indian in Latin American history: Resistance, resilience and acculturation*. Wilmington, DE: Scholarly Resources.

Knight, A. 1990. Racism, revolution, and *indigenismo*: Mexico, 1910–1940. In *The idea of race in Latin America, 1870–1940*, ed. R. Graham. Austin: University of Texas Press.

———. 2002. *Mexico: From the beginning to the Spanish conquest*. Cambridge: Cambridge University Press.

———. 2007. Mexico's three fin de siècle crises. In *Cycles of Conflict, Centuries of Change, Crisis, Reform, and Revolution in Mexico*, ed. E. Servin, L. Reina, and J. Tutino. Durham, NC: Duke University Press.

Leon-Portilla, M. 1963. *Aztec thought and culture*. Norman: University of Oklahoma Press.

Lockhart, J., 1992. *The Nahuas after the conquest: A social and cultural history of central Mexico, sixteenth through eighteenth centuries*. Stanford, CA: Stanford University Press.

MacLachlan, C., and J. E. Rodriguez O. 1980. *The forging of the cosmic race*. Berkeley: University of California Press.

Madsen, W. 1967. Religious syncretism. In *Handbook of Middle American Indians*, Vol. 6, ed. R. Wauehope. Austin: University of Texas Press.

Mallon, F. E. 1995. *Peasant and nation: The making of postcolonial Mexico and Peru*. Berkeley: University of California Press.

Mann, C. C. 2005. *1491: New revelations of the Americas before Columbus*. New York: Vintage.

McNeil, C. 2006. *Chocolate in Mesoamerica: A cultural history of cacao*. Gainesville: University Press of Florida.

McWilliams, C. 1990[1968]. *North from Mexico: The Spanish-speaking people of the United States*. Westport, CT: Greenwood Press.

Menchaca, M. 2001. *Recovering history, constructing race: The Indian, black, and white roots of Mexican Americans*. Austin: University of Texas Press.

Meyer, M., and W. Beezley, eds. 2000. *The Oxford history of Mexico*. Oxford: Oxford University Press.

Miller, M. E. 2001. *The art of Mesoamerica: From Olmec to Aztec*. London: Thames and Hudson.

Morner, M. 1967. *Race mixture in the history of Latin America*. Boston: Little, Brown.

————. 1989. *New world soundings: Culture and ideology in the Americas*. Baltimore: Johns Hopkins University Press.

Morse, R. M. 1989. *New world soundings: Culture and ideology in the Americas*. Baltimore: Johns Hopkins University Press.

Muldoon, J., ed. 2004. *The spiritual conversion of the Americas*. Gainesville: University Press of Florida.

Ortiz de Montellano, B. 1990. *Aztec medicine, health, and nutrition*. New Brunswick, NJ: Rutgers University Press.

Padden, R. C. 1967. *The hummingbird and the hawk: Conquest and sovereignty in the Valley of Mexico, 1503–1541*. Columbus: Ohio State University Press.

Paz, O. 1961. *The labyrinth of solitude*. New York: Grove Press.

Raat, W. D. 1992. *Mexico and the United States: Ambivalent vistas*. Athens: University of Georgia Press.

Ramos, S. 1962. *Profile of man and culture in Mexico*. Austin: University of Texas Press.

Reina, L. 2007. Local elections and regime crises: The political culture of indigenous peoples. In *Cycles of conflict, centuries of change, crisis, reform, and revolution in Mexico*, ed. E. Servin, L. Reina, and J. Tutino, pp. 91–128. Durham, NC: Duke University Press.

Restall, M. 2005. *Beyond black and red: African-native relations in colonial Latin America*. Albuquerque: University of New Mexico Press.

Ricard, R. 1966. *The spiritual conquest of Mexico*. Berkeley: University of California Press.

Robinson, W. I. 2004. *A theory of global capitalism: Production, class, and state in a transnational world*. Baltimore: Johns Hopkins University Press.

Rodriguez O., J. E., ed. 1989. *Mexican and Mexican American experience in the 19th century*. Tempe, AZ. Bilingual Press/Editorial Bilingue.

Romanell, P. 1967. *Making of the Mexican mind*. Notre Dame, IN: University of Notre Dame Press.

Romanucci-Ross, L. 1986. *Conflict, violence, and morality in a Mexican village*. Chicago: University of Chicago Press.

Ruiz, R. E. 1992. *Triumphs and tragedy: A history of the Mexican people*. New York: W. W. Norton.

Ruiz Medrano, E. 2006. *Reshaping New Spain: Government and private interests in the colonial bureaucracy, 1531–1550*. Boulder: University of Colorado Press.

Sanchez-Albornoz, N. 1984. The population of colonial Spanish America. In *The Cambridge history of Latin America, Vol. 2: Colonial Latin America*, ed. L. Bethell. Cambridge: Cambridge University Press.

————. 1988. *Españoles hacia América: La emigración en masa, 1880–1930*. Madrid: Alianza Editorial.

Schroeder, S., and S. Poole, eds. 2007. *Religion in New Spain*. Albuquerque: University of New Mexico Press.

Schwartz, S., ed. 2000. *Victors and vanquished: Spanish and Nahua views of the conquest of Mexico*. Boston: Bedford/St. Martin's.

Servin, E., L. Reina, and J. Tutino, eds. 2007. *Cycles of conflict, centuries of change, crisis, reform, and revolution in Mexico*. Durham, NC: Duke University Press.

Sierra, J. 1969. *The political evolution of the Mexican people.* Austin: University of Texas Press.

Simpson, L. B. 1966. *The encomienda in New Spain.* Berkeley: University of California Press.

———. 1967. *Many Mexicos.* Berkeley: University of California Press.

Skidmore, T. E., and P. H. Smith. 1992. *Modern Latin America.* New York: Oxford University Press.

Smolenski, J., and T. J. Humphrey, eds. 2005. *New world orders: Violence, sanction, and authority in the colonial Americas.* Philadelphia: University of Pennsylvania Press.

Sokolov, R. 1991. *Why we eat what we eat: How Columbus changed the way the world eats.* New York: Simon & Schuster.

Spicer, E. 1962. *Cycles of conquest.* Tucson: University of Arizona Press.

Stein, S., and B. Stein. 1970. *The colonial heritage of Latin America.* New York: Oxford University Press.

Suchlicki, J. 2001. *Mexico: From Montezuma to the fall of PRI.* Washington, DC: Brassey's.

van den Berghe, P. L. 1967. *Race and racism: A comparative perspective.* New York: John Wiley & Sons.

Van Young, E. 2001. *The other rebellion: Popular violence, ideology, and the Mexican struggle for independence, 1810–1821.* Stanford, CA: Stanford University Press.

Vasconcelos, J., and M. Gamio. 1926. *Aspects of Mexican civilization.* Chicago: University of Chicago Press.

Vaughn, B. 2009. My blackness and theirs: Viewing Mexican blackness up close. In *Black Mexico: Race and society from colonial to modern times,* ed. B. Vinson and M. Restall, pp. 209–219. Albuquerque: University of New Mexico Press.

Vigil, J. D., and F. Lopez. 2004. Race and ethnic relations in Mexico. *Journal of Latinos and Latin America Studies* 1(1): 49–74.

Villegas, D. C. et al. 1974. *A compact history of Mexico.* Los Angeles: University of California, Latin American Center.

Vinson, B., and M. Restall, eds. 2009. *Black Mexico: Race and society from colonial to modern times.* Albuquerque: University of New Mexico Press.

Wagley, C., and M. Harris. 1958. *Minorities in the New World: Six case studies.* New York: Columbia University Press.

Wasserman, M. 2000. *Everyday life and politics in nineteenth century Mexico: Men, women, and war.* Albuquerque: University of New Mexico Press.

Weber, D. J., and J. M. Rausch, eds. 1994. *Where cultures meet: Frontiers in Latin American history.* Wilmington, DE: SR Books.

Whetten, N. L. 1969. *Rural Mexico.* Chicago: University of Chicago Press.

Wills, W. H., and R. D. Leonard, eds. 1994. *The ancient Southwestern community: Models and methods for the study of prehistoric social organization.* Albuquerque: University of New Mexico Press.

Wolf, E. R. 1959. *Sons of the shaking earth.* Chicago: University of Chicago Press.

———. 1966. *Peasants.* Englewood Cliffs, NJ: Prentice-Hall.

———. 1982. *Europe and the people without history.* Berkeley: University of California Press.

Wood, S. G. 2003. *Transcending conquest: Nahua views of Spanish colonial Mexico.* Norman: University of Oklahoma Press.

Zavala, S. 1943. *The Spanish colonization of America*. Philadelphia: University of Pennsylvania Press.

Zorita, A. 1963. *Life and labor in ancient Mexico*. New Brunswick, NJ: Rutgers University Press.

Mexican Independence and Nationalism 1821–1846

The era of Enlightenment increased autonomy and made natives and the budding mestizo peoples demand still more independence. Gradually, this feeling also led to the use of Mexicano as a source of ethnic identity—one name, one people. This was a stage characterized by bold experimentation, by excursions further and further from earlier influences. Yet, it was also a time of great confusion, where the shifting sands of cultural variation had not yet settled. Peasant lifeways were further forged from this time of ferment and flux and began to show signs of permanence in some regions.

Part of the people had one foot in the past and desired to maintain that connection for a sense of security, if not the comforts of that time period. In contrast, others looked only to the future and to some vaguely defined goals because the past was so harsh and mean. In addition to these internal sources of ambiguity, the external environment often imposed sharp limits on unbounded innovations and even inflicted sometimes cruel punishment for mishaps and miscalculations.

"Parts" of a nation, of course, are much more concrete than are the competing aspects of economic, social, and political forces and changes. The land, the people, the manner of subsistence, a reliance on the system of values established in America, represented a semblance of stability in the midst of ill-defined and poorly conceived strivings for nationhood. In this rather abrupt transition to a broader and more

sophisticated social and economic network, peasantry became more of a factor in the lives of the indigenous and mestizo peoples. Storm and stress characterized this time period. At times, reformist leaders attempted to move the country toward major (if ill-defined) social and economic revampments. As often occurs, more conservative elements thwarted such intrusions, turning the society and economy back toward institutional forms established during the colonial period. As these reform and counterreform contests continued, many people left the centers of political strife to colonize the frontier regions of Mexico. In these new locales, they often patterned their social establishments on those that predominated in the land of their origin. Amid this activity, Mexico was also threatened by the expansionist tendencies of powerful foreign nations, the United States and France in particular.

In the flurry of changes, major turning points often emerged in strange and unpredictable ways. The Anglo-American acquisition of Mexico's northern provinces was one of the more severe blows suffered by Mexico in the years between independence in 1821 and the 1910 Revolution. For the Chicano people within the territories annexed by the United States, an abrupt and earth-shattering end had come to their strivings to remake themselves. While Chicanos in the United States continued to be affected by events in metropolitan Mexico, other social forces and places became more important in their everyday lives.

In anticipation of that importance, our study of this tumultuous period will focus considerably more attention on events in the Mexican frontier regions than has been the case in previous chapters. Because the era was full of surprises and unpredictable turns and lasted until the 1910 Revolution for Mexicans living in Mexico, this stage includes some discussion of late nineteenth-century events in Mexico, such as the role of land tenure under the regimes of Benito Juarez and Porfirio Diaz.

Chapter 6

INTACT AND STABLE SOCIAL ORDER

Class: Ideological Struggle between Liberals and Conservatives

Mexico under Criollos

Independence seemed to produce little change for the masses. The gachupines were removed from the socioeconomic structure, but they were replaced by the criollos. The nature of social relations thus remained the same (Hamnett 2006). "Mexico still retained many elements of her colonial heritage. Her economy was essentially dependent on foreign markets, her social structure was defined along racial lines, and colonial institutions such as the Catholic Church and the hacienda continued to function in traditional ways" (Sinkin 1979:11). In short, "The basic infrastructure of the economy remained the same, and growth was halting. But at least growth was endogamous, and no surplus was siphoned off to Spain" (Knight 2007:158). Peasant society was sharply reordered in this phase, and gradually some peasants joined the proletariat—a more unstable urban labor sector, often referred to as surplus labor. Nevertheless, some opportunities were also opened for mestizos and culturally assimilated Indians (Cline 1963). Barriers to social mobility still remained after decades of struggle, but isolated breaches of the barriers did occur.

Political confrontations between conservative and liberal leaders and their followers dominated the scene, and even within liberal ranks debate contin-

ued. The puros were uncompromising in their beliefs, whereas the moderados were open to negotiations with the church (Sinkin 1979; Gomez-Quinones
1994a). At the center of this political discord was the issue of how to recon-
struct the social and economic sectors to best enhance Mexico's future, especially in light of the three major wars that marked the century: the War of
Independence (1810–1821), the Mexican–American War (1846–1848), and the
French Intervention (1861–1867). Liberals accepted both the event and the
spiritual promise of independence, while conservatives struggled to preserve
past practices and renegotiate independence teachings (Meyer and Beezley
2000; Gomez-Quinones 1994a).

Minor as well as major issues were intensely debated among the powers
competing for leadership. The groups were often unable to come to an understanding. These indecisions had disastrous effects on Mexico for the first 50
years following independence (Meyer and Beezley 2000; Cockcroft 1990;
Gomez-Quinones 1994a). Haciendas, debt peonage, and sharply defined class
differences continued during this period of ferment. There was a move toward a
redefinition of the status and role of the peasant, in part through the incorporation of Indians into a class society as "citizens" in an effort to rid the country of
the constraints of a caste system and to integrate natives into the new urban proletariat (Knight 2007; Frye 1996). Nevertheless, this restructuring did little to
reduce social and economic inequality. "Instead of achieving a nation of free and
equal Mexicans, the country was almost entirely in the hands of a class of white
hacendados and of national and foreign investors. . . . The country belonged
politically, economically, and culturally to the few" (Lomnitz-Adler 1992:277).

Peasant Conditions

In the political arena, the liberal and conservative viewpoints presented
contrasting ideological perspectives. Yet, when the time for policy implementation arrived, liberals also followed self-interest motives. As a result, the
majority of Indians and mestizos remained exploited and powerless. Leaders
of all persuasions followed the customs of a former age, while the majority,
despite changes in their formal legal status, continued to suffer (Tutino 2007).

From 1820 to 1850, the republicas de indios were still holding on, but from
1850 to 1890, they began to lose out due to liberal reform laws, especially during the Porfiriato (the reign of Porfirio Diaz) (Knight 2007). The downside of
the creation of the Mexican state was the diminution of what little self-rule
and autonomy the Indians held. A gradual breakdown of the communal pattern began to unfold. Meanwhile, the mercantilist orientation of the colonial
economy gradually gave way to a more fully capitalist system, exacerbating
the problems of the expanding peasantry (Semo 2007; Whetten 1948).

Indeed, before the end of the nineteenth century, under the dictatorship of
the mestizo Porfirio Diaz, the situation deteriorated. Eleven thousand hacen-

dados managed to gain control over about 57 percent of Mexico's land by dispossessing villagers previously covered by colonial protective legislation. As a result, approximately 15 million people were left without land, some of them in rural villages once controlled by peasants (Servin 2007; Vanderwood 2000; Cockcroft 1990) The liberal Benito Juarez had initiated the sale of Indian communal and mission lands to promote reform and individual ownership by the peasants (Bazant 1977), but instead the holdings went straight to wealthy private buyers. The Indians did not surrender their holdings without protest. Peasant uprisings took place throughout the 1840s and early 1850s in Michoacan, Oaxaca, Puebla, and the state of Mexico (Officer 1987; Cockcroft 1990; Redfield and Villa Rojas 1990; Vanderwood 1992; Hu-DeHart 1993; Taylor 1993; Potter et al. 1967).

Benito Juarez.

Republicas de Indios

Even with all the external and internal conflicts and strains nearly everyone enjoyed the aura of freedom from colonial rule. Indians and mestizos participated in the struggle for independence but were unable to enjoy its fruits. The Indians did not involve themselves in the public life of the new independent country, and many avoided contact with the white man. They continued to seek out their living in the missions or by working as peons, and carried on living in their republicas de indios (Wolf 1965; Potter 1967; Meyer and Beezley 2000).

It has been argued that the republicas were the most tradition-bound units in Mexican society, each maintaining a system of internal government that had undergone very few changes since the early colonial period (Tutino 2007). Wolf, however, argues that peasant communities have always had some contact with the rest of society through state taxes, church tithes, or through working in local haciendas; "these communities were given organizational form by the colonial bureaucracy, as integral components of the Hispanic state and its economic system" (Wolf 1982:145).

A white person or mestizo rarely lived in a republica, except for an occasional parish priest (Meyer and Beezley 2000). A remarkably deeply rooted lifestyle pervaded the Indian towns. Rising at 6:00 AM and returning from tending the *milpa* (maize fields) in the late afternoon the peasant barely subsisted. Tortillas and beans flavored with chile sauce were the main staple of the day. On special days (festivals, patron saint days) and holidays there was pulque or *aguardiente,* a poor version of sugarcane rum, which usually resulted in a drunken collective affair. Dutiful and patient beyond compare, the Indian peasant was the social mainstay of rural Mexican society (Kearney 1996).

Haciendas

The expansion of haciendas required more cheap labor, supplied by dispossessed Indians, and further broadened the power of the hacendados (Wolf 1965). These transformations incorporated the peasantry into a larger regional and later a national political economic network (Knight 2007).

The hacienda system turned Indian peasants into part-time laborers; their traditional economic means of survival now became dependent upon their wages. Hacendados also frequently ran out of money. This resulted in a policy in which only the best land was farmed and production was reduced to keep wages down and allow the land prices and rents to be raised (Wolf 1965, 1982). Mexico City and a few other large cities started importing less agricultural products from distant regions, relying on local production. Many large haciendas went bankrupt (Tutino 2007). Both domestic and foreign investments in agriculture were encouraged, but in the late nineteenth century this pattern was disrupted.

The major innovation of haciendas was in the organization of labor, as technology played a relatively unimportant role in a labor-intensive system. Outside interference with this human apparatus was rigidly opposed (Wolf 1965; Nutini 1995). Thus, the hacienda remained the same internally in the midst of swirling social upheavals and political struggles. Granted citizenship on paper, the Indian was bound to the same lowly status. "The problem was compounded by the fact that the Mestizo leadership, adhering to the imported European and American models of industrial liberalism, considered them an impediment to the development of the country" (Nutini 1995:285–86).

Within this socioeconomic tangle, the changes from a colonial caste to a modern class system were filled with new additions and arrangements. Viewed separately, these alterations meant very little, but as a whole they spelled the beginnings of a major shift to a market system that overlapped with past practices. Cultural lag was reflected in the ways that Indians maintained certain customs and language habits as broader economic networks were being introduced (Meyer and Beezley 2000; Nutini 1995).

Peasant Economy and Ideological Changes

The peasant household, in Mexico as elsewhere, is a productive unit that is "horizontally" involved with other households like it and "vertically" involved with superordinate power holders (Wolf 1966).

> The peasant's economic activities are related to the larger society of which he is a part. The grain, fruit, meat, wine, pottery, fish, cotton, or flax he produces go not only to feed and clothe his family, but also to maintain the priests, artisans, merchants, bureaucrats, kings, and soldiers who make up the urban population or who are the carriers of the Great Tradition of his society. He is tied into a system of distribution and taxation in which his goods and services become part of a regional and national network of economic exchanges. In many cases he participates in an impersonal market where prices respond to supply and demand. (Diaz 1967:51)

As indicated above, peasant producers during this period were being remade into free wage laborers, adding new variations to the rural masses.

> Many became pauperized and survived by begging, engaging in day labor, farming on a tenant or sharecropping basis, or tilling subsistence parcels granted them by *hacendados*, whom they served as debt-peons. Those attaching themselves to the haciendas were sometimes better off than their job-seeking counter-parts. . . . A few peasants managed to succeed as rancheros. (Cockcroft 1990:53)

The Role of Women

Independence for peasant women was not liberating; they were still considered arbiters of the "internal government of the families" (Haidt 2009:79). Economic difficulties during this time drove more and more peasant women into the city in search of work. A third of the labor force of Mexico City was made up of women, 82 percent of whom were Indians or mestizas (Hamnett 2006). The shift from the hacienda to the city still entailed that women would be the domestic workers, but women could also work in other jobs, for instance as spinners in the textile mills, food preparers, waitresses, and vendors on the streets and in the marketplaces (Jaffe and Lewis 2009). Employment, however, was not an emancipating experience; the working woman was widely stigmatized. Peasant women were forced to accept work that was considered degrading and that questioned their honor. One of the few careers that earned women respect and prestige was midwifery (Arrom 1985).

Events in Northern Mexico

Debate on the future of Mexico also occurred in the northern territories (see Bannon 1974). Although the issues took on a different complexion and were discussed within a smaller circle of participants, there appeared to be a clear tendency toward a liberal solution. Some leaders even went so far as to suggest that a Mexican nationalist program should be patterned after the United States. This was particularly true in California and New Mexico, two fully established settlements. California's situation (not forgetting the importance of New Mexico and, later, Texas) serves to sharpen our understanding of key social-class patterns, especially in light of the 1846 war, its aftermath, and modern historical developments.

Conditions in the borderlands, especially California, were similar to those in Mexico. A smaller-scale hacienda system prevailed, with land ownership again determining social rank and role. The Colonization Act and the Reglamento of 1828 allowed land to be settled and owned privately (Lake 2006). Landowners were known as gente de razon (people of reason, and usually all non-Indians), and social life revolved around their privileged circle. Some worked their ranchos, but most preferred the traditional hacendado role. Captain Jose Bandini noted in 1828 that most of the gente de razon preferred to spend their days socializing, gambling, and riding. Indians were relied on to do the work around the hacienda, as many of the owners had neither a trade nor a profession (Weber 2009; Hutchinson 1969; Phillips 1993; Monroy 1990). Mestizo and Indian *pobladores* (settlers) usually worked as vaqueros (cowboys) and foremen, but if they were independent, they often operated *ranchitos* (small ranches) for themselves. Many also served gente de razon as household domestics (Vigil 1974; McWilliams 1990[1968]).

Mexican urban workers at the time of the revolution.

It has been argued that the social structure of Spanish California was similar to that of the Deep South, with the gente de razon being the equivalent of the plantation owners; the native California Indians, the slaves; and the Mexicans, the "poor white trash" (McWilliams 1990[1968]). Such a mixture of classes and ethnic groups generated tension; that is why: "a deep structural weakness of Spanish frontier colonies contributed to the native rebellions. . . . When the demands of friar, soldiers, settlers, government officials weighed more than the natives wished to bear, they rebelled" (Weber 2009:91).

Later, mestizo and Indian immigrants became transient, unskilled laborers. They spoke poor Spanish, and their lot was often little better than that of the California Indian, except that they had hopes of future improvement. They were known as cholos (Indians in transition from one culture to another and considered marginal to both). In Mexico, they would have occupied the lower level in the social-class hierarchy. However, in California there were others who occupied this rung, allowing the cholos to ascend the social ladder (Borah 1970). The lowest group, of course, was the California Indians. Most of them could not improve their social status, as they were caught in a vicious cycle of poverty, racism, and oppression. City officials of pueblos like Los Angeles even sold Indians. As previously noted, native women were even lower, as sexual conquest and violence often accompanied or followed military and political subjugation under a patriarchal colonial society that shaped gender relations (Jaffe and Lewis 2009; Castaneda 1993). "There was a hierarchy within the female community. Indian women and girls living at the missions were accorded lower status than Spanish and Mexican women . . . as Indian women had no rights under colonial law" (Lake 2006:83).

Economic Enterprises in the North

Gente de razon, pobladores, cholos, and California Indians comprised the class system. Other borderland regions used different class labels, but essentially the same unequal system obtained (Mitchell 2005; Kessell 2002). For example, in New Mexico two classes existed: *ricos* (rich) and *pobres* (poor) (McWilliams 1990[1968]; Oboler 1995). In contrast to California Indians, New Mexico Indians were much less integrated into Mexican society because they had more effectively resisted total Spanish subjugation. The central government of that era had tried to improve opportunities for all Indians (Weber 2009), but the program that sought to integrate them into the national culture was poorly implemented.

Before Mexico's independence, California Indians were widely dispersed geographically, and the Spanish soldiers had to locate and capture them to force them to work on colonial enterprises and accept Christianity (Jackson and Castillo 1994). According to a British observer of those events: "If . . . any of the captured Indians show a repugnance to conversion, it is the practice to imprison them for a few days . . . and thus they continue to be incarcerated until they declare their readiness to renounce the religion of their forefathers" (Moquin and Van Doren 1971:133). With Indian aid, 21 missions had been founded in California, each strategically located one-day's ride from another. While the missionary goal was native religious conversion and training, much energy was also expended on making the socioeconomic unit self-sufficient. This scheme mirrored Mexico's hacienda system in thoroughness and severity (Lake 2006; Phillips 1993). Over a period of 200 years, the Spanish in America had perfected the use of the mission as an instrument for binding Indians to the state (Weber 2009).

Housing over 30,000 Indians and with holdings valued in millions of dollars, the missions flourished as religious-economic centers. The colonists introduced Spanish and Mexican technology and products, making them the mainstays of economic and social life (Lake 2006; Mitchell 2005). Some of the new subsistence products were cattle, sheep, pigs, grapes (both wine and raisin), citrus fruits, avocados, olives, pomegranates, pears, wheat, flax, alfalfa, beans, and cotton. Indian labor cared for and produced them. Indians were also trained for various occupations, such as vaquero, shepherd, blacksmith, horticulturist, brick and tile maker, irrigator, miner, and church attendant (Weber 2009; Hass 1995). As noted previously, Hispanicized Indians were given better jobs, and after the secularization of mission lands, they served the gente de razon.

Breakup of California Missions

After Mexican independence, the anticlerical movement affected colonists in the northern region. Many wealthy Californians, including both long-time criollo settlers and newcomers, sought to weaken church power. Since the seat of religious authority was so far away, making administration nearly impossible, gente de razon stepped in to improve their fortunes. Secularization of the missions took place from 1834 to 1843, resulting in a society where the church and religious beliefs were of little significance in guiding the actions of individuals (Archer 2000; Hale 1968; Hutchinson 1969; Moquin and Van Doren 1971; Officer 1987; Gomez-Quinones 1994a). "Making the church a major reform target, the . . . government moved to control clerical appointments, canceled civil obligations to pay tithes, eliminated the enforcement of monastic vows upon friars and nuns, and began to disentail church estates and other properties" (Archer 2000:330). Soon after, church land came under civil control and was redistributed by government grants.

Immediately after secularization, nearly 500 land grants created from the former mission lands were distributed to newcomers. Many of the earlier land-grant residents also benefited by adding more land to their estates. Land grants were of two types: individually owned, or controlled in common by a community of residents, usually as a grazing range for livestock. In California, the primary unit was the individual estate. Within their land-grant boundaries, some patron Californians allotted smaller parcels, ranchitos, to their faithful workers and supporters (Lake 2006).

Variations of the System in New Mexico

The New Mexico land system developed along different lines. After 1598, settlers had carved out large land units and often set aside communal landed estates (more here than in California) for settlers engaged in raising sheep or cattle (Sanderson 1986; Gomez-Quinones 1994b). As a result of this early beginning, socioeconomic life flourished, and despite the persistent conflicts with neighboring dissident Indians, some degree of stability (and some racial mixture) had been established by the time Mexico became independent (Gomez 2007).

In 250 years, the Spanish-speaking population of New Mexico swelled to 60,000, the largest colony in the north. A rico/pobre dichotomy prevailed, with Indians in the lowest position, of course, but intense conflict had subsided as the social relations between the groups stabilized. Within this relatively quiet setting, the large and small rancheros and their workers carried on an independent, self-sufficient life. Many surrounding Indian groups, however, had resisted full Hispanic control and maintained a semblance of autonomy in the region, although there was some diffusion of Hispanic culture (Carter 2009; Dunbar Ortiz 2007).

Independence did not have a great effect on New Mexicans; New Mexico had always been far removed from the centers of power. The greatest effect was the removal of the strict trade embargo placed on Mexico by colonial Spain; this opened up the northern region to commerce and communication, accelerating the rate of changes that already were taking place and leading to an increased Anglo immigration (Gutierrez 1991; Gomez-Quinones 1994a).

The first Anglos to arrive in New Mexico were merchants selling their wares. They were followed by trappers hunting for pelts in New Mexico's Rockies. Pioneers in search of land came next. Finally, the soldiers came to annex New Mexico. The Anglos continually slandered the Indians and Hispanos of New Mexico, claiming divine rights of conquest and asserting what they viewed to be their own moral and cultural superiority (Kessell 2002; Gomez-Quinones 1994a). The "nineteenth-century Protestant apostles of American democracy found in New Mexico a depraved people who wallowed in promiscuity, whose devilish fandangos corrupted, and whose addiction to vice had created an indolent and mongrel race" (Gutierrez 1991:338). New Mexicans were now in conflict with Anglos over the very same issues they had been in conflict with when the Spanish arrived—religion, labor, land, and water. It was a clash over America's modernism and Mexico's traditionalism, the English and Spanish traditions creating different trajectories for the countries.

Rancho Life

Much of the rancho life in California resembled that of the missions before it, but with some variations and important additions. Almost nation-sized in extent, the ranchos became centers of cattle raising, which soon mushroomed into a lucrative commercial network. All of the activities and paraphernalia associated with this industry surfaced here: rodeos, vaqueros, branding, and so on. Trade with New England merchants developed, in which hides and tallow (used in the manufacture of soap and candles) were exchanged for manufactured products from the eastern seaboard. Cattle hides became popularly known as "California bank notes," and the United States leather industry flourished. Mexicans who carried the balls of tallow to the waiting clipper ships were left with a slick mess of grease on their backs. They came to be known as "greasers," an opprobrious label eventually used toward all things Mexican (Lake 2006).

Women were also active participants of the cattle-ranching society. It has been noted that the working woman, *la mujer trabajadora*, in actual fact did more manual labor than the ranchero himself. She wove clothing and blankets, made

A family of Californios at the turn of the century pose in their Sunday best in front of their home.

cheese, and bleached beeswax, in addition to performing all her household duties. Before modern capitalist growth, women were actively engaged in agricultural production and related income-producing activities, as well as being property owners (Heidenreich 2007; Fowler-Salamini and Vaughan 1994).

Interestingly, the early Yankee settlers (mountain men, traders, seamen, and adventurers) were readily accepted by gente de razon. They did not view the Anglos as enemies, and much intermarriage took place with the Mexicans (de la Torre and Pesquera 1993; Blea 1992). Most of the immigrants became Hispanicized and acquired their own land grants. Afterward, as a result of intermarriage, many Yankees inherited large parcels of land that gente de razon had willed to their daughters. General George Patton of World War II fame is a descendant of one such marriage. Assimilated Yankees became the social equals of Californios, with the cholos and Indians remaining in the lowest position (Lake 2006).

Mexican Texas

For a variety of reasons, Texas was an interesting region of northern Mexico. Initially settled in the early eighteenth century by soldiers and civilians, in addition to having a tenuous mission system, the area was one of the hardest environments of the frontier. Particularly noteworthy was how Indians there, armed with weapons that were secured from French sources in Louisiana, were able to fend off Spanish soldiers and colonists. As a result, the Spanish presence was shaky (Weber 2009). As compared to California and New Mexico, the experience of Texas with immigrants from the United States was also different. Anglo settlers first came into Texas in 1821, when the Mexican government granted colonization rights (De Leon and Griswold del Castillo 2006; Gomez-Quinones 1994b). These newcomers sought to regenerate the Tejanos who had been swallowed up by the wilderness (De Leon and Griswold del Castillo 2006). These views carried over into their treatment of Mexicans during the brief period that Texas became a republic: "Texas Mexicans suffered from forced marches, general dispossession, and random violence" (Montejano 1987:27). In what is now east Texas, over a hundred Mexican families were forcibly uprooted, losing their homes and lands (Montejano 1987; Oboler 1995).

Culture: Budding Mexicanismo

First Steps toward National Unity

In Mexico, the early nineteenth century was a time of scores to be settled and new realities to react to, combined with the goal of attaining national unity. However, the populace adhered to old customs to maintain some semblance of stability, as patterns of language, religion, family structure, and many other traditions persisted. The overriding societal theme was that all citizens should be consolidated into the nationality both spiritually and economically, thus facilitating national cohesion (Chavez 2005). While liberals and conservatives were locked in a power struggle, with the ideological contest in doubt for decades, the liberals sought educational reform for natives. However, the legislation on education was soon rejected by Santa Ana, the Attila of Mexican Civilization (Servin, Reina, and Tutino 2007), who became president of Mexico in 1832 and later gained notoriety in the Texas war of secession from Mexico.

The conservatives adamantly opposed social transformations. Neither political group's policies clearly dominated before 1860, with the exception of the liberal reforms of the mid-1850s. A last-ditch conservative effort to reassert control ended disastrously. By inviting the French archduke Maximilian to establish a Mexican monarchy in 1864, some conservatives incurred the animosity of patriotic Mexicans of all political shades (Hamnett 2006; Bazant 1977). After the foreign intervention failed, liberals took over national leadership.

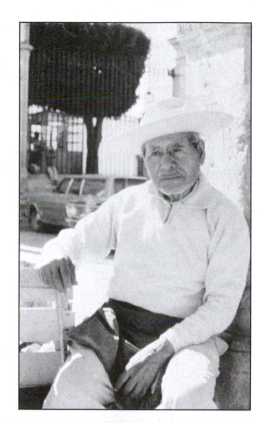

Modern peasants. *Top left:* unemployed urban nomad; *top right:* street vendor in central Mexico; *bottom:* muleteers loading maize in Guanajuato, Mexico.

Social reform writers were adamant in their expectations, but the application of their ideas fell far short of what they intended, and these ink-and-paper innovations were never implemented. Indians and mestizos were consistently barred from joining the mainstream. Current political practices are surely derived from these earlier beliefs. Children of mixed descent and Indians who had become both linguistically and culturally acculturated were placed in the social category of Indian and were not accepted as being Mexican. The only way to counteract this and be called Mexican was to move to another area, where one's personal history was unknown. Mexican leaders were concerned more with shaping a national identity and establishing an entrepreneurial class than with improving conditions for the masses or with encouraging them to contribute to the national debate on the future of the nation.

Repercussions were experienced in other realms of Indian, peasant life, namely, religion. Religious syncretic alterations had retained many Indian practices and beliefs that emphasized the group and community affairs. Rituals and ceremonies still balanced social needs with economic activities in the governance of villages. "While the Indians stress equality, personal relationships and mutual aid, capitalist ideology encourages competition, individuality and the subordination of personal feelings to rational self-interest" (Cubitt 1988:71). A change from the cooperative/communal to the competitive/individual made Indians even more vulnerable to subjugation. Religion and religious practices had always provided a salve to the aching Indian spirits. In these new times of outside pressures and increased exploitation, religion became even more important.

In this ideological and economic miasma, peasants were integrated into something new that would eventually transform them into a proletariat, whose lives were dominated by wage labor (Kearney 1996; de Janvry 1981:95–96; de Rouffignac 1985; Cubitt 1988; Fowler-Salamini and Vaughan 1994).

> Agricultural laborers worked in what critics described as a "slave mode of production." Although labor conditions varied greatly throughout Mexico, it was overwhelmingly the case that workers were now spending an increasing percentage of their shrinking wages on food. (Buffington and French 2000:419)

Psychocultural Aspects of Peasantry

Authors have often described peasants as having a certain "peasant mentality," with the following characteristics: fatalism, passivity, conservativism, distrustfulness, and superstition. However, the view that peasants are conservative and reluctant to change has been challenged (Meyer and Beezley 2000). George Foster (1988) created the image of the "limited good" to describe the fact that Mexican peasants tend to "see their social, economic, and natural universes—their total environment—as one in which almost all desired things in life" (Foster 1988:124) are found in finite qualities. Thus, there was a pervasive competition among villagers to acquire what little resources that existed and this strain led to envy (envidia) among them.

Various other terms have been used to describe peasant society. "Closed communities" refers to those peasant communities with land ownership and distinctive cultural traits. The harmony and reciprocity of peasant life is often emphasized in these accounts, with little attention being paid to how outside influences and the hardships of poverty and rural life came to be (see, for example, Foster 1988; Kearney 1996; Duren 1992).

Peasants relied on folk medicines to cure ailments and illnesses. They believed in witchcraft and magic. However, each area within Mexico had a distinct cultural tradition. "Cultural patterns . . . may also be distinctive of particular communities. All the villagers in a region speak the same indigenous language, but they may have their own particular costumes, jewelry, dances or other customs" (Cubitt 1988:67). A trip through several peasant towns could bring you in contact with copper, silver, leather, seashells, and tequilas.

Peasants were known for establishing solid social networks with their family and through fictive kin, known as *compadres* or *comadres*. Compadrazgo is "the particular complex of relationships set up between individuals primarily, though not always, through participation in the ritual of Catholic baptism" (Mintz and Wolf 1967:174). It furthers social solidarity both "horizontally," across the same class, and "vertically," across classes (Mintz and Wolf 1967). This custom of co-parenthood is still widely practiced in contemporary times in both sides of the border.

As mentioned previously, national reconstruction was blocked by political turmoil. The socioeconomic structure suffered from the lack of concern political leaders showed over the poverty-stricken majority of the population. Class differences were as sharp as they had been 100 years previously (Servin, Reina, and Tutino 2007; Chavez 2006).

Decline of Cultural Imperialism

Increasingly concerned with their national image, Mexican leaders sought to build on Enlightenment thinking. They did this by applying European concepts to the nation's evolving cultural style (Buffington and French 2000). Efforts at emulation, however, added to the contentious divergence already prevalent. The source of friction was that each individual or group championed one European attribute or another, all of which were equally unrelated to a nation built on an indigenous base. The comment of one liberal spokesman, Jose Maria Luis Mora, highlights an attitude that ran counter to the needs of the people of that time. He claimed that "the glory of the legislator does not consist in being an inventor, but in guiding his subjects (*comitentes*) toward happiness" (Hale 1968:155). As it turns out, these "subjects" were the upper-crust, liberal elite. However, a few leaders continued to strive toward social integration and shaping a truly national culture.

The outstanding cultural themes of this period were the evolution of a political philosophy and the rise of a nationalist consciousness (Servin, Reina, and Tutino 2007; Chavez 2006). Internal military upheavals affected the achievement of these goals, sometimes helping them and other times slowing them or stopping them altogether (Meyer and Beezley 2000; Sierra 1969). During the approximately 70-year period following the break from Spain to the beginning of the Diaz government, Mexico was in a state of disarray in the struggle for national freedom. There was no stable government during this time (Katz 2007; Gomez-Quinones 1994b; Nutini 1995), and the period (1810–1867) experienced upheaval from three major wars.

Eventually Mexico stopped mimicking other nations and charted a course of its own making (Knight 2007; Gomez-Quinones 1994b), but not without several difficulties. For example, the weakness shown by a fledgling nation such as Mexico created the opportunity for foreign intervention. The previously mentioned French-imposed monarchy was one example. The Mexican–American War of 1846 was even more disastrous and ended with over half of Mexico's territory lost to the United States (Vazquez 2000). Both destabilizing events, coming at a vulnerable time for Mexico, increased public support for a nationalist path and solution (Meyer and Beezley 2000; Sierra 1969). Furthermore, the growing sense of cultural and racial homogeneity encouraged nationalist awareness (Wasserman 2000). The 1910 Revolution would bring this about much faster.

Cultural Variant in Northern Mexico

Northern Mexican settlers were strongly influenced by the shifts in feeling from the center of Mexico. Government and military officials had been sent to rule and maintain order in the north, thus complementing missions in the religious sphere (Pitt 1998). The mission, *pueblo* (civil rule), and *presidio* (military defense) affected cultural life in many ways. The pueblo and presidio ensured that native laborers would be kept in check and that foreign intruders would be resisted. When foreign interlopers pressed, the Mexican government countered by increasing defenses.

Even at this early date, 1846, California and other parts of northern Mexico represented a dual heritage. The syncretic experience that shaped Mexico was repeated here, but, as might be expected, with different causes and results. Hispanic culture was brought to California mainly by the Mexicans, rather than the Spaniards (Weber 2009; Spicer 1962). Also, in the eighteenth century, the Spanish were having difficulties with the Indians in what would now be northern Mexico and the Southwest of the United States (Griffin-

Pierce 2000; Kessell 2002). During the late sixteenth and seventeenth centuries, a successful Indian countermovement to the Spanish had surged in the area (Mitchell 2005; Officer 1987).

A combination of Spanish and Indian vocabulary and names for rivers, mountains, deserts, and other geographical features resulted. The names of the southwestern states are a carry-over from this period. California, New Mexico (a syncretic name), Nevada, and Colorado are from Spanish words, and Arizona, Texas, and Utah are named after Indian tribes. In California, many place names originated from Indian sources, including Lompoc, Malibu, Pacoima, and Pismo.

In colonial California, Indian laborers had built many buildings following a syncretic style, for instance, Indian adobe bricks with Spanish tile roofs (Samora and Simon 1977). The changes in New Mexico were even more profound as the mixed heritage took on a life of its own and became popularized as a new cultural style (Weber 2009). Much of the terminology identified with the United States Southwest, such as that used in agriculture, raising livestock, and mining, is borrowed from the Spanish and Mexicans.

Economic Influences on Cultural Patterns

The Spanish-Mexican legacy includes more than words alone. Raisin culture (that is, making raisins out of grapes), vineyards, wheat, flax, cotton seeds, as well as the many other resources noted previously were introduced by the Spanish. The successful California vineyards, with 30 million vines producing over seven million gallons of wine after 1848, were actually planted in or near the original Spanish vineyards (Lake 2006; McWilliams 1990[1968]). Indian labor contributed greatly to agricultural expansion and maintenance. Spaniards, Mexicans, and later other groups benefited from plentiful, cheap Indian labor, which made labor-saving technology unnecessary. The aim was for the Indians to maintain the missionaries and provide most of the food for the presidios, while also being able to provide for themselves (Lightfoot 2005; Monroy 1990).

As a result of native labor, rancho social life bustled in the postcolonial period, especially for richer criollos and mestizos. In the lucrative livestock industry, for instance, the cattle roundup season involved several weeks of work, followed by a time of feasting and drinking. The work ethic was not oriented to preparing for future needs, but to working hard in the present in expectation of the fun that would come immediately after. This ethic, as well as the good climate, cheap Indian labor, and plentiful supply of land, meant that the ranchos ran smoothly (Jackson 2005; Sanderson 1986; Pitt 1998).

Even the work was designed for entertainment and included numerous contests of roping and bull-dogging. Fiestas for religious, marital, baptismal, and other important occasions were common and sometimes lasted a week.

Often, rancheros throughout California were invited to the affair. Hired hands, vaqueros, and some domestic servants also participated, though they might celebrate in separate rancho buildings.

Like politics and philosophy, ranchero social habits were patterned on those of upper-class Mexico City residents. A formal social etiquette prevailed, which seems pretentious or bizarre in a region far removed from a more advanced civilization. A rustic environment had generally not prevented criollos and mestizos from enjoying the social rituals of their antecedents in spite of the difficult circumstances. This was less true of New Mexicans, who over two centuries had fashioned a sociocultural life suited to their more rugged environment (Sanchez 1967).

Color: Mestizaje and Lingering Racism

First Challenges to Racism

Interracial unions were more common in Mexico after independence than during colonial times. However, although in 1822 legal distinctions as to race were ended, racial terminology continued to be used in official documents in many cases, especially regarding marriage statistics, until 1940 (Knight 1990; Navarro 1970). The race question became even more important with the spread of mestizaje (Esteva-Fabregat 1995). The racial composition of Mexico during the nineteenth century began to change greatly with the increase in numbers of mestizos due to miscegenation, intermarriage between Indians and whites, and socioracial passing (Sandstrom 1991). According to census figures, mestizos rose from 27 percent of the population in 1824 to 53 percent in 1900, becoming the majority group in Mexico. Although disputed by many who claim that Mexico is a *mestizocracia* (a mixed-race democracy) the rise of mestizos appears to stem from socioracial passing (see chapter 4) when many Indians claim to be mestizo as part of their acculturation strivings (Vigil and Lopez 2004).

In such areas where mestizaje was common and prominent, one could observe the racial variations from white/mestizo to Indian, which also corresponded to matters of acculturation and location. Certain regions and cities were very Spanish culturally and racially (i.e., the Mesa Central, Jalisco, Guanajuato, and Queretaro) and some mestizos with typically Indian appearances (southern Mexico and Yucatan) were better able to accommodate to the dominant culture by moving to these places (Knight 1990)—because in these regions, the Spanish people were poor and powerless. Importantly, this same process of miscegenation was unfolding in northern Mexico, especially among Africans and Native Americans (Forbes 1993).

Criollos and some mestizos who passed for white were the first to challenge racism. Motives for their actions varied, but racial tolerance was the primary reason for many; also, enlightened philosophical viewpoints had become fashionable. Equally significant was the fact that criollos linked their egalitarianism with the notion of human progress (Miles 1993; Bazant 1977).

Problems of Redefinition

The hidden motive for the criollos' nondeprecating view of mestizos may have been that they, too, were of mixed racial background. Perhaps they felt guilty about hiding this fact, but more likely they wanted to eliminate the barriers that had kept them from advancement during the colonial period. Unfortunately, they were not motivated enough to nullify the conditioned psychological effects of the colonial past. Even radical liberals such as Lorenzo Zavala continued to support racist practices, as his argument for the expulsion of Indians shows: "he urged them to 'force the barbarians to organize themselves into regular societies or leave the national territory, as the North Americans are doing with their Indians'" (Navarro 1970:147).

Although criollos became more inclined to reevaluate the effects of racism, they were too imbued with the past to break with it completely. While seeking improvements, they still agreed that the lower classes prevented full national development because of their cultural and racial backwardness. Latin American elites would smugly state that it was the "apathy, indolence and improvidence" of the masses that led to underdevelopment (Stein and Stein 1970:183; see also Knight 1990).

Role of Mestizos

Despite a national mood bent on curbing racism, mestizos attempted to pass as whites and became repressive fixtures of the social order (Vigil and Lopez 2004; Stein and Stein 1970; van den Berghe 1967). This continued to be the case during the Anglo period, when mestizos adopted a "fantasy heritage" (McWilliams 1990[1968]) of racial purity, posturing to be "Hispanic" to gain acceptance, which was more than likely one of their strategies for maintaining their status and power within the Anglo racial hierarchy that devalued "color" (Acuna 2011). In fact, Mexico's "middle class of politicians, professionals, military officers, tradesmen, and assorted urban and rural segments was essentially a Mestizo population" (Nutini 1995:286). As a result, the criollos formed "an unspoken alliance with an essentially Mestizo [i.e., real or passing] political leadership; a shaky peace henceforth constituted the cornerstone of the political and economic life of the nation until the Revolution of 1910" (Nutini 1995:280; see also Banton 1998).

Mestizos generally fell in with this attitude, and so, with independence, the mestizos became the "Gachupines of the Indians" (Navarro 1970:148). They created even more suspicion among Indians by mistreating them in order to obtain more favorable positions for themselves. As previously noted, social conditions forced mestizos into this path. Casual farmers, middlemen, workers, and others who had no legal position in the colonial regime set up residence on the outskirts of Indian villages and other communities near haciendas, mills, or mines. Their marginality (cholo) often compelled them to adopt antisocial patterns of behavior (Wolf 1965). Underemployment of the racially mixed contributed to the creation of urban slums, with a poverty-stricken population always welcoming any opportunity to make money by whatever means (Cumberland 1968). Groups of "guerilla brigands" wreaked havoc in Mexico during Independence and after (Buffington and French 2000; Vanderwood 1992; Joseph 1992). "Haciendas were looted and burned; cattle stolen and dispersed. The followers of bandits . . . became infamous for their crimes" (Vanderwood 1992:23–24).

Race and Class Linkages

The abolition of "Indian" as a legal category meant that caste now "became secondary to class as a form of social identification" (Knight 1990:72). However,

> the use of the term "Indian" became synonymous with a combination of material poverty and cultural "backwardness." Class distinction was again framed in racial terms, so that poor mestizos—especially peasant mestizos—were called "Indians" by the upper classes, while rich mestizos were "whitened." (Lomnitz-Adler 1992:276)

Indianness, however, was "not defined solely or even primarily in somatic terms. A range of other characteristics determined 'racial' . . . identification: language, dress, religion, social organization, culture and consciousness" (Knight 1990:73). Indians, therefore, could move up the social scale if they changed their social habits, which could occur with migration, education, and occupational shifts (Knight 1990; Cubitt 1988; Lomnitz-Adler 1992). Migration within Mexico, of course, was central to socioracial passing (Wagley 1965).

Individuals nevertheless were ranked in the social-class system on the basis of their racial appearance, unless their behavior clearly contradicted such indicators. Generally, the darker and more Indian-appearing one was, the lower the social class position, and the whiter, the higher. Furthermore, many leaders, such as Mora (a prominent liberal politician), sought to encourage the immigration of Europeans in order to "whiten" the population, while at the same time restricting the entrance of Asians and Negros. Mora's plan in the mid-nineteenth century was that white foreigners should be given preference over the "colored" races in "everything that did not constitute a 'clear violation of justice'" (Navarro 1970:154). This "provoked a valorization of whiteness . . ." (Lomnitz-Adler 1992:276).

The modifications that occurred were mostly in people's awareness of racism, not in any substantive changes that were made concerning it. Previously, a closed class system existed. "Opaque partitions" kept colonial classes separate, blocking out the vision one class had of another. Public awareness was limited in viewing social class distinctions based on racial differences. With independence, the opaque partitions were exchanged for transparent (or maybe merely translucent) ones. Classes still were separate, but now people became more aware that the white Europeans were on top, the medium-hued mestizos in the middle, and the dark Indians and Afro-mestizos at the bottom. The people on top or in the middle would not break the partitions, and as a result, racist ideology and practices persisted.

The Latin American elite flourished during this period, while the situation for the working class, mostly the dark-skinned population, worsened (Morner 1967; Bustamante 1994). They still were affected by the social mobility barrier, which emphasized facial features and the color of one's skin. An exception to that centuries-old social rule was rare indeed—although one rare case was the presidency of the assimilated Indian Benito Juarez.

Indians in the North

The words of a Franciscan missionary illustrate native conditions in California and generally throughout the northern region: "The Indians of California may be compared to a species of monkey . . . they are careful to select vice, in preference to virtue. This is the result, undoubtedly, of their corrupt, and natural disposition" (Heizer and Almquist 1971:4). Further,

> missionaries and soldiers constantly scrutinized and modified Indian behavior. . . . Disobedient Indians were flogged, put into stocks, and locked up at night. . . . Whipping with a barbed lash, branding, and solitary confinement were other punishments used to enforce military and Catholic discipline. (Lake 2006:153; see also Heidenreich 2007)

Pseudoscientific racial theories of the time contributed to racist attitudes; it was believed that persons of mixed race inherited not the best characteristics of each race, but the worst (Gutierrez 1991). Taking into account the experiences of the Mexican Indians and mestizos, it is no wonder that those who were racially different became ingrained with an inferiority complex and negative self-image; no wonder socioracial passing became such a strong option, perhaps the only one.

Chapter 7

BREAKUP AND TRANSFORMATION OF THE SOCIAL ORDER

Contact: Anglo-American Expansionism

Roots of Contact

While Mexico was struggling with internal problems, increased contacts with foreigners, particularly Anglo-Americans, led to further disruptions. Initial interactions with the Anglo-American north familiarized Mexico with concepts of democracy and social revolution. These traditions were far different from the Spanish social and ideological heritage. While helping to expand the horizons of emergent Mexico, further contacts soon introduced a decidedly less favorable pattern: Manifest Destiny, the fated expansion westward of the United States to the Pacific coast and even beyond. This orientation first made its appearance in America in the mid-1840s and soon became a popular slogan (De Leon and Griswold del Castillo 2006; Heidenreich 2007). To Mexico's misfortune, America expanded westward toward Alta California, New Mexico, and Texas, the three insufficiently protected Mexican provinces (Henderson 2007; Gomez 2007; Heidler and Heidler 2003). Driving this expansion was the idea that Anglos (and whites) held superiority over Mexicans as a people and race (De Leon and Griswold del Castillo 2006; Montejano 1987)—an attitude embraced by the mostly southern-based American newcomers who held disparaging views toward "darker" people (Almaguer 2008). Manifest Destiny also had an economic rationale that explains why traditional, agricultural society had to give way to a far superior modern industrial system (and people!) (Heidenreich 2007; Montejano 1987), a process that shaped the peasant-to-immigrant transformation.

The belief that some superhuman power has ordained imperial expansion is not new; such ideas often motivate those who carry forth the flag of conquest. It is undoubtedly true that the underlying goal of expansion is to obtain new land and wealth for the victors, even as words and actions pretend it is for ideals. Thus, the Moorish and Christian conquests and the spread of Spanish Catholicism to the New World were accompanied by both idealistic motives and material rewards. After World War II, Marxian governments fell into a similar pattern. The expansionism of the United States in the nineteenth century also plainly exhibits a desire for land and resources (Gomez 2007). Although different from the peasant situation in Mexico that came later, it gives some indication of how landed farmers in some parts of northern Mexico were to be transformed under the United States into wage laborers. The latter had nothing but their sweat to bargain with. The migration of labor soon became more of a factor in the workers' lives, just as it would later for the Mexican peasants in the early part of the next century (Castaneda 2007; Tabler 1988).

Expansionist Tradition in the United States

Inspired by Enlightenment thinking, the U.S. sought to remake the world and everything before it. It was manifest that the Americans felt an obligation to spread from the Atlantic coast to the Pacific coast (Conway 2010). Thomas Jefferson moved American boundaries toward Mexico by maintaining that the 1803 Louisiana Purchase included territory extending to the Rio Grande (De Leon and Griswold del Castillo 2006; Griswold del Castillo 1990:11). Even before Mexican independence, Americans had settled in Texas and, in some cases, had participated in attempts to seize control of the region (Heidler and Heidler 2003). One observer stated that racialism "was planted in the unique psychohistorical experience of the white Texas pioneers and settlers" (De Leon 1983:12). As noted in chapter 6, American merchants in the same time period had established a major commercial presence in California. Many had settled there, intermarried with the local aristocracy, and added their own antipathy to Mexican control to the Californios' desires for greater autonomy (Gomez 2007; Pitt 1998).

Background to American Takeover

The years following Mexico's independence from Spain were marked by increased American immigration into the Mexican frontier provinces. Many—

perhaps most—of the immigrants carried with them the conviction that their new homes would eventually become part of the United States, and their activities helped to promote that belief. Americans in Texas and New Mexico chafed under Mexican government policies and spread their discontent among the local aristocracy (Dunbar-Ortiz 2007; Teja 2010). Communications from Hispanicized Yankees in California further whetted the eastern entrepreneurs' desire for good seaports and expanded trade and also—whether intentionally or unwittingly—provided important strategic military information (Pitt 1998:12; Bauer 1974:12).

Mexican authorities attempted to secure the northern provinces by developing land-grant policies to encourage Mexican citizens to settle in the frontier regions. American immigrants were also given land and citizenship rights in an effort to win their loyalty to the Mexican government. While these policies led to prosperity for many settlers, some Americans viewed them as an expression of the government's weakness, and they continued their efforts to subvert Mexican rule. Mexican leaders were working from a position of weakness and freely accepted all grantees, but the end result found that "we made a present of Texas to the Americans of the North" (Castaneda 1976:310) and thus hastened the transition from a traditional to a modern society, with far-reaching consequences for the mass of the Mexican people, especially women (Chavez-Garcia 2004).

Officials of the American government encouraged intrusions into Mexican territory and sought, both openly and surreptitiously, to promote American incorporation of Texas, New Mexico, and California. With the exception of the displacement of the American Indians, it was the first major imperial thrust by the United States and the beginnings of a militarization of American society (Gomez 2007). As early as 1825, the government sent Joel Poinsett (whose name is now remembered for the Mexican flower he brought back) to Mexico to attempt to purchase Texas (Jones and Rakestraw 1997). A later envoy from President Andrew Jackson offered Mexico five million dollars for the territory (Acuna 1988). In California the United States consul, Thomas Larkin, worked on persuading Californians to reject the Mexican government, both in name and in practice (Rosenbaum 1981). As a respected and influential figure, he was confident that California would become American territory through peaceful means (Pitt 1998). Some observers have likened these events to American dealings with the North American Indians and, as noted above, with African slaves (Almaguer 2008; De Leon and Griswold del Castillo 2006). There was little difference between Indians and Mexicans, according to American leaders, and this attitude undermined diplomatic relations between the two countries (Heidler and Heidler 2003).

Repercussions of Annexation

In time, these developments led to open warfare despite fierce, if disorganized, resistance by Mexico. In addition, there was some opposition in the

United States Congress to American annexation of the territories that comprise the present southwestern states (Heidenreich 2007). Another major foreign intrusion, continuing hostilities along the northern border, and increased bitterness and suspicion toward the American government were setbacks that contributed to further instability in Mexico (see Gutierrez Ibarra 1987 and Martinez Caraza 1991 for the Mexican version of the account in the Spanish language). For Chicanos living in the newly American territories, the annexation brought a new layer of oppression, but with a decidedly different macrostructural arrangement. One author offers this assessment of how early American immigrants thought of Mexicans, quoting an American observer:

> The Californio's mixed racial background is a constant theme in Farnham's narrative. It is also the focus of his blunt comment on women, of whom he states "The ladies, dear creatures, I wish they were whiter, and that their cheekbones did not in their great condescension assimilate their manners and customs so remarkably to their Indian neighbors." (Castaneda 1999:163)

Conflict: End of the Mexican–American War, Continuation of Strife

Texas as Prelude

Texas was the first battleground in the Mexican–Anglo conflict. Although it was the American government that endorsed the policy of westward expansionism, Mexico, in fact, contributed to its momentum by allowing Anglo-Americans to own Mexican territory (Dunbar-Ortiz 2007; Griswold del Castillo 1990; Castaneda 1976). Anglo settlers had no intention of obeying Mexican authority, whom they considered inferior. Moreover, Mexican control was tenuous; the center of power was hundreds of miles from this outpost, which made political and military directives nearly impossible. When Mexico sent in troops to stop the generous Anglo colonization program, it was too late. The clamor for a free and independent nation was led by influential Anglo leaders and dissident Mexicans. After a major, if bloody, Mexican victory in 1835 in which General Santa Ana demolished the Alamo defenders, an army led by Sam Houston caught Santa Ana napping at San Jacinto. The defeat of Santa Ana's forces necessitated his acceptance of Texas independence (Meier and Ribera 1993), and the Lone Star Republic was born in 1836.

The loss of Texas led almost directly to Mexican military conflicts with the United States (Fuller 1936:38; see map on p. 158, showing the major battles of the war). From 1836 to 1846 there were constant battles, forays, and skirmishes between the rebel Texans and the Mexicans, most ending in a stalemate. To the advantage of the Texans, the Mexican government was too greatly occupied by domestic affairs, so that troops were sent to the border several years after the defeat of Santa Ana at San Jacinto. The policy of some Texan leaders was to create a constant war at the frontier until Mexico would be ready to negotiate (Vargas and Paterson 1999; Webb 1935). The Mexican congress never legally ratified a treaty to give Texas an independent status. Although the United States feigned neutrality to avoid a free vs. slave state squabble, Texas was admitted to the union as soon as approval could be secured. This annexation occurred despite congressional opposition based on fears of upsetting trade relations with Mexico and on northern antislavery sentiment (for Texas was admitted as a slave state).

Texas Annexation and Intrigue

By annexing Texas, the United States was now faced with a state where conflicts persisted. In fact, the Mexican government regarded the annexation as a declaration of war. By following the 1844 Democratic Party platform, which advocated western expansion and Texas annexation, the newly elected President James K. Polk placed the United States on a collision course with Mexico (Henderson 2007; Price 1967). However, a new dimension was added to the acquisition of Texas: Polk's emissaries were instructed to offer anywhere from $15 to $40 million for the territories of New Mexico and California! In the eyes of the Mexicans, this overture added insult to injury. The Mexicans considered the American annexation of Texas illegal because Mexico had never ratified Texas independence. Moreover, the annexation of Texas was in violation of the terms of the 1819 Adams-Onis American treaty with Spain, which specified that the western boundary of the United States was to be the Sabine River, the present-day border of Louisiana. This line was clearly outside the area of Mexican Texas (Conway 2010; Gomez 2007). To complicate matters further, the United States government accepted the Texas claim of the Rio Grande as the boundary between the alleged independent Texas and Mexico proper. In fact, to encourage Texan leaders to accept annexation, Polk promised them that the American government would support their claim to the Rio Grande. This was a risky step, as the recognized border of Texas was the Nueces River, about 150 miles to the north (De Leon and Griswold del Castillo 2006; Griswold del Castillo 1990). The American offer to purchase additional territory, without negotiating the status of Texas, was viewed as a subterfuge. To the Mexicans it seemed plain that the United States intended to take it anyway. Anglo-American expansionist strategy resorted to "war as diplomacy by other means."

Declaration of War

Polk was prepared for war in any event. An engagement involving the American and Mexican armies that took place between the two rivers was the excuse he needed. His May 11, 1846, declaration of war message to Congress stressed that "American blood was shed on American soil" (Merk 1963:88). This stands out as one of the most duplicitous phrases ever spoken by a president. War was declared—even though Mexican soldiers had lawfully defended Mexican territory from foreign intrusions.

The Mexican–American War was speedily brought to a conclusion. By 1848, the United States had forced its version of the disputed Texas boundary on Mexico and had seized additional Mexican lands extending beyond the Rocky Mountains. With each Yankee victory, expansionist enthusiasm flourished. What Castaneda (1976:307) has described as American "plans to acquire what belongs to their neighbors" and Livermore (1969:13) labels "this lust for territory" was publicly proclaimed in many circles. Nevertheless, the annexation of Mexican territory was justified in terms of extending civil and religious liberty, and industrial and commercial enterprises (Livermore 1969:12). A pop-

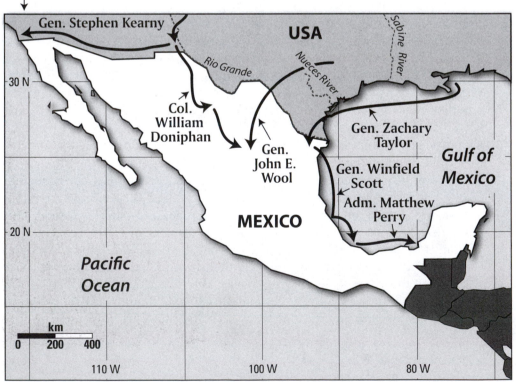

Area of river border controversy and American military campaigns.

American marines storming the Chapultepec Castle.

Mexico City under attack.

ular idea at the time was that the Mexicans were being "rescued" by the Americans (Fuller 1936:81). Northern congressional opposition—whose ranks included the young politician, Abraham Lincoln—could not reduce this fervor.

Skirmishes and Resistance

It was a short war with lots of battlegrounds. Mexican resistance was encountered in both Mexico and the borderlands; over 50,000 Mexicans, most of whom were peasants, lost their lives in this affair (Cockcroft 1990; see battlefield map on p. 158). Several episodes in California show that the Mexicans fought bravely and successfully (Pitt 1998). The revolt in Los Angeles, a skirmish at Chino (just south of Los Angeles), and the Battle of San Pasqual (near San Diego) are three examples of well-organized, well-executed victories over American forces. The affair at San Pasqual was a humiliating defeat for United States forces, who lost over 20 men, with more wounded, particularly since it involved the General of Western Operations, Steven Kearney, and his scout, the famous Kit Carson. Furthermore, there was not one Mexican casualty (Bancroft 1888). In New Mexico, the revolt of 1847 by disgruntled pobres (peons and Indians) further underscores native resistance (Dunbar-Ortiz 2007; Gomez 2007; DeLay 2008). However, Anglo numerical and technological superiority won out in the end.

The battle was lost, the war formally ended, but fighting raged on. Conflict had in fact been present in this area since 1846 and continued long after the Treaty of Guadalupe Hidalgo was signed (DeLay 2008; Dunbar-Ortiz 2007; McWilliams 1990[1968]). The Mexican elite, gente de razon and ricos, who believed they would benefit from the new rule, were surprised when in only a few years their land was taken from them (Dunbar-Ortiz 2007; Heidenreich 2007; Montejano 1987). Subsequent political struggles in the United States Congress over what to do with this land brought another, bigger war: "In the immediate aftermath, internal tensions were exacerbated to the point that the Civil War became more probable" (Gomez-Quinones 1994b:182). In fact, most of the North and South leaders in the latter conflict had fought in the Mexican–American War.

Unfortunately, those who caught the initial post-war onslaught were the poorer Mexicans, the pobres, peons, and cholos. Since they were on the first line of defense, they were brought into contact and conflict much sooner. The few ranchitos they possessed were occupied immediately. Now within the U.S. Southwest, the Mexican elites lost their land piecemeal until they were entirely dispossessed of it (Pitt 1998; Dunbar-Ortiz 2007).

Outlaws or "Social Bandits"?

Although the actions taken by these Mexicans were sporadic and disorganized, the conflict sometimes reached a revolutionary level. Instead of fighting against soldiers in full military uniform, the rebels battled law enforcement officers such as Texas Rangers and sheriffs in the towns and hinterland (Harris and Sadler 2004; Stout 2002; Montejano 1987; Webb 1935). This friction and antagonism had its peculiar Mexican-Anglo touches, but historically nations who share a border generally live in a zone of conflict (Vargas and Paterson 1999; Dunbar-Ortiz 2007). In addition to this, there was the frontier violence that marked the period, in which outlaws of all races made life miserable for settlers and entrepreneurs. One writer referred to them as "prairie pirates, seizing any property that comes in their way, murdering travellers, and making descents upon trains and border villages" (Taylor 1934:31). Such Wild-West conditions only worsened Mexican–Anglo relations.

Mexican guerrilla or resistance activity persisted through the nineteenth century; similar repercussions and ripple effects occurred in Mexico proper in various regions where peasant unrest and disturbances challenged the government until 1910 when a full-blown civil war erupted (Chavez 2006; Raat 1992; Cockcroft 1990). Anglos angrily maintained that the Mexican rebels were nothing but common, ordinary bandits (Thompson 2007; Acuna 1975; Webb 1935). However, many of the resisters became folk heroes to the oppressed Mexicans, and some observers maintain that this social banditry was revolutionary in character (Hobsbawn 1959; Vigil 1974; Gomez-Quinones 1994b). Social bandits usually flourish after a war, when their group has been subjugated. Native resistance mounts because the whole social order is changed in favor of the victor (Gomez 2007; Dunbar-Ortiz 2007; Pitt 1998). Interestingly, the agrarian unrest among Mexican peasants at this time was also considered criminal by Mexican authorities.

There were dozens of social bandits in the border regions (Thompson 2007; Harris and Sadler 2004; Rosenbaum 1981). Joaquin Murietta and Tiburcio Vasquez in California, Sostenes L'Archeveque in New Mexico, and Cheno Cortina in Texas are only a few of the more famous ones. Murietta's career apparently began because of the abuse he and his family received (Vigil 1974:34–37). Furthermore, he had resisted the discriminatory treatment meted out to Mexicans in the mining region of California, where gold had recently been discovered (Ridge 1969; Pitt 1998). His acts of resistance lasted from 1851 to 1853. Accounts of his death (or escape?) vary.

Another social bandit was Tiburcio Vasquez. Some accounts have him riding with Murietta, but it is certain that by 1854 he was branded an outlaw by Anglo justice authorities (Greenwood 1960). Before he was captured and hanged in 1876, he said: "Given $60,000.00 I would be able to recruit enough arms and men to revolutionize Southern California" (Greenwood 1960:13).

The situation in New Mexico was somewhat different because many Indians joined the Mexican resistance (Dunbar-Ortiz 2007; Gomez 2007; Swadesh 1974). It was because of the initiatives of Anglo-Americans, rather than Mexi-

Joaquin Murietta.

Tiburcio Vasquez.

Juan "Cheno" Cortina.

can Americans, that lawlessness took place. The Anglo-Americans were for-tune-seekers who profited from the fact that American law and order were not yet effective in the area (Gonzalez 1993; Zeleny 1974). The revenge of Sos-tenes L'Archeveque, one among many who resisted, is illustrative. "After his father was shot down by Anglo-Americans in . . . eastern New Mexico, the young man lost little time in acquiring twenty-three 'gringo' notches on his gun" (McWilliams 1990[1968]:120–21). Later, a group known as Las Gorras Blancas (the White Caps) (Acuna 2011) became famous when they stood up against land barons, particularly since they escaped capture and punishment (Rosenbaum 1981:112; Weber 1973:234). The following highlights key points of the Gorras Blancas platform:

> Not wishing to be misunderstood, we hereby make this our declaration. Our purpose is to protect the rights and interests of the people in general; especially those of the helpless classes. . . . We want no "land grabbers" or obstructionists of any sort to interfere. We will watch them. . . . We are down on race issues, and will watch race agitators. We are all human brethren, under the same glorious flag. (Vargas and Paterson 1999:182)

Juan "Cheno" Cortina, the Tejano (Texan), was another Mexican who fought injustice and inequality (Thompson 2007; Montejano 1987). His life exemplifies the widespread resistance of the period and also the continued ties of Chicanos in the United States with Mexico. Cortina has been both praised (Paredes 1958) and condemned (Webb 1935; Clendenen 1969). His career was an unusual one. He survived all attempts to stop him, finally end-ing up as a top official in the northern Mexican state of Tamaulipas. Early in his life, Americans labeled him the "Red Robber of the Rio Grande"; later, fel-low government officials in Mexico distrusted him, and it was alleged that he plotted conspiracies (Hamnett 2006; Bazant 1977). He even fought on the Union side during the Civil War, clearly an instance of political expediency.

> Cortina had personally witnessed the fraudulent transfer of lands from Mexican to Anglo hands during the 1850s. . . . Hundreds responded, see-ing him as the hero who would bring redress to their grievances. . . . His bold leadership had made him a folk personage, one admired and respected for facing the hated enemy, for attempting to uphold his name, and for defending the integrity of the downtrodden. (De Leon and Gris-wold del Castillo 2006:34)

So went the pattern of conflict—some claimed that antisocial acts were pure and simple criminality, while others argued that it was a resistance based on historical injustices (Rosenbaum 1981). As De Leon has maintained, however, it was the most violent era in Texas history, reflecting the "ingrained contempt Anglos had for 'greasers'" (De Leon 1983:88; see also De Leon and Griswold del Castillo 2006; Mirande 1987).

Conflict as Pattern

The Mexican people generally supported the individual acts of social bandits. In all the regions where Vazquez and Murietta operated, they were aided both morally and physically by their countrymen. Frequent crowd protests erupted in which accusations were made about the dual system of law enforcement—Mexicans were punished and Anglos went free. The solidarity of the Mexican people was reflected in countless episodes during the 1850s and 1860s (Gomez 2007; Dunbar-Ortiz 2007; Stout 2002; Vigil 1974; McWilliams 1990[1968]). After 1848, opposition to the courts mounted when a similar double standard was practiced: The gente de razon found their titles at risk, losing both in the courts and to their American lawyers (Paredes 1958). Furthermore, Anglo reactions to this resistance often entailed the creation of a special corps of law enforcers, sometimes amounting to a private army. None were more formidable in seeking out and persecuting Mexicans than the Texas Rangers (Harris and Sadler 2004; Raat 1992:74; Webb 1935)—"los rinches" as the Tejanos called them.

In the former Mexican territory, there were many adventurers, mostly Anglos but some Mexicans, who planned and carried out filibustering missions against Mexico (Stout 2002; Harris and Sadler 2004). Some even attempted to conquer Central American republics (Rippy 1926). An undeclared war pervaded the entire border region, along the 2,000-mile line now technically separating the two countries, and this state of affairs continued until well into the twentieth century (Montejano 1987; Clendenen 1969). The chaos and conflict associated with cattle raids and filibustering in the first decades has continued to the present, manifested now as problems regarding immigration and drug trafficking.

These and other notable events increased Mexican awareness of their station in society. One avowed champion of the people in Los Angeles was Francisco P. Ramirez, the editor of the newspaper *El Clamor Publico* (The Public Outcry). His coverage of events and personalities of the 1850s attests to a tension-filled climate (De Leon and Griswold del Castillo 2006; Pitt 1998; Vigil 1974). While the newspaper carried the usual fare, it also took up the cultural, economic, and political problems of the Mexican people. An especially newsworthy item on September 16, 1856, concerned the United States government's refusal or reluctance to live up to the Treaty of 1848, a document that was clearly intended to protect Mexican rights (Vigil 1974), but even at that early date the legal agreement was nothing but a piece of paper.

Change: New System for Mexican Americans

Treaty of 1848

Mexicans and Indians are the only minority groups in the United States who were conquered and whose rights were protected by treaty provisions (Henderson 2007; Gomez 2007; McWilliams 1990[1968]:103; Chavez 1984). The Treaty of Guadalupe Hidalgo (1848) resolved several issues and established a political boundary. Through it, a huge region that was formerly the northernmost province of Mexico became the southwestern province of the United States—a geopolitical area that was split in two by the war. The most noteworthy articles in the treaty concerned the protection of land grants and cultural rights, especially the protocol added later, which referred to the Louisiana Purchase stipulation of 1803 (De Leon and Griswold del Castillo 2006; Griswold del Castillo 1990; Ross 1928). According to this treaty, some Mexican practices would be protected. Land grants and tenure rights established during the Mexican period would be respected on the basis of international law (Ross 1928). A legal scholar has maintained that "Congress compromised by ratifying the treaty of Guadalupe Hidalgo to achieve two ends: the cession by Mexico of half its territory, but with the barest guarantees regarding the citizenship and property rights of the Mexican people living in those lands" (Gomez 2007:18). On paper, the treaty serves as a guarantee for legitimate land grants in Texas, New Mexico, Arizona, and California, but it never was seriously embraced by the United States government (Griswold del Castillo 1990). "It joined the ranks of hundreds of other treaties that the United States made with Native American tribes in

Mexican cession.

the nineteenth century that have been almost totally ignored since then" (Griswold del Castillo 1990:173; see also Weber 2009; Dunbar-Ortiz 2007; Heidenreich 2007).

In addition, Mexican cultural customs and patterns were to be given equal consideration with Anglo culture; this meant recognition and accommodation of the Spanish language and Catholic religion (Cockcroft 1990). For example, in California the first state constitution was written in Spanish and English (Pitt 1998). In other regions there was a definite trend, at least initially, toward respect for the Spanish language (Gomez 2007; Zeleny 1974). This policy came to an end somewhat abruptly when a backlash occurred on several fronts. In addition to the conflict conditions already noted, Mexican Americans began to be subjected to prejudice and discrimination on the basis of their cultural customs and language (Meier and Ribera 1993). What began as human rivalry and competition over land and resources took a decidedly racist bent and now added language and cultural differences.

Ethnic Rivalry and Hostility

It was not mere coincidence that land rights and cultural accommodation declined sharply at the same time, a double practice of actions paralleled by thoughts (Vigil 1999). There is clear evidence of Anglo encroachments and eventual absorption of both small and large parcels of Mexican property (Vargas and Paterson 1999; Zeleny 1974; McWilliams 1990[1968]; Heidenreich 2007). One observer of Texas says: "But it is certain that the traditional belief in unfair deprivation of private property in land remains an element in the background of Mexican emotional hostility to Americans. Both Mexicans and Americans told me their versions of what happened, the Americans often corroborating the Mexicans" (Taylor 1934:188). After the Mexican–American War of 1846, a dual economy with a dual wage system evolved.

> Chicanos were excluded from education, or their education was inferior. Political participation was impossible, and they lost the land (the basis of their wealth). Chicanos suffered religious discrimination, shootings, hangings, and general violence. Many women were raped and otherwise violated. . . . Women, men, and children resisted the hated and feared Texas Rangers. (Blea 1992:46–47)

Moreover, the dominant Anglos became increasingly convinced that socioeconomic and cultural privileges should not belong to a "culturally and racially inferior" people; they were a "mongrel race that not only incorporated the genes of the 'redskin' but also those of the 'nigger'" (De Leon 1983:15). For example, Anglos complained that the large ranchos were poorly developed by the Mexicans (Moquin and Van Doren 1971; Ross 1928). They also believed that Mexican customs retarded the full use of land and natural resources; that is, too many fiestas and fandangos hindered large-scale development. The new leaders maintained that civilization would advance with land control in Anglo-American hands, and that "if Mexicans could not keep pace with Yankee progress, or improve their standard of living, it was their own fault" (De Leon 1983:26–27).

In this era of Anglo–Mexican relations, Manifest Destiny provided a cultural reason to expropriate land and continue the growth and development of the United States, as "territory lost by Mexico to superior arms was used by the United States to launch its own industrial revolution" (Raat 1992:55–56; see also Heidler and Heidler 2003). During the war, hostile attitudes were sown and nurtured by each ethnic group (Acuna 1988). When competition over land intensified, there was an increase in invective on both sides. During the war, Anglo soldiers, many of them rowdy backwoodsmen, took special joy in killing "greasers," desecrating Mexican churches, and raping the women; Mexican women were also stereotyped as sluts who would willingly sleep with any man (De Leon 1983). The word "greaser" became a commonly used derogatory term for Mexicans. According to one writer, it referred to their greasy food (Paredes 1978:69). As noted in chapter 6, Mexicans who carried the balls of tallow to the waiting clipper ships and were left with a slick mess of grease on their backs were called greasers. To Jeremiah Clemens, an 1840s observer, the ethnic label described the whole Mexican group: "The people look greasy, their clothes are greasy, their dogs are greasy, their houses are greasy—everywhere grease and filth hold undivided dominion" (Dobie 1969:179). Somewhat less offensive, and not to be outmatched, Mexicans referred to Anglos as gringos, a corruption of the Spanish word *griego*, meaning one who speaks Greek (gibberish) (McWilliams 1990[1968]). Thus, postwar attitudes were set, epithets were invented, and the behavior that followed was a vicious display of how territorial conflict can set human against human.

Roots of Friction: Economic Competition

Anglos first took over the land. Soon after, Mexican labor was sought, secured, and dominated. With land and labor under Anglo control, it obviously followed that wealth (capital) would also fall into their hands (De Leon and Griswold del Castillo 2006; Samora and Simon 1977). As a result, the Mexican people were left largely without resources, almost destitute. It is now fairly clear that these initial changes paved the way for a more capitalistic system where the cattle, mining, railroad, and agriculture industries were built and commercialized for export with entrepreneurs exploiting Mexican labor (Dunbar-Ortiz 2007; Montejano 1987; Cockcroft 1990:53; Raat 1992). "This transition took longer in New Mexico than in California or Texas, but the result was the same" (Raat 1992:73; see also Gomez 2007).

On the surface social and cultural issues appeared to dominate the relations, but underneath, and the real source of the problem, was clearly economic competition. Racial and cultural practices that establish a dominant/subordinate relationship are often obvious, but there is a reason why one group discriminates against another racially or culturally (Vargas and Paterson 1999; Price 1967; Acuna 2011). The Anglo discrimination only added to the previous burden of racial and cultural oppression experienced by the Mexican people. As Wolf states, it reflected the effects of "North American Capitalism," a juggernaut that demolished "unproductive" societies, burying traditional commercial and social practices and replacing them with new ones (Wolf 1969:288).

Variance in Treatment of Mexicans

A complex situation arose. Those Mexicans who could not look and act the part of Europeans were accorded a subordinate status. Generally speaking, some gente de razon had a somewhat easier time because of their Latin background; but in Texas the distinction between Castilian and Mexican soon lost its usefulness (Menchaca 2001; Montejano 1987). It was the poor, darker individuals unassimilated to the European model who suffered more abuse. In the words of a modern writer: "One cannot understand the discrimination that has been visited upon Mexican Americans without taking into account the color of their skin and the fact that they look like Native Americans or part Native American" (Forbes 1964:4). The treatment received by the socially immobile, dark, and Indian-acting Mexicans further underscored the Anglo attitude that "the only good Indian is a dead Indian" (Price 1967:17; see also Almaguer 2008). Contributing to this fixed belief, many of the lighter-hued

Mexicanized Apache warriors led by Geronimo.

Spanish types felt superior to the other Mexicans. The descendants of gente de razon still, to this day, deny their mestizo heritage and the fact that their ancestors acquired Mexican, rather than Spanish, land grants (Pitt 1998), similar to modern populations who prefer to be called Hispanic to emphasize the European heritage.

A Mexican intragroup split resulted. Because the more oppressed elements suffered considerably, they tended to group together against those who were above them on the social scale (Menchaca 2001; Montejano 1987). To protect their interests (McWilliams 1990[1968]), many gente de razon joined Anglos in opposing the resistance stance of the Mexican masses (*Evening Free Lance* 1927). Despite this uneasy alliance, they, too, lost out in the end, becoming bankrupt and poverty-stricken in many instances. They continued to be viewed by Anglo-Americans as being Mexicans, except in ceremonial occasions when certain traits became "Spanish" (McWilliams 1990[1968]). This post-war dynamic was even more pronounced among the Mexican women (Bouvier 2001; Chavez-Garcia 2004), as suggested in how these changes

> had a far-reaching effect, altering the most intimate aspects of . . . women's lives . . . and led them to live out of wedlock . . . some living in common-law marriages. . . . Others were forced to find employment outside the home in unskilled and labor-intensive jobs, working as washerwomen, seamstresses, or housekeepers. Some were even found to resort to begging or stealing to make ends meet. (Chavez-Garcia 2004:172–173)

New Dimension to a Sense of Inferiority

The Mexicans' racial makeup was the primary obstacle placed in the path of socioeconomic mobility. If that barrier was not enough, then cultural criteria were used to undermine their advancement. For many, it was truly a perplexing situation, since they were only beginning to master the Spanish language when a new dominant one was substituted for it. However, the new social structure was not so new after all, since it generally resembled the old colonial one in at least one respect: Native Mexicans were on the bottom. Where it differed is in the nature of the macrostructural revampments. How they were situated on the bottom was new, especially in the piecemeal ways they were being stripped of their traditional lifeways and relegated to a different role in an industrial economy. (See Gomez 2007, chapter one, for her double colonization analysis.)

Basis of New Cultural Blending

The native cultural style was being replaced by a new one. There was some trepidation among natives concerning the Anglo slogan "time is money" and the "cold materialism" ethic (Pitt 1998), meaning that profit trumps human feelings. Although some features of the Anglo social structure and belief and practice ethos contrasted sharply with earlier systems, enough was similar to remind natives of past experiences and adjustments. For example, natives were introduced to a new language, customs, beliefs, and values. Regional subcultures within northern Mexico now formed part of the Southwest U.S. (Paredes 1978), especially in the border area where there were constant interactions and exchanges over a long frictional history (Alvarez 1995). Many Mexican traditions, such as Catholicism, were altered, and along with other developments, further added to the confusion and growing sense of powerlessness in the new era. Anglo-Americans took over all the administrative, trade, and cultural activities. This meant that the newly conquered Mexicans in the area had little say in government policy (Vargas and Paterson 1999). Obviously, certain beliefs concerning the family, work, child-rearing, and the nature of individual and group life had to change if the Mexicans were to survive (Chavez-Garcia 2004). But as noted in earlier chapters, the changes from an indigenous to peasant way of life, constituting a new hybrid culture, were beginning to take root and become routinized as traditional. This syncretic process covering several hundred years was now undergoing another interruption and alteration. It both complicated and aggravated cultural evolution for the Chicano people, making human adaptation hard won and fought.

An example of this mixed, uneven change is how Spanish and Mexican society underwent transformations in the area of patriarchy and command and control of the household, especially the subordination of women as an ideal (Bouvier 2001; Chavez-Garcia 2004; Castaneda 1999). Spanish customs under the Catholic Church definitely granted power and authority to the patriarch, but interestingly, the legal system gave women a number of rights and privileges, such as the ability to inherit property and titles, sign contracts, and so on. With the settlement of northern Mexico, where a harsh environment required new roles and responsibilities for everyone, women found themselves doing things that heretofore were the prerogative of men (Gonzalez 1993). Farming, ranching, and household chores were arranged quite differently as the circumstances of everyday life dictated. These adaptations became particularly acute during the 1821–1848 period. This cultural transformation resulted because of the trade and diplomatic relations between Mexico and the United States and in larger order because of the egalitarian currents of the time. Matriarchal households and an increase in female employment were a sign of the times. In short, "family life increasingly became a mixture of the old and the new values regarding paternal authority and the proper sphere for women" (Griswold del Castillo 1989:99; see also Chavez-Garcia 2004; Gomez-Quinones 1994b). Late in the century, women also played a role in some of the progressive and radical politics of the labor movement (Gonzales 1999; Gomez-Quinones 1994b).

Cultural accommodation for the new U.S. citizens was out of the question, except for a few gestures toward Spanish elites. Mexican culture in the South-west was crushed by the American socioeconomic belief system. Mexicans felt morally defeated during these early years of subordination (Almaguer 2008; Gomez 2007; Dunbar-Ortiz 2007; Robinson 1963). Over time, a more accommodating cultural reintegration finally took place (Robinson 1963). As noted before, many Anglo-Americans were Hispanicized or mestizacized, thus taking the lead in cultural integration and becoming exemplars of bilingual-bicultural strategies of change.

Cultural Accommodation or Disintegration

For most natives, a successful life was based on their adoption of new values and norms; refusal to do so often meant failure. In some respects, the earlier Spanish experience had prepared them for such choices. Perhaps it is universally true that subjugated native peoples must shift and readjust to changing sociocultural conditions. In this prevailing Anglo world, numerous types of native reactions were possible, and most transpired. It must also not be forgotten that "all minorities must cope with the fact of Anglo domination; that is what being a minority in the United States means" (Rosenbaum 1981:151). Notwithstanding this truism, Gomez-Quinones suggests that "the people's sense of identity led them to consider themselves as Mexicans regardless of citizenship or of the boundary line between countries" (1994a:194).

More and more Anglo-Americans and European immigrants poured into the Southwest, especially California. This was particularly true after the gold rush (1850s) in the north and the completion of the railroads (1870s and after) in the south. Finding themselves in the way, the Mexicans at the outset began to establish their own communities. Since they played such an important role in the growing economy, they remained close to fertile land, jobs, and the homes of the wealthy. This choice was made in order to survive (Camarillo 1979; McWilliams 1990[1968]). But also, "Throughout this period, Mexicans north of the imposed border continued to maintain their ties, contacts, and mutual influences in many aspects of socioeconomic life with Mexicans south of the border" (Gomez-Quinones 1994b:207). Thus, a sense of binationalism prevailed at the beginning.

It was necessary for Mexicans to integrate somehow into United States society, even if only selectively. All-out resistance was futile. Some reasoned that if this route were followed and held to, they would surely suffer the fate of the American Indians. One avenue eventually taken, the era of social bandit activity notwithstanding, was for Mexicans to group together for defense. Many Mexicans were still being abused without provocation (Teja 2010). Suspicion and distrust characterized the Anglo attitude, for Mexicans were perceived as deceitful, treacherous people. Therefore, staying within their own spatial and social boundaries, both groups—Anglos and Mexicans—became isolated from each other (Villa 2000; Vigil 2009; Grebler, Moore, and Guzman 1970; Camarillo 1979).

Growth of Economy

During this time the Anglos built a great economic empire. As mentioned previously, many Indian-Spanish-Mexican practices were borrowed by Anglo entrepreneurs. These traditions, readapted by the Anglos, became the mainstays of the Southwest—mining, irrigation and riparian rights, ranching and cattle raising, and so on (Vargas and Paterson 1999; McWilliams 1990[1968]). Moreover, "by 1900, the mineral output alone of the lost territories amounted to more than the national income of the Mexican Republic" (Raat 1992:78).

In keeping with the dominant/subordinate system of economic relations, the Mexicans were employed in and contributed to many enterprises (Vargas and Paterson 1999; Forbes 1964). Often they did not receive equal pay for equal work (Taylor 1934). Economic competition between the two groups generated conflict and violence, and initially, for example, Mexicans were driven out of the mining region to stem the turmoil. When Anglos eventually gained control, they began to enlist Mexican workers, not as equals but as subordinates. This was only the first of many occupational adjustments. If gente de razon were having difficulties adjusting to the changes, Mexicans were doubly suffering. The occupations they had been trained for were being taken away from them, as the vaquero industry was absorbed and became cowboy culture. They were then reappearing on the job market as farm laborers and livery-stable hands (McWilliams 1990[1968]). Since Mexicans had to eat, they worked at any job, which usually meant the lowest. In Texas, the transition was a classic example of how traditional farmers are challenged and undermined and overrun by the cattle industry and commercial agriculture. The end result was a social system that devalued them as a people but welcomed their labor in the buildup of "a farm society based on contract wage labor and business rationality" (Montejano 1987:104).

Doing farmwork as field-hand peons was not new to Mexicans; it was similar in some respects to the Spanish colonial pattern. And as noted for Texas, the difference here was that *campesinos* (field hands) participated in the building of an agricultural empire; in California, agribusiness later became unequaled in the world. In addition, when the railroad and mining industries spread throughout the Southwest, section laborers were needed to lay and

Decaying rancho in the late nineteenth century.

Field hands at an old mission in the 1880s.

care for the tracks and miners were needed to dig up and process the ore. For this purpose, towns owned and supervised by the railroads and mining companies sprang up, inhabited mostly by Mexicans. So as traditional culture gave way to modern technology and occupations, a new cultural orientation came with it.

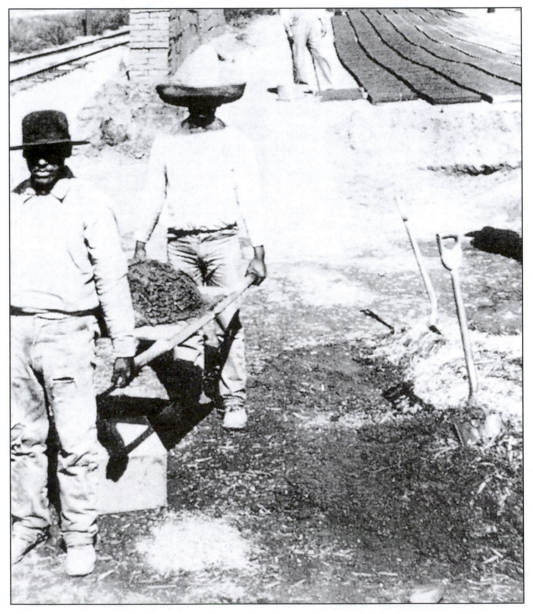

Adobe brick makers.

Adaptation Strategies

As noted before, there were several types of adaptations to these changes: Some people were assimilated into American culture; others remained loyal to the Mexican community; and still others survived through crime (Pitt 1998). Many variations of these strategies were possible (Montejano 1987; Stewart and De Leon 1994). For example, some followed a separatist route and stayed as far away from Anglos as possible. Eventually, though, the Anglo-American population expanded and settled there, making the respite short-lived. Those who wished to protect and maintain ethnic traditions founded town *barrios* (ethnic enclaves) or rural *colonias* (colonies) (Vigil 2009). The colonias evolved from small ranchito settlements. When hostilities ran high, Mexican resisters or social outlaws found sanctuary in such places.

Many of the elite Mexicans, especially in places like New Mexico and California, sought and maintained a semblance of power under the new Anglo political order (Pitt 1998; Gomez-Quinones 1994a). Holding elective offices such as mayor, supervisor, sheriff, and city councilman, they generally defended the constitutional rights and properties of their compatriots; some even pushed for bilingual education and the accommodation of cultural differences between the two groups. Oftentimes these individuals were in the middle of some rather volatile political situations, such as the Santa Fe Ring (a corrupt power broker group that controlled political and economic life in New Mexico for most of the nineteenth and early twentieth centuries) in New Mexico, where elite Mexicans and Anglos forged a machine that lasted until well into the next century.

Although assimilation was difficult, especially for Indian-appearing Mexicans, many selected that approach. In large measure, the lighter the skin and the better the English, the smoother the change. However, conflict between the two cultures did not always occur; cooperation was needed for daily life (Paredes 1978:72). Recognizing the benefits of the dominant culture, many Mexicans learned the English language and Anglo customs. And yet, particularly in border regions such as Texas, they also retained important Mexican language and sociocultural traits. Unlike assimilationists, they adopted a nativist type of acculturation—learning the dominant culture but not unlearning the native one. For some the adjustment was shaky, especially since dominant group institutions worked against cultural accommodation and ethnic diversity. In many instances, the result was a sense of marginality to both cultures. This was a repetition of the native experience in the colonial period, which sometimes had a positive result (a new hybrid culture) and sometimes ended in confusion or choloization.

Thus, some Mexicans rejected separatism, assimilation, and acculturation—or were forced out of these patterns by poor treatment—and continued a life of resistance. Obviously, there were serious problems for those who took this militant path: resisters faced death or jail. All of these reactions to change became integrated into the already broadly based Mexican sociocultural character. But "the fact remains that most Mexicanos in the United States lost the freedom to live in the way they wanted to live in during the nineteenth century" (Rosenbaum 1981:157). As the years passed, a new cultural synthesis developed.

STAGE III REFERENCES

Acuna, R. 1975. Mexican-American history: A reply. In *The Chicano*, ed. N. Hundley. Santa Barbara, CA: ABC-CLIO.

———. 2011. *Occupied America: A history of Chicanos*, 7th ed. New York: Pearson.

Almaguer, T. 2008. *Racial fault lines: The historical origins of white supremacy in California*. Berkeley: University of California Press.

Alvarez, R. R., Jr. 1995. The Mexican–U.S. border: The making of an anthropology of borderlands. In *Annual Review of Anthropology* 24: 447–470.

Archer, C. I. 2000. Fashioning a new nation. In *The Oxford history of Mexico*, ed. M. C. Meyer and W. H. Beezley. Oxford: Oxford University Press.

Arrom, S. M. 1985. *The women of Mexico City, 1790–1857*. Stanford, CA: Stanford University Press.

Bancroft, H. H. 1888. *California pastoral*, vol. 34. San Francisco: The History Co.

Bannon, J. F. 1974. *The Spanish borderlands frontier, 1513–1821*. Albuquerque: University of New Mexico Press.

Banton, M. 1998. *Racial theories*, 2nd ed. Cambridge, MA: Cambridge University Press.

Bauer, K. J. 1974. *The Mexican war, 1846–1848*. New York: Macmillan.

Bazant, J. 1977. *A concise history of Mexico: From Hidalgo to Cardenas, 1805–1940*. New York: Cambridge University Press.

Blea, I. 1988. *Toward a Chicano social science*. New York: Praeger.

———. 1992. *La Chicana and the intersection of race, class, and gender*. New York: Praeger.

Borah, W. 1970. The California mission. In *Ethnic conflict in California history*, ed. C. Wollenberg. Los Angeles: Tinnon-Brown.

Bouvier, V. M. 2001. *Women and the conquest of California, 1542–1840: Codes of silence*. Tucson: University of Arizona Press.

Buffington, R. M., and W. E. French. 2000. The culture of modernity. In *The Oxford history of Mexico*, ed. M. C. Meyer and W. H. Beezley. Oxford: Oxford University Press.

Bustamante, J. 1994. Racismo Mexicano. *Frontera Norte*, January 24.

Camarillo, A. 1979. *Chicanos in a changing society: From Mexican pueblos to American barrios in Santa Barbara and Southern California, 1848–1930*. Cambridge, MA: Harvard University Press.

Carter, W. B. 2009. *Indian alliances and the Spanish in the Southwest, 750–1750*. Norman: University of Oklahoma Press.

Castaneda, A. I. 1993. Sexual violence in the politics and policies of conquest: Amerindian women and the Spanish conquest of Alta California. In *Building with our hands*, ed. A. de la Torre and B. M. Pesquera. Berkeley: University of California Press.

———. 1999. Sexual violence and the politics and policies of conquest in Alta California. In *Major problems in Mexican-American history*, ed. Z. Vargas and T. Paterson. London, UK: Houghton Mifflin College Division.

Castaneda, C. E. 1976. *The Mexican side of the Texan revolution (1836) by the chief Mexican participants.* New York: Arno Press.

Chance, J. K. 1994. Indian elites in late colonial Mesoamerica. In *Caciques and their people: A volume in honor of Ronald Spores,* ed. J. Marcus and J. F. Zeitlin. Anthropological Papers no. 89. Ann Arbor: Museum of Anthropology, University of Michigan.

Chavez, J. R. 1984. *The lost land: The Chicano image of the Southwest.* Albuquerque: University of New Mexico Press.

Chavez-Garcia, M. 2004. *Negotiating conquest: Gender and power in California, 1770s to 1880s.* Tucson: University of Arizona Press.

Clendenen, C. C. 1969. *Blood on the border: The United States Army and the Mexican irregulars.* New York: Macmillan.

Cline, H. F. 1963. *Mexico: Revolution to evolution, 1940–1960.* New York: Oxford University Press.

Cockcroft, J. D. 1990. *Mexico: Class formation, capital accumulation, and the state.* New York: Monthly Review Press.

Conway, C. B., ed. 2010. *The U.S.–Mexican war: A binational reader.* Indianapolis: Hackett.

Cotera, M. P. 1976. *Diosa y hembra: The history and heritage of Chicanas in the U.S.* Austin, TX: Information Systems Development.

Cubitt, T. 1988. *Latin American society.* Harlow, UK: Longman Group UK Limited.

Cumberland, C. C. 1968. *Mexico: The struggle for modernity.* New York: Oxford University Press.

de Janvry, A. 1981. *The agrarian question and reformism in Latin America.* Baltimore: Johns Hopkins University Press.

de la Torre, A., and B. Pesquera. 1993. *Building with our hands: New directions in Chicana studies.* Berkeley: University of California Press.

DeLay, B. 2008. *War of a thousand deserts: Indian raids and the U.S.–Mexican war.* New Haven, CT: Yale University Press.

De Leon, A. 1983. *They called them greasers: Anglo attitudes towards Mexicans in Texas, 1821–1900.* Austin: University of Texas Press.

De Leon, A., and R. Griswold del Castillo. 2006. *North to Aztlan,* 2nd ed. Wheeling, IL: Harlan Davidson.

de Rouffignac, A. L. 1985. *The contemporary peasantry in Mexico: A class analysis.* New York: Praeger.

Diaz, M. N. 1967. Introduction: Economic relations in peasant society. In *Peasant society: A reader,* ed. J. M. Potter, M. N. Diaz, and G. M. Foster. Boston: Little, Brown.

Dobie, F. J. 1969. *Guide to life and literature of the Southwest.* Dallas: Southern Methodist University Press.

Dunbar-Ortiz, R. 2007. *Roots of resistance: A history of land tenure in New Mexico.* Norman: University of Oklahoma Press.

Duren. 1992. Los Indios de Mexico en la Sociedad Mexicana. *Cuadernos Americanos* 50(6–7).

Esteva-Fabregat, C. 1995. *Mestizaje in Iberio-America.* Albuquerque: University of New Mexico Press.

Evening Free Lance. 1927. Crimes and career of Tiburcio Vasquez: The bandit of San Benito County and notorious early California outlaw. Hollister, CA.

Forbes, J. D. 1964. *The Indian in America's past.* Englewood Cliffs, NJ: Prentice- Hall.

———. 1993. *Africa and Native Americans: The language of race and the evolution of red-black peoples*. Norman: University of Oklahoma Press.

Foster, G. M. 1988. *Tzintzuntzan: Mexican peasants in a changing world*. Long Grove, IL: Waveland Press.

Fowler-Salamini, H., and M. K. Vaughan, eds. 1994. *Women of the Mexican countryside, 1850–1990: Creating spaces, shaping transitions*. Tucson: University of Arizona Press.

Frye, D. 1996. *Indians into Mexicans*. Austin: University of Texas Press.

Fuller, J. D. P. 1936. *The movement for the acquisition of all Mexico, 1846–1848*. Baltimore: Johns Hopkins University Press.

Gomez, L. 2007. *Manifest Destinies: The making of the Mexican American race*. New York: New York University Press.

Gomez-Quinones, J. 1994a. *Mexican American labor: 1790–1990*. Albuquerque: University of New Mexico Press.

———. 1994b. *Roots of Chicano politics, 1600–1940*. Albuquerque: University of New Mexico Press.

Gonzalez, D. 1993. La Tules of image and reality: Euro-American attitudes and legend formation on a Spanish-Mexican frontier. In *Building with our hands: New directions in Chicana research*, ed. A. de la Torre and B. M. Pesquera. Berkeley: University of California Press.

Grebler, L., J. Moore, and R. Guzman. 1970. *The Mexican-American people*. New York: The Free Press.

Greenwood, R. 1960. *The California outlaw: Tiburcio Vasquez*. Los Gatos, CA: Talisman Press.

Griffin-Pierce, T. 2000. *Native peoples of the Southwest*. Albuquerque: University of New Mexico Press.

Griswold del Castillo, R. 1989. Patriarchy and the status of women in the late nineteenth century Southwest. In *The Mexican and Mexican American experience in the 19th century*, ed. J. E. Rodriguez O. Tempe, AZ: Bilingual Press.

———. 1990. *The treaty of Guadalupe Hidalgo: A legacy of conflict*. Norman: University of Oklahoma Press.

Gutierrez, R. A. 1991. *When Jesus came the Corn Mothers went away: Marriage, sexuality and power in New Mexico, 1500–1846*. Stanford, CA: Stanford University Press.

Gutierrez Ibarra, C. 1987. *Como México perdió Texas*. Mexico D.F.: Instituto Nacional de Antropologia e Historia.

Haidt, R. 2009. The wife, the maid, and the woman in the street. In *Eve's enlightenment: Women's experience in Spain and Spanish America, 1726–1839*, ed. C. M. Jaffe and E. F. Lewis. Baton Rouge: Louisiana State University Press.

Hale, C. A. 1968. *Mexican liberalism in the age of Mora*. New Haven, CT: Yale University Press.

Hamnett, B. 2006. *A concise history of Mexico*. Cambridge, UK: Cambridge University Press.

Harris, C., and L. Sadler. 2004. *The Texas rangers and the Mexican revolution: The bloodiest decade, 1910–1920*. Albuquerque: University of New Mexico Press.

Hass, L. 1995. *Conquest and historical identities in California, 1769–1938*. Berkeley: University of California Press.

Heidenreich, L. 2007. *"This land was Mexican once": Histories of resistance from northern California*. Austin: University of Texas Press.

Heidler, D., and J. Heidler. 2003. *Manifest Destiny*. Westport, CT: Greenwood Press.

Heizer, R. T., and A. J. Almquist. 1971. *The other Californians: Prejudice and discrimination under Spain, Mexico, and the United States to 1920*. Berkeley: University of California Press.

Henderson, T. 2007. *A glorious defeat: Mexico and its war with the United States*. New York: Hill and Wang.

Hobsbawn, E. J. 1959. *Primitive rebels*. New York: W. W. Norton.

Hu-DeHart, E. 1993. Yaqui resistance to Mexican expansion. In *The Indian in Latin American history: Resistance, resilience, and acculturation*, ed. J. E. Kicza. Wilmington, DE: Scholarly Resources.

Hutchinson, C. A. 1969. *Frontier settlement in Mexican California*. New Haven, CT: Yale University Press.

Jackson, R. 2005. *Missions and the frontiers of Spanish America: A comparative study of the impact of environmental, economic, political, and socio-cultural variations on the missions in the Rio de la Plata region and on the northern frontier of New Spain*. Scottsdale, AZ: Pentacle Press.

Jackson, R. H., and E. Castillo, eds. 1994. *Indians, Franciscans, and Spanish colonization*. Albuquerque: University of New Mexico Press.

Jaffe, C. M., and E. F. Lewis, eds. 2009. *Eve's enlightenment: Women's experience in Spain and Spanish America, 1726–1839*. Baton Rouge: Louisiana State University Press.

Jones, H., and D. Rakestraw. 1997. *Prologue to Manifest Destiny: Anglo-American relations in the 1840s*. Wilmington, DE: SR Books.

Joseph, G. M. 1992. On the trail of Latin American bandits: A reexamination of peasant resistance. In *Patterns of contention in Mexican history*, ed. J. E. Rodriguez O. Wilmington, DE: Scholarly Resources.

Katz, F. 2007. International wars, Mexico, and U.S. hegemony. In *Cycles of conflict, centuries of change: Crisis, reform, and revolution in Mexico*, ed. E. Servin, L. Reina, and J. Tutino. Durham, NC: Duke University Press.

Kearney, M. 1996. *Reconceptualizing the peasantry*. Boulder, CO: Westview Press.

Kessell, J. L. 2002. *Spain in the Southwest*. Norman: University of Oklahoma Press.

Knight, A. 1990. Racism, revolution, and *indigenismo*: Mexico, 1910–1949. In *The idea of race in Latin America, 1870–1940*, ed. R. Graham. Austin: University of Texas Press.

———. 1994. Popular culture and the revolutionary state in Mexico, 1910–1940. *The Hispanic American Historical Review* 74(3): 393–444.

———. 2007. Mexico's three fin de siècle crises. In *Cycles of conflict, centuries of change: Crisis, reform, and revolution in Mexico*, ed. E. Servin, L. Reina, and J. Tutino. Durham, NC: Duke University Press.

Lake, A. 2006. *Colonial rosary: The Spanish and Indian missions of California*. Athens, Ohio: Swallow Press/Ohio University Press.

Lightfoot, K. G. 2005. *Indians, missionaries, and merchants: The legacy of colonial encounters on the California frontiers*. Berkeley: University of California Press.

Livermore, A. A. 1969. *The war with Mexico*. New York: Arno Press.

Lomnitz-Adler, C. 1992. *Exits from the labyrinth: Culture and ideology in the Mexican national space*. Berkeley: University of California Press.

Martinez Caraza, L. 1991. *La intervención Norteamericana en México*. Mexico D. F.: Panorama Editorial.

McWilliams, C. 1990[1968]. *North from Mexico: The Spanish speaking people of the United States.* New York: Praeger.

Meier, M. S., and F. Ribera. 1993. *The Chicanos: A history of Mexican Americans.* New York: Hill & Wang.

Menchaca, M. 2001. *Recovering history, constructing race: The Indian, black, and white roots of Mexican Americans.* Austin: University of Texas Press.

Merk, F. 1963. *Manifest Destiny and mission in American history.* New York: Random House.

Meyer, M. C., and W. H. Beezley, eds. 2000. *The Oxford history of Mexico.* Oxford: Oxford University Press.

Miles, R. 1993. *Racism after "race relations."* New York: Routledge.

Mintz, S. W., and E. R. Wolf. 1967. An analysis of ritual co-parenthood (compadrazgo). In *Peasant society: A reader,* ed. J. M. Potter, M. N. Diaz, and G. M. Foster. Boston: Little, Brown.

Mirande, A. 1987. *Gringo justice.* Notre Dame, IN: University of Notre Dame Press.

Mitchell, P. 2005. *Coyote nation: Sexuality, race, and conquest in modernizing New Mexico, 1880–1920.* Chicago: University of Chicago Press.

Monroy, D. 1990. *Thrown among strangers: The making of Mexican culture in frontier California.* Berkeley: University of California Press.

Montejano, D. 1987. *Anglos and Mexicans in the making of Texas, 1836–1986.* Austin: University of Texas Press.

Moquin, W., and C. Van Doren, eds. 1971. *A documentary history of the Mexican American.* New York: Praeger.

Morner, M. 1967. *Race mixture in the history of Latin America.* Boston: Little, Brown.

Navarro, M. G. 1970. Mestizaje in Mexico during the national period. In *Race and class in Latin America,* ed. M. Morner. New York: Columbia University Press.

Nutini, H. G. 1995. *The wages of conquest: The Mexican aristocracy in the context of Western aristocracies.* Ann Arbor: University of Michigan Press.

Oboler, S. 1995. *Ethnic labels, Latino lives: Identity and the politics of (re)presentation in the United States.* Minneapolis: University of Minnesota Press.

Officer, J. E. 1987. *Hispanic Arizona, 1536–1856.* Tucson: University of Arizona Press.

Paredes, A. 1958. *With his pistol in his hand: A border ballad and its hero.* Austin: University of Texas Press.

———. 1978. The problem of identity in a changing culture: Popular expressions of culture conflict along the lower Rio Grande border. In *Views across the border: The United States and Mexico,* ed. R. S. Ross. Albuquerque: University of New Mexico Press.

Phillips, G. H. 1993. *Indians and intruders in central California, 1769–1849.* Norman: University of Oklahoma Press.

Pitt, L. 1998. *The decline of the Californios: A social history of the Spanish-speaking Californians, 1846–1890.* Berkeley: University of California Press.

Potter, J. M. et al. 1967. *Peasant society: A reader.* Boston: Little Brown and Company.

Price, G. W. 1967. *Origins of the war with Mexico: The Polk-Stockton intrigue.* Austin: University of Texas Press.

Raat, W. D. 1992. *Mexico and the United States: Ambivalent vistas.* Athens: University of Georgia Press.

Redfield, R., and A. Villa Rojas. 1990. *Chan Kom: A Maya village.* Long Grove, IL: Waveland Press.

Ridge, J. R. 1969. *The life and adventures of Joaquin Murrieta.* Norman: University of Oklahoma Press.

Rippy, J. F. 1926. *The United States and Mexico.* New York: Alfred A. Knopf.

Robinson, C. 1963. *With the ears of strangers: The Mexican in American literature.* Tucson: University of Arizona Press.

Rosenbaum, R. J. 1981. *Mexicano resistance in the Southwest.* Austin: University of Texas Press.

Ross, I. B. 1928. *The confirmation of Spanish and Mexican land grants in California.* Berkeley: University of California Press.

Samora, J., and P. V. Simon. 1977. *A history of the Mexican-American people.* Notre Dame, IN: University of Notre Dame Press.

Sanchez, G. I. 1967. *Forgotten people: A study of New Mexicans.* Albuquerque, NM: Calvin Horn.

Sanderson, S. E. 1986. *The transformation of Mexican agriculture: International structure and the politics of rural change.* Princeton, NJ: Princeton University Press.

Sandstrom, A. R. 1991. *Corn is our blood.* Norman: University of Oklahoma Press.

Semo, E. 2007. The left in the neoliberal era. In *Cycles of conflict, centuries of change: Crisis, reform, and revolution in Mexico,* ed. E. Servin, L. Reina, and J. Tutino. Durham, NC: Duke University Press.

Servin, E. 2007. Another turn of the screw: Toward a new political order. In *Cycles of conflict, centuries of change: Crisis, reform, and revolution in Mexico,* ed. E. Servin, L. Reina, and J. Tutino. Durham, NC: Duke University Press.

Servin, E., L. Reina, and J. Tutino, eds. 2007. *Cycles of conflict, centuries of change: Crisis, reform, and revolution in Mexico.* Durham, NC: Duke University Press.

Sierra, J. 1969. *The political evolution of the Mexican people.* Austin: University of Texas Press.

Sinkin, R. N. 1979. *The Mexican reform, 1855–1876: A study in liberal nation-building.* Austin: University of Texas at Austin, Institute of Latin American Studies.

Spicer, E. 1962. *Cycles of conquest.* Tucson: University of Arizona Press.

Stein, S., and B. Stein. 1970. *The colonial heritage of Latin America.* New York: Oxford University Press.

Stewart, K. L., and A. De Leon. 1994. *Not room enough: Mexicans, Anglos, and socioeconomic change in Texas, 1850–1900.* Albuquerque: University of New Mexico Press.

Stout, J. A. 2002. *Schemers and dreamers: Filibustering in Mexico, 1848–1921.* Fort Worth: Texas Christian University Press.

Swadesh, F. L. 1974. *Los primeros pobladores: Hispanic Americans of the Ute frontier.* Notre Dame, IN: University of Notre Dame Press.

Tabler, H. W. 1988. Peasants and the shaping of the revolutionary state, 1910–1940. In *Riot, rebellion, and revolution: Rural social conflict in Mexico,* ed. F. Katz. Princeton: University of Princeton Press.

Taylor, P. S. 1934. *An American-Mexican frontier.* Chapel Hill: University of North Carolina Press.

Taylor, W. B. 1993. Patterns and variety in Mexican village uprisings. In *The Indian in Latin American history: Resistance, resilience, and acculturation,* ed. J. E. Kicza. Wilmington, DE: Scholarly Resources.

Teja, J. F. de la, ed. 2010. *Tejano leadership in Mexican and revolutionary Texas.* College Station: Texas A&M University Press.

Thompson, J. 2007. *Cortina: Defending the Mexican name in Texas*. College Station: Texas A&M University Press.

Turner, F. C. 1968. *The dynamics of Mexican nationalism*. Chapel Hill: University of North Carolina Press.

Tutino, J. 2007. The revolutionary capacity of rural communities: Ecological autonomy and its demise. In *Cycles of conflict, centuries of change: Crisis, reform, and revolution in Mexico*, ed. E. Servin, L. Reina, and J. Tutino. Durham, NC: Duke University Press.

van den Berghe, P. L. 1967. *Race and racism: A comparative perspective*. New York: John Wiley & Sons.

Vanderwood, P. J. 1992. *Disorder and progress: Bandits, police, and Mexican development*. Wilmington, DE: Scholarly Resources.

———. 2000. Betterment for whom? The reform period, 1855–1875. In *The Oxford history of Mexico*, ed. M. C. Meyer and W. H. Beezley. Oxford: Oxford University Press.

Vargas, Z., and T. Paterson. 1999. *Major problems in Mexican American history*. London, UK: Houghton Mifflin College Division.

Vazquez, J. Z. 2000. War and peace with the United States. In *The Oxford history of Mexico*, ed. M. C. Meyer and W. H. Beezley. Oxford: Oxford University Press.

Vigil, J. D. 1974. *Early Chicano guerrilla fighters*. La Mirada, CA: Advanced Graphics.

———. 1999. Streets and schools: How educators can help Chicano marginalized gang youth. *Harvard Educational Reviews* 69(3): 270–288.

———. 2009. Community dynamics and the rise of street gangs. In *Latinos: Remaking America*, ed. M. Suarez-Orozco and M. Paez. Berkeley: University of California Press.

Vigil, J. D., and F. Lopez. 2004. Race and ethnic relations in Mexico. *Journal of Latino-Latin American Studies* 1 (2): 49–74.

Villa, R. 2000. *Barrio logos: Space and place in urban Chicano literature and culture*. Austin: University of Texas Press.

Wagley, C. 1965. On the concept of social race in the Americas. In *Contemporary cultures and societies in Latin America*, ed. D. B. Heath and R. N. Adams. New York: Random House.

Wasserman, M. 2000. *Everyday life and politics in nineteenth century Mexico: Men, women, and war*. Albuquerque: University of New Mexico Press.

Webb, W. P. 1935. *The Texas Rangers: A century of frontier defense*. Austin: University of Texas Press.

Weber, D. J. 1973. *Foreigners in their native land*. Albuquerque: University of New Mexico Press.

———. 2009. *The Spanish frontier in North America*, the brief ed. New Haven, CT: Yale University Press

Whetten, N. L. 1948. *Rural Mexico*. Chicago: University of Chicago Press.

Wolf, E. R. 1965. Aspects of group relations in a complex society: Mexico. In *Contemporary cultures and societies of Latin America*, ed. D. B. Heath and R. N. Adams. New York: Random House.

———. 1966. *Peasants*. Englewood Cliffs, NJ: Prentice-Hall.

———. 1969. *Peasant wars of the twentieth century*. New York: Harper and Row.

———. 1982. *Europe and the people without history*. Berkeley: University of California Press.

Zeleny, C. 1974. *Relations between the Spanish-Americans and Anglo-Americans in New Mexico*. New York: Arno Press.

Anglo-American and Mexicanization Period 1846–Present

The complex historical developments of rural society and peasantry in Mexico reached a new crisis with the civil war of the twentieth century; the remaining fragments of an indigenous past were about to change again. For those Mexicans living in the northern territories annexed by the United States, it came much earlier, and with equal force, at the end of the Mexican–American War. It was a highly variable process in each place and in both time periods. In the United States, the resident Chicano population confronted and participated in a society that passed through a major civil war, abrupt and strife-ridden industrialization and urbanization, two world wars and several lesser wars, and periods of capitalistic expansion and depression. Chicanos in the United States made a transition to the new industrial order and settled primarily in cities. With their uprooting from the land and the subsequent civil war upheavals and other disruptions in Mexico, migration and immigration marked the lives of a people buffeted about by the economic and political forces of the time. Urbanization and modernization were processes that characterized the migrant and immigrant experience, and considerations of time and place are integral elements in understanding developments in this historical phase.

The civil war in Mexico impelled thousands of rural inhabitants northward into the United States. The transition from peasant life to immigrant status is filled with strains and stresses. Human movement on such a massive scale brought many uncertainties for the future. Caution and worry became natural instincts as people struggled to find a place in a rapidly changing world. False starts and missteps occurred with regularity, but with trial and error, most learned from the experience. Nevertheless, a sense of familiarity and control over the new situation came about very unevenly for Mexicans in both the United States and Mexico.

In the United States, the transformations set in motion by Mexico's independence were abruptly moved in new directions. Imposition of a new Anglo-American order made Mexicans aware of other groups and other social systems, especially in regard to important human links to the environment—jobs, homes, and health. However, earlier struggles and successes had given Mexicans a sense of confidence and awareness. As a result, the momentum to make decisions, learn from mistakes, and plan a new life course, within limits, was definitely under way.

The factors affecting human migration show how economic systems and networks transcend nation-state boundaries, incorporating more resources and more people in their expansion. After the 1910 Mexican Revolution, and continuing to the present, immigration has been a major contributor of human resources to support this "globalization" of the economy.

The Mexican people grew and evolved from this experience to take their place among modern populations. Showing autonomy to win independence put them in good stead to make the shift to a modern, urban lifestyle. For some Mexicans the event took place after 1848, and for many more it occurred after the 1910 Revolution and throughout various ebbs and flows of the middle and late twentieth century. The Mexican people were dedicated to taking control of their destiny. Too much blood had been spilled, too many lives had been lost, and too many centuries had passed for them to passively accept the tumultuous changes and new and different symbols of authority. Freedom whets the appetite for more of the same and encourages defiance of anyone who threatens to take away what has already been gained. In spite of the numerous setbacks that occurred during this period, the Mexican people continued to move ahead.

Chapter 8

INTACT AND STABLE SOCIAL ORDER

Class: Industrialism and Urbanization

Background to Capitalism, Roots of Inequality

As the Chicano people entered the twentieth century, the economies of the United States and Western Europe were becoming full-blown capitalist systems. Capitalism is a system in which the means of production and distribution (that is, land, factories, mines, railroads, and so on) are privately owned and operated—more or less competitively—for profit. Capitalism is the culmination of previous systems such as mercantilism, colonialism, and racial/cultural imperialism and, in its short history, has undergone its own internal shifts and leanings—e.g., laissez-faire, monopoly, mixed, and global. The contemporary social-class structure was formed in response to changes in the structure of capitalism, creating opportunities for some and hindrances for others. As noted at the beginning of this book, changes experienced by the Chicano people were intricately entwined with historical and cultural developments. This chapter chronicles the more recent phase of these macrohistorical developments.

Soon after 1860, when intense Mexican ethnic resistance was subsiding, the United States moved into a new age of commerce, investment, and speculation (Gonzalez 2004). Mexico, too, was caught in the web of late nineteenth-century economic expansion, as important United States capitalists invested hundreds of millions of dollars in railroads, mines, oil wells, and agricultural enterprises (Meier and Ribera 1993; Servin, Reina, and Tutino 2007). Thus, Mexicans on both sides of the recently established border were anchored in these transformations with the effects occurring a little earlier and in a slightly different way for those Mexicans on the northern side of the border. Ultimately, the revampments made populations on both sides of the border subject to shifts in the availability of jobs, thereby triggering spatial mobility as migrants moved in search of employment (Meier and Ribera 1993). Mexican labor had always been the cornerstone of the evolution of the economy, except now the first phases of globalization and the movement of capital also required the *movement* of Mexican labor.

It was an age characterized by intense class conflict in both the industrial and the agricultural sectors of the United States. Strikes, bombings, arrests, and intervention by government troops regularly appeared on the front pages of newspapers. Mexicans graced these pages too: cowboy protests, agricultural strikes, urban disturbances, and school walkouts. These developments were closely linked to the rise of industrialism and the increasing urbanization of the population. Under these conditions, different types of laborers were employed in varying settings. For a few, the economic expansion, industrialization, and growth of cities brought great wealth; for others, a comfort-

Foreign-owned oil field in late nineteenth-century Mexico.

able living; and for many, poverty. Chicanos, along with other minorities, were more often found in the last category. As a result of this system, by the mid-twentieth century, 20 percent of America's families controlled 76 percent of the wealth, which means that the remaining 80 percent of the people were left with 24 percent of the wealth (Spencer 1977). Put another way, the top 1 percent of the population owned 48 percent of the nation's wealth, and the bottom 80 percent had just 6 percent (Wolff 1996). Obviously, this method of resource acquisition and distribution causes problems. These figures have hardly changed today (see chapter 10).

One result was that 30 or 40 million U.S. citizens in the 1950s were poor, or below the poverty line of a $3,200 annual income for a family of four (Harrington 1962:177). Within this category, the percentage of Chicanos was disproportionate to their total population. Nearly a third of the Chicano population in the Southwest, a total of 1,082,000 people, was officially classified as being below the poverty line in 1960 (Gonzales 2009; Briggs 1973). The figure was really higher because many individuals were uncounted, especially unmarried immigrant males.

Still, the largest number of poor people in the United States has always been white: at that time, whites comprised over half of the poor, or more than 12 million people (Harrington 1962). Despite the significance of ethnic connotations, as verified by the high incidence of poverty among Chicanos, the fact that white people also experience inequality and deprivation emphasizes the importance of the class factor. This fact cannot be overstated. As noted previously, the wealthiest families are comparatively few, but commensurate with their resources they have a considerable influence on social and political sectors of American life. Lack of wealth and thus limited social and political resources is a fact of life for many citizens and especially for minorities such as Chicanos (De Leon and Griswold del Castillo 2006; Meier and Ribera 1993).

The national class structure that evolved in this period can be divided into three main categories, each one having two subcategories: (1) upper (upper-upper, lower-upper), (2) middle (upper-middle, lower-middle), and (3) lower (upper-lower, lower-lower) (Gordon 1964). These strata were based on income, occupation, housing, and various other factors. One's location within the system determined power, esteem, and prestige—or lack of them, in the lower levels. Most people were somewhere in the middle sectors.

It is this middle sector that set the pattern for national thought and action. Cultural membership notwithstanding, Mexican Americans lived a middle-class lifestyle once they became white- and blue-collar workers, resembling other Anglo Americans rather than Mexican newcomers (Varzally 2008; Penalosa 1973; Sanchez 1993). It is this lifestyle that many lower-class, socially mobile people wanted to emulate. However, because of their typically lower-class standing, Chicanos had to reach higher to attain that level. One statistical study of selected workers, which controlled for education and occupation, found that the total income difference in 1959 between Anglo and Mexican male workers was $2,050. Of this total difference, $1,141 was attributable to the differing educational and occupational distributions of Anglos and Mexican Americans. The remaining portion of the difference could be attributed to discrimination against Mexican Americans as a minority group (Telles and Ortiz 2008; Poston, Alvirez, and Tienda 1977).

Chicano Role in the Economy

The foundation for Chicano poverty was set in the nineteenth century (Romo 1983). Chicanos in several regions worked in jobs that contributed to building up the capitalist economy (Monroy 2008; Montejano 1987). When mining enterprises dwindled, for example, many mine workers joined farm laborers toiling in the fields. In addition to the labor contributions Chicanos made in the cattle and railroad industries, they worked in many other unskilled jobs as well (Bortz 2008; Gomez-Quinones 1994a). According to Manuel Gonzales:

> Still, the most compelling attraction exerted by the Southwest was the abundance of jobs. Mexicans found work as laborers, on construction sites, in public works systems, in service and food establishments, in lumbering camps, and on ranches. The overwhelming majority, however, came to work in three main industries: mining, railroad maintenance, and agriculture. (Gonzales 2009:121)

Millions of dollars of investment capital were dependent on Mexican labor. Once again, the Chicano masses, Indians, and mestizos, who in earlier stages of their history had participated in building up other empires, did not appreciably benefit from the emerging capitalist system.

At the same time that economic growth was changing the availability of jobs and the distribution of wealth in the United States, significant changes were occurring in Mexico during the regime of Porfirio Diaz. Nowhere were these changes more dramatic than in the role of women (Mitchell and Schell 2007). Under a peasant economy, males and females had shared many of the productive activities of the household, of which the male was in charge. As noted previously, the migration to cities undermined these patterns. City life in an industrial economy resulted in males becoming more dependent; that is, while men were away at work, women took complete charge of the household. Later, when women, too, joined the factory labor force, they were subjected to lower wages and worse working conditions than the males (Segura 1990). In time, these role and working-condition experiences led to a more assertive posture as women became involved in efforts to improve and advance their cause (Ruiz 1999; Vallens 1978; Macias 1982; Soto 1979; Arroyo 1977).

Farmworker in the United States and peon in Mexico.

Further, Indians and mestizos, mostly peons and low-paid urban workers, remained in a postcolonial state even though a degree of liberation had occurred (Gonzalez 2004). The hacendados and the peons (found mostly in southeastern Mexico), tenants, and sharecroppers (found in central and northern Mexico) took social inequality for granted (Beezley and MacLachlan 2009; Bazant 1977). The *porfiriato*, as this era was called, emphasized "unequal economic growth . . . based on increasing exports and a dramatic opening to foreign investment . . ." (Hinojosa-Ojeda 1994:111; see also Cockcroft 1990). In addition, the hacendados, comprising approximately one thousand families, controlled 90 percent of the land, while 85 percent of the rural population was landless (Cumberland 1968). The peasants felt that their land had been stolen from them by the hacendados and that it was only just to demand that their means of production be restored to them (Bazant 1977). Thus, conditions were ripe for revolt. While Diaz had appeased the ideologies of conservative and liberal members of the dominant population, others, mostly peasants, Indians, and city laborers, were far from content (Beezley and MacLachlan 2009; see Katz 1988 for a review of peasant movements and rebellions).

The 1910 Mexican Revolution, then, had the earmarks of a common people's revolt. Before the civil war erupted, however, there were several attempts by opposition leaders to unseat Diaz. The sentiment against him mounted, and eventually a coalition overthrew his rule. One member of the opposition, Diaz Soto y Gama, had this to say in 1910:

> Mexico was ruled by a narrow, unpatriotic, dictatorial clique, which catered to the interests of foreigners and especially the Catholic Church, [and] were conspiring to take over the nation and destroy every last remnant of earlier revolutionary reforms. . . . The ultimate target of . . . the attack was Porfirio Díaz: the Caudillo who betrayed democracy. (Cockcroft 1968:98)

In terms of the larger picture, one modern Mexican historian has observed that in Mexico's transition to capitalism, "with its violent upheavals in 1810, the 1850s to 1860s, and 1911–17 . . . the mobilization of peasant participation in these conflicts had long-lasting effects on social, economic, and political development" (Coatsworth 1988:62; see also Knight 2007).

The Mexican civil war lasted throughout the decade and even into the 1920s. Agrarian reform was a key issue for the masses. The military leaders—Villa, Obregon, Zapata, Calles, Amaro, and others like them—were all unknown children of peasants and Indians. The revolution made them famous, as it did many women, who both fought alongside the men and led contingents of their own (Mitchell and Schell 2007; Cockcroft 1990; see Salas 1990 for a full review). Many of the demands of the masses were granted totally, others only partially, and still others not at all. Like most revolutions, the Mexican Revolution broke the bondage of earlier ages. But, as with many revolutions, unresolved questions remain to this day (Servin, Reina, Tutino 2007).

Few would disagree that the Mexican masses generally benefited from the upheaval. Although other observers have used different frameworks in discussing postrevolutionary Mexico, the following summary will suffice here. The Institutional Revolutionary Party (PRI) has been the ruling party of contemporary Mexico, and its spokesmen maintain that every presidential regime—each one lasting six years—is part of a "continuing, permanent revolution." After the PRI was instituted in the 1920s, political turmoil quieted. During the 1930s, President Lazaro Cardenas led the nation toward improving social conditions. From 1940 to 1960, the Mexican government emphasized economic and technological development. But after 1960, there was a turn to a "balanced revolution": a pragmatic mix of political, social, and economic reforms as needed, according to the leaders (Servin, Reina, Tutino 2007; Beezley and MacLachlan 2009).

The revolutionary sloganeering was all rhetoric, however, as the communal landholding system (i.e., *ejidos*) was a cornerstone in the aftermath of the

Porfirio Diaz.

Pancho Villa.

Emiliano
Zapata.

Soldaderas.

revolution, but suffered from 1940 onward. Accordingly, the state moved in new directions, undermining *ejidatarios* as a new "agroindustrialism" (or neo-latifundismo!) took over. Peasants first became migrants in their own country, moving from region to region to gain a livelihood. Increasingly, however, they soon had to migrate to another nation, the United States, especially after the 1970s (Monroy 1999; Sanderson 1988). Mexico had been brought into the capitalist network, but in a special way. There was a "dependence on foreign capital, [and] domestic capital's reliance on cheap labor . . . contributed to the great divisions between rich and poor that characterize Mexico today" (Cockcroft 1990:139; see also Gonzales 2009).

Effects of the 1910 Revolution on the United States: The Push-Pull Factor

The 1910 Revolution that profoundly transformed Mexico also had a profound impact on the United States. For one thing, social unrest in Mexico and the destruction of human ties to the land brought internal and external migration. Many adult Chicanos living in the United States have or had a relative who migrated to the United States during that time. It must be underscored, however, that this process of "U.S. employers . . . seeking inexpensive labor" began in the late nineteenth century and accelerated in the aftermath of 1910 (Cockcroft 1986:36; see also De Leon and Griswold del Castillo 2006). The presence of immigrants reinvigorated the Mexican culture in the United States and added a more determined, militant element to the labor struggle. Here we will focus on immigration, however.

Along with the "push" factor stemming from the strife in Mexico, an economic "pull" force was simultaneously operating in the United States (Hinojosa-Ojeda 1994). The economic development of the American Southwest drew many Mexican workers to the United States (Bortz 2008; Driscoll de Alvarado 1999; Reisler 1976). This push-pull reciprocity in large part explains why Mexicans immigrated, some with permission papers and others without them, but always with the aid of intermediaries, both formal and informal. Indeed there were also other reasons. The United States had closed the door to Asian immigrants and soon after, in 1924, placed immigration quotas on southern and eastern Europeans, who had served as the United States labor reservoir for over 50 years. As a result, a new pool of workers was needed, and the Mexicans filled this need.

Because of the history of problems with Mexicans (war, conflict, resistance, hostility, economic competition, and so on), there was a general reluctance to admit this new "brown horde." There was even a movement to include them in the 1924 immigration quotas, and in the meantime, the Border Patrol was created to monitor them (Monroy 1999, 2008; Weaver 1994). Mexican labor was desired, but the permanent settlement of Mexicans was not. An immigration policy that allowed the temporary use of Mexican labor was advocated (Cardenas 1977).

Economic motives won out over social attitudes, and the farmers and ranchers of the American Southwest welcomed Mexican laborers regardless of whether they were legal or not (Vargas and Paterson 1999; Stowell 1974). Nevertheless, rampant racism resulted in Mexican workers receiving lower pay than whites and unfair treatment by police; border conflicts re-erupted in this time period, and in El Paso, 391 Mexicans were killed between 1911 and 1919 (Cardoso 1980). The developing industrial order required "a mass of unskilled workers who could be hired cheaply and dismissed freely . . ." (Hinojosa-Ojeda 1994:111). In time, this initiative would encompass the western hemisphere in an expansionary mode that later incorporated large portions of the globe (Robinson 2004).

The ebb and flow of immigration continued for decades; it actually increased when it became clear that the Mexican government had little interest (acting as a further "push") in assisting the peasants/Indians with communal land development (Katz 2007; Hinojosa-Ojeda 1994). Immigration policy

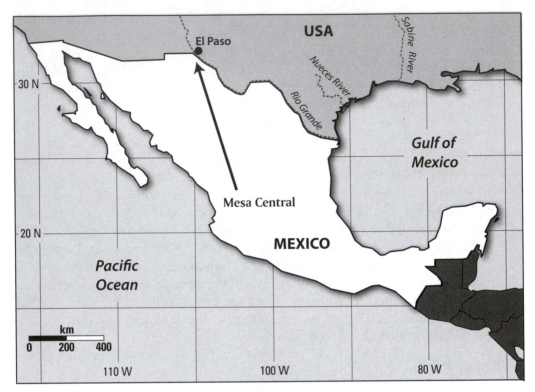

Major immigration route in the 1920s.

has also been greatly affected by the influence of agribusiness on state and federal legislation (Chavez 1998). Immigration restrictions on Mexicans have been periodically relaxed—for example during World War I and the Bracero (literally "arm" or field hand) Program, initiated during World War II (Driscoll de Alvarado 1999; Bortz 2008). An additional burden was placed on women in peasant communities during these peak immigration periods, as males typically left the household to find work, leaving matters entirely under the supervision and care of their wives, even to the point of making them responsible for the food on the table (Mitchell and Schell 2007; Stephen 1991; Vigil 1990).

Living conditions for these workers were poor, with no appreciable changes forthcoming for many years. Even when the situation was brought to public attention, few significant efforts at improvement were made. Mexican immigrants were paid lower wages than other local laborers; their income was barely at the subsistence level (Gonzales 2009; Cockcroft 1986; Galarza 1964; Reisler 1976). They were subjected to substandard housing and hygienic conditions, and constant job insecurity. Often, settlement patterns produced separate villages or appendages to towns and ranches (Gonzalez 1994).

Life in an Urban Environment

The influx of immigrants occurred during the United States' rise to industrial prominence. A concomitant development was more workers moving to urban areas. Mexicans were a part of this process. Some businessmen went so far as to state "that were immigration to cease, or be cut much below the present average by a quota, they would be left on the verge of bankruptcy" (Gamio 1969:30; see also Alvarez 1976). As Mexicans became increasingly urbanized, they were additionally affected by the problems of urban life; within cities they dwelled in pockets of poverty plagued by health problems and crime (Vigil 2001, 1988; Moore and Vigil 1993). Their communities appeared as appendages, urban villages, and struck an obvious chord of distinctiveness as spatially separate and visually blighted (Vigil 2001, 1988; Gonzalez 1994). Either as barrios (urban) or colonias (rural colonies), such settlement patterns were noted early in the century (Romo 1983; Taylor 1934).

Urban life and routines are an entirely new experience for many newcomers to the United States, and making the necessary adjustments is not an easy task (Velez-I. 1996; Vigil 2001). The work environment can provide a range of new experiences: new technology, machines, office equipment, and modes of transportation affect how time is organized and whether one joins other peoples and groups, such as unions. Participation in this transition affected Mexicans in several ways. In California, in 1931, 11 percent of wage earners in manufacturing industries were Mexicans. Toward the end of the twentieth century the proportion of Mexicans in various industries ranged from 2.4 to 66.3 percent (Sanchez 1993). While a rural–urban transformation is in itself dramatic, the Chicano case must be viewed in a magnified form and on a broader scale because it also involved a shift across national and cultural lines; it was an ecological and cultural switch that was ironic for a people who once claimed the same area. In any event, the Chicano tendency to establish ethnic neighborhoods (colonias and barrios, which were similar to other immigrants' ethnic enclaves or ghettoes) was continued and even enlarged (Vigil 2008).

As previously mentioned, this settlement pattern functioned in two basic ways: it insulated and preserved cultural lifeways, and it helped temper the social abuse and discrimination that were everyday realities. Many social problems that originated with the first groups to arrive were, in turn, transmitted to the new arrivals. A group of recent Mexican immigrants either meant a new settlement or an old one enlarged, and since the majority of Mexican immigrants were very poor, various social problems emerged in each of the settlements (Villa 2000; Bogardus 1934; Stowell 1974; Samora 1971). In short, it seemed that unskilled, low-paying jobs translated into inferior places to live and raise families. Besides suffering from an oppressive labor position, Mexicans became victims to serious social ills that further undermined their development and well-being. For example, what began as a

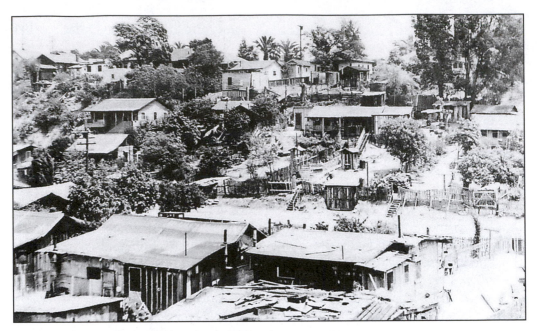

El Hoyo in east Los Angeles (Fickett's Hollow).

The courts near Los Angeles' Olvera Street.

Mexican street railworkers in Sonora Town (Los Angeles).

Farmworkers' "mobile" house.

palomilla (cohorting) adolescent tradition of male bonding evolved into street gangs. The pressures of urban life and the social isolation and neglect of several decades transformed mischief and adventure into dangerous and criminal behavior. Problems with crime, alcohol, and drugs similarly intensified during this period.

Additional problems arose with attempts by dominant Anglo institutions to thoroughly re-enculturate the Chicano populace. These efforts, known as "Americanization" programs (Valencia 2010; Gonzalez 1990), were similar to those directed toward Native Americans. Anglo values were taught by the educational system, through regular contact with members of the dominant culture and by those Chicanos who had already been acculturated. However, remnants of the Mexican way of life were kept alive in the home. This mixing of new and traditional cultures stunted opportunities to raise one's social and economic status.

Internal Colonialism

Economic and social problems existed internationally as well as nationally. For example, 35 percent of the world's population earned 93 percent of the total income, leaving the remaining 7 percent of the wealth for 65 percent of the population, figures shockingly similar to the national proportions (Starr 1978). These inequities, in large part, stemmed from European expansionism, as colonizers harnessed and controlled resources, both natural and human, and the products of human labor were unevenly distributed. While Chicanos had their own unique role in this world drama, struggling against domination and manipulation of various sorts, it is striking to note how similar their situation and experiences are to other colonized peoples (Gonzalez 2004; Bustamante 1978).

Indigenous peoples were subjected to this treatment by the United States, as land, labor, and wealth arrangements were revamped. The Chicano variant of this experience has sometimes been called "internal colonialism" (Barrera, Munoz, and Ornelas 1974). This characterization must be applied carefully to each time period, place, and people. For instance, south Texas has had an especially destructive and oppressive history—characterized by, for example, the Alamo, border conflict and filibustering, and social and political ostracism of Mexicans (Harris and Sadler 2004). For some elites in both New Mexico and California, for example New Mexico's Santa Fe Ring, the experience was more one of cooptation and collaboration with Anglos over the Indians and peasants of the area (Dunbar-Ortiz 2007; Monroy 1999). Nevertheless, Acuna's apt summarization (2000) of this dominant/subordinate system highlights economic, cultural, and racial inequalities and injustices that occur after a war of conquest in which the victors thoroughly overwhelmed the vanquished. This model can be applied to Chicanos and other national ethnic minorities (primarily blacks and Indians) in several ways: (1) isolation in separate ethnic communities (barrios, ghettos, reservations); (2) poor educational preparation; (3) lack of political power; and (4) as a function of the first three, inability to improve their social and economic conditions (Valencia 2010).

Early in their American experience, Chicanos had begun to exercise their rights as workers. "Strike activity with ethnicity as a cohesive element was evident wherever Mexicans constituted a significant segment of the workforce. It occurred throughout cities and farms, along railroads and mines, and in the construction, canning, and meat-packing industries" (De Leon and Griswold del Castillo 2006:74; see also McWilliams 1990[1968]; Valdes 1991; Driscoll de Alvarado 1999; Bortz 2008; Gomez-Quinones 1994a). Many strikes occurred because Chicanos were unhappy with receiving a lower wage than whites for similar work. However, Mexican trade-union activities were fraught with difficulties: for example, language discrimination in union proceedings. During the early twentieth century, with the expansion of industrial capitalism, there was an increasing trend toward the participation of Mexican laborers in radical and organized labor movements (Monroy 2008; Gomez-Quinones 1994b; Sanchez 1993).

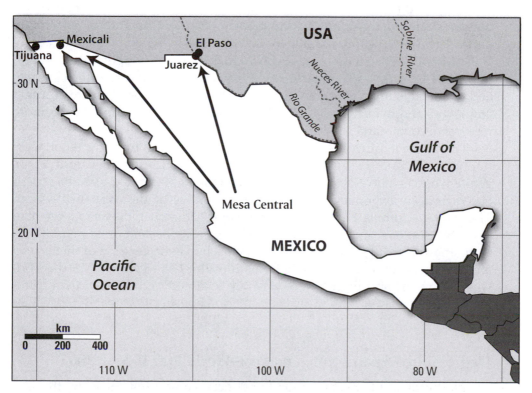

Immigration routes in the 1940s.

Chicanos led a series of farmworker strikes beginning in the early twentieth century. In most cases, throughout the century, they were the majority of the workers and therefore had the power to repeatedly challenge agribusinessmen. Overall, Mexicans constituted a major part of the migratory agricultural labor between 1900 and 1940 (Gonzalez 2000; Weaver 1994), and some rural towns with an agricultural base were comprised primarily of Mexicans (Bortz 2008; Driscoll de Alvarado 1999; Menchaca 1995; Gonzalez 1994). The improvements Chicanos sought were slow in coming, however, for in some areas Chicanos were held in low esteem. For example, in Texas, "Many expressed the views that Mexicanos were a poor, simple, childlike group that needed guidance and close supervision. . . . Both patron and worker accepted the belief that the natural order of things was the superior-subordinate relationships of the rancho" (Foley et al. 1977:15). Similar attitudes prevailed in California, despite the union activity. Growers always desired permanent and reliable Mexican workers, even if they had to tolerate occasional social discontent and periodic rumblings (Shaw 2008; Gonzalez 1994; Menchaca 1995).

With increasing urbanization of the Chicano people, strike activity spread to other occupations (Gomez-Quinones 1994b). Other problems resulting from urbanization and severe economic inequality were poor sanitation and housing conditions, inadequate health services, crime and juvenile delinquency, strains on the family structure, unemployment, and an overwhelming dependence on the capitalist elite for the means of livelihood (Telles and Ortiz 2008; Moore 1978; Moore and Pachon 1985). Workers sought better wages, improved housing and sanitary conditions, a decent education for children, and many other improvements. This righteous stance aroused the ire of Anglo employers and the general public and in many instances brought even more repressive counterattacks.

The inherent difficulties of a Mexican–Anglo cultural transformation were multiply marginal because of the effects of urbanization (Penalosa 1973). White workers in Western Europe and the United States had already experienced or were experiencing the endemic features of the capitalist system. They suffered similar hardships and met repression when they sought to alleviate or eliminate inadequate and unfair conditions and treatment. There were important differences for the Chicanos, however, because of their racial and cultural experiences in the aftermath of the 1846–1848 war. In the Midwest, Mexicans and blacks were generally charged higher rents than European immigrants for similar or even inferior housing (Escobar 1999; Valdes 1991; Reisler 1976).

Depression, Repatriation, and Post–World War II Mobility

Workers gradually left agricultural occupations for those in the city (Galarza 1964). During this transition, however, the United States was hit by one of its periodic economic crises: the 1930s depression. The Great Depression led to large numbers of Mexicans being deported (Balderrama 1995; Weaver 1994). The public recognized the need for reform, but Mexican pleas were ignored as they were excluded from the debate to improve living conditions. One irritant to the public stemmed from Chicano migrant worker organizations and demonstrations against the usual poor working and living conditions. This was particularly true in the highly productive San Joaquin, Coachella, and Imperial Valleys of California. Nevertheless, it took decades of constant struggle before basic improvements were made.

By 1940, a New Deal compromise had been worked out with the Anglo majority workers. In contrast, Chicanos were deported wholesale. This deportation program, known by the less offensive word "repatriation," was originally initiated against dissident farmworkers (Balderrama 1995; Weaver 1994; McWilliams 1990[1968]). Eventually,

> pressure mounted to remove aliens from the relief rolls and, almost paradoxically, from the jobs they were said to hold at the expense of American citizens. In the Southwest, immigration service officers searched for Mexican immigrants, while local welfare agencies sought to lighten their relief load by urging Mexican indigents to volunteer for repatriation. (Hoffman 1974:2)

Under this program, several hundred thousand Chicanos, including thousands born in the United States, were "repatriated" to Mexico.

The government's failure to respond to the needs of agricultural workers only served to stiffen Chicano opposition:

> The Mexican nationalism of immigrants often intensified in the United States. "I would rather cut my throat before changing my Mexican nationality," declared a laborer who had resided in the United States for twenty-five years. "I prefer to lose with Mexico than win with the United States." (Reisler 1976:114; see also Monto 1994)

Even though the Chicano population suffered great setbacks, increasing numbers of them were able to move out of the barrios and into the middle-class bracket (Telles and Ortiz 2008; Moore and Pachon 1985). Social mobility was aided by industrial productivity and urban growth in the United States after World War II (Gomez-Quinones 1994b; Alvarez 1976). In this "boom" period, many Chicanos moved to the suburbs, with a few attaining higher socioeconomic levels after pursuing educational and professional career goals (Sanchez 1993). In proportion to the total number, these individuals were few, but they reflect how aspirations of social mobility are joined with strategies of assimilation and acculturation. Chicanos, despite many obstacles, were steadily moving away from lower-class traditional Mexican culture toward middle-class Anglo-American culture, even syncretically recombining traditional lifeways with the better material resources available in the United

States. This transformation came in stages, starting with the first generations of Mexicans, as early as the late-nineteenth century (Sanchez 1993). With large-scale immigration in the 1920s it continued in an accelerated fashion. After World War II when a larger, more determined population pushed for change, the movement toward middle-class culture accelerated again. In most instances, these developments combined social mobility aspirations with increased adoption of the dominant Anglo culture (Penalosa 1973). It also brought with it social upheavals and strains that replayed episodes of resistance of earlier times (Alvarez 2008; Pagan 2003; Leonard 2006).

Improvements during the post–World War II period can be easily exaggerated; since the previous immigrant generation started with nothing, any upward shift in the subsequent generation appeared to be progress (Telles and Ortiz 2008; Alvarez 1976). Although some Chicano socioeconomic mobility had taken place, the average yearly family income in the Southwest was only $4,164 in 1960, compared to the average Anglo income of $6,448. In addition, the figure of $4,164 includes wages earned by all family members, not just the household head. It was very common for youth to leave school at an early age in order to seek gainful employment and contribute to the household income, even handing their check over to the household head (Knouse, Rosenfeld, and Culbertson 1992; Grebler, Moore, and Guzman 1970). This appeared to be a pattern with each wave of immigrants since the nineteenth century, as peasant society valued family and group solidarity and reciprocity, particularly under the adverse circumstances dictated by urban life and the demands of an industrial economy.

Trade unionism also benefited the urban working class, including some Chicanos. While many unions have practiced overt discrimination, as well as more subtle forms of exclusion, especially with the better paying, more prestigious blue-collar occupations, Chicanos have still made inroads and taken their place alongside other workers (Gomez-Quinones 1994b; Romero 1979). Because of continuing Mexican immigration, however, there has been an increase in the proportion of Spanish-speaking male workers' "service" and "operative" job categories. Service occupations tend to be low paying, low in prestige (Grebler, Moore, and Guzman 1970), and without fringe benefits and career advancements. As we will note, the occupational strata became more common and a sore spot in coming decades.

Failure of the Political System

Since shortly after the 1848 War, Chicanos have been nearly powerless in the political arena (de la Garza and DeSipio 1996; Griswold del Castillo 2008; Meier and Ribera 1993). Constant streams of immigration contribute to this, as new immigrants must familiarize themselves with the American political system. However, it is equally true that the two-party political system historically failed to provide Chicanos with adequate representation. This, in turn, created and perpetuated a sense of discouragement and apathy among Chicanos. With Roosevelt's New Deal, Democratic politicians were popularly perceived as supporters of Chicano interests, although since World War II, politicians have appeared to direct attention to the group only during election time. Programs to benefit Chicanos typically failed to materialize and turned out to be empty promises.

Chicanos lacked the basic education and the college-trained leadership so necessary for political participation. Specific training and awareness programs, such as widespread voter registration efforts, were sporadic and almost nonexistent (Griswold del Castillo 2008; Garcia and de la Garza 1977). Much of Chicano political activity sprung from street protests and worker strikes. Although there were sporadic and courageous organizational efforts on the part of certain individuals and groups (Marquez 1993; Gomez-Quinones 1990), the Chicano political landscape was almost barren—a situation that was exacerbated by gerrymandering.

Gerrymandering was used to redraw state and national legislative district boundary lines in order to favor one interest group, usually one of the two major political parties (Gomez-Quinones 1990). The Chicano ethnic interest group was sliced, trimmed, and snipped into political oblivion. Greater East Los Angeles, with several hundred thousand Chicanos in 1960, provides a clear example of gerrymandering. The region was deliberately divided to ensure that no state assemblyman or senator would be able to rely on a majority Chicano vote to win. Chicanos were a minority in every district. Because the Chicanos were unable to elect leaders who reflected their interests, their voice went unheeded. This situation changed when the U.S. Commission on Civil Rights concluded that Chicanos in California had been gerrymandered out of opportunities to elect their own representatives to the state legislature or the United States Congress—government bodies that in no way reflected Chicanos' percentage of the state population (Gomez-Quinones 1990; Garcia and de la Garza 1977).

Different political methods were used to dilute or stamp out Chicano votes in other states. For example, in Corpus Christi, Texas, in 1915, there are indications that Mexicans were directed to vote in certain ways by Americans who paid their poll taxes (Taylor 1934). In addition, where Chicanos comprised a clear majority (sometimes close to 90 percent of the populace), Anglo leaders would handpick Spanish-surnamed candidates, "ringers," to run in the election. When such candidates won, they were "supervised" by Anglos during their tenure. But even in their defeat, the Anglos won, for their candidate took votes away from other Chicanos, who perhaps were running with the intention of serving their own community.

Chicanos in Texas took steps to change this state of affairs, even if only on a small scale. In the early 1960s, PASO (Political Association of Spanish-speaking Organizations), together with some non-Mexican groups (the Teamsters and the Catholic Bishops Committee for the Spanish Speaking), successfully managed to depose the Anglo political structure in Crystal City, Texas. This is a classic example of the reintroduction of democracy to the people, who in this case were 90 percent of the electorate. Other political activities in the Southwest during the 1960s finally led to the election of three Spanish-speaking congressmen and one U.S. senator.

In short, lack of political education and awareness, undemocratic political districting, and "rigged" elections all led to political disempowerment. Organizational efforts in the aftermath of the civil rights movement have somewhat altered this situation (Griswold del Castillo 2008). However, it is no secret that the outcome of many U.S. elections is almost directly dependent on the amount of money spent. Money is typically a requisite for political power, and abundant money is not usually one of the Chicanos' possessions. Jesse Unruh, a California Democratic leader, stated, "Money is the mother's milk of politics." Chicanos, however, "will enjoy very little political success if they must depend upon economic power to promote their political objectives" (Garcia and de la Garza 1977:67).

In summary, Chicanos have historically been members of the exploited laboring population, kept in a dependent, underdeveloped, and disadvantaged state. In the years between the 1848 Mexican–American War and 1960, those relatively few Chicanos who managed to escape such conditions usually had to abandon much of their cultural heritage to do so. With the large-scale immigration beginning in 1910 and continuing to this very day, the situation has become more complicated and difficult (as we will note later). For both Chicano natives and Mexican immigrants, the adoption of Anglo-American patterns of success often entailed giving up Mexican lifeways. Many denied their heritage—claiming instead a Spanish background—to escape from economic and social disadvantages (Telles and Ortiz 2008; Weaver 1994; Moore and Pachon 1985). Personal and group problems abound in this context of class struggle and intense culture conflict, where economic survival is wedded to cultural adjustments and revampments. An awareness of Chicano acculturation and even assimilation to the dominant mode of thought and action is crucial to understanding this period. Was a cultural transformation a prerequisite to socioeconomic advancement? Did such a transition ensure material betterment? If so, has this changed? The answers have fundamental implications for the continuing Chicano struggle (Telles and Ortiz 2008; Vigil 1997; Moore and Pachon 1985).

Culture: Assimilation vs. Nativist Acculturation

The Shifts and Pulls of Middle-Class American Culture and the Ebbs and Tides of Mexican Immigration

Well over 130 years since the incorporation of the Chicano into the United States, American cultural life experienced a major transformation. A primarily agrarian society shifted to one that was industrialized and urbanized, forging the path to becoming an international military and political power. Conflicts engendered by these processes contributed to the development of cultural differences among socioeconomic classes, and especially ethnic minorities. Moreover, the prosperity born of industrialization also brought about a numerically and culturally dominant middle class, alongside a working class that tended to mimic it. The core values of the middle class became widely accepted as typical of American culture—i.e., what you are or what you should become—and mass communications strengthened that characteristic.

One element of this value system was the ethnocentric notion that American culture was superior to any other, implying that American people were superior to any other. While values can be simply defined as the "ought-tos" of society and the norms the "blueprints for action," the stage was set for newcomers from different, contrasting cultural traditions to undergo miscues and react in unsteady but also creative ways.

As wave upon wave of immigrants poured into the country to farm the frontiers, work in the factories, and build the railroads, the average American greeted them with disdain, at least until they learned the values and norms of the dominant group. Although the immigrant groups contributed greatly to the enrichment of American language, arts, philosophy, and cuisine, the "100 percent American"—as Linton (1975) noted satirically—refused to recognize that his or her daily life included the use of behavior, beliefs, and materials derived from hundreds of different cultural traditions. Each new wave of different ethnicities in succeeding eras helped change American culture, some even contributing their own values and norms as a subset of the dominant ones (Gordon 1964).

Social and economic sanctions were therefore fashioned to impede ethnically and culturally "different" people from entering into and participating fully in mainstream American society. To complicate matters, this was in the context of a rapidly changing society. Such contending developments created pressures on the newcomers to assimilate—to discard the "different" traditions of their countries of origin and accept the values and beliefs of the American middle class, including discrimination toward subsequent arrivals who insisted on clinging to old lifeways (Telles and Ortiz 2008; Castaneda 1974). Such barriers and restrictions, especially discrimination in employment and housing, contributed to the creation of distinct ethnic enclaves and the maintenance of ethnic pride through nativist revivals and practices. While the common message to immigrants was to assimilate, the external barriers effectively undermined their efforts to do so; it was a mixed message that seriously hindered their integration into American society. Simply stated, immigrants embraced the values that were presented to them but were prevented from acting out the norms.

The decline of massive immigration from Europe and Asia after World War I was a watershed in American immigration history. Ethnic enclaves of these groups gradually faded away as they acculturated and assimilated American patterns through subsequent generations. For a complex of reasons, a distinctively Mexican tradition continued to flourish in the United States. The original imprint of Mexican culture before the conquest of 1846–1848, and more significantly the continued immigration of large numbers of Mexicans, led to a different ethnic minority experience. More obvious racial differences between the majority of Mexican immigrants and most Americans also contributed to the perseverance of Mexican culture. Unlike the sons and daughters of European immigrants, the children of most Mexican immigrants, with Indian or mestizo heritages, were noticeably different in appearance from the white majority and were less freely accepted by its members. Similar constraints also operated with regard to Asians, American Indians, and blacks. Thus, from the first large waves of immigrants to the present continuing flow from Mexico, Central America, and Asia, cultural adaptation as mediated by racial appearance has played a key role in the remaking of American culture.

Although retaining a distinctly Mexican flavor, the culture that developed among Mexican Americans nevertheless was affected by somewhat the same processes at work in other cultural minorities. The result was a hybrid culture mirroring a wide range of elements from both Mexican and American backgrounds (each of which is itself a complex of various origins), as well as unique patterns created through a fusion of elements from both traditions. Language usage is one example. "Such a complex continuum has given rise to four types of cultural-linguistic personalities: the monolingual in Spanish, the monolingual in English, the bilingual, and then . . . there is the child who speaks a patois" (de Leon 1970:36; see also Valencia 1991; Emiliano 1976).

The strength of Mexican-American culture lay in the fact that it could draw from these two rich cultural traditions, the mestizaje style of Indian and Spanish motifs and the entrepreneurial industrialism of modern life in the United States. Yet that opportunity also gave rise to grave problems, for important aspects of the two traditions were in conflict, and many Chicanos found themselves unable to successfully sort out the valuable traits from the harmful ones, according to Weber (2009), and the borderlands turned into a complex, mestizo frontier (Velez-I. 1996). In that setting, cultural syncretisms had generated a whole range of ethnic identities (Bernal and Knight 1993). When cultural moorings were loosened, however, a kind of cultural impoverishment sometimes resulted—empty marginality, with young people in particular turning to antisocial and self-destructive values and behavior (Vigil 1988).

The culture of the dominant majority in the United States was modeled from many themes, partly because of the large size of American society (Varzally 2008). Nevertheless, certain core values, rooted in what has been labeled a "white Anglo-Saxon Protestant ethic" (giving rise to the acronym "WASP" or, less commonly, "McWASP" to emphasize its middle-class identity), have been of particular importance (Gordon 1964). Individualism, a work ethic, competition, an achievement orientation, and a sense of communalism are some of the central tenets of this pattern (Bellah et al. 1985). Work, and the value symbols associated with it, played a significant role in American middle-class culture. Work also played a significant role in Chicano culture, but it featured other characteristics that crossed social-class categories (Telles and Ortiz 2008; Romero 1979) and combined with habits based on the way work was structured in a colonial economy built on indigenous labor and traditions.

Nevertheless, cultural life was heavily influenced by class status and the new industrial economy. The organization of the productive labor in an industrialized society and the ability to procure the goods produced are two of the most salient aspects of U.S. culture (Fernandez 1977; Vigil forthcoming). In this atmosphere of material production and consumption, people demanded a certain type of food, clothing, and shelter that they could select from a seemingly endless array. The necessary cultural accoutrements that accompany these possessions—words to describe them, values to guide human energy in obtaining them, customs and rituals involving them, and so on—led to further cultural divisions that were based on class criteria. While these standards motivated many United States citizens, including Mexican Americans, not all people had the same attitudes toward motivations for success.

Differing Styles of American and Mexican Cultures

The middle-class American ethic was an industrial society's reworking of western and northern European cultural traits that arrived with the early English-speaking immigrants to America. Besides the cultural customs, northwestern Europe contributed Protestantism, a tradition that subsequently evolved from a collection of religious beliefs and practices into a general philosophy of life emphasizing hard work, individualism, and frugality (Gamio 1969; Marger 1994). Implicit in that philosophy and explicitly stated by some of its proponents is the concept that material success is a sign of God's blessing, and failure a sign of his displeasure.

Several other points highlighted American culture. First, values emphasized a universe in which humankind had full mastery. Every person in society had an equal opportunity in all matters. If inequalities existed, it was because some people did not strive to reach their potential. In other words, it was one's own fault if he or she failed to achieve success. Furthermore, by work and achievement, one could gain control over natural forces. Because of this optimistic opportunism, societal members conformed to a standard that would bring material advancement for each individual (Diaz-Guerrero 1975). If everyone adhered to this pattern, group success would be enhanced (Inkeles 1977; Diaz-Guerrero 1978; Kluckholm and Strodtbeck 1961). While individual effort and achievement were extolled, unbridled personal aggrandizement interfered with the common good (Bellah et al. 1985).

The age of industrialism proved that machines could master previously unheard-of tasks. This technical achievement infected the human spirit, causing humans to strive to make nature bend to their wishes. The Protestant ethic complemented this goal, for it stems from the deeply held belief that God rewards those who work hard and struggle against any obstacle. Humans thus receive earthly success and, most importantly, spiritual salvation (Bellah et al. 1985; Foley et al. 1977). In facilitating hard work and earthly achievements, new tools and techniques shaped and cultivated a new way of thinking and became part of the legacy of the industrial revolution.

Traditional Mexican cultural characteristics contrast with those just cited in major respects, some sharply and others only slightly. The cultural contrasts between Mexico proper and its northern settlements in the nineteenth century were previously mentioned, and these contrasts have continued to the present (Moore and Pachon 1985). While American culture involved hard work, individual achievement, accumulating wealth, and technological advancements, all accompanied by God's blessing, Mexican culture has been extremely heterogeneous because of mestizaje, and the waves of immigrants varied in the cultural style that each brought to the United States (Chavez 2008; Cockcroft 1986; Portes and Bach 1985). Nevertheless, most Mexicans emphasized the importance of family, and there was a strong tendency toward stressing work and the production of goods for the group rather than the individual. This fact deserves special mention because Mexicans also valued the work ethic, but not for its own sake (Briggs 1973; Velez-I. 1996). Their past and present performance in agriculture and light industry has underscored this fact (Zavella 1987; Bortz 2008), despite former California Senator George Murphy's pejorative remark in the 1960s that "Mexicans are good farmworkers because they are short and built low to the ground" (Servin 1970:140).

Generally, work organization and group cooperation were aimed toward fulfilling basic needs, with an emphasis on material gain not for its own sake but for the sake of survival (Weaver 1994). The present was valued more than the future, and people were admired for who they were, rather than what they did (Kluckholm and Strodtbeck 1961). Females were subordinate to males, and there was a clear preference for a patriarchal family head. While accepting the everyday struggles of life, people had learned to assuage disappointment and look beyond defeat and failure (Velez-I. 1996). Coming from a peasant background with these traditions to a modern urban one was a major change, but when coupled with the strife and strain associated with immigration conditions and barriers, the adjustment was momentous (Chavez 2008; Kearney 1996). A clash of values was a predictable outcome, for how could a rural, almost communal outlook mesh with a fast-paced industrial style?

These sketches of American middle-class and traditional Mexican cultures are of course incomplete, but they provide some indication of the major styles that influenced Mexican-American culture and point to some of the syncretisms and conflicts within that culture. To fully describe Mexican-American culture is a difficult chore (Telles and Ortiz 2008; Gutierrez and Zavella 2009; Velez-I. 1996), and some observers (e.g., Romano-V. 1973) have raised important questions challenging such an endeavor. The assessment of personal values would vary with each individual, whether middle-class, white, Mexican, or a mixture (Keefe and Padilla 1987). However, the basic values of future goals versus present needs and doing rather than being are clear contrasts; gender inequalities and patriarchal fixtures are somewhat similar but are arranged in different ways for varying purposes between the two groups (Mirande and Enriquez 1979). For example, Mexican culture has formalized terms to reflect gender roles and attitudes, such as *machismo* (manliness, social and sexual dominance, and so on) (Mirande 1997); *hembrismo* (subordination of females), and *marianismo* (motherhood, sacred spiritual superiority associated with the Virgin Mary). Machismo is a very controversial and debated issue among Mexicans, especially among women who feel that this belief system has worked to suppress and demean them (Macias 1982; Gonzales 2009).

In these and other beliefs and patterns, what is unusual in the case of Mexican Americans (a people who blend several cultures) is that these contrasts were present within one person (Ramirez 1985; Arvizu 1974). Many individuals had independently fashioned a cultural style that combined values, giving them "situational" consideration as the time and place warranted (Vigil 1997).

George Sanchez, a Mexican-American educator, spoke on the issue of cultural openness or accommodation and championed the contribution Mexican culture could make. Other writers have supported this position, with one suggesting that the "psychology of the Americas" facilitates this orientation (Ramirez 1985). The "psychology of the Americas" is a reference to the ideas of Jose Vasconcelos in *La Raza Cosmica* (1926[1977]), in which he champions the ability to function in more than one language and culture—multiculturalism, as it is called today. Along with the more obvious material cultural items and practices of Mexican culture such as language, music, folklore, architecture, foods, crafts, and customs, there are deeper attributes to consider. Some of these would include the formal respect accorded a person, the sense of loyalty to family and nation, the profound spiritualism that undergirds religious beliefs, and particularly, the kind of stoic strength that assists in overcoming burdens and obstacles (Sanchez 1967). In some areas of the Southwest and border regions, this cultural accommodation is happening (or has already happened) and is in direct contrast with the sometimes negative appraisal some critics have given to Mexican culture (Kluckholm and Strodtbeck 1961).

A few Mexican Americans, and even some Anglos, were able to syncretize aspects of both cultures; they learned to plan for the future and live the present fully. They enjoyed work for its own sake, remembering that work was only a means, not an end, and therefore they could benefit from the fruits of their labor immediately. Increasingly, more observers and writers are touting this reflexive, more cosmopolitan cultural style, and have added support to the burgeoning awareness of cultural pluralism and multicultural education (Gibson, Gandara, and Koyama 2004; Spindler and Spindler 1990; Gibson and Ogbu 1991; Vigil 1997). Today, researchers have discovered that this multicultural and bilingual experience can combat Alzheimer's.

Strategies and Problems of Adaptation

In the "Stage IV" time period, acceptance of aspects of both cultures was a positive response to the problem of culture conflict and the potential for marginality. The fact that it was a hit-or-miss occurrence made it difficult and frustrating for many people. As noted, acculturation is a broad process of change taking place in one or both cultures, and this varied with time and place conditions and the ethnic makeup of the population. In addition, there was considerable variation in the types of reaction people had to change and adaptation. Compounding matters during phases of rapid change were class and gender transformations, where opportunities for upward mobility often entailed extreme cultural strains and adjustments (Chavira 1994; Vigil 2008).

Many Mexicans took the route of assimilation (Monroy 1999; Kluckholm and Strodtbeck 1961). This strategy began after the American annexation, when Mexicans lost their land rights and began to familiarize themselves with the new cultural standards in order to maintain or improve their economic conditions (Monroy 1993; Zeleny 1974). Assimilation usually occurred after long exposure to the dominant culture, but there were some who decided to accelerate the process. If they had lighter complexions, for example, they might first prefer to be called American, but if forced to commit themselves, they would claim a "Hispanic" descent (Menchaca 1993, 2001). Although there were many mestizos among them, the Hispanos in New Mexico and California, in the early twentieth century, started calling themselves Spanish Americans or Californios in order to differentiate themselves from

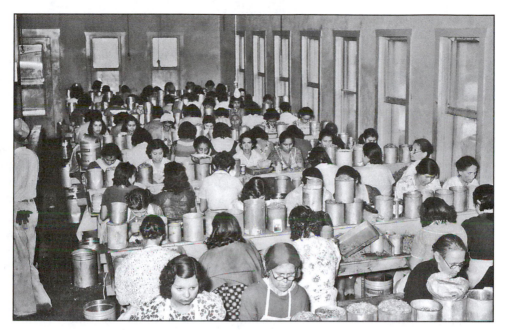

Pecan shellers in Texas.

Making parachutes in San Diego, California, for the World War II effort.

other Mexicans (Almaguer 2008; Alvarez 1976). Within the intracultural variation among people from Mexico, there also were European-oriented individuals whose racial appearance and cultural bearings were closer to the Anglo (Kluckholm and Strodtbeck 1961). Minimally, they were certainly accustomed to dominating those below them.

In some instances, this assimilation reached extremes in which people became flag-waving superpatriots and worked to master perfect English. They socialized their offspring to this end. In their efforts to rid themselves of Mexican culture, however, they often aroused the wrath of fellow Mexicans. "No Mexican is so despised as he who denies his race" (Gamio 1969:93).

Assimilation entails the complete transformation from one culture to another (Telles and Ortiz 2008; Gordon 1964; Bernal and Knight 1993; Castaneda 1974). There was no mistaking what assimilated Mexicans did politically, economically, religiously, and socially, even seeking marriage partners from the dominant group. Interestingly, in New Mexico the Hispanos were able to effect a coalition with the Anglos because of the Hispanos' willingness to accept the new culture (Gomez-Quinones 1994a). This alliance, known as the Santa Fe Ring and somewhat patterned after East Coast political machines, dominated the state up to the modern times, that is, post–World War II. In this case, assimilation meant retention of political and economic power.

For many Mexican Americans, however, assimilation was a sad experience because dominant Anglo society was so exclusionary. Mexican elites were obviously of a higher status and thus had a somewhat easier time of it, but even they suffered instances of blatant rejection. Thus, the assimilated Mexicans often were in limbo; they had changed, but no one cared to find a place for them in middle-class white society. Many even changed their telltale Spanish surname: Martinez to Martin, Ramirez to Raymer, and Barajas (meaning cards) to Cards.

Another adaptive alternative for Mexicans was to change their secondary social allegiances while maintaining the primary ones; this occurred in the initial phases of contact with Anglos. This meant functioning in all the important secondary Anglo areas to improve life's opportunities but keeping a primary Mexican ethnic identity, social relations, and cultural traditions (Gordon 1964; Spindler and Spindler 1991). Such people would take the path of acculturation—i.e., a bilingual/bicultural stance (Vigil 1997)—but maintain a primary, private life by speaking Spanish within their families and following Mexican customs. During work hours, at school, or in any place outside the primary area, they would adopt an appropriate English-speaking, Anglo-acting posture. According to a lifelong advocate of this strategy, "Cultural buffer areas do exist and people living within their boundaries belong to both civilizations culturally" (de Leon 1970:43). Patricia Phelan and Ann Davidson (1993) have referred to these people as "border crossers." Acculturation of this sort means living one's private life one way and public life another—or because of whim or need, mixing them up with almost equal dexterity. Of course, there were already people who had managed to assimilate some of the positive functional aspects of both cultures. In the modern period, such a strategy entailed a reversal of the assimilation process, with many reconnecting with their parents' and grandparents' roots. This dual process has been referred to as nativist acculturation, or additive rather than subtractive acculturation (Gibson and Ogbu 1991): learning a new culture but not discarding the old one (Vigil 1997).

Ethnic identification processes and ethnic identity labels involve birthplace, language usage, and customs and practices, among other facets. For this reason, they are controversial, and there are as many schools of thought and theories about labeling as there are labels (Suarez-Orozco and Paez 2009). Whatever labels people apply to themselves, or others use to designate them, it is important to underscore the dynamic nature of acculturation since it often involves constant reshufflings and revampments (Telles and Ortiz 2008; Sanchez 1993). Individuals who took this additive acculturation approach could refer to themselves as Mexicans if they wished, or, to reflect the bilingual and bicultural nature of their existence, as Mexican Americans, or, to emphasize their secondary participatory rights, as Americans of Mexican descent. Whatever their choice of label, they were reasonably good at habituating to both types of cultural standards. As many other ethnic minorities in different times and places have discovered, however, there are psychological consequences for anyone who functions in both worlds (Suarez-Orozco and Suarez-Orozco 1994).

What occurred in this regard was a continuation of the Chicano marginal syndrome that dated from colonial times, with the conquest of indigenous groups and the transformation of much of the population into peasants. Especially hard hit were the cultural moorings of the people in each time period. In the early colonial period, cholo became a pejorative label that characterized an Indian who was only partly (marginally) acculturated to the Spanish way of life. (This word has survived to the present and is currently used to describe street youth, especially those who belong to gangs [Vigil 2002; 1988]). Thus, over time a person often found him- or herself in a state of flux. For example, one southern Texas Chicano noted: "I think like an Anglo and I act like an Anglo but I'll never look like an Anglo. Just looking at me, no one could tell if I am an American or one of those blasted Mexicans from across the river. It's hell to look like a foreigner in your own country" (Madsen 1964:8).

Drinking, fighting, anomie (normlessness), using drugs, and other forms of cultural disorientation were behaviors often exhibited by individuals who were unable to fashion a stable bilingual and bicultural world and who were not securely rooted in either Mexican or Anglo culture (Suarez-Orozco and Suarez-Orozco 1994; Bernal and Knight 1993; Saldana 1995). This phenomenon sometimes involved cultural conflict between generations (Telles and Ortiz 2008; Sanchez 1993; Alvarez 1987; Vigil 1997; Gamio 1969) and had several sources. For some it was a personal choice resulting from the pressures of cultural conformity and discrimination. One of my former students from the 1960s once expressed it in this way:

> "I didn't know you were Mexican." "I'm not, I'm Italian." I can actually remember saying this to my friends in school yards, dances and anywhere else the dreaded question would pop up. I tried as hard as possible not to be a Mexican, for that was the only way I thought I could be happy. Due to my light color and height I could easily pass for a white with the right clothes on. When the "surfer" craze was on I was right in there, wearing the latest surfer get-up I could find; but the funny thing was that I always felt so self-conscious, the fun was gone from acting this way. You must understand that at that age I never thought about who I really was, but just what I wanted to be, which changed from white fad to fad. In history class I remember being totally embarrassed when we studied Mexico. They would show films of old adobe huts with the mother patting tortillas and the father working in the fields. Everyone thought this was funny and I remember wishing that Mexico was all skyscrapers to show the others how great we really were.

Perhaps the most forceful factor stemmed from socioeconomic issues. Research on ethnic identity often stresses the telling effects of environmental forces and socioeconomic pressures on the psychological well-being of individuals undergoing cultural change (Polo and Lopez 2009; Suarez-Orozco and Suarez-Orozco 1994; Padilla 1995; Melville 1994). Frustration and discouragement often resulted when someone competently mastered his or her job but was paid lower wages than the others doing the same work or was passed over when the time for promotion arrived. Chicanos increasingly began to feel alienated as a result of the antagonism toward Mexican culture and the racial discrimination expressed by Anglos (De Leon and Griswold del Castillo 2006; Gonzales 2009; Weaver 1994; Moore and Pachon 1985).

The combination of forces interfered with the attainment of middle-class status for many. Worse yet, self-racism was exacerbated when members of the subservient culture accepted and internalized the cultural superiority views of the dominant group and began to believe that they were incapable of any meaningful action (Almaguer 2008; Menchaca 2001; Melville 1994). This accounted for much of the intragroup ethnic "sensitivity" to imagined and real slights, whether from language differences, surname changes, or a contrast in cultural lifestyles and customs (Bernal and Knight 1993; Rubel 1966). One novel, titled *Pocho*, a term for a Mexican American with Anglo mannerisms, emphasizes the concern with resisting self-hate when a father tells his son: "Promise me—that you will be true unto yourself, unto what you honestly believe is right. And, if it does not stand in your way, do not ever forget that you are Mexican" (Villarreal 1970:169).

As mentioned before, a strong contributor to this self-hate was the social snubbing one received because of racial appearance. It was particularly offensive to those who had learned the new culture and were prepared to contribute but were unable to change their race or appearance. Of course, some elements within American society challenged such ethnocentric practices. For example, anthropologists were among those who advocated "cultural relativism," that is, a belief that each world culture is intrinsically worthy of respect and appreciation, and that race is strictly a social construct. Also, many humanitarian people and organizations accepted those who were ethnically different and sometimes offered aid in their defense.

In addition to the discrimination experienced on an individual basis, discrimination against Mexican Americans as a group also contributed to and exacerbated the situation. Law enforcement personnel, for instance, often mistreated and physically abused Mexican Americans because they lived in the barrio or colonia community (Rios 2011; Escobar 1999). It was fairly common for the police to stop any Mexican for questioning, without cause or provocation (Vigil 1988; U.S. Commission on Civil Rights 1970). Residence in an area considered to have a high crime rate meant the increased possibility of police questioning and perhaps harassment. One former Los Angeles police chief was frank about it: "Police deployment is heaviest in minority sections of the city because, based on statistical reasons [the police chief] believes it to be a fact that racial minority groups commit more crime" (Morales 1972:48). While this occurred mainly in the low-income areas, it also frequently occurred in "better" sections of the city, especially if someone appeared out of place in an upscale neighborhood.

New Syncretism: Pachucos

Mexican Americans knew they were not accepted in many parts of town and so created their own world and tried to make it as self-sufficient as possible (Monroy 2008; McWilliams 1990[1968]). Thus was born a unique, defensive, and creative reaction to marginality. A new culture was invented to soften the confusion. No doubt this syncretic process began earlier, and the most easily recognizable example is with cattle ranching, which was a blend of Northern Mexican ranchero culture with Anglo-American innovations (Weber 2009; Paredes 1978, 1993). However, the syncretic cultural variant that sprang up in the 1930s and 1940s following large-scale Mexican immigration was especially significant. It was a step, perhaps an unsteady one, toward what later became known as Chicano culture (Velez-I. 1996; Barker 1972).

Pachucos was the name given to this generation of Mexicans who attended Anglo schools in large numbers (*pachucas* were the females of this generation and lifestyle) (Ramirez 2009). Their lifestyle was innovative. Some observers criticized this pattern as an ostentatious variant of the zoot-suit style (the zoot suit is discussed below) of that time, but with a decidedly Mexican turn (Alvarez 2008). Unjustly perceiving the pachucos as rebels and outlaws, many observers neglected to consider the cultural-conflict aspects of their predicament. Pachucos wanted neither to integrate into American culture nor to become Mexican again. It has been said that a pachuco's "whole being is sheer negative impulse, a tangle of contradictions, an enigma. Even his very name is enigmatic" (Paz 1961:14). Others, while not championing the pachucos' cause, expressed a more sympathetic view: It was racial segregation, economic exploitation, and cultural insensitivity that thwarted Mexican integration into American society. Pachuco youth were forged out of this tense, uneven cultural experience (Ruiz 1993; Sanchez 1993; Sanchez 1974).

Much of what became recognized as *pachuquismos* (pachuco inventions) was in many instances *pochismos*—chopped up English or Spanish, or simple word mixing (Galarza 1971). Still, the style became widespread, because pachucas and pachucos strove to make something good out of a bad situation. The style seemed to resonate with youth who identified with the feeling and attitude then emerging, as it eventually spread to different regions of the Southwest. Tensions between home and school were the main source for these developments. The young student was caught in a cultural squeeze between school measures to induce students to adopt Anglo traits and home instruction to retain Mexican customs (Valencia 2002; Barker 1972). Rather than accept this state of confusion, many drew from both cultures to form a new one. Pachuco language symbolizes this trend. English was Hispanicized and Spanish was Anglicized, as these words attest: *Ay te watcho* (I'll be seeing you), *chante* (shanty), *daime* (dime), *brecas* (brakes), *bote* (jail, "can" translated into Spanish), and *ganga* (gang) (Griffith 1948). In Texas there evolved a Tex-Mex argot, often created by adding a Spanish sound at the beginning or end of an English word (*cookiar, watchiar, parkiar, marketa,* and so on); Anglos in close contact with Mexicans along the border region have adopted some of this style (Alvarez 1995), but Spanish-speakers are usually more pressured to adapt to English.

Other pachuco characteristics involved dress, manners, and social attitudes, for pachucos took pride in their creations. For example, the zoot suit (a suit that the hip urban crowd wore in the 1940s) became the pachuco uniform, with male and female versions (Alvarez 2008; Ramirez 2009). It is interesting that the modern version of the pachuco, the low-riding cholo, has also developed a peculiar lifestyle, much of which is borrowed from the pachuco innovators. However, the cholos' situation is noticeably different from that of the 1940s generation. Some have fashioned or adopted debilitating cultural patterns, including much more frequent drug use and gang killings that became widespread in the 1960s and 1970s (Vigil 1988, 2003).

The pachuco adaptation was an attempt to resolve the implicit contradictions of two cultural worlds. When a "critical mass" of second-generation Mexican Americans emerged in the 1940s, a presence was established to carry culture change and acculturation to another level (Macias 2008). Many of the pachuco generation escaped the worst effects of marginality and, as a result, became fairly stable bilinguals. Furthermore, there was a long history behind the pachuco. The pachuco dialect, for example, although it included Hispanicized English, Anglicized Spanish, and invented words in Nahuatl and Archaic Spanish, was mainly made up of Calo—Spanish gypsy slang, supposedly popularized by bullfighters. Although the pachucos and their creations were castigated and stigmatized for their behavior—for they conformed neither to Mexican nor to Anglo-American cultural standards—a generation later, many observers changed their opinion and pointed out the significance of this generation (Sanchez 1993; M. T. Garcia 1989). Luis Alvarez offers a revisionist interpretation of the style and era: "Zoot suiters in Los Angeles, New York, and elsewhere, however, did not always accept being kept in their places. They challenged their own dehumanization and creatively found ways to claim dignity, much as defense workers, social activists, and many other Americans did" (2008:235).

Separatism

There were other cultural adaptive responses. Except in isolated areas such as certain northern reaches of New Mexico or south Texas, there has always been a tendency for some to defiantly challenge the U.S. presence in the Southwest. Thus, in a decidedly self-conscious manner, some Mexican Americans took a separatist approach, turning their backs on assimilation, acculturation, marginality, and syncretism, especially if they could not handle the pressure or refused to accept the burdens of cultural conflict. Separatism entailed either returning to Mexico (Vigil 1974) or promoting the reconquest of the Southwest. Separatist initiatives were used throughout the twentieth century by those who advocated an aggressive, militant stand against the Anglo system. To the south, in Mexico, peasants had fought for justice in the 1910 Revolution. Struggles for justice, however, were not confined to Mexico, as the Southwest was perking with political activity (Monroy 1999; Gomez-Quinones 1994a). During World War I a group of Mexican Americans, led by a barber, formulated the San Diego Plan (named for a small town in Texas) (Gomez-Quinones 1994a; Webb 1935). This plan, albeit grandiose, aimed to overthrow the United States government and advocated the return of all territories once belonging to Mexico and freedom and land for similarly oppressed American Indians, blacks, and Asians.

Another separatist scheme, the Sinarquista movement, was more widespread, especially in California. During World War II the Union Nacional Sinarquista, a group of political activists, supported an Axis victory, with the goal of regaining sovereignty over the Southwest. There were two thousand members in the United States by 1942. Active groups existed in Southern California and Texas communities (McWilliams 1990[1968]). Despite the "falangist" (Spanish fascist party based in Mexico), right-wing orientation of the

Sinarquistas, Mexican Americans of various political persuasions rallied behind this "nationalist" program; again, the organizational efforts involved more "talk" than action, but it, too, reflected the hidden resentment some Mexicans had toward the United States. A further reminder of this historical memory is that until 1943, the maps used in some Mexican schools had the words "Territory temporarily in the hands of the United States" printed over the United States Southwest. It was no coincidence that these two thrusts transpired during World War I and World War II, when the United States was most vulnerable (Griswold del Castillo 2008).

Mexican Background: Effect of Time and Place on Culture and Identity

Time and place issues make understanding Mexican Americans a very complicated task. As Mexican natives living in or immigrating to the United States became overwhelmed by American forces, many antagonisms and resentments festered and set the future tone of Mexican–American relations. As noted, the transition from indigenous to peasant to immigrant charts a macrohistorical evolution and transformation of nearly 500 years to create different cultural currents. According to a 1930 study, three basic cultural traditions were prevalent in Mexico at that time: modern European, indigenous, and mestizo (a mixture of the first two). The indigenous and especially the mestizo traditions accompanied most Mexican immigrants to the United States (Weaver 1994; Gamio 1969). As a result, the changeover from an indigenous or culturally mixed background to a "modern" way of living was very abrupt and of multiple dimensions (Gamio 1969)—tantamount to a horizontal (moving to the United States) and vertical (facing urban life) adjustment simultaneously. The profound problems that accompany cultural adaptation were softened somewhat as early immigrants usually settled in rural areas, but by 1930, 57.5 percent of the total number of immigrants were living in urban areas (Romo 1983; Sanchez 1993). This trend continued and strengthened throughout the 1940s (J. H. Alvarez 1973).

Time and place factors figure very prominently in an examination of these processes (Vigil 2001; N. L. Gonzales 1967; Moore and Pachon 1985). Mexican immigrants brought a culture that reflected their time (historical or cultural tradition) and place (regional variations). Their new cultural life was strongly influenced by where they settled—what state in the Southwest, or in a rural or urban area—and how long they lived in the United States—generational distance from Mexico. It is also fair to state that amount of time in the United States affected and usually improved their occupational mobility (Knouse, Rosenfeld, and Culbertson 1992; Sanchez 1993; Gomez-Quinones 1994b; R. Alvarez 1973). Similarly, aspirations of social mobility and increases in income would operate to alter the cultural adaptation strategy.

One way to determine the changing strategies is to look at cultural habits of the past and perhaps examine the motives behind a person's chosen ethnic label (Menchaca 2001; Melville 1994; Bernal and Knight 1993). For example, two important Mexican cultural traditions are compadrazgo and, to a lesser degree, machismo, a topic of extreme importance in considering questions of gender (Telles and Ortiz 2008; Chavira 1994). Machismo has been discussed already, so a brief comment will suffice. The changing work pattern caused by industrialization and urbanization revised this cultural trait, as it has done for other gender patterns. Women have played important roles under these technological and lifestyle changes, doing factory work as well as excelling in other occupations generated by the industrial economy. In addition, urban problems have added to the diminishing effects of machismo. In former times, the patriarch, for good or bad, dominated and maintained stability in the family. In the city, where unemployment and street crime often undermined the male role, many women took over as household breadwinners and household heads (Mirande 1997; Moore 1991). Thus, for both positive and negative reasons, gender expectations and roles were changed (Mirande 1997; Chavira 1994; Ruiz 1993; Del Castillo 1990), and eventually women began to challenge the abusive and detrimental effects of machismo.

Likewise, compadrazgo—an intense bond of cooperation and friendship among parents and godparents—was affected by cultural changes. As Mexican Americans more fully integrated into urban middle-class culture, the nuclear family structure became reordered (Grebler, Moore, and Guzman 1970; Telles and Ortiz 2008; Moore and Pachon 1985; Foley et al. 1977). Compadrazgo has been both disparaged as impeding adaptation to American culture (Briggs, Fogel, and Schmidt 1977), especially in an industrial economy that values individualism and personal achievement, and championed as an aid for collective survival (Grebler, Moore, and Guzman 1970). Time and place as well as generation have certainly altered this extended family orientation (Alvarez 1994). However, it appears that it has remained an important part of Chicano lifeways anyway. In this context, an open, fluid family network works as social capital where respect and devotion are enhanced for a person who is dutiful and helpful.

Cultural alterations and revampments became the common lot of Mexicans, sometimes a painless affair and in other moments a traumatic episode, depending on the circumstances. The factors of time and place were operating here. Researchers have found that the amount of time spent in the United States has a definite effect on cultural adaptation, especially because of discriminatory experiences (Almaguer 2008; Weaver 1994). Studies on self-image find that Mexican immigrants often have a more positive perception of themselves than do Mexican Americans (Suarez-Orozco and Suarez-Orozco 1994; Vigil 1997); this may be true despite the low self-image they might have in Mexico if they are dark mestizo or Indian. Although acculturation can be a means for an individual to escape a situation of domination, it doesn't guarantee status equality. Particularly noteworthy is how Chicanos were able to retain or maintain a semblance of their past culture as they learned the new one (Gibson, Gandara, and Koyomo 2006).

Not only is "time" in the United States a factor, but the time element is instrumental in Mexico as well (Beezley and MacLachlan 2009). Compadrazgo and machismo patterns definitely shift from generation to generation (De Anda 1996; Vigil 1997; Moore and Pachon 1985; Grebler, Moore, and Guzman 1970). Today, Mexican compadrazgo, machismo, and other aspects of Mexican culture generally are different from what they were even 20 years ago. In part, this is a result of evolutionary change, one that began as a by-product of the 1910 Revolution and, more importantly, the globalization of the economy—as economic exchanges and networks are often a precursor to cultural ones. Mexicans, especially at the middle-class level, have been increasingly abandoning their old traditions in favor of new ones created by their desire to become more like Americans (Zolov 1999; Weaver 1994; Penalosa 1973).

Acculturated Mexican Americans showed a range of cultural responses in the Stage IV time period (Varzally 2008; Vigil 1997; Trueba 1991). The ethnic label they selected was often indicative of their cultural style and orientation, as noted earlier, although generation, language usage, and other factors were also important components of cultural style. Time and place obviously played a role, but Anglicization tended to occur when there was the predisposition to change and a lack of barriers to prevent it. Thus, some "Spanish-appearing" individuals might identify more with white people, as the latter might be more receptive and open to them as members of the European phenotypes. Other prompters to assimilate might include shame of culture, avoidance of extended family members, and desire to get ahead. It has also been noted that growing up outside a Mexican neighborhood can aid access, exposure, and identification with Anglo culture (Vigil 1997; Penalosa 1973). In other words, when Mexicans moved geographically closer to Anglos, they tended to select a more Anglo ethnic identity. Thus, it is reasonable to assume that ethnic identification can be tied to cultural practices (Bernal and Knight 1993; Romanucci-Ross and De Vos 1995).

In the case of marginal individuals, the variance is much more unpredictable. This is the case particularly during the cultural transitional phase of familiarity with and integration into Anglo culture, which typically occurs sometime between the first and second generations. Some people never quite anchor themselves in the dominant culture nor do they totally remove themselves from the native culture. Without a set pattern, these people might alternate between being extremely Mexican at certain times and being very Anglo at other times. A subtle tension appears to have developed in their minds: sometimes Mexican, then Anglo, then a fleeting mixture of the two, and finally perhaps neither one (i.e., anomie, normlessness). *Choloization* is what the author has called it elsewhere (Vigil 1988, 1997), and a whole range of ethnic labels reflect it.

Strengths and Weaknesses of Mexican Culture

In spite of the inherent pitfalls in cultural transformations or the overall materially poor life of Mexican Americans, there remain some valuable cultural features. It has been suggested that Anglos could learn many things from Mexicans, especially "to do with the business of how to live life better" and also, perhaps, how to live life better with death in the offing (Diaz-Guerrero 1978:306). In general, Anglos tend to avoid thoughts of death, knowing that it is there waiting but not wanting to think about it. In contrast, Mexican Americans have long accepted the presence of death and, as a result, have lived each day as if it were their last; *Dia de los Muertos* is just one of the celebratory events associated with this belief. This could be a legacy from the Indian belief in the dual nature of life whereby one extreme cannot be understood, much less lived, unless its opposite is also embraced. A contributing factor most certainly is a life of poverty, which inclines Mexican Americans to live their lives more fully and enjoy the small things.

The ways work and recreation are thought of and conducted are worthy of examination. It has been said that "Anglos work full-time and enjoy life part-time, and Mexican Americans work part-time and enjoy life full-time." As noted, Mexicans have a strong work ethic (Briggs 1973); in contrast to the Puritan ethic, however, Mexicans view work as a means of survival rather than as a value in itself. Material objects are also viewed as necessities rather than as ends in themselves (Murillo 1976).

Many observers have remarked on the frequency of parties in Chicano life, but few have noted the religious nature of many such affairs, with an almost "complete form of communication with the spiritual world and with others involv[ing] the mind, body, and soul" (Najera-Ramirez 1994:328; see also Weaver 1994). This might be an inheritance from pre-Columbian times or from religious fiestas of the Spanish colonial period (Kluckholm and Strodtbeck 1961). In any case, when someone arranges a baptism, birthday party, wedding, or funeral wake, a great deal of effort goes into ensuring that the guests can drink and eat to their heart's content. Although this custom has been criticized as too ostentatious for "poor people," it continues in a somewhat altered form. Similar customs are practiced among working-class people in other parts of the world. The various elements and symbols in the *Fiestas Patrias* (patriotic holidays), such as food, folk costumes, music, dances, the Cura Hidalgo, the Virgen de Guadalupe, the Grito de Dolores, and *charreadas* (vaquero rodeos) serve to reinforce and affirm Mexican cultural identity (Melville 1978; Najera-Ramirez 1994; Sands 1993; Pena 1985).

Besides the symbolic significance, such events have a sound economic and historical basis, stemming from both indigenous and peasant influences. The habit of sharing material resources helps other family members and friends even if it might take away from the already meager belongings of the immediate family (Murillo 1976). At the same time, however, it reinforces bonds with others and builds up what is sometimes called "social capital," that is, an assurance that others will try to assist you when you need help (Velez-I. 2010). Mesoamerican peasant Indians still practice economic redistribution through civil-religious ceremonies (Rus, Hernandez Castillo, and Mattiace 2003; Foster 1988). For example, whole communities may celebrate for a week or more, commemorating the pueblo's patron saint. The fiesta typically involves parading the saint's image as well as feasting and dancing, with well-off constituents playing prominent roles. An affluent person extends an open invitation to the community to share in his good fortune as a demonstration of community involvement and dedication. This is more a sharing than a showing off of wealth and is a different way to attain status. Great pleasure is derived from providing guests with enjoyable relief from their daily, arduous work.

The above are examples of positive traits, despite the criticism and negative stereotyping some have directed at them. In contrast to the positive features discussed above, a long history of oppression and domination by separate forces has generated many destructive Chicano cultural features, such as joblessness and poverty. "East Los Angeles had become the major entry point for immigrants. . . . Unemployment stood at double the county average and one-quarter of the area's residents lived below the poverty level" (Bauman 2008:91). Poverty especially has helped to produce generations of poorly educated, low-skilled, unemployed, and marginal people. Cultural imperialism on the part of white America is primarily responsible for their plight (Paredes 1978).

Education: An Aspect of Cultural Imperialism

Barriers to the acquisition of American culture were nowhere more rigid and detrimental than in schools and in the whole educational system (Valencia 2010). Schools are next in importance to the family as a socializing agent, and for newcomers from a peasant, rural background, schools are *the* gateway to the dominant culture. How the children of these immigrants have been received, integrated, accommodated, and cultivated educationally remains a dark page in American history. Separate schooling for Mexicans and Americans, although not legally institutionalized, has long been the custom in many southern California cities (see Alvarez 1987, on which the film *The Lemon Grove Incident* is based). The fact that these "Mexicans" are American citizens does not seem to be of importance (Gonzalez 1990). This historical pattern is true for most of the Southwest (Valencia 1991; Grebler, Moore, and Guzman,

1970; U.S. Commission on Civil Rights 1971). Mexican Americans have for many years completed less schooling than any ethnic group of Americans except American Indians. In 1960, Anglos averaged 12 years of school; blacks, 10 years; and Mexican Americans, eight years (Grebler, Moore, and Guzman 1970; see Telles and Ortiz 2008 for an update of the Grebler et al. book). Furthermore, it is clear that many more Mexican Americans start school than finish it, which means that parents send their children, but, unlike past times when young people purposely left school to help support their family, the schools cause them to drop out, or worse, push or kick them out (Valenzuela 1999; Valencia 2010). Mexican Americans themselves have often been blamed for their learning deficiencies, under the "cultural deficiency" rationale (Buriel 1984). Some researchers have suggested that Mexican-American children are mentally inferior to American children of the same age (Sanchez 1967). However, these early "scientific" reports failed to factor in how racial barriers and attitudes and socioeconomic realities are related to educational performance (Valencia 1991; Gamio 1969).

In conjunction with other factors, cultural imperialist programs have hindered Chicano educational advancement; the Anglo's sense of cultural superiority was a factor in the post-1848 period but accelerated and reigned supreme during the first decades of immigration in the twentieth century. For example, after arriving at school, a young child's first lessons were in English, and if he or she spoke Spanish inside or outside the classroom, the child was typically scolded (Briggs 1973). Often, students who spoke Spanish were threatened with having their mouths washed out with soap; many stopped talking to avoid such treatment. Schools continually refused to recognize that Mexicans were culturally different and so needed educational programs that were suited to these differences (Sanchez 1967). This was not an unusual practice, since Americanization programs have affected most ethnically different people (Gonzales 1990; Sanchez 1966). Beginning in the late nineteenth century, Americanization efforts were a common educational practice in cities filled with immigrants.

Many children were left behind academically because they could not understand the learning tasks given in English. The problem with Mexican-American children was not the fact that they spoke Spanish, but that most teachers in the school system could not understand the children's language or their culture. This linguistic and cultural divide made authorities think that students were mentally retarded, so they were placed in special classes (Valencia 1991). By ignoring different cultural standards and educational needs, schools were adding to the confusion and disorientation of the students who already were lost in this new world. The words of the student quoted earlier on marginality elaborate on this problem:

> I remember in the fifth grade studying Spanish and when we had to do
> class conversations out loud it was always traumatic for me. Most of the

kids in my class were Anglo, so when I spoke Spanish I was careful not to have an accent, so I would not be laughed at. Perhaps I should have showed more will power, but it's awfully damned hard when even the teacher snickers. This kind of experience gave me a shyness I have never been able to get rid of. Instead of mastering the language, it was, instead, taken away from me and replaced by the knowledge that Columbus discovered America and that Indians were savages.

Countless incidents of this nature have been cited throughout the Southwest to underscore the institutional insensitivity and damaging nature of such mistreatment (U.S. Civil Rights Commission 1971; Valencia 1991; Parsons 1971).

An integral aspect of cultural imperialism was the ethnocentric attitude of teachers. It is important to note that most teachers felt they were helping the children learn American culture, even if it meant disparaging Mexican culture. This misguided and insensitive attitude infected the classroom atmosphere and promoted a poor self-image among the students (Valencia 1991). But matters did not end there, for many teachers harbored other feelings and showed them in insults and physical abuse. How could anyone learn when made to feel slow, dirty, and deficient because someone else thought it was true? The imperialist basis of these attitudes was often explicit:

> A teacher, asked why she had called on "Johnny" to lead five Mexicans in orderly file out of a schoolroom, explained: "His father owns one of the big farms in the area and . . . one day he will have to know how to handle the Mexicans." Another teacher, following the general practice of calling on the Anglos to help Mexican pupils recite in class, said in praise of the system: "It draws them (the Americans) out and gives them a feeling of importance." (Parsons 1965:219)

Socioeconomic forces dictated the above treatment, but cultural insensitivity was a part of it, too. Other educational areas were similarly affected by this attitude. There has been a gross underrepresentation of Mexican Americans among teachers. In the Southwest, about 17 percent of students in the 1970s were Mexican American, but only 4 percent of their teachers were Mexican American. In addition, the curriculum emphasized the perspectives of the dominant group and denigrated those of minorities. For instance, public school history books often ignored the Mexican–American War and the Treaty of Guadalupe Hidalgo, and this omission gave the impression that the Southwest was always a part of the United States. Many critics have questioned the lopsided nature of this "quest for truth" and what it does to the identity formation of a child. To complicate matters, coming from a different historical tradition, Mexican Americans found it difficult to identify with dominant cultural themes.

> I'm sitting in my history class,
> The instructor commences rapping,

I'm in my U.S. history class,
and I'm on the verge of napping.

The Mayflower landed on Plymouth Rock.
Tell me more! Tell me more!
Thirteen colonies were settled.
I've heard it all before.

What did he say?
Dare I ask him to reiterate?
Oh why bother.
It sounded like he said,
George Washington's my father.

I'm reluctant to believe it,
I suddenly raise my mano.
If George Washington's my father,
Why wasn't he Chicano?

The preceding verse by Richard Olivas (included in Romano-V. 1968) shows that at least some students were aware of the discrepancies in cultural cues and images being fed to them; more militant students would question why monocultural education is useful if we are a nation of immigrants.

Those who overcame the learning barriers were usually very bright or lucky and often felt that they had to turn their backs on their culture (Rodriguez 1988). Notwithstanding these successes, there were additional obstacles that further restricted the development of their innate potential. Poor counseling, ability tracking, and the biased attitudes and behavior of other students toward them are some of the hindrances (Valencia 2002). For example, thousands of students have been counseled into vocational or trade courses, even if they were capable of professional career training. Two notable graduates of Roosevelt High School in East Los Angeles, The Honorable Edward Roybal, who served as a Democratic congressman in Washington, D.C., and Dr. Julian Nava, who was a Harvard professor and a diplomat, were successful despite counseling advice to pursue a career as a body-and-fender worker and an auto mechanic, respectively. This advice, unfortunately, is rooted in the centuries-old belief that Mexicans (and Indians) are "good with their hands" and nothing else. One fact that allowed these practices to continue, making them seem reasonable on the part of the dominant group, was that few Chicanos had risen to higher status positions in the 1960s.

In time, as for millions of other members of minority groups that have gone through generational change, improved learning levels came with familiarization with the Anglo culture. However, what sets Mexican Americans apart from the others is the almost steady influx of Mexicans into the United States throughout the mid-nineteenth and twentieth centuries. This regular "human infusion" replenished and regenerated fading Mexican cultural attributes; that is, Mexican culture spans the generations because there has been constant cultural immigration to remind even the assimilated ones of the Mexican presence. The same cannot be said of many of the European ethnic groups who immigrated to the U.S. in several waves, which ended in about the 1920s.

Color: Inter- and Intragroup Racism

Ethnocentrism

The Chicano experience in the United States unfolded in the context of a society preoccupied with racial distinctions. Critics of the Mexican–American War noted the racist implications of the conquest (Acuna 2000), and soon thereafter the United States was almost dissolved by a war focused on slavery. A century after the Civil War, "people of color" were still subject to discrimination and social, economic, and even legal sanctions against their progress. This situation, of course, was not unique to the United States.

In the aftermath of the 1846 war until the 1910 Mexican Revolution, conditions and practices of racism permeated Anglo–Mexican relationships. The Mexican was considered an Indian, looked the part, and was held in low esteem just like the American Indian (Menchaca 1993). Mexican racial attitudes and practices from the colonial era still played a role in this new context; one faced a double dose of racism if he or she was Indian racially and Mexican (Spanish!) culturally (Vigil and Lopez 2004). This reality persisted for many decades after the 1910 Mexican Revolution; however, some profound and far-reaching changes were introduced, and they continued to ebb and flow for most of the twentieth century. Mexican immigration simultaneously increased the population and regenerated Mexican culture in many major cities of the Southwest. Faced with this steady influx and changes in the economy that led to stagnating conditions for wage workers, many Anglo-Americans became angry and blamed Mexicans for the economy and the cultural problems of the nation (Gonzales 2009; Melville 1994). Thus, the embers of past racism were kept alive and fanned into an intense antiforeign, anti-immigrant sentiment, diverting attention from major macrostructural changes: for example, why the U.S. had such a major need for immigrant labor.

Behind all these developments was ethnocentrism, an attitude that exists in all cultures, but operates at its most dangerous levels within societies that have a subordinate minority population.

> The belief that one's own customs, language, religion, and physical characteristics are better or more "natural" than those of others is termed ethnocentrism. Minor and minute cultural and physical differences may often be

given exclusive attention to prove the inferiority of another people. (Wagley and Harris 1958:258)

A cultural (and often a racial) group attitude of feeling good about oneself can represent a benign form of ethnocentrism. But when one moves to block or stop the movement or freedom of another person or group of people, then it is malignant ethnocentrism.

Ethnic minorities in the United States have encountered a type of malignant ethnocentrism that has frequently turned into racism. After socioeconomic changes rearrange the social structure, and cultural justifications form as barriers to status equality, then racial prejudice and discrimination ensure that a superior/inferior understanding and relationship is solidified.

Although the experience varied for each ethnic minority in the United States, there were some clear similarities. Emphasis on racial features is one of them. Another is the use of racial standards as a justification for economic exploitation. At first the goal was simple—one human group benefiting at the expense of another—but it soon grew, for ethnocentrism finds many avenues to relegate and maintain status and distance between groups. It should be understood, however, that such attitudes and actions to gain and maintain economic advantages are not consciously formulated. Rather, the rationale is probably developed subconsciously to assuage the dominant group's conscience; it is a subtle form of racism, or "aversive" racism, that still affects the deeper feelings, if not the behavior, of those on the "inferior" side of the ledger (Lopez 2011; Dovidio et al. 1992).

Racist practices were initiated in the colonial period, and these customs evolved to be elaborated upon and exacerbated in the modern period. Many downtrodden people carry racist perceptions of themselves that are formulated through a series of contacts with dominant group members (Varzally 2008). Adding to all the barriers that Mexicans struggled to overcome was the U.S. government's decision to get tough on immigration.

> Legislation—laws that made unlawful entry a felony and lifted the statute of limitations on deportations—not only criminalized illegal entry but also racialized such behavior as "Mexican." Illegal, in other words, became associated with Mexicans, regardless of their citizenship or immigration status. (Varzally 2008:28)

Roots of Prejudice and Discrimination

Prejudicial attitudes gave rise to discriminatory behavior. To anchor Mexicans in the lowest positions, the dominant group prejudged their behavior negatively (prejudice) and set up social barriers (poor-quality schools, housing, and so on) to impede their social mobility (discrimination). Thus, discrimination is prejudice turned into action. In a very short time, dominant group members believed Mexicans were so obviously inferior that their sub-ordinate status was really of their own making. Mexican workers were seen as irresponsible, lazy, and undependable. There was, therefore, a ready associa-tion between Mexicans and menial labor (Monroy 1999; Simmons 1973). Such imagery, similar to that used with regard to black slaves (and later sharecrop-pers), was widely disseminated in American society at the time of the Mexi-can–American War. This type of racism extended to the point of denying Mexican Americans citizenship (Menchaca 1993).

Even white ethnic groups have had trouble overcoming barriers that for a long time prevented their advancement. Mexicans, however, have had to wait even longer. Indeed, the problem was a dual one for Mexicans: The dominant group believed in their inferiority and rejected them, and many Mexicans learned to agree with the dominant group's verdict and internalized a negative self-image (Bernal and Knight 1993; Phinney 1995). Few people understood that racial ideologies originated with the colonial encounter of Europeans with people from Africa, America, and Asia. Europeans justified their political and economic domination on the grounds that they were dealing with inferior races (Frazier 1957). As one observer remarked, "Color is neutral; it is the mind that gives it meaning" (Bastide 1968:34). Unfortunately, this meaning has been far more sinister for Mexicans and other people of color than it has for Euro-pean white ethnics (largely Eastern and Southern Europeans) (Varzally 2008).

Class relationships were at the root of racial policies in the countries that emerged in the Americas, "particularly those with capitalist economies" (Mel-ville 1994:88). Such policies eventually generated sociopsychological prob-lems, including poor self-esteem, self-hatred, and marginality. In addition to class and cultural difficulties, the strain of gaining social acceptance made Mexicans in the United States work harder and longer than average U.S. citi-zens. The Mexican experience was an attenuated continuation of a U.S. colo-nial pattern that began with the Indians. For most, it was also a persistence of the discrimination suffered under the ethnic elite of Mexico. During the Mexi-can–American War, Senator John C. Calhoun said:

> "I know further, sir, that we have never dreamt of incorporating into our union any but the Caucasian race—the free white race. To incorporate Mex-ico, would be the very first instance of the kind of incorporating an Indian race; for more than half of the Mexicans are Indians, and the other is com-posed chiefly of mixed tribes." (Weber 1973:135; see also Menchaca 2001)

The historical sequence and context of color discrimination against Chicanos thus began with subduing the Indians and subsequently included the impor-tation of African slaves (Restall 2005; Vigil and Lopez 2004), the inclusion of Mexicans after the 1846 war, the enticement of cheap Chinese labor from Asia, and large-scale southeastern European immigration in the late-nineteenth century (Varzally 2008).

"Pigmentocracy"

Anglos often insisted that a light-skinned Mexican was Spanish rather than Mexican. This was based on their conviction that Mexicans were very dark (Simmons 1973). Anglo feelings of superiority were so pernicious that only lighter-hued Mexicans might escape the worst effects of racism, and even "swarthy" Spaniards were looked down upon (Almaguer 2008). "The term 'racism' can be considered shorthand for the phrase 'pejorative social discrimination based on phenotypic (observable biological) characteristics'" (Melville 1994:92). According to Americo Paredes (1978), the late professor of folklore, the superiority syndrome is ethnocentrism perfected: a strong nationalist inclination that diminishes other people's sense of self-respect in many ways, such as always making the "good guys" Anglos and the "bad guys" Mexicans (and other people of color) in motion pictures (Noriega 1992).

Although this was the pattern of racism, it must be underscored that many American leaders and groups fought against this practice. The civil rights struggles in the United States have generally found progressive elements leading the way in this regard. The 1964 Civil Rights Act is an example of this type of striving for equality. Nonetheless, such hard-won victories were few and far between for most of our history, as the majority group's attitudes remained mired in the past even as they toned down overt racism (Dovidio et al. 1992).

Cultural imperialism was easy to practice with racial cues, and once activated, the worst attitudes and behavior of the dominant group often emerged. Sometimes just hearing the ethnic group's language, as in the case of lighter Mexicans, would be enough of a catalyst. In large part these visual and linguistic "markers" are responsible for hindering Mexican entrance into the social mainstream of the United States. Often the degree of assimilation or white appearance of the minority-group member does not matter to the white middle class. A Mexican is still a Mexican no matter how refined in speaking English or stylishly dressed. In fact, in early legal cases, the interplay between physical appearance and cultural habits played havoc in the courts, and in one instance led to a strange ruling: "White Mexican students . . . could be segregated only if they did not speak English" (Menchaca 1993:598). The social and political environment thus cursed the Mexican in many ways (De Leon and Griswold del Castillo 2006).

Institutional Racism

Branding with prejudicial words and labels might affect any minority group, but in the case of Mexican Americans it was accompanied by stronger discriminatory actions. No doubt this began in the period after the Mexican–American War (1848), when anti-Mexican feelings were deeply entrenched. In time these feelings and actions became built into the structure of society. Thus, the "authorities"—law enforcement officers particularly, but others, too—did not wait for Mexicans to go wrong but acted precipitately to keep a tight rein on the population and asked questions afterward (Escobar 1999; Morales 1972). As in the earlier colonial confrontation, the struggle over resources—land, labor, and wealth—and "social power" (Melville 1994:97) was an important reason for this behavior.

Racist ideology, and later, institutions, operated to prevent Mexican acquisition and retention of land and wealth. Their poverty was then frequently used, in a vicious circle, to justify continued mistreatment. A Los Angeles police chief remarked that

> poor people who are of darker skin are under greater suspicion of committing crime—even more so if they communicate in a "foreign" language. . . . It seems just, however, to say that Mexicans are unmoral rather than immoral since they lack a conception of morals as understood in this country. Their housing conditions are bad, crime is prevalent, and their morals are a menace to our civilization. They are illiterate, ignorant and inefficient and have few firm religious beliefs. (Morales 1972:33)

Imagine how these words translated into attitudes and actions toward Mexicans on the part of the rank-and-file police officers, as reported not only in Los Angeles but also in other regions of the Southwest (Harris and Sadler 2004; U.S. Civil Rights Commission 1971).

Mexican-American efforts to obtain rights blocked by institutional racism had occasional success, especially in the celebrated cases involving segregated schools: The Lemon Grove (Alvarez 1987) and the *Mendez v. Westminster* cases (Strum 2010; Gonzalez 1990). For example, the *Mendez* case was instigated by situations such as this:

> The Vidaurri girls were light-skinned. The Mendez children, however, were visibly darker and, to the teacher, their last name was all too clearly Mexican. They would have to be taken to the "Mexican" school a few blocks away. Little Gonzalo Jr. would remember the teacher telling his aunt. "We'll take those," indicating the two Vidaurri girls, "but we won't take those three." "We were too dark," Gonzalo recalled. (Strum 2010:1)

Nevertheless, the well-structured program of suppression required only periodic supervision for maintenance (Simmons 1974). As mentioned earlier, schools and teachers were instruments that fostered this arrangement. Most other societal sectors were interwoven with racial standards that were implicitly or even explicitly aimed at the exclusion of ethnic minorities. Earlier generations of ethnic minorities who had learned these lessons socialized their children with a dose of second-class citizenship stories even before they might experience it themselves.

Public Barriers

Racism continued in social realms outside the school. The community swimming pool might be especially reserved for Mexicans and blacks on a set day. There were even reports that the pool was drained and refilled for white use for the remainder of the week; while this placated blind Anglo racists, it probably was a symbolic draining of a small proportion of the water. In addition, lighter-hued Mexicans might be welcomed on "regular" days if they could "pass." More often, it was a mixed affair, as this example shows: "In 1939, it was revealed that, although the swimming pool at Chaffey Junior College was used on an integrated basis during the academic year, when it was open to the general public during the summer, Chicanos were allowed to use it only on Mondays" (Acuna 2000).

A similar experience awaited Chicanos at the movie theater (Taylor 1934), where sometimes the front rows or whole balcony was known as the "Mexican" section (Menchaca 1995). One Texas town limited the types and amount of ice cream a minority person might buy. Even something as mundane as a haircut was touched by racism: In 1945, it was revealed in the U.S. Senate hearings that Chicanos from McCarney, Texas, had to travel 45 miles in order to get a haircut. Why? Two reasons: (1) Anglo barbers refused to cut their hair, and (2) Chicanos could not legally become barbers in McCarney (Guzman 1974). A Texas barber had earlier explained his understanding of this practice:

> "No, we don't wait on Mexicans here. They are dirty and have lice, and we would lose our white trade. The Mexicans also have venereal diseases, most of them, but of course some whites do, too. The Mexicans go to their own barber shop. The Negroes barber each other." (Taylor 1934:250; see also Almaguer 2008; Varzally 2008)

Reactions to Mistreatment

Social discrimination, along with inadequate education and unfair political practices, such as poll taxes and gerrymandering, built up a backlog of resentment among Chicanos. Many Chicanos lived with this reality and developed acute self-hatred. They had learned to despise their ethnicity and all that it entailed (Almaguer 2008; Moore and Pachon 1985). However, the resistance and resilience of many more are equally important.

It must be underscored that Chicano resistance as a reaction to racism erupted in the nineteenth century. It took the form of social banditry, social protests, and boycotts and has continued in different ways to the present. Some incidents were minor scrapes involving a handful of people, while others were major riots and disturbances where hundreds, even thousands participated (Monroy 2008; Mazon 1983). The so-called pachuco riots of the early

1940s in Los Angeles, one of several major race riots taking place in American cities at that time, is a modern example of this stand against racist persecution.

On that occasion Mexican Americans grouped together for defensive purposes, as the community was subjected to angry attacks by both authorities and civilians, and rioting continued for several days. Anglos confronted youth who wore the zoot suit, as younger Chicanos had begun to dress that way. Luis Alvarez says that "zoot suiters regenerated style, fashion, and wartime popular culture to make their lives more livable, meaningful, and dignified in the face of poverty, patriarchy, and violence, as well as discrimination in war industries" (2008:79). Originally, the zoot-suit dress and label applied across class and ethnic lines to all those who dressed in this particular style, but on this occasion, it became equated with Chicanos (Guzman 1974). At first, only "zoot-suit pachuco" types were beaten by armed mobs, then anyone Mexican, and finally any other easily recognizable people of color.

The attacks on members of the Chicano community met strong resistance and even counterattacks over several days. Despite the violence, however, there were no deaths associated with the strife (Mazon 1983). The authorities, overlooking the actions of the predominantly white mobs, tended to blame the entire episode on the Mexican Americans. Captain E. Duran Ayers, chief of the Foreign Relations Bureau (!) of the Los Angeles County Sheriff's Department, summed up the dominant public attitude toward the affair: "The biological basis is the main basis to work from. . . . This total disregard for human life has always been universal throughout the Americas among the Indian population" (Morales 1972:41). The events that occurred during this episode showed, if nothing else, that the Chicanos were not docile people and would fight back when pushed. Chicanos salvaged a certain amount of pride and dignity from this, and Anglo authorities grudgingly afforded a new respect for a group that stood up for its rights (Mirande 1987). Furthermore, the episode sparked the formation of a number of youth social programs, mostly from the Catholic Church, one of which was the Catholic Youth Organization (CYO).

Returning Mexican veterans from World Wars I and II reinforced the battle against racist institutions (Allsup 1982; Melville 1994). They were dissatisfied with first-class citizenship on the front lines and second-class citizenship at home. Mexican Americans were the United States' most highly decorated ethnic minority (Allsup 1982; Morin 1966), and they resented being on the receiving end of discrimination. Consequently, they steadily challenged the racist policies that often characterized real estate operators, restaurants, movie theaters, and other establishments.

Institutional discrimination was reinforced by the proliferation of derogatory images of Chicanos and by labels such as "greaser" and "Mecskin." One early book about Mexican travel had these words: "There are two things I

Zooters and sailors battle.

could never understand, why the Lord made mosquitoes and Mexicans" (Stowell 1974:116). Claims of superior status are often accompanied by a vocabulary of insult to flaunt and fortify the power that dominant groups have amassed. The early labels were joined by "beaners," "wetbacks," "chili chokers," "tacos," "chukes," "half- breeds," and many others (Almaguer 2008; Kirk 1979). Ironically, poorer whites who lived near Mexicans, often sharing similar poverty conditions, were usually the ones who used the labels. Although they were just as destitute, they felt relieved to have someone below them, a practice that was also present in certain areas of the South, between poor whites and blacks.

There were also more sophisticated ways of negatively portraying an ethnic minority. These carried more weight because social-science writers and other academicians, who have since purged their remarks, created them to rationalize the experiences of the ethnically defined underclass. Mexicans were described as lazy, dumb, dirty, bloodthirsty savages, immoral, breed-like-rats, culturally deficient, and a host of other demeaning stereotypes (Martinez 1973). One needed only to look to movies and television programs to document such stereotyping. Mexican (as well as Indian) characters were portrayed in a lower-status jobs such as gardener, waiter/waitress, babysitter, and janitor, or in underworld roles such as bandit, terrorist, or gang member. If given a higher status, it might have been as a dictator or leader of a global crime syndicate, and for females, as the sinister femme fatale. Moviegoers far removed from real Mexicans came away thinking the worst of the people (Noriega 1992).

Similarly disparaging images were fed daily to national television audiences. Misinformation on racial and cultural characteristics was common. Advertising especially showed very demeaning images, and viewers learned how to be racist even without knowing any Mexicans (Martinez 1973). One blatant example was a deodorant commercial that depicted Mexicans as reeking of body odor.

Reverse Racists

Chicanos have over time adjusted to this treatment and fashioned a self-protective shell to become "reverse racists," even toward other racial minorities. Put-down words such as "gringo," "paddy," "*gavacho*" (meaning foreigner, used initially toward the French), and "*bolillo*" (a hard-crusted loaf of white bread) were hurled back at whites. More sophisticated Chicanos labeled Anglos as aggressive, competitive, money hungry, exploitative, and insensitive. This racist attitude was probably one of the adaptive mechanisms Mexican Americans used to survive with some self-dignity (Almaguer 2008). In contrast, the lower classes in Mexico are much more tolerant of those who are racially different, possibly because that segment of the Mexican population was racially mixed. Lest we forget, even after immigration to the United States, intragroup racism persisted among Mexicans, with the darker-hued people still considered and treated shabbily.

Toward that end, intragroup relationships have also been affected by generational distance from Mexico. To some degree, Mexicans in the United States have mistreated and verbally abused Mexican immigrants on the basis of cultural attributes, calling them *"chuntaros," "mojados"* (wetbacks; or wet-packs for children wearing knapsacks), "T.J.s" (from Tijuana, and suggesting riffraff border residents), and so on. On occasion, Mexican-American leaders have made an effort to reduce this animosity (Weber 1973). According to Julian Samora, economic causes lay behind this friction: "the hiring of cheap alien labor has [had the effect] of pitting Mexican Americans against Mexicans" (Samora 1971:130). Immigrant Mexicans reacted by calling Mexican Americans "pochos," *"agringados"* (having gringo traits), and "cholos."[1]

Although the labels aim at cultural phenomena, the terms are implicitly racist. The more Mexican-looking (Indian!) may resent those who are lighter and thus more employable by Anglo standards; often a great deal of time and energy have been expended in worry and concern over job prospects. Racial attitudes probably did, in fact, play a role in Anglo hiring practices (Reisler 1976). Another source of intra-ethnic conflict is the contrast in backgrounds. Mexican immigrants compare their socioeconomic status to the status they had in Mexico, whereas the Mexican Americans born in the United States compare their status to that of Anglos. The relative advantages and disadvantages that each group perceives may thus affect their self-images and attitudes toward one another (Monroy 2008).

Roots of Intragroup Racism

Not all Chicano racism is attributable to experiences in the United States, nor does it stay at the inter- or intragroup level. Families have been known to favor the *guero* (light-skinned) child over the *prieto* (darker) offspring. This appears to be a Spanish colonial practice that carried over into the present day. In New Mexico, there is clearly a defensive attitude about being part Indian. Intermarriage with Indians is looked down upon, and, when it does occur, the children of the union are stigmatized with the terms *lobo* (wolf) or coyote (Kluckholm and Strodtbeck 1961).

Many who were lighter in color called themselves Spanish and sought to marry Anglos, often looking down on their own group in order to gain the allegiance and respect of Anglo acquaintances (Simmons 1974). However, having light skin did not guarantee that this would happen, for a light complexion was not always equated with better socioeconomic conditions; many poor Mexicans were very white, as sections of Mexico's Mesa Central attest (Jalisco, Guanajuato Queretaro). In addition, darker-skinned Mexicans sometimes sought a status change through intermarriage. Generally it is true that Mexicans have attempted to emulate whites, if only because opportunities for social mobility were increased in this way. Nevertheless, there was always a certain amount of pragmatic switching. The distinction between Indian and Hispanic features in certain individuals is difficult to make. These individuals are, therefore, able to claim to be of either Spanish or Indian descent, depending on the group of people they are dealing with (Almaguer 2008).

Thus, at the end of this period, the Chicano community still faced tremendous problems stemming from racial discrimination. Barriers to advancement in employment and social standing continued. The mass media either ignored or disparaged Chicanos. Furthermore, for too many Mexican Americans, the vacillation over self-image led inexorably to self-hate. And even more within the community had incorporated an intrapsychic mode of self-repression. Nevertheless, resistance to these situations and conditions also survived and even grew, and the stage was set for change.

Note

[1] An earlier definition of this word throughout Latin America meant someone in cultural transition, such as a native acculturating to the Hispanic mode, but the word is now used to describe a Chicano subcultural, street-gang style; perhaps it is also indicative of the transition from Mexican to Anglo-American culture.

Chapter 9

BREAKUP AND TRANSFORMATION OF THE SOCIAL ORDER

Contact: Civil Rights Ferment

Shaping the Chicanos

From the time of its incorporation in the United States, the Mexican-American community has encountered forces that bred change in its lifeway and expectations. The Civil War and Reconstruction, the settling of the West, the rise of industrial capitalism and urbanization, labor unions and economic crises, and two world wars affected Chicanos along with other Americans, although in different ways. Social and economic discrimination and policies aimed at coerced assimilation afflicted Chicanos and other ethnic minorities, but in different ways. Continuous contact with Mexico uniquely affected the Chicano people, at once affording more cultural stability and also exposing them, more than most other Americans, to the revolutionary ideas of the late-nineteenth and early-twentieth centuries. This was especially true in the 1910 Revolution and its aftermath (Gonzales 2009; Pulido 2006; Rendon 1971).

Chicanos were not passively buffeted about by these social forces. Many fought their way against great odds into the middle-class mainstream of American society. Others, with equal vigor, resisted the social pressures to

241

"Americanize and abandon traditional ways." Followers of both strategies won victories, large and small, in pushing for equality and justice. As Cynthia Orozco (2009:40–41) has noted in rebutting the notion that the events of the 1960s were without precedent, "ideological influences generated by several events, movements, and policies that included the Mexican Revolution beginning in 1910, the Plan de San Diego episode of 1915, the Progressive movement of the 1910s and 1920s, the Americanization movement in the post-1915 era, World War I, waves of Mexican immigration, the eugenics movement, and the talk of the 'Mexican Problem' in the 1920s" all contributed to the historical memory and motivations for action among Chicanos.

Modern Chicano resistance to unequal treatment is rooted in the legacy left to the community from colonial times (Rochin and Valdes 2000; Vigil 1978; R. Alvarez 1973). What Octavio Romano-V. (1973:54–55) has labeled the "seemingly endless decades" of Mexican and Mexican-American involvement in labor uprisings against unjust exploitation is an example of the continuity of the Chicano's quest for social justice, "conflict which involved literally tens of thousands of people of Mexican descent and which at one time spread to eight different states in the Union—conflict which was met with massive military counteraction." Of course, not all these events were full-blown affairs, like social banditry, that captured the public eye. They were more often localized, sporadic, spontaneous eruptions, such as a group of people gathered around a jail, clamoring for the release of a prisoner unjustly detained; workers from railroads, mines, or farms organizing to improve living conditions; or political rallies to support a candidate who reflected Chicano interests. Chicanos participated in many of these activities in unison with other members of American society.

In their own way, Chicanos carried a banner of protest throughout the twentieth century. Spontaneous and sporadic efforts improved living and working conditions. This evolved into a self-conscious organizational discipline that brought public attention to the plight of the Chicano population. Only when repressive actions were stepped up did resistance issues and programs decline. In some instances such activities were crushed completely. Nonetheless, despite temporary slowdowns, each revival of resistance brought on renewed discussion and planning in Chicano leadership circles (Rochin and Valdes 2000; Romano-V. 1968). Early efforts at resolving basic contradictions were made, and many leaders worked to spread their insights, programs, and goals. Social and political recommendations varied from moderate to radical, but it is clear that previous generations of Chicanos did not passively accept their socioeconomic situation. For example, one study of the Chicano youth movement mentions how those who started organizing in the 1930s later helped the present generation move toward similar goals (Gomez-Quinones 1978).

Beginning in the late nineteenth century, *mutualistas* (mutual aid societies) were established for self-help purposes, often promoting the sense of ethnic unity and mission for other activities. Chicanos pooled their resources and helped each other economically by, for example, providing low-interest loans and low-cost funeral and insurance benefits. Subsequent groups followed these self-help patterns, also. For example, Mexicans and Chicanos have begun operating *tandas*, rotating credit associations, based on *confianza* (trust) (Velez-I. 1983, 2010). Moreover, they have broadened the goals to encompass other issues. Organizations such as the League of United Latin American Citizens (LULAC) (Orozco 2009), the Community Service Organization (CSO), and G.I. Forum (Griswold del Castillo 2008) are a few illustrations of this historical pattern (Marquez 1993). (These organizations are discussed in the section, "Precursors of Change.") A biography of Bert Corona and his career as a California activist clearly documents several decades of socioeconomic strife that pervaded Chicano communities (Garcia 1994). Corona's role predates the official Chicano movement and illustrates how there has been a continual struggle for improvement and justice. Such local and focused activities, when it was not yet possible or popular to organize on a larger scale, served a twofold purpose. First, they kept the light of protest burning during the quiet, incubating years. Second, these groups formed a core from which later organizations gained inspiration to continue the struggle.

Effects of Modern Urban Industrial System

Despite the historical precedents, the modern period is unique for several reasons. Modern technological systems brought former peasants into the mainstream of work and urban growth. These developments are clearly evident in the Chicano experience. In 1930 nearly half of all employed Chicanos worked in agriculture; by 1982 this figure decreased to less than 7 percent. Between 1950 and 1990, the percentage of Chicanos living in urban areas increased from 66 percent to 94 percent (Meier and Ribera 1993). Previously, most of the world's people were locally organized and nationally controlled. Then the spread of capitalist enterprises and networks developed what was in many ways an international social system and a global economy. In their drive to acquire raw resources and more workers, capitalist leaders made a large part of the world's population more homogeneous, through, for example, the mass media. Thus, modernization has also meant ideological revision and, perhaps, congruence and conformity in thought. This experience tended to pull the interests, concerns, and needs of modernizing people into the same orbit; what happens to one group or in one part of the world generally has repercussions on other groups and regions (Robinson 2004; Wallerstein 1974). Because of a system's macrolevel influences, observers began to seek macrolevel solutions to conditions and problems. Chicanos united with other groups that had similar interests. Labor resistance to exploitation offers an example: labor unions, which have had a heavy Chicano representation, were increasingly working together to develop strategies for socioeconomic and political change. More recently, Chicanos are uniting with other Latinos to fight for educational and political reform.

Precursors of Change

Three major developments helped to make the 1960s a watershed period within the Chicano movement and community. One was the inroads made by the black civil rights movement; another was the United States government's efforts under President Lyndon Baines Johnson to eliminate poverty in the nation (Bauman 2008; Farnen 2002; Harrington 1962); and the third was the Vietnam War and its consequences.

> Mexican American political activism in relation to the War on Poverty during this period shifted from inclusion and representation to self-determination and community control . . . [and] inspired . . . Young Chicano/as for Community Action. . . . These young people's experience in neighborhood and community improvement increased their awareness and pride in their ethnic identity, and they began to create events focusing on Chicano culture, history, and politics. (Bauman 2008:94)

Each operated to restimulate the ethnic solidarity struggle, which at this time snowballed into the first relatively united national Chicano effort. The achievements of the black civil rights movement sparked renewed organization in the Chicano community, often modeled in large part on earlier black campaigns. The political power mustered by the civil rights campaigns also paved the way for stronger ties between Chicano leaders and national political organizations. The presidentially endorsed War on Poverty led to new job opportunities in the Chicano community and to the recruitment of Chicanos in government and the universities on a scale never previously reached (Chavez 2002). This, in turn, had two effects: it increased the number of highly visible middle-class Mexican Americans, and it brought Chicano intellectuals into contact with the activist social reformers and revolutionaries then concentrated in the universities. The War on Poverty soon worked as a catalyst to awaken the political actions of barrio dwellers and their sympathizers (Rosales 1997; Magana 2005; Romo 1990; Forbes 1973). The war in Vietnam brought to the Chicano community the same dissension it sparked elsewhere in the nation. Newly radicalized Chicano students were quick to note the discrepancy between their community's underrepresentation in the social, political, and economic power structure and their overrepresentation in war casualty statistics (Vigil 1999).

Chicanos generated their own leadership and methods aimed at problems unique to them. By the late 1950s, discontent within the Chicano population became noticeable, especially within the CSO. The CSO, formed in Los Angeles in the 1940s, began with a concerted effort to register voters and win elections. With some early successes, especially in advancing the career of Congressman Edward Roybal, the CSO eventually became a community agency that provided social services (Alaniz and Cornish 2008; Moore and Pachon 1985). With the increasing support of the Chicano community, the first steps to social change could now be effected (Gonzales 2009; Dunne 1967). The main goal of the CSO was to prod government into alleviating serious social problems. Through political networking, Roybal focused on civil rights and immigrant cases, which helped generate community interest and support. After some moderate successes, especially in breaking down some of the housing covenants in segregated areas, the CSO settled into a role primarily as a service provider and continued to develop new leaders (Gomez-Quinones 1990).

LULAC, organized in the 1920s by World War I veterans primarily to combat prejudice, also built a platform to aid Mexican integration into the body politic (Marquez 1993; Orozco 2009). With some moderate shifts in orientation over the decades, LULAC has now expanded considerably. Nevertheless, the organization still remains moderate to conservative in its

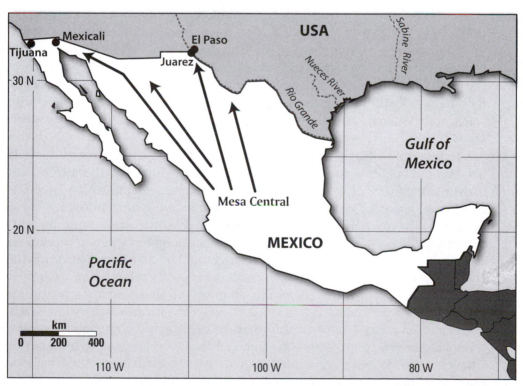

Immigration routes in the 1960s.

approach to political issues. For instance, LULAC now generally follows a middle-of-the-road path that champions community programs and sometimes has corporate support.

The G.I. Forum was founded by World War II and Korean War veterans who pushed for equal access to economic and political opportunities.

> Soon the American G.I. Forum involved itself in a dramatic case of discrimination, that of Felix Longoria. In 1948, after Felix Longoria had been killed in action in the Philippines during the war, his remains were finally sent to his hometown of Three Rivers, Texas. When the local undertaker refused to hold services in his chapel because it was for "whites only," Texas Mexican Americans launched a campaign to have Longoria buried in Arlington National Cemetery. (Griswold del Castillo 2008:101)

This event made national headlines.

Because of the inroads the G.I. Forum made, it was able to develop a southwestern regional organization that later expanded its goals to include educational issues. At present it still plays a role in electoral politics as well as other matters. During the 1960s War on Poverty, both the G.I. Forum and LULAC helped start Project SER (Service, Employment and Redevelopment) programs throughout the Southwest (Gomez-Quinones 1990).

The G.I. Forum gained support among Chicanos, and one of the premier politicians, Congressman Henry B. Gonzalez from San Antonio, Texas, was one of its strongest supporters. Gonzalez had a long and varied career in Democratic politics in local, state, and national arenas. Always a champion of the poor and dispossessed, he has remained outspoken to his last days. Beginning as a probation officer, he rose through the elective ranks, winning city, state, and national offices and showing remarkable ingenuity in capturing votes from several sectors, especially Latinos and blacks. Recognized as a "New Deal" Liberal, he nonetheless at times angered Chicano activists with his non-nationalist stance. Nevertheless, he and others in the 1970s were instrumental in bringing together all Latino congressmen into an organization called the Hispanic Congressional Caucus (Meier and Ribera 1993).

Cesar Chavez was one Chicano who learned how to organize in the CSO (Bruns 2005; Shaw 2008; Pawel 2009). Chavez's long-term effort to organize farmworkers was helped considerably after the United States' Mexican Bracero Program ended in 1964, which had long been a goal of labor and liberal political forces (Watt 2010). Under this program the United States government had officially recruited and sanctioned the use of Mexican workers in a guest-worker arrangement, which made it more difficult for Chavez to mount a unionization campaign. Thus, the United Farm Workers Union, founded by Chavez and Dolores Huerta (M. T. Garcia 2008), focused first on American-born or naturalized Chicanos. Generally they were more familiar with the union idea and working conditions in the United States, and presumably they

Union leader Cesar Chavez.

UFW cofounder Dolores Huerta (*left*) joins in prayer for Cesar Chavez outside the Monterey County jail in Salinas, California, in 1970. Chavez was jailed for violating a court injunction prohibiting a lettuce boycott. Mrs. Ethel Kennedy (*right*) marched to the rally with hundreds of Mexican farmworkers before attending the mass and visiting Chavez in jail. Larry Itliong (*right of Huerta*) was an early farmworker who founded NFWA (National Farm Workers' Association).

were easier to organize. In addition, their extended exposure to conditions and consumer standards in the United States may have driven them to improve on their underclass role, but with a special leadership philosophy guiding them.

One commentator noted: "It is a paradox that the termination of the Bracero Program is the only way in the long run of helping Mexican as well as American workers" (Nelson 1966:17). However, the continued immigration of undocumented laborers and community opposition to the suppression of immigration later led Chavez to alter this strategy and attempt to organize the immigrant workers as well. The UFW initiated strikes and boycotts against lettuce and vegetable growers. Strikers demanded higher wages, a means to alleviate grievances, and a cessation in the use of pesticides, among other issues. Chavez emphasized nonviolence as a strategy and, following the tactics of such previous leaders as Mahatma Gandhi, went on several fasts to bring attention to the farmworkers' cause (Griswold del Castillo and Garcia 1995).

> In terms of his political persona, Chavez presented urban Chicanas [Mexican-American women] and Chicanos with a form of masculinity virtually unknown outside the Catholicism of their *abuilitas*. At its very core was the principle of "militant nonviolence.". . . Nonviolent change, therefore, is to be sought not only at the level of institutions but in the very attitudes of the antagonist. (Mariscal 2005:146)

Chavez is gone now, but the farmworkers' struggle continues under UFW leadership to this day, with gradual success despite strife and many obstacles (M. T. Garcia 2008; Griffith and Kissan 1995). Additionally, the Farm Labor Organizing Committee (FLOC), founded in 1967, expanded the struggle to improve migrant farmworker life in the Midwest (Rochin and Valdes 2000; Valdes 1991). They negotiated an agreement with Campbell Soup and Campbell's tomato and cucumber growers in Ohio and Michigan to improve working conditions (Watt 2010; Barger and Reza 1994).

Reis Lopez Tijerina was an activist in the land-grant movement (1960s and 1970s), a collective demand for the return of communal land grants and a considerably radical idea for the time. Communal land grants from the crown were very common in the late Spanish colonial period. New Mexico was the leader in this practice when land was given to groups of petitioners, each made up of at least ten families from a pueblo. The grant was to enable the petitioners to establish a farming community (Dunbar-Ortiz 2007; Gardner 1970). Following the takeover by the United States in the nineteenth century, such lands fell under new ownership. Tijerina, an evangelical Protestant minister, and his followers had been active in attempts to reclaim title to these lands that once belonged to early Mexican settlers.

The efforts became much more militant in 1966 when Tijerina and many members of his Alianza armed themselves in a highly publicized series of "re-occupations" and other protests (Nabokov 1969; Oboler 1995). Detailing the abrogation of Chicano land and cultural rights, and basing their program on the 1848 treaty ending the Mexican–American War, they subsequently took a memorial signed by thousands of Chicanos to Mexico to hand over to then President Lopez Mateos. The document demanded the Mexican president to intercede with the United States government to fulfill the terms of the Treaty of Guadalupe Hidalgo. These efforts ended in failure, with Tijerina and his followers being arrested on numerous charges related to the protests. Literally hundreds of Alianza members were involved in these activist incidents and protracted legal processes.

Although no land grants were obtained, the national eye was riveted on New Mexico. Chicano activists, of course, were encouraged by this stirring of the national memory. Many Chicanos rallied behind these goals. The labor and land demonstrations led by Chavez, Tijerina, and others raised the social consciousness of Chicanos and generated a host of additional actions in various other sectors.

Tijerina and followers petitioning Governor Fages of Arizona.

Patsy Tijerina.

While urban life had its problems, overall it aided Chicanos in reaching higher. Life's rewards were now close at hand. Previous expectations were low, for Chicanos had inherited a meager standard of living with little hope for the future. The post–World War II years were good for the economy in general, and many Chicanos similarly benefited. Movement from the barrios and into a higher social status broke the pattern of low aspirations. One middle-aged man, comparing the economic difference between the time of his youth and the 1960s, noted that: "Now you see bread lying in the streets. When I was a boy you never saw bread in the streets" (Grebler, Moore, and Guzman 1970:343). Thus, with one dream fulfilled, there was a rising expectation for the satisfaction of previously unheard-of possibilities. Chicanos who experienced this feeling grouped together to have their wishes recognized and met (Ruiz 2008; Smith 2009; Romero 1979). The urbanization process was in large part responsible for bringing Chicanos onto the center stage of national life.

Nature of Inequality

Urbanization brought Chicanos into contact with other people, some of whom had been similarly relegated to a life of low status and poverty. In spite of the differences among all of them, there were some who began to perceive that strong threads held them together. Complementing this new mood of national interethnic awareness were the first attempts to draw parallels with colonized peoples in the Third World of the Americas, Africa, and Asia. Many Chicanos began to view their situation as that of an "internal colony." It was rightly believed that worldwide colonization had created certain common features—external conquest and subjugation, economic and racial imperialism, and inequality and poverty. Chicanos were either Indians, and thus the original inhabitants of this hemisphere, or Mexican settlers before the United States expansion into Mexican territory. Thus, it was necessary to explain their presence in the United States in a framework other than that applicable to other immigrants or poor ethnic minorities. Like so many people in other parts of the world, they were incorporated into a new society by a war of conquest. Thus, they became an internal colony, within which barrio life was affected at all levels (Gutierrez 2000, in Rochin and Valdes; Barrera, Munoz, and Ornelas 1974; Moore 1973). Although far from uniform throughout the southwestern states, this belief is premised on: As indigenous residents of the area, Chicanos were involuntarily incorporated into the United States; thus, contemporary ethnic relationships are colored by these superordinate/subordinate beginnings (Gonzales 2009; Alaniz and Cornish 2008).

There were enough Chicano leaders who understood this fact and began to develop new insights and gain the strength necessary to build alliances with other similarly affected peoples. At that time, and to this day, other Chicano leaders disliked this idea and instead never completely embraced this concept of human solidarity, preferring a strict La Raza nationalist program. Neverthe-less, the sentiment of reaching out persists for the simple reason that similar conditions (or contradictions) necessitate coordination among the "powerless."

Conflict: 1960s Chicano Movement

Movement Background

The Chicano movement was the recipient of all that came before, and by the mid-1960s it coalesced. However, it is difficult to pinpoint exactly how the movement started or who initiated it; there were too many contributors—stu-dents, teachers, community activists, intellectuals or old "pols" (experienced political insiders)—and too many key issues (Chavez 2002; Mora 2007; Mar-iscal 2005; Munoz 1989; Gomez-Quinones 1990). The Chicano movement "was a creative and revivalist cultural surge, it was a civil rights struggle, it was an effort for political recognition and economic rights by middle-class elements, and it had intimations of an incipient national liberation struggle" (Gomez-Quinones 1978:29).

There was no start-off date, but the example and momentum of the Chavez farmworkers and Tijerina's Alianza (Alliance) land initiatives cer-tainly caught on. In a remarkably short period of time, many organizations and activities had blossomed (Rochin and Valdes 2000; Orozco 2009; Vigil 1999; Meier and Ribera 1993). These groups focused their energies mostly on the issues and conditions that were discussed in the earlier stages. The farm union fought to correct injustices against workers, and the Alianza sought the return of treaty-guaranteed land; both issues, land and labor, were at the cen-ter of this historical account. These targets generally directed the movement for the longest time and were instrumental in heightening Chicano aware-ness. Other organizations brought attention to another core problem: the lack of resources and wealth among the Chicano population. Some groups concen-trated their efforts on a single sector, such as education or politics. Others, with varying success, confronted most social-situation conditions that ham-pered Chicano development.

Groups and Actions

The earlier reform groups were joined by others. The Crusade for Justice in Denver, led by Rodolfo "Corky" Gonzales in the mid-1960s, was a broadly based thrust for community control, mainly economic and political (Vigil 1999; Gomez-Quinones 1990; Gonzalez 2000). Under his leadership, links were established with other groups throughout Colorado and later in other areas of the Southwest. Gonzales forged strong bonds within the network he had assembled under the rubric of "cultural nationalism" and self-determination. It was his group that popularized the idea of an "Aztlan" nation.

The Brown Berets emerged in 1967 from a group of young students who worked for the VISTA program, a government-sponsored initiative to resolve urban problems (Haney-Lopez 2003; Rosales 1997; Bauman 2008). As the foremost militant unit within the Chicano movement, the Berets were instrumental in organizing protests and demonstrations that confronted educational policies and police practices, often with the assistance of young barrio gang members and other disaffected youth who reveled in direct action. For example, they were one of the primary organizers of the largest of the Chicano Moratoriums. The Chicano Moratoriums of the 1970s were nominally anti-Vietnam War but took on a broader front, addressing the whole social system (Mariscal 1999, 2005; Chavez 2002; Munoz 1989). Internal struggles for leadership and differences over issues, as well as infiltration by police agents, led to the Berets disbanding in 1972. They are still recognized, however, as a group that shook the political establishment, including many moderate and middle-class Chicanos (Haney-Lopez 2003; Trevino 2001; Acuna 1988).

United Mexican American Students (UMAS) and other Southwest student organizations, such as the Mexican American Youth Organization (MAYO) in Texas, helped generate university student involvement in all areas, exerting demands to establish Chicano Studies programs and effective minority student recruitment (Mora 2007). The activities of these and similar student groups later led to the formation of the National Association for Chicana and Chicano Studies (NACCS), a faculty and student organization that has subsequently expanded in size and strength. They were key leaders, along with the Brown Berets, in planning and executing the Los Angeles high school walkouts aimed at improving education (Chavez 2002; Gomez-Quinones 1978; Munoz 1989). Later, as participants in a youth conference sponsored by Corky Gonzales in Colorado, MAYO merged with other student organizations to form the Movimiento Estudiantil Chicano de Aztlan (MEChA) with local affiliates throughout the Southwest (Vigil 1999). MEChA is still in existence today, with some campus units continuing the direct and confrontational actions of the 1960s, while others now act principally as social clubs, with only occasional efforts at protecting special programs for minority students when challenged.

The political goal of Jose Angel Gutierrez's La Raza Unida Party (United Peoples Party) in Texas was to build an independent third party throughout the country (Shockley 1974; Garcia and de la Garza 1977; I. Garcia 1989). This brash move stemmed from a series of successful local election campaigns in small towns in Texas, elections that in some cases sought to gain representation for 90 percent of Chicanos in a town. For a while, Raza Unida gained adherents throughout the Southwest, but ultimately where political under-representation was a problem, like most other third-party movements in the

United States, it collapsed. The dominant political parties, both Democratic and Republican, were able to undermine the "nationalist" appeal of Raza Unida's platform by working finally to represent the people. Nevertheless, this attempt at a third party encouraged Chicanos for the first time to think of a national, coordinated campaign to participate in the political system. This experience was invaluable, in the sense that subsequent events gained impetus from its example. More people got behind voting and political parties and more fully attempted to become part of the Chicano electorate.

Catolicos Por La Raza (Catholics for the People) demanded somewhat tumultuously that the church be made responsive to the needs of the Spanish-speaking poor (Acosta 1973). In the past, the Catholic Church usually could take for granted the faithful participation of the Mexican population in religious affairs. Thus, when Catholic activists joined the movement and demanded that the church respond to the social and economic needs of the barrio communities, church leaders stiffened in opposition to such disobedient and unruly behavior. Only after some priests had become involved in the farmworkers movement and anti–Vietnam War protests in the United States, did the church become more responsive. (Interestingly, this coincided with the Theology of Liberation movement among Catholic priests in Latin America begun in 1969.)

Actually, the Catholic Church in the post-zoot episodes had generally initiated and supported, with moderate success, social and cultural programs addressing poverty and social isolation. The Catholic Youth Organization (CYO) provides a prominent example of these efforts. Due to the American dictum of the separation of church and state, the church seldom played an overt role in political organizing in the Chicano communities. It wasn't until after the 1960s that community-based units such as United Neighborhood Organization (UNO) in Los Angeles and Communities Organized for Public Service (COPS) in San Antonio were formed with participation of church leadership. Although strong numerically, usually such groups concentrated on tangible local issues—for example, reducing auto insurance rates and gang violence—and have only recently expanded to focus on political candidates and their platforms, and thus push for political change.

An example of the momentous events of the period is provided by the 1968 walkouts in which several thousand students boycotted classes. (See HBO 2006 film, *Walkout*, for a dramatic portrayal of this event.) This incident is important for several reasons: It was the first major urban confrontation in the largest Chicano-populated area in the nation. It was coordinated by numerous groups—teachers, students, and community activists—and afterward, other individuals and organizations of various ideological shades rallied to their defense (Munoz 1989; Mora 2007; Urrieta 2009). Most importantly, the event and subsequent developments sparked debate and action not only on the educational front but in a number of different related areas, such as job training, sports, and recreation programs. However, education was the pivotal rallying issue. The public educational system historically served to oppress the Chicano population, both culturally and economically (Valencia 2010). Students subject to this treatment soon became part of the struggle (Gomez-Quinones 1978). Two high school student leaders at that time wrote that "the situation created a climate . . . where students started questioning things. . . . Schools are supposed to service the community and they weren't. Rather, they were more like prisons in the community. They were just doing custodial things as far as keeping students together" (Santana and Esparza 1974:1).

Consciousness-Raising

The reform activities show how far-reaching contacts brought many groups into conflict with the social system, as walkouts, protests, demonstrations followed one after the other in different cities and states in the southwest U.S. Furthermore, these were not merely sporadic, apolitical confrontations, but well-organized challenges to the power brokers. Young leaders were born in these episodes of struggle. Participation in the movement allowed adolescents as well as adults the opportunity for positive identity formation, as dedication and loyalty to an ideological position is a normal part of that development (Romero et al. 1997). Protest activity served as a psychological catharsis in assuaging the effects of inferiority and marginality (Oropeza and Espinoza 2006). Militancy became the rallying banner for those who confronted Anglo-American institutions. As noted previously, Chicanos challenged every sector, although the extent and nature of the challenges varied from community to community (Knowlton 1975). A small number of groups even advocated taking up arms and went on a spree of terrorist bombings.

The groundswell also enveloped less militant organizations. One was the Association of Mexican-American Educators (AMAE), a moderate group that championed educational reform. Although accused of adhering to an "establishment" orientation, many in this group helped organize the students (Urrieta 2009; Ericksen 1970). Some of the more progressive teachers, such as Sal Castro, a major leader and spokesman of the walkouts, led the way for change (Garcia and Castro 2011). However, even the less-threatening suggestions of the AMAE moderates created suspicion in the eyes of the authorities. Both moderate and progressive elements were in open conflict with the system at different levels. "In fact . . . the differences between them are less important than the similarities that bind them" (Garcia and de la Garza 1977:43).

An old-line (1959) political group, the Mexican-American Political Association (MAPA), steadily evolved under Bert Corona into a more militant organization as the movement spread (de la Garza and DeSipio 1999; Garcia and de la Garza 1977; Gomez-Quinones 1978). The original goals of MAPA were rather moderate, for they stressed ethnic identity, direct electoral politics, and electoral independence. Centered around the personage of Edward Roybal, MAPA had tired of the Democratic party's nonchalant attitude toward the always reliable Mexican voting bloc. The campaign work of MAPA helped elect Roybal to Congress, where he became an influential leader until retiring in 1991. MAPA still plays a role in the state politics of California (Gomez-Quinones 1991).

Countless individuals and groups remained in the background but contributed immensely to the cause. For example, the Mexican-American Action Committee (MAAC) was founded in 1966 in Los Angeles by young professionals who spanned the political spectrum but agreed on one goal: social action. Because of or despite this ideological diversity, by 1968 they were responsible for helping other groups and causes that caught the public eye. Members of MAAC played instrumental roles in MEChA, the Brown Berets, the high school walkouts, and various educational and political reform actions. Among the participants of this group were individuals who subsequently became political officials, several prominent activists, and even local judges who got their start in public life during this time. Further reforms came from a University of California campus, the Plan de Santa Barbara, which advocated that the university begin to serve the community.

Step-Up in Militancy: Aztlan Nation

The formation of the southwestern regional body known as Movimiento Estudiantil Chicano de Aztlan (MEChA; the Chicano Student Movement of Aztlan) emphasized the increasingly common use of the word "Aztlan." This ancient Aztec name for the Southwest came to symbolize the Chicano destiny (Chavez 1984). A recent book's (Velez-I. 2010) front cover shows a trade route map of Aztlan, now the border nexus of the U.S. and Mexico.

Student groups, meeting in Denver in 1969, developed a historically based type of nationalism (El Plan Espiritual de Aztlan 1970). Their goal of an Aztlan nation was one instance of the recurrent call for Chicano separatism. (Other examples are the Sonora Immigration in 1856, the San Diego Plan in 1914–1915, and the Sinarquistas in the 1940s.) However, separatism in this case meant more than a return to earlier, perhaps indigenous, sociocultural traditions. It also implied the use of modern resources and techniques for community control and development (I. Garcia 1989). Corky Gonzales, one of the spokesmen for the plan (1967:3), wrote an epic poem that explained an aspect of the Chicano trajectory, as this excerpt shows:

> I am Joaquin,
> Lost in a world of confusion,
> Caught up in a whirl of a
> gringo society

Confused by the rules,
Scorned by attitudes,
Suppressed by manipulation,
And destroyed by modern society.
My fathers
have lost the economic battle
and won
the struggle of cultural survival
and now
I must choose.

Gonzales, the poet-politician, chose a separatist Aztlan. Others resolved the dilemma by working for cultural retention but a fairer economic integration, to obtain what they viewed as the best of two worlds. Still others sought total social and economic equality for Chicanos in the United States, with or without the retention of distinct cultural traditions. This coterie of strategies in some ways characterizes the ways in which the two major political parties have responded to the Chicano population. Democratic leaders have generally espoused the need for social and economic programs to help the less advantaged members of the minority community. However, the strings attached to this advocacy often entail that Chicanos forgo cultural and nationalistic goals and follow an assimilationist path as strict "Americans." Republicans, on the other hand, have only recently attempted to woo Chicanos, but the enticement for support is that Chicanos buy into "corporate" America and all that this entails, including the interventionist policies of the United States government in Central and Latin America, as well as other parts of the troubled world. Nevertheless, part of the Chicano population is attracted to Republican conservatism and its emphasis on family moral values. Thus, the Chicano vote has become a "swing" vote in the United States, with presidential candidates often becoming involved in what has been termed "fiesta politics" (Moore and Pachon 1985).

The Chicano reform movements were viewed with suspicion by much of the American public, who often misinterpreted the self-determination efforts of Chicanos as attacks on democracy, and by the political and economic elite, who correctly viewed Chicanos as a threat to some of the privileges they controlled.

August 29 Moratorium

Various actions were taken to stem the new wave of Chicano self-determination. Throughout the Southwest there were dozens of incidents, but one example will suffice here. On a hot summer day, August 29, 1970, the largest Chicano demonstration of the period took place, an event organized by the "Brown Berets" as a result of a larger goal of a "National Chicano Moratorium Committee" to protest the war (Alaniz and Cornish 2008). The peaceful marchers were protesting the Vietnam intervention policies of the United States, and in particular the high Chicano casualty rate there (Vigil 1999; Mariscal 1999, 2005). Over 30,000 people from throughout the Southwest congregated at an east Los Angeles park for a rally. After a short time, sheriff's deputies broke it up (Chavez 2002; Morales 1972; Sanchez 1978). When the police lined up to intimidate the protesters, some monitors attempted unsuccessfully to hold the crowd back. Nevertheless, several hundred policemen drove the people from the park. In the aftermath, some people rioted, destroying over a million dollars in property on Whittier Boulevard, a main thoroughfare. Three people were killed, including Chicano reporter Ruben Salazar, and hundreds of others arrested (Salazar 1995; Shorris 1992). Scores of people were harassed, and one leader, Corky Gonzales, was apprehended and jailed because he "suspiciously" was carrying $300 in cash (Marin 1975:114; Vigil 1999).

A program of indoctrination was a major thrust of the counter-measures to protest, demonstrations, and other acts of civil disobedience. The media, politicians who preached "law and order," local and federal law enforcement officials, the court system, and other establishment functionaries began to paint a negative picture of the social ferment. At times their criticisms were correct. More often, however, they missed the mark. They characterized public protest as un-American and unlawful, despite protest organizers' efforts to ensure legal compliance at rallies and meetings. Some government leaders considered even minor differences of opinion to be an attack on the United States. A Mexican-American congressman, generally regarded at the time as a liberal, nevertheless felt it necessary to disavow any ties to the protests: "It may well be that I agree with the goals stated by the militants; but whether I agree or disagree, I do not now nor have I ever believed that the end justifies the means" (Gonzalez 1974:260). That the protest organizers had never suggested otherwise, and had in fact maintained discipline until police intervention, was apparently lost on the national leadership. The Brown Berets, prominent among the organizers of the protest, began to lose support and popularity in its aftermath (Chavez 2002; Acuna 1988). Nevertheless, the event on August 29 turned out to be a major turning point for the Chicano movement: it attracted supporters from all over the Southwest; it was a disciplined, peaceful affair; and it struck fear in the hearts of adherents of the status quo.

Opposite page: A mass of interlocked hands forms a pyramid, classic symbol of Mexican heritage. By the late 1960s communities of color were actively opposing the Vietnam War, and a series of national demonstrations at more than 20 cities by Chicano and Latino activists were organized for August 29, 1970. The Los Angeles rally drew tens of thousands. Massive police presence resulted in a clash that left many tear gassed and beaten, as well as the death of award-winning Chicano journalist Ruben Salazar.

LA RAZA

VIVA

NATIONAL CHICANO
MORATORIUM AUG. 29
E.L.A.

BELVDERE PARK — RALLY STARTS AT 10:00 A.M.

Rioting after the Moratorium and the death of Ruben Salazar at the Silver Dollar.

Comparisons with Other Groups and Counterreactions

Chicanos were not alone in their protests during this time, for other groups—blacks and Indians in particular—were taking issue with similar features of the social structure. As a result, many minority group members began to perceive the social-class roots of inequality and injustice for all (Vasquez and Torres 2003; Gomez-Quinones 1978). They were joined by white radicals in articulating and acting out their criticisms of government actions.

A number of countermeasures tended to undermine the social movements. For example, many Chicanos, particularly those who were moderate or more conservative, were co-opted into various institutional networks and given jobs or made leaders; therefore the movement did not have the opportunity to recruit them. Some observers correctly viewed this as a deliberate plan and pointed to the aftermath of the 1968 walkouts. The school board had established a community group, the Educational Issues Coordinating Committee (EICC), which succeeded in excluding the militants involved in the protests. Thus, those who governed the schools solidified their position of power over the Chicano community (Munoz 2007). In other social or political arenas authorities also supported Chicano groups favorable to the status quo in order to counter advocates of social change—thus creating intragroup fighting and slowing progress (Haney-Lopez 2003; Foley et al. 1977). In short, cooptation and accommodation worked in tandem to blunt the tip of the social movement. What one pundit referred to as the politics of putting someone into your hip pocket was very much the order of the day, and there were plenty of people eager to be bought off. Indeed, it is safe to state that the Democratic Party picked up what pieces were left from the disgruntled left and helped redirect much of what energy remained in the Chicano community; often this meant keeping a moderate lid on social ferment in order to play it safe (de la Garza and DeSipio 1999).

Furthermore, the Chicano organizations that were making the most headway attracted another type of law enforcement attention. Like other militant organizations, these groups were infiltrated by undercover agents, or agents provocateurs, who managed to disrupt and misdirect them. One way they did this was to encourage internal conflicts between the organizational leaders (Munoz 1974; Chavez 2002; Vigil 1999). These provocateurs became full-time "militants" (with long hair, beards, and other visible paraphernalia) in order to redirect the movement into unlawful activities. David Sanchez (1978:6), former prime minister of the Brown Berets, had this to say about the problem: "The infiltrators were one of the main reasons why the Brown Beret organization was so often misinterpreted and misrepresented. The infiltrators served as agitators of violence!" Intimidation, harassment, and arrests characterized this period. Ernesto Vigil from Colorado gives this view of one such event, the arrest of protesters at the Nuevas Vistas conference at the Biltmore Hotel in Los Angeles where Governor Reagan's speech was interrupted:

> The key prosecution witness was undercover officer (LAPD) Fernando Sumaya, who had infiltrated the National Brown Berets and was present at the Biltmore protest, where, Sumaya claimed, the activists conspired to disrupt the conference and start fires. The defendants, however, held Sumaya himself responsible for advocating violence and setting the fire. (Vigil 1999:150)

Factionalism and Aftermath of the Conflict

As in most historical periods of ferment, there were also intragroup struggles. In addition to the macrolevel struggles, there were microlevel differences that set Chicano against Chicano. Sometimes these conflicts were as heated as those occurring in the national arena (Haney-Lopez 2003; Vasquez and Torres 2003; Gomez-Quinones 1978). Essentially the contention was over ideology and how to bring about change. Programs for change ranged from total assimilation to white middle-class America to separatism, and they were vociferously debated at national conferences or in smaller units such as college MEChA chapters (Chavez 2002; Munoz 2007). Almost as much energy was expended in these intragroup conflicts as in united actions. Many people and organizations were casualties as a result, and with normal burnout added to the mix, there were many friendships and allegiances taxed beyond repair. Besides the fragmentation of some worthwhile organizations, the toll was often that Chicanos were alienated from each other and, worse, from themselves. Intragroup conflicts had some good aspects, though, as indicated by Juan Gomez-Quinones (1978:5): "Factionalism is a part of development, positive or negative; if positive it strengthens progressive ideological clarity and organizational coherence. Negative factionalism causes confusion and weakens organization." As we will note shortly, CASA (Centro de Accion Social Autonomo), which rose from these ashes, made some important contributions and inroads (Chavez 2002).

A movement can be considered as a battle in a long protracted war to address and transform the fissures and potholes of a long history of upheavals and subjugations that created gaps and voids. In terms of a major structural and political overhaul of the establishment, movement activists assuredly missed their mark. Munoz (2007:120) points out the movement's shortcomings, which were largely due to "the lack of a critical analysis on the part of Movement leadership of the nature of Chicano oppression." Nevertheless, mass protest did have some beneficial outcomes. One such gain was in the learning and experimentation that transpired and the knowledge that people thus acquired. With this insight they could be better prepared for another day, or perhaps be able to more successfully penetrate the closed political system that drove them to such extreme measures. Furthermore, other developments were generated by the movement, as Hurtado and Gurin state: "New ways of thinking about ethnicity were added while older ways were refined and retained. Thus, each successive generation had a richer cultural repertoire of identity construction to draw upon. Multiplicity of ethnic labeling is the cultural and historical legacy of U.S. Mexican descendants" (Hurtado and Gurin 2004:91) In summary, the 1960s movement made its mark, and the process is still unfolding—and so, of course, is a proper understanding of it (Vigil 1999; Munoz 2007; Rochin and Valdes 2000; Montejano 2010). Clearly, a careful assessment of the impact of the "battle" is in order.

Change: 1970s and Beyond

State of the People

It is difficult to speak of an aftermath of the Chicano movement and the conflict surrounding it, for both the movement and the conflict continue in abated fashion. There were certainly initial victories as there were also set-backs. Some measures have withstood the test of time and blossomed. Even with major changes and improvements, many of the conditions that gave rise to the movement are still present—for example, underrepresentation of Chi-canos in social, economic, and political positions of leadership; discord between the community and local authorities; and lower-than-average income and education. The dramatic headlines of the 1960s are gone and an air of general normality has returned to the Chicano community, although activism still erupts periodically to address unresolved issues. However, the norms have changed, although in many instances only subtly, with Chicanos now having more direct participation in the political process. The movement definitely knocked down doors.

The movement altered the consciousness of Mexican Americans with a ferment that began after World War II but peaked in the civil rights era. The highly publicized assertions of Chicano rights and cultural legacies have led some in the community to goals similar to those stemming from yet another larger blip, the Mexican Revolution: "the people refuse all outside help, every imported scheme, every idea lacking some profound relationship to their inti-mate feelings, and . . . instead they turn to themselves" (Paz 1961:147). Others have built on the earlier militancy in more traditionally American reform efforts, directing their energies toward fuller Chicano participation in the ben-efits of the larger society. As Julian Samora and Patricia Vandel Simon noted, Chicanos have learned the maxim of American democratic politics—that "the wheel that squeaks the loudest gets the most grease" (1977:227). (They have also learned its corollary of what happens when one begins to seriously threaten the ruling elite, as the old Asian adage has it: the nail that sticks out gets hammered.)

Others have sought to redirect the focus of the 1960s to even more far-reaching efforts, including critical analyses of the basic structures of society and socioeconomic stratification. Finally, there are still a few who continue to attribute Chicano problems to Chicanos themselves. A noted scholar sums it up in this way:

> Chicanos reasoned that their oppression was not only personal but structural, not only individual but institutional. Racism was deeply historical, rooted in legacies of conquest and colonization, and in personal and systematic effects of poverty, segregation, and white skin privilege . . . [and in Chicanos] demanding equal access to better education, to fair housing and employ-ment, and to full membership in American society. (Gutierrez 2009:95)

Chicanozaje

The development of Chicanozaje or Chicanismo, as it is sometimes called, is the most pervasive sign of the altered consciousness of Mexican Americans.

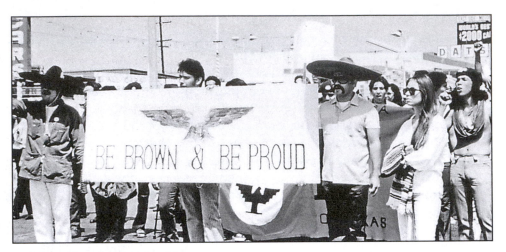

Marchers claiming racial pride.

The term "Chicano" was seized upon by militants, especially youth, in the 1960s to express disdain for their "hyphenated" status as Mexican Americans and to reconnect with their Mexican heritage. While many in the Mexican-American community rejected the term, associating it with the vulgarities of street life, its use spread until even establishment figures, white middle-class leaders included, had begun to use it. In recent years more sophisticated objections to Chicanozaje have been raised. Some challenge the machismo, mostly male thrust to its labeling. There particularly has been a backlash from those who argue that a "noble savage" interpretation of Chicano culture must be resolutely avoided, as there are still many unresolved problems to be addressed and many cultural traits still in gestation. These viewpoints, however, downplay the importance of the all-encompassing scope of the word "Chicano," which covers the diversity of Mexican-American lifestyles (Gomez-Quinones 1978). Chicana feminist, poet, and cultural theorist Gloria Anzaldua (2007) has underscored the reality of the multidimensionality of Chicano/a individuals and culture—and the struggles that individuals have in keeping their identity intact.

Generally, Chicanozaje includes a historical awareness of the Chicanos' role as oppressed members of society. Chicanos stress the acts of being (how the past shaped them) and becoming (how they will shape the future). Equally important, they now realize that their past is a complex one of multiple heritages, both ancient and new, made up of Indian, Spanish, Mexican, and Anglo elements (Gonzales 2009; Vasquez and Torres 2003). The historical record shows that a succession of different identities reflects the laboring role and social status of the people at different time periods, suggested in the categories and in the passage of time from indigenous to peasant to immigrant.

Moreover, this complex, multilayered background was taken off the shelf to which it had been consigned, full of negative implications, and was now extolled as a true world virtue. Much of this regeneration of cultural awareness and broadened ethnic identity awareness aided political developments and maturation (Varzally 2008; Gutierrez 1995). Chicano students and activists made pilgrimages to Mexico to recapture their "lost" heritage. These contacts motivated Mexican leaders in high positions to establish cultural and student exchange programs that allowed Mexicans to reconnect with the vast territory of the north. For a while, a strong current of international, albeit informal, cooperation began to emerge, with each group showing interest and involvement in the political situation in their respective countries to help close gaps. In large part, these activities comprised a move to rekindle connections with the territory and people stripped from Mexico over 100 years ago. This striving added to wave after wave of immigration from Mexico, which brought more Mexicans to the U.S. to further challenge the one people, two nations thesis.

Because of their complex background, a whole range of cultural styles is possible for Chicanos. Some can favor the European side, others the Indian, or they can move in between, seeking the cultural style that fits them (Alaniz and Cornish 2008; Bernal and Knight 1993; Sanchez 1976). Chicanozaje thus expands the boundaries of the age-old mestizaje tradition of Mexico. It is a fluid, dual cultural membership that gives a deeper meaning to the term "Chicano." This fluid sense of identity has been referred to as *personas mexicanas* (the many identities of Mexicans): "Pigeonholing oneself with just one ethnic identity may have been appropriate during earlier phases of our American and international history, but our current period of introspection is drawing us together into a 'global village.' . . . It is incumbent on all of us to think multiculturally and transnationally; to become 'border crossers'" (Vigil 1997:2; see also Zentella 2009).

Chicano Arts

Both aspects of Chicanozaje, the past and the future, are apparent in the blossoming of Chicano arts since the 1960s (D. G. Garcia 2008). Contemplative artists incorporated a change of consciousness. In very profound and complex ways, the processes of acculturation through several historical eras have helped generate various cultural influences, which Chicanos can claim for inspiration. With the modest support cultural pluralism is now receiving in the United States, this regenerative and innovative quality has grown. Contemplative artists have incorporated into their art a consciousness of political change. Poets, writers, filmmakers, and muralists are known to create and maintain this state of mind in East Los Angeles (Trevino 2001).

Chicano painters and muralists, and others as well, have interpreted the cultural-historical legacies of barrio dwellers. By creating a work of art, they

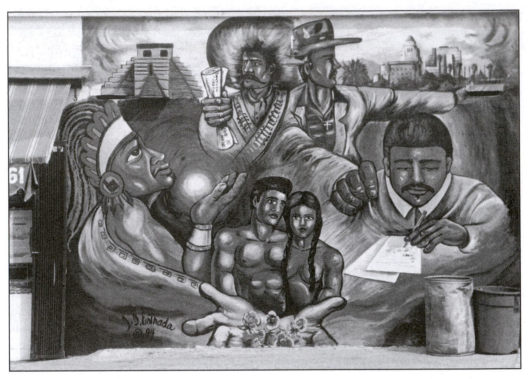

Cultural heritage and diversity.

have brought a new awareness and focus to people's experiences. They have especially reflected the interests and concerns of the people and neighborhoods where this art is found, showing the pride, anger, and futility in the faces of its characters. The murals draw especially from historical inspirations such as the Mexican Revolution and the Indian legacies, thus reminding viewers of the rich past and revolutionary potential of the Chicano people (Cockcroft and Barnet-Sanchez 1993; Griswold del Castillo, McKenna, and Yarbro-Bejarano 1991).

This type of consciousness-raising can be found in several areas of expression. For example, the Teatro Campesino (Rural Workers Theater) began as a medium to inform farmworkers and others about the 1965–1970 grape boycott (Broyles 1990; Broyles-Gonzales 1994). Later it became a model for teatro groups for youth throughout the nation. These theater groups used dramatic interpretation to expose the conditions of the Chicano people. Theater in the Southwest has always served to entertain and instruct, and so it became an effective means of raising cultural and political awareness (Bacalski-Martinez 1979). Teatros have combined humor and satire to portray the multiple Chicano heritage (Hernandez 1991). In this manner, a consciousness is generated. People laugh, cry, or feel pain at the same moment, as if they were all of a sim-

A scene from *Zoot Suit* by Luis Valdez at the Center Theater Group/Mark Taper Forum in Los Angeles.

ilar mind. "All of the dramatic techniques used by the teatro were directed toward depicting the political situations and offering alternative solutions. The goal of the techniques was to produce immediate empathy in order to motivate action. They were symbolic of what 'ought' to have been done in reality" (Garcia 1978:40). The original Teatro Campesino, led by Luis Valdez (1992), presented the successful play *Zoot Suit*, and later *La Bamba*, which familiarized audiences with Chicano urban experiences. Culture Clash, a more recent theater group, has continued this tradition of political education (D. G. Garcia 2008).

Educational Transformations

Similar changes took place in the Chicano educational experience. From Operation Head Start to the university, teachers and students compared notes on the past and present (Samora and Simon 1977). In this exchange, each learned from the other. Since most of the teachers were middle class in the midst of the movement, students regularly reminded them of community needs. As a result, teachers found themselves responding to subtle pressures, even though they may have left the barrio years before. Eventually, many of these same students became teachers and helped reshape the learning landscape. Student awareness was also altered as teachers presented knowledge previously unavailable to them. Garfield High School in East Los Angeles exemplifies this change, as students now compete on an equal basis with all other city students in mathematics and other college-prep courses. Students have embraced a new social concern, as initially heralded by El Plan de Santa Barbara in the 1970s, continuing to call for the university to serve the community (Gomez-Quinones 1978).

One program offered by reformers was for bilingual education, an idea that garnered increasing support from Anglo officials. According to experts, Chicano educational liabilities have stemmed from a cultural and, specifically, a linguistic source. To correct this, schools were to give equal time and attention to English and Spanish. Thus, Chicanos and others would learn to appreciate their culture and language. Gradually, it was reasoned, the sense of Chicano inferiority engendered by traditional schooling would give way to a positive attitude toward themselves and education, and traditional Anglo ethnocentrism would begin its demise.

Government-supported experimental bilingual education programs began to tackle the "cultural" problem. It is no coincidence that most of these pro-

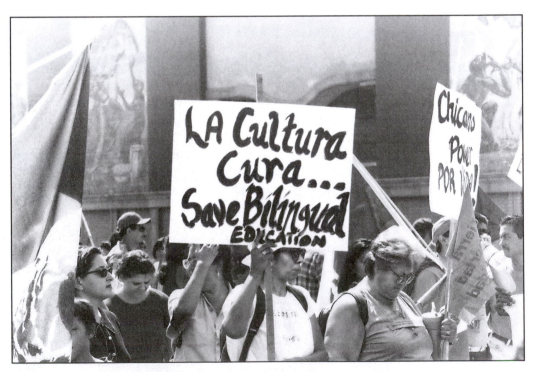

Defending bilingual education.

grams were started at the height of the movement in the 1960s (Magana 2005; de la Garza 1979; Valencia 1991), although even reformist notions based on cultural criteria were previously considered too radical. After the programs were initiated, however, it was too late to rescind them. Both Anglo and Chicano educators found that the bilingual programs in large part improved student school performances (U.S. Commission on Civil Rights 1975). Parents and community leaders strongly supported bilingual education, for they had participated in its creation and implementation. The battle is not over, however. Counterattacks on bilingual education are mounting, as critics (sometimes including parents) underscore how these programs slow learning in English and retard integration into American society. An "English-language-only" movement has also gained national media attention. In spite of these attacks, research continues to show the success of bilingual education programs.

Revolution or Reform?

While reforms made a contribution, some claim that leaders of these efforts exploited the Chicano movement (Munoz 1989; Gutierrez 1995). Rocco (1974:168) argued that wider use of the Spanish language, including bilingual education, has been helpful but has not changed the institutions in power. Thus, it is said, while such reforms and others—the Southwest is now dotted with Chicano agencies and centers—have certainly ameliorated suffering in Chicano communities, in that Chicanos have been afforded the opportunity for more familiarity with dominant institutions, they have also allowed the

Protest to save old Mexican pueblo of Los Angeles.

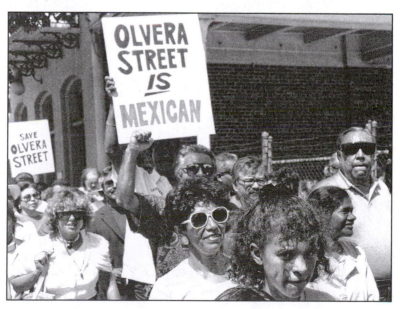

same institutions to "co-opt" community leaders. Indeed, it may be argued that some of these leaders came to the table "pre-co-opted," and thus motivated primarily by self-interest. Activist critics were quick to point out that in most instances, reformers' purse strings were not in the hands of Chicanos.

Nevertheless, the changes wrought with the Chicano movement have created fertile ground for other important developments. Hopes and opportunities for social class mobility and advancement improved for earlier generations of Mexicans. As Telles and Ortiz (2008) remind us, however, the number of people who transitioned from the "generations of exclusion" still did not catch up with the remainder of the U.S. population. Further, the situations and conditions in Mexico—that is, the up-and-down nature of the economy and political system there—made immigration to the U.S. a continuous process. Starting off as peasants or poor, unskilled urban workers, the newcomers brought the total Mexican-American income and status back to ground zero. Similarly, educational levels were also lowered with the influx. On one hand, there were improvement and inroads, but with millions of new Mexicans there were drawbacks, and matters were brought to a standstill. As we will note in the next chapter, there was certainly growing Chicano strength and, just as clearly, many areas that still needed attention.

Chapter 10

A POSTSCRIPT TO THE ANGLO-AMERICAN AND MEXICANIZATION PERIOD

THE THREE C's

Class

It is now close to 40 years since the height of the Chicano movement. The changes that unfolded in the aftermath of that era are significant on several fronts (Hernandez-Leon 2008). However, because of macrostructural changes in the last decade, it is time to talk about a new Three C's: Class, Culture, and Color in the twenty-first century. Key to this era is the issue of immigration and the Mexicanization of the Chicano population. The 2010 census shows that there are now 308 million residents in the United States, of whom 50.5 million are Hispanic. Over 31 million of the Hispanics of Mexican heritage (44 percent) are foreign born; plus, the millions who are undocumented were not counted. The presence of such large numbers of Mexicans and other Latinos makes for a new ball game and the beginnings of a new contact, conflict, and change sequence.

The macrostructural identity of immigrants that defines the last Anglo-American period has been expanded. Large-scale immigration has profoundly altered the social and cultural landscape. The Southwest is no longer "the" population center for migrant Mexicans; cities such as Chicago and New York now have large Hispanic populations as do regions such as Dixie—the South. In March 2006 the largest protest and demonstration of a group championing immigrant rights in the history of the United States occurred in all the places noted above (Chavez 2008:154–157). Media and print coverage ensured that the world was informed about the plight of millions of Mexicans (and other Latinos and ethnic groups) and their objections to being the backbone of labor but the stepchild of political leaders and U.S. citizenry in general. Since then, the American public's outcry to oust Mexicans from the country has risen to high decibel levels. The mean-spirited legal and political actions to prevent Mexicans from becoming citizens and deny citizenship to babies born in the U.S. to undocumented mothers are some of the examples of this xenophobia.

All acculturation and generational change studies (Vigil 1997; Telles and Ortiz 2008; Chavez 2008) indicate that Mexicans are here to stay. "Findings suggest that in terms of education, income, and home ownership, each subsequent generation of Latinos is increasingly integrated into U.S. society and its economy. This does not mean that inequalities in access to education or the

Immigration routes shift and expand in the 1990s.

job market cease to exist" (Chavez 2008:55). The days of sojourners are a thing of the past. Even though unrest and violence in Mexico has brought the country closer to a failed state and the push to leave is stronger than ever, in recent years there has been a turnabout. An increase in jobs and education in Mexico has kept people home, and the immigration tide has slowed almost to a stop (Cave 2011). However, until 2009, the proportion of immigrants in the Mexican population in the U.S. was about three times what it was at the time of the Chicano movement. The goal in the minds of the twenty-first century immigrants is to gain respect and be treated with civility as they contribute to a country that they look up to.

Though U.S. citizens complain that immigrants take away jobs from fellow Americans, the actual truth is that Mexicans do many jobs that Americans don't want to do, and Mexicans are the lowest paid workers in the lowest, mostly service, jobs in the country. As longtime immigration expert Wayne Cornelius maintains: "There is no question that U.S. employers have learned to use low-skilled Latino immigrant labor extensively and productively to fill the kinds of jobs that are shunned by most native-born workers, especially the young" (Cornelius 2009:167). Whereas New York once had immigrants from a variety of nations in the back of the kitchens in its fine selection of restaurants, when you visit New York today it is Mexicans who fill those jobs (Smith 2006, 2009). Similarly, jobs in chicken factories in the U.S. Southeast are now filled by Mexicans, mostly indigenous peasants from southern Mexico who were uprooted when the North American Free Trade Agreement (NAFTA) went into effect and Mexico selected a neoliberal path.

All of this need for cheap, service labor from south of the border comes at a time when inequality and poverty are at an all time high. As Professor Pastor states: "The striking fact is that the Latino poverty rate is nearly 40 percent—almost half of the California's Latino population lives in conditions most observers would term quite challenging . . . even households headed by U.S.-born Latinos earn only about 80 percent of their Anglo counterparts" (Pastor 2009:22). Not to be ignored, "The richest 1 percent of Americans now take home almost 24 percent of income, up from almost 9 percent in 1976" (Kristof 2010).

In short, this groundswell in immigration has elicited quite different reactions as a result of the recent economic crises in Mexico and increases in unemployment in the United States. Anti-immigrant attitudes in the 1990s to the present have become more widespread and fueled political debates in many regions in the United States, especially in the Southwest.

Social Class and Gender Equality

The median family income of the Spanish-surnamed population in 1969 was $7,080 and that of Anglos was $10,750—a sizable gap (Briggs, Fogel, and

Schmidt 1977). Ten years later, Chicano family income was still about 70 percent of that for whites, or $11,742 as opposed to approximately $16,000 (Thurow 1979; Daniels 1991). By 1990, Chicano families earned an average of $21,025 versus $33,142 for non-Hispanic families, that is, only two-thirds as much (Segura 1992). Moreover, the 1990 census showed that while family incomes had improved, 25 percent of Chicano families were still below the poverty line (Meier and Ribera 1993). In Los Angeles between 1969 and 1985, there was an overall increase in poverty, with almost all of it stemming from the Chicano population (Moore and Vigil 1993; Ong 1988). Statistics also indicate that Mexican male workers in the late 1980s earned only 57 percent of the earnings of white males (Reimers 1992). Even controlling for generational change and social mobility to the middle class through skilled and white-collar occupations, there is still a relative gap in income. Several researchers have emphasized the persistence of discrimination as the primary barrier (Bean and Tienda 1987; Romero 1979). Today, there is still a decided income gap between U.S. whites who earn $49,777 annually, as opposed to $38,039 for Hispanics, not counting the millions of undocumented Mexicans (Pastor 2009:23).

The upward mobility of earlier generations continues (Telles and Ortiz 2008) as doctors, professors, and dentists begin to fill the ranks of Chicano occupations. Still, the greatest increase in jobs is in the service sector as janitors, gardeners, domestics, child- and senior-care workers, day laborers, dry-

Homeboys mural in east Los Angeles.

The barrios
today.

wallers (a high percentage in southern California), dishwashers, car washers, and busboys; other low-paying, unskilled construction and light industries jobs also dominate the scene. In addition to low wages for most of these occupations, there is also the issue of health coverage: "the percentage of Latino households lacking health insurance was [in the early 2000s] 40.1, about twice the rate of Anglos" (Pastor 2009:34).

Closely associated with this economic marginality is how particularly stressed families have lost the battle to the streets due to pressures that hamstring them from effectively guiding and supervising their children. As scholars have noted, rising inequality has repercussions in other related realms. Financial distress, for example, can take a toll on families and contribute to family breakdowns and attenuated child-rearing patterns. As such, inequality isn't just an economic issue but can shape inadequate living conditions, stressful personal and family changes, and cultural and psychological adjustment in schools. Multiple marginality is thus produced where place, status, sociocultural surroundings, and self-identity become betwixt and between mainstream and fringe realities. For children, this placement makes for gangs and gang members (Vigil 2002, 2007; Miranda 2003). Immigration and poverty are unfortunately closely connected. It is no accident that the rise in gangs stems from the overcrowded poor sections of cities and towns having to integrate the influx of newcomers (Vigil 2009).

A national issue that has been steadily gaining attention in recent decades deals with equal opportunity for women, another class factor (Hondagneu-Sotelo 1994, 2007). Chicanas are very much involved in that struggle, and in fact their role affects important cultural and socioeconomic dimensions (Romero, Hondagneu-Sotelo, and Ortiz 1997; Del Castillo 1990; Melville 1980). In the 1980s there was a tremendous jump in Chicana participation in the labor force, more than double the rate for women generally (Segura and Zavella 2007; Segura 1992). Since historical conditions have relegated Chicanos to the lowest positions, Chicanas are even more disadvantaged than non-Chicana women (Gonzales 1979). In 1969, the earnings of working Chicanas averaged to be only a third of those of white female workers. This discrepancy in wage levels has diminished but it does still exist. In 1990, Chicanas earned much less than non-Hispanic women (Meier and Ribera 1993): average earnings for 1990 were: Chicanas, $8,110; non-Hispanic women, $11,245 (Segura 1992). (The pay gap for men was even larger: Chicanos, $12,107; non-Hispanic men, $21,267.) The wage gap for Chicanas is largely due to the usual relegation to low-wage, low-status jobs, such as domestic and agricultural work, which offer little opportunity for promotion (Hondagneu-Sotelo 1994, 2007; Segura 1990). Chicanas and women from Mexico, like their male counterparts, are part of a "transnational" reservoir of labor, adding further to the importance of migration and immigration to any discussion of social-class issues

(Ruiz and Tiano 1987; Martinez and McCaughan 1990). For females, "these jobs have entered the global marketplace and immigrant women from developing nations around the globe are increasingly represented in them in major metropolitan centers throughout the country" (Hondagneu-Sotelo 2007:303; see also Suarez-Orozco 2009).

However, the Chicano movement as a whole has been hesitant to address gender issues and problems of male domination. When Chicanas began to raise the issue of gender inequities, some movement activists responded by arguing that feminist concerns diverted attention from the "real" issues of racism and class exploitation. Chicano intellectuals "interpreted the condition of Mexican men and women to be synonymous; gender was irrelevant in determining life experience and power" (Orozco 1990:12). Feminism was also viewed to be Anglo, middle-class, and bourgeois, and Chicanas were thus denounced as being traitors to "la causa" (Oboler 1995). This resulted in many Chicanas initially being reticent in voicing their demands. Slowly and inexorably, however, a more concerted feminist perspective developed to generate increased information and insights to fill the ethnohistorical gap of knowledge about the obviously neglected half of the Chicano people.

Confronting these difficulties, Chicanas have fought for equality and justice within their community organizations. Demands have included welfare rights, rehabilitation programs for *pintas* (female ex-convicts), safeguards against male violence, access to birth control, and the right to refuse forced sterilization (Oboler 1995). One Chicana, Francisca Flores, played a major role in politics and other Chicana issues by founding the California League of Mexican American Women (Meier and Ribera 1993).

The heroine of the classic labor film *Salt of the Earth* underscores the Chicana plight with these angry and insightful words (aimed not only at her husband but presumably at all minority men): "Do you feel better having someone lower than you? Whose neck shall I stand on to make me feel superior? And what will I get out of it? I don't want anything lower than I am. I'm low enough already. I want to rise. And push everything up with me as I go." Chicanas and other minority women have been actively pursuing the end of their position as "twice a minority" (Melville 1980).

United States, Mexico, and Undocumented Immigrants

Chicano economic inequality is intertwined with the continuing saga of "as the United States goes, so goes Mexico!" Since the 1960s the growing complexity of problems resulting from multinational corporate entanglements has evolved into something else. Transnational capitalism has taken over, and as we shall see, free-trade innovations like NAFTA, which was formed between the U.S., Mexico, and Canada in 1993, underscore this development. Mexico is now completely at the mercy of the United States. As William Robinson maintains in his investigations of global capitalism, "The accelerated incursion of capitalist production into the countryside around the world in the second half of the twentieth century uprooted hundreds of millions of peasants and threw them into the capitalist free labor market, often as unemployed or underemployed workers" (Robinson 2004:149). Chiapas, a southern state in Mexico, is a case in point. Since the aftermath of the 1910 Revolution the government had dutifully subsidized peasant indigenous communities to ensure their survival. After NAFTA, however, the neoliberal policies effectively undermined the rural, peasant lifestyle, sending tens of thousands of Maya peoples to join the migratory stream, with many landing in the Southeast United States.

Earlier, in an effort to escape from U.S. labor unions and environmental restrictions, many corporations (then known as multinationals because they transcend national boundaries and move to any nation that provides the cheapest workers) have built plants (*maquiladoras,* about 2,700 of them) just across the Mexican border, to tap the cheap source of labor (Cornelius 2009; Marcelli and Cornelius 2001; Pastor 2009). Many of these maquiladoras, to gain added advantage from wage disparities, employ mostly women who, in Mexico as in the U.S., tend to receive lower wages than men. Maquiladoras have increased urban growth, with the rise of "sister" border cities along the United States–Mexican boundary (Arreola and Curtis 1993). On the Mexican side, residents might earn only 20 to 30 percent of what they would for comparable work in the United States (Price 1973; Gann and Duignan 1986). As an upshot of these economic ties and transactions, social relations and cultural exchanges between Americans and Mexicans on both sides of the border have multiplied exponentially. In 2003, there were 9.1 million pedestrian border crossings in Arizona, and 32 million in California, the San Ysidro section of San Diego.

A whole new literature devoted to the phenomena of "border culture" has arisen, with some observers even coining a new regional term, MexiAmerica (Alvarez 1995:4, 2001; Martinez, 1996; Mora-Torres 2001). Both sides of the border have become important, as northern Mexico now is the source of many agricultural products targeted for U.S. communities (Heyman 1991; Alvarez 1995, 2001). For example, in 2005 Mexican exports to the U.S. totaled $50 billion, not counting the near $40 billion of illegal drugs smuggled into the U.S. by drug cartels.

Mexico's move to join NAFTA not only furthered the economic integration of the U.S., Canada, and Mexico, it also added uncertainty to workers' futures on both sides of the U.S.–Mexico border. While the agreement somewhat stabilized Mexico's free fall in the world market, it also created 21 new billionaires in the country to further aggravate the gap between rich and poor and instill rancor in the working population. Organized labor in the United States expressed concerns that NAFTA would lead to loss of jobs there, and environmentalists feared an increase in pollution because of less stringent environmental regulations in Mexico. In January of 1994, as NAFTA took effect, the Zapatista Army of National Liberation (or EZLN, Ejercito Zapatista de Liberacion Nacional) dramatically surfaced in one of the neglected indigenous peasant regions of southern Mexico to challenge the Mexican government (Collier and Quaratiello 1994). Their demands for attention and access to resources included mention of NAFTA. The latter was a strategy to shake the Mexican government and correct the serious state of underdevelopment in the region. Such a reaction serves to underscore the importance of macro-structural developments in transnational economic growth and globalization, including large-scale and continuing migration (Cornelius 2009).

The 1970s witnessed the largest increase in the number of undocumented Mexican workers in the United States; in the 1970s there were anywhere from 2 to 12 million undocumented Mexicans (Chavez 2008; Cornelius 1978), and this transnational process has continued, with the figures remaining more or less the same for the 1990s and 2000s. Previous periods of high immigration were the 1920s, the 1950s, and the 1960s. Significantly, in each immigration wave through the twentieth century, most of the newcomers originated from the same central and northern regions and states of Mexico. More recently, however, many more immigrants come from the urban areas of these regions,

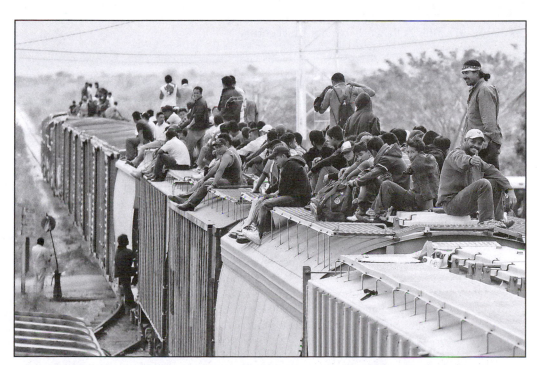

Migrants from southern Mexico ride a train bound for the U.S.–Mexico border.

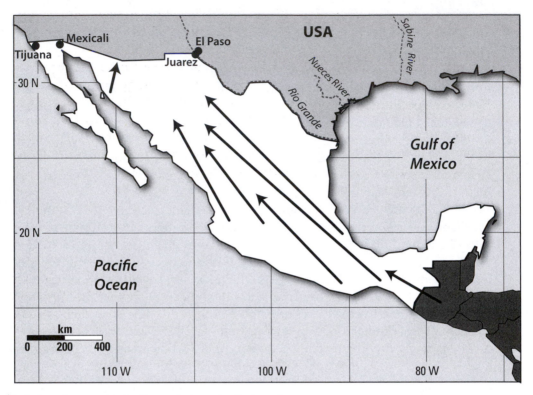

Immigration routes in the early twenty-first century.

and a much larger number of indigenous peasants from southern Mexico (and Central America) have begun to alter the figures (Martinez 1996; Segura and Zavella 2007; Chavez 2008; Cornelius and Bustamante 1989).

These workers fill the low-paying, unskilled jobs that no one else desires and, indeed, provide important services; furthermore, they often settle in whatever open spaces are available near work locations (Chavez 1998, 2008). More important is the Mexican labor force's "flexibility and disposability" to accommodate a fluid and volatile economic system subject to periodic recessions and downturns (Cornelius and Bustamante 1989). In fact,

> such labor is regarded simply as a windfall to a greedy minority of U.S. employers intent on protecting or enlarging their profit margins; a subsidy to middle-class U.S. consumers who do not want to pay more for their restaurant meals, clothing, agricultural produce, and personal services; and a social safety valve—an employment-welfare program—for Mexico. (Cornelius and Bustamante 1989:26; and also Marcelli and Cornelius 2001)

In this assessment, economic restructuring in the U.S. and consumer demands have made a reliance on immigrant labor that much more necessary

(Massey et al. 1987). American citizens, who object to increased immigration, fail to acknowledge that it is "the political economy that creates a demand in the U.S. labor market for immigrant labor" (Chavez 2008:135).

Immigration has nevertheless become a central concern for many people, including government officials, and some of the solutions to the "problem" fostered continuing attitudes of a discriminatory nature. The passage of Proposition 187 in California in 1994 aimed to bar undocumented immigrants from certain health and education services, but the higher courts stopped this effort. In an earlier example, in the 1970s, Congressman Peter Rodino presented a bill that would allow employers to ask for place of birth identification from anyone "appearing" to be Mexican. Obviously, such a measure would infringe on the civil rights of millions of Mexican Americans born in the United States. To resolve this difficulty, one naive apologist suggested that native Mexicans could wear badges. Congressional struggles over this issue mirrored the national mood until the Immigration Reform and Control Act (IRCA) was passed in 1986. The passage of IRCA was intended to resolve this problem but failed to do so. Many Chicano activists challenged this legislation, some aspects of which they considered racist and discriminatory. Nevertheless, Cesar Chavez argued that IRCA would improve working conditions by allowing undocumented immigrants to unionize (Griswold del Castillo and Garcia 1995). Meanwhile, anti-immigrant fervor has once again reached a panic level, especially with the passage of state and federal legislation curtailing services to noncitizen immigrants. This disposition has engulfed affirmative action and other hard-won civil rights laws and regulations to fan a general mood of antipathy toward ethnic minorities.

Since the mid-1980s, a whole series of laws has been enacted. Congress has debated and passed the Immigration Act of 1990, allowing a few more newcomers every year and the development of a lottery system to select them. In 1996, the Illegal Immigration Reform and Immigrant Responsibility Act attempted to streamline the status of the undocumented immigrant, but mostly created confusion. Welfare reform legislation enacted in 1996 aimed to restructure the social welfare system, especially AFDC (Aid to Families with Dependent Children), but instead it put further restrictions on poor immigrants, even though undocumented ones were denied participation. So it went into the beginning of the twenty-first century, with the House of Representatives' 2005 Border Protection, Antiterrorism and Illegal Immigrant Control Act (which did not pass in the Senate) and the Senate's efforts to provide a path to citizenship for undocumented residents. In contrast, the state of Arizona enacted the 2010 Support Our Law Enforcement and Safe Neighborhoods Act (SB 1070), which provided law enforcement with the right to verify legal status of undocumented workers. In 2011, Alabama enacted similar provisions.

For the first time in American history, there are as many noncitizen Mexicans (and other Latinos) as there are registered Mexican voters in the United

States. This means that numerical superiority cannot translate into political power unless all Latinos, that is both documented and undocumented, have the opportunity to participate in the political process. NALEO (National Association of Elected and Appointed Officials) and SVREP (Southwest Voters Registration and Education Project) are striving toward this goal and expend much energy on informing unregistered Latinos of the importance of voting in the United States. NALEO has progressively grown through the decades from 3,743 officials in 1996 to 5,736 in 2010. Democrats and Republicans alike are watching these developments with increasing interest, knowing that in certain sections of the nation—mainly in the Southwest, but also the Midwest, Florida, and the Northeast—Mexicans (and Latinos) can influence election outcomes. In fact, the portents of the future might duplicate a 1996 election in a Republican stronghold of Orange County, California, where a Chicana defeated a hard right-winger in a close contest. The event caused a furor on several levels, not least because of the discovery that a small number of the newly naturalized Mexicans had voted prematurely, before being sworn in (Valle and Torres 2003). Despite the potential for such political influences, however, are concerns in the apparent lack of forceful leadership. Valle and Torres (2003:397), for example, maintain that "timid Latino political leaders . . . cannot capture the cultural space to articulate a transnational human rights agenda . . . [and] risk reinforcing the existing hegemonic order."

Currently, the debate continues on various political fronts as to whether American labor will benefit from immigration reform in keeping down the competition from foreign labor. Screening job applicants for proof of citizenship or legal resident alien registration cards, a part of IRCA stipulations, is also proving to be a difficult task for employers. Meanwhile, the anti-immigration rhetoric has risen with some observers comparing the millions of undocumented workers with that of an invading army threatening American security (Chavez 2008).

The movement of large numbers of immigrants, legal and undocumented, continues. Fewer undocumented immigrants applied for legal residence under IRCA (1986) than some observers expected, but enough (about 3.8 million) did, demonstrating that making a home in the United States is important. Lest we forget, "the march [demonstrations in 2006] was a political statement, a taking over of the village square, to claim recognition as social and cultural citizens, and to show support for legislation that would allow them to eventually become legal residents and citizens of the United States" (Chavez 2008:152).

Opposite page: Thousands of demonstrators crowd the streets in Los Angeles, March 2006.

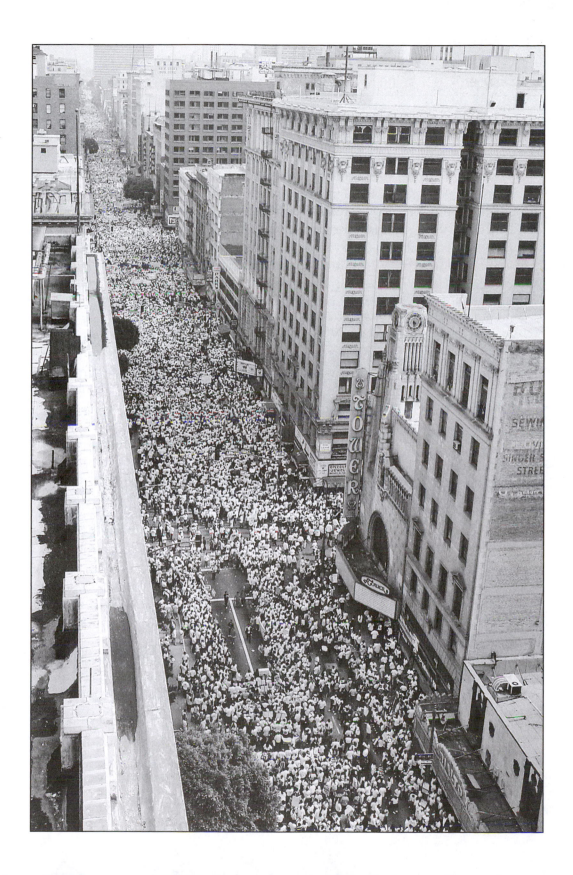

Culture

Tied to how immigration increased the Mexican population and that of other Latinos to over 50 million in 2010, making this group the number-one ethnic minority group in the United States, are other cultural and social developments. For one, this massive change brought about a cultural ethos that transformed certain cities and regions to create a Mexicanization current. Acculturation processes have radically changed because of the thrust of the Chicano movement clamoring for bilingual/bicultural education. When an increase in population occurs simultaneously with this push, then whole generations of newcomers' children become raised and educated with a true bidirectional acculturation path to guide and direct them (Suarez-Orozco and Suarez-Orozco 2001). Today, one can hardly find young Chicano high schoolers who are unable to speak some form of Spanish and who still are able to speak a form of English. The Mexicanization current has also fortified the groundwork initiated in the aftermath of the Chicano movement and set the direction and tone of ethnic self-identification among Mexican students of all generations. For example, Spanish language usage and pride in Mexican/Latino cultural habits and customs have become the "norm."

To encourage this sentiment, the Mexican government has moved in the direction of binationality, allowing immigrants to maintain Mexican citizenship with full rights while also becoming American citizens. The renewed interest on the part of the Mexican government to keep ties with the millions of Mexicans who reside on the U.S. side of the border is a recent development. Previously, Chicano leaders and intellectuals had firmed up a connection for mostly cultural and educational purposes. However, it is apparent today that both Chicano and Mexican leaders realize that a continuing flow of information and other exchanges are essential to political situations on both sides of the border. Testimony to the importance of this budding relationship is seen in the Mexican electoral campaigns when candidates visit U.S. cities to curry favor with the transplanted citizens. This habit has grown since the 1980s and even includes a Mexican presidential campaign.

Mexicans, however, are not a "generic" population, and a single label cannot address the variability within the group (Suarez-Orozco and Suarez-Orozco 1994). Thus, we need a broader framework that encompasses the differences in time, place, and people. The time period reflects the economic, social, and political habits that shape people and events, whereas place, such as the neighborhood or institutions, reflects changing realities. People change over time and in places, and new and/or different forces, such as immigration or economic restructuring, can significantly alter an individual's feelings, thoughts, and actions. As the Spindlers have noted (Spindler and Spindler

Chicano power!

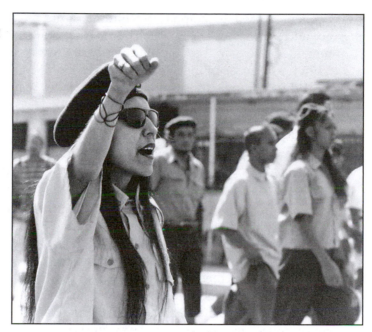

1990), such shifts can tax and strain enduring (past), situated (present), and endangered (stress between first two) notions of self.

During the late 1980s and the early 1990s, Chicano student groups began again to struggle for educational reform. In large part, this reclamation effort was headed by a new generation of Chicano students. Most of these leaders and participants came from the "1.5 generation"—immigrants who arrived in the United States as children, and were raised in a bilingual and bicultural setting (Vigil 1997). UCLA students mobilized in the spring of 1993 to push for a separate Chicano Studies Department. A coalition of student, faculty, and community activists went on a hunger strike to convince the university's administrators that this change was long overdue. Public and media attention focused on this event, which ended with a partial victory for the activists; a new Chicano Studies Department was established and named the Cesar Chavez Center, but other demands (such as for more faculty) went unmet. This thrust for educational changes and reform has continued throughout the nation, particularly in states with large concentrations of Chicanos, as more programs are initiated and expanded with student and faculty members shaping and pushing the agenda.

So far only the reform efforts within a cultural nationalist framework have been discussed. Other factors and forces also were important, as Chicanos were committed to improving their overall standard of living—schools, jobs, and so on—and they worked hard for these goals. Nevertheless, it seems that the spirit of the times and primary impetus for change was culturally based.

Leaders tended to emphasize cultural rights as a precondition leading to advances in other areas, such as in the political arena. This orientation remained strong in the Chicano community, as even the Brown Berets enjoyed a brief resurgence in the late 1980s and early 1990s.

While cultural transformations were under way, some weak (even barely perceptible) class and color changes occurred. The spirit of the Mexican Revolution was instrumental in this slight stirring since cultural nationalists drew on the egalitarian revolutionary ideas of such leaders as Emiliano Zapata, Pancho Villa, and Ricardo Flores Magon. This imagery and call to action has continued its appeal with time and was renewed by the Zapatista army revolt in Chiapas in 1994 (Vasquez and Torres 2003). In contrast, there is still a strong ideology that possessions and material wealth are more important than people, even though the 1960s movement gave hope for future generations to champion a more communal style.

Of great significance to the growth in the Chicano population and rise in consciousness is the understanding associated with "macrostructural identities." In other words, there may have been cultural differences among the earliest Mexicans, such as Aztecs varying from Tarascans or Maya, but nearly all of them became peasants in the Spanish era and remained so in the subsequent Mexican period. Later, with further regional and worldwide economic and political revamping, regional variation among peasants from places such as Oaxaca, Yucatan, or Morelos became blurred when they joined the massive migrations of the twentieth century (Kearney 1996). While holding culture constant over the centuries, the macrostructural identities of indigenous (Indian), peasant, and immigrant arose to fit the ever tightening regional and global economic networks that gradually took root.

There is little doubt that the Chicano movement made an impact on the initial time period and in subsequent generations. Some activists have continued to carry the banner pushing for radical change, while others advocate a progressive approach with the charged political realities of today. Thus, the process of change is weaving a newly distinct, yet diverse, pattern (Lux and Vigil 1979).

Growing Chicano Strength

The resistance mounted against IRCA, although unsuccessful, nevertheless shows the building strength of the Chicano community. Chicanos are increasingly outspoken in American politics and more adept at forming alliances with liberal whites and others. Earlier demonstrations of this resolve include the successful (but short-lived) outcome of the United Farm Workers' call for a boycott of California grapes and lettuce—farmers eventually recognized the union and California enacted progressive farm labor laws. While most of these changes were partially turned back in the 1980s, the UFW con-

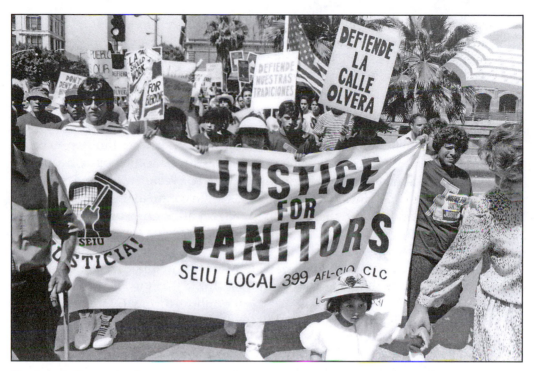

Service workers organize.

tinues to draw attention to issues affecting migrant workers and supports their needs. Similarly, the third-party thrust of La Raza Unida at times influenced local elections—even winning several—and since then, Chicano elected and appointed officials have increased in number at all levels of government (de la Garza and DeSipio 1999). The Catholic Church has successfully organized barrio families into large neighborhood groups such as Communities Organized for Public Service (COPS) in San Antonio, The Organization of the Northwest (TON) in Chicago, and the United Neighborhood Organization (UNO) in Los Angeles. Increasingly, the large and vocal immigrant community has become a part of this community-based organizing. The 1992 Los Angeles upheavals and subsequent smaller-scale protests were characterized as a poor-people's rebellion, and many of the participants were Mexican or Latino, which shows the intense disenchantment of part of this population.

Both small and large demonstrations of discontent and strength have by no means overcome all institutional discrimination against Chicano leadership, and factionalism among Chicano politicians has also interfered with advances. Still, the few protests and eruptions are sufficient to prove that a growing awareness and a sophistication in tactics and strategy are being amassed in dealing with the barriers and obstacles in U.S. society.

Indeed, there is ample reason to expect Chicano consciousness and political influence to continue to blossom. Presidential cabinet-level officers have served in the administrations of both Bill Clinton and Barack Obama, and even the George W. Bush era had more Hispanics in high positions than in previous Republican controlled periods. Already a number-one minority population, some observers are predicting that the Chicano population of Los Angeles will soon grow sufficiently to make California the first "minority-majority" state in the contiguous United States. The continuing massive immigration from Mexico will not only enlarge the Chicano population in the United States, but it will strengthen the links between the Chicano community and Mexico (Hurtado and Gurin 2004; Gomez-Quinones 1978). Moreover, it will add luster to Chicanozaje imagery (Gutierrez and Zavella 2009; Ramirez 1985).

In fact, for a while, especially in the 1980s "Decade of the Hispanic," it was thought that sheer demographic increases in the population would force changes; later, one observer quipped, "now that the Decade of the Hispanic is over, what do we do now?" Furthermore, during the 1980s Chicanos somewhat acquiesced to the conservative atmosphere, even as major increases in Chicano political representation occurred (Vasquez and Torres 2003; Gomez-Quinones 1990; de la Garza and DeSipio 1996). To reiterate, in 1996, there were more than 3,700 elected and appointed officials nationwide (these increased to over 5,700 in 2010), and in California, the fastest growing Mexican/Latino state in the nation, representatives in the state legislature increased from seven in 1991 to 21 in 2011. Although the number of representatives has increased, many have joined the Republican Party, while others, now secure in the middle class, identify with conservative forces in the Democratic Party who shun social programs for the disadvantaged. Even organizations with long records of activism have formed commercial alliances with very conservative business firms in return for contributions to their social programs.

One significant outcome of the lull in progressive changes was the effort on the part of Latino politicians to organize a national Latino network, primarily comprised of Chicanos and Puerto Ricans, but inclusive of other Spanish-surname, Spanish-speaking pressure groups. NALEO (National Association of Latino Elected and Appointed Officials) successfully attempted in the late 1970s to establish a common meeting ground for lobbying for Latino issues, such as political underrepresentation, low average income and education levels, and so on. NALEO then broadened its agenda and took on the work of encouraging immigrants throughout the country to become naturalized citizens. Interestingly, former Congressman Edward Roybal from Los Angeles was instrumental in starting this group, just as he was with the CSO in the late 1940s and MAPA in the late 1950s.

Another move, led by Willie Velasquez from Texas, was to coordinate a region-wide voter-registration drive. The Southwest Voter Registration Education Project (SVREP) successfully targeted Mexican-American districts with low registration and voter-turnout patterns, and increased the size of the voting bloc over the years. Gradually, the organization gained a wider appeal among Chicanos and won respect from established politicians, who, of course, wanted to facilitate access to the Chicano vote. Much of this activity was aided by the Voting Rights Act in 1965, which was expanded in 1975 to include language minorities. As an example of the growing strength of the Latino vote, two-thirds of Latinos voted for President Barack Obama in 2008.

Equally important to the push was the work of the Mexican American Legal Defense and Education Fund (MALDEF) and the National Council of La Raza (NCLR). MALDEF had formed in the early 1970s to assist local agencies and organizations in providing services to the community. As it grew in stature and expanded its base, it eventually focused on political issues. One of them was to challenge political district boundaries, which historically had been gerrymandered to dilute the Chicanos' vote, a widespread practice throughout the Southwest. This problem still plagues the Chicano community; the 2010 U.S. Census gave Texas four new congressional seats, and Anglos (and Republicans) are working to gerrymander these districts to benefit themselves.

In Los Angeles, MALDEF, along with other plaintiffs, succeeded in getting the courts to redraw county supervisory district lines to better reflect the large, concentrated Mexican-American neighborhoods. Not one of the five supervisors was Chicano (or other minority), and none was female. In a subsequent election to fill a vacant seat on the Board of Supervisors, then Los Angeles City Councilwoman Gloria Molina won and her victory became a cause celebre. The National Council of La Raza (NCLR), begun in 1968, has become recognized as a Washington, D.C., lobby force for Latino issues. While there is some disagreement on just who NCLR represents, there is no doubt that its presence in the nation's capital has placed Latino national concerns in the forefront.[1]

Many hazards still accompany such cultural changes. There persists, for example, the problem of marginality; some people are unable to function adequately in any culture, much less become creative cultural innovators. Many variants to this situation of conflict and confusion reflect a type of "multiple marginality" (Vigil 1988) in which economic forces predominate. High dropout rates, learning difficulties, self-image problems, drug and alcohol use and abuse, and family strains are among the offshoots of these conditions (Hurtado and Gurin 2004). For example, the barrio problems with gang warfare stem from many sources, but one cannot explain the lifestyle of cholo gang members without considering cultural criteria. As previously noted, the cholo or chola is marginal to both Mexican and Anglo cultures and is mainly a street-

Cholo montage.

raised person. Some have patterned a life based on *la vida loca*—the crazy life. This is a subcultural model that over the years has become so institutionalized that "crazy" acts are considered acceptable. Fathoming the conditions that created this *vato loco* (crazy dude) tradition, it is no wonder that many who feel wronged by society believe it is the only way to survive in the United States. In recent years, problems associated with this lifestyle have spiraled almost out of control, partly because society's solution for these multiple problems has largely emphasized suppression at the expense of prevention and intervention (see Vigil 2010 for a more balanced anti-gang strategy). However, it must also be noted that the majority of those who appear to be cholos are "wannabes" who follow a less destructive path, cruising with the cholas, getting high, and generally presenting an image of urban Chicano cool. Many simply dress and behave like cholos because it is stylish and the "in thing" to do.

Chicanos: Additive Acculturationists

The Chicano community on the whole has sought a more rewarding route in insisting that something positive is linked to their background. Those favoring the label "Chicano" have chosen a name that stems from indigenous sources, and when a generic label is needed, "Latino" is favored over "Hispanic," the latter promoted by the federal government for all Spanish-speaking, Spanish-surnamed Americans. Using the label "Chicano" (and "Latino") is partly a declaration of independence, of the desire and self-determination to no longer be treated as a second-class citizen. It challenges the stereotype that Chicanos are inferior or culturally deprived (Alaniz and Cornish 2008; de la Garza 1979). The term "Chicano" implies pride in a background of many and mixed heritages and the versatility to widen one's sociocultural persona. This orientation of additive acculturation, in which the dominant cultural mode is learned and the native style kept, will help to lead American citizens away from ethnocentrism (Gibson and Ogbu 1991; Vigil and Long 1981). "Biculturalism is of tremendous advantage . . . for it carries with it . . . the ability to pick and choose constructively and eclectically from two different and useful cultures" (Arvizu 1974:125–126).

Another way to look at it is that a person can have "multiple" identities and not just "one self per customer" (Shweder and Markus 1995); a notion that has been recognized by some researchers who advocate a multidimensional measure for an individual's "selves" (Felix-Ortiz, Newcomb, and Myers 1994). I have referred to this strategy of cultural expansion and incorporation as "personas mexicanas" (connoting many masks of Mexicans) because it reflects the history and cultural evolution of Mexicans and Mexican Americans (Vigil and Hanley 2002), a people of many cultural and linguistic influences; it closely approximates the "American Cultural Dialogue" notions proposed by the Spindlers (Spindler and Spindler 1990).

This pattern is based on cultural democracy: everyone's way of life is right and proper (Ramirez 1985, 1976). As a socioculturally diverse population within the United States and perhaps leading the Western Hemisphere in this regard, Chicanos are in the forefront of this new age of "panhuman" awareness, in which a global economy requires, minimally, an open mind to the development of a global culture.

Color: Persistence Generates New Ways to Dissect Race

Most of the changes on race and racism in the last several decades were "part of the larger worldwide egalitarian impulse to eradicate the most egregious forms of racial discrimination in the 1960s" (Gutierrez 2009:109). The Chicano movement generated a lot of attention, energy, and insight on how a people were barred and prevented from having the same opportunities afforded members of mainstream society, and relegated to the margins of society on the basis of their racial appearance and phenotypic characteristics. While most of us agree "that race matters" we have not yet agreed on how it has persisted and taken on new forms. Racial formation theory (Omi and

Winant 1994; Lopez 2011) is fairly explicit on outlining how race relations are fundamentally grounded as an organizing principle in American society. There are both macro and micro situations and conditions that contribute and perpetuate racial inequality.

Thus, daily practices reflect behavior that show prejudices, and legal rulings emerge to reshape how people are to behave toward each other. Racial profiling, like DWB (Driving While Black, or Brown) is a recent innovation of racial inequality that legal experts have addressed because it has become so commonplace in our society (police stopping motorists on the basis of color, appearance or type of automobile; or teachers holding different unequal attitudes and expectations of students and treatment of same). Further, "illegal alien," used as a descriptor denoting someone in the U.S. without legal documents, has become code for a not-so-feigned racial stereotyping label. To counter and account for these developments, CRT (Critical Race Theory) (Delgado and Stefancic 2000) has become a scholarly enterprise for unraveling how race and racism figure in the affairs and institutions of humans in societies all over. The point of all this for us is how these developments play a role in the contemporary *color* experiences of the Chicano population, including other Latinos who share similar phenotypic traits (Healey 2010).

The first order of business is to quickly recount the past historical dynamics that have produced a miscegenated population of Indians, Spaniards, and Africans. Many racial attitudes and self-identification dynamics of the past continue to the present. Laura Gomez (2007) has referred to an aspect of this heritage as "double colonization" because of the Spanish conquest and the much later Anglo takeover of the Southwest. It is like racism through a prism, with light and angles making deep or nuanced rays across ones eyes. The received popular wisdom in Mexico today is one of "mestizocracia" (Vigil and Lopez 2004) or the "mestizo myth" where racism is a thing of the past, erased by the progress and revolutions that broke and eliminated the color barrier.

This would be true except for "socioracial passing" became such a pattern that even towns that were 100 percent Indian became mestizo overnight just because residents claimed that heritage (Vigil and Lopez 2004). Burying one's past became so common that barely now have Mexicans begun to deal with their African racial roots, and, more importantly, their racism (Villarreal 2010); witness the uproar in Mexico when a cartoon character, Memin Pinguin, was exposed as that country's pet version of Little Black Sambo, the latter, by the way, an interesting variation on the Spanish label for an Indian/African admixture, Zambo. Africans, as noted in the Spanish colonial section of this book, were a sizeable segment of the Mexican population in that era. They did not just disappear. According to recent experts on the subject, Africans took up residence in selected interior and coastal regions but generally just melded into the population through racial mixing (Vaughn 2005, 2009; Dulitzky 2005). So much for mestizocracia!

A recent study (Menchaca 2001) creatively and definitely laid out the African admixture in the Mexican population. So the double conquest whammy Gomez suggested is compounded with another one in the racial experience. Moreover, in openly showcasing that "open" hidden secret, researchers are beginning to document how race affects other realms in a person's life, such as schooling and academic achievement, self-identity, inequality (Lopez 2003, 2011; Bonilla-Silva 2003; Feagin 2005; Pizzaro 2005). To underscore the point, racism has manifested itself in old ways and researchers continue to unravel what these ways are and, more interestingly, discover new variations on the theme.

Racial discrimination always has some type of psychological consequence. Already mentioned are the racial stigmas and socioracial passing practices associated with cultural contacts and changes. According to researchers, most people who assimilate are left with psychological trauma if their racial appearance interferes with being accepted (see Stonequist 1937 for the classic study on this subject). Despite Mexicanization, on one level there is still a deeper process for many where they despise their own culture and racial group in order to conform to the national ideology. This becomes a very complex situation for the minority person to confront, a commonly traversed path of marginality, conflict, and ambiguity that is still a reality for Mexicans in the United States.

Because close to one-half of the current Mexican population is Mexican born, the baggage of the past has arrived in the United States. Thus, the colonial mentality that still persists today in the psyche of Mexican society means a personal preference for light skin colors over the darker ones even for the Mexicans in the United States. Ortiz Pinchetti (1998) argues that the preference of skin color reflects that Mexican racism has not been overcome despite the modernization that has taken place in Mexico; as noted, it is mestizocracia without the elimination of racism. He further points out that the status quo in Mexico is defended by people quickly pointing out that racial mobility in Mexico has been enormous in this century.

Yet, in some Mexican households favoritism is still given to the fair-skinned children. Barros (1997) writes, "Many of us have been witness to the predilection of a mother or of a father for their children who are *güeritos* (light skinned) and of the irreparable damage that has been made to the brown or not so white [children] of the family." Sandstrom also indicates that "in Mexico to be *güero,* or light skin complexioned, gives a person advantage over his or her dark peers" (1991:64). Jorge Bustamante (1994) notes the importance given to skin color when he writes that racist ideology has been filtered in many aspects of social life in Mexico and in the aesthetic values. Bustamante thinks that to analyze ourselves self-critically, we must take our skeletons out of their closets. He writes, "I would like to propose as a premise for that auto-criticism to examine the following: we Mexicans are racists" (1994:44).

Indigenous migration to urban places in both Mexico and the United States is now commonplace and has been increasing in recent years. Mestizos in both nations had little contact with such darker Mexicans, but as expected, once history is factored in, the renewed contact has revealed the anti-indigenous sentiment among mestizos. The treatment of indigenous people in the northern parts of Mexico has included human rights violations, which have received little attention. In the transition to a modern society—the shift of a largely peasant society to an urban, industrial one—the issue of race becomes even more complicated. Indians came from villages where the belief/practice construct was not in full use, but with migration and immigration it resurfaced in new ways but always with the socially constructed use of racism (Miles 1993). In short, the racial miscegenation and racist practices of the past have worked to muddle and sometimes undermine the integration of the Indian into Mexican society, and now in the U.S. the problem is exacerbated.

Note

[1] The Tomas Rivera Center, a California-based think tank named after a deceased Chicano scholar and prolific writer, has more recently contributed to the movement toward reform with a series of studies and initiatives aimed at policy formulation and implementation on such pressing issues as education, politics, and economic conditions.

STAGE IV REFERENCES

Acosta, O. Z. 1973. *The revolt of the cockroach people*. San Francisco: Straight Arrow Books.

Acuna, R. 1988. *Occupied America*, 3rd ed. San Francisco: Canfield Press.

———. 2000. *Occupied America*, 4th ed. New York: Canfield Press.

Alaniz, Y., and M. Cornish. 2008. *Viva la raza: A history of Chicano identity and resistance*. Seattle: Red Letter Press.

Allsup, C. 1982. *American G. I. Forum*. University of Texas Press.

Almaguer, T. 2008. *Racial fault lines: The historical origins of white supremacy in California*. Berkeley: University of California Press.

Alvarez, L. 2008. *The power of the zoot: Youth culture and resistance during World War II*. Berkeley: University of California Press.

Alvarez, R. 1973. The psycho-historical and socioeconomic development of the Mexican-American people. In *Chicano: The evolution of a people*, ed. R. Rosaldo, R. A. Calvert, and G. L. Seligmann. Minneapolis: Winston Press.

———. 1976. The psycho-historical and socioeconomic development of the Chicano society in the U.S. In *Chicanos: Social and psychological perspectives*, 2nd ed., ed. C. A. Hernandez, M. J. Haug, and N. N. Wagner. St. Louis: C. V. Mosby.

Alvarez, R. R., Jr. 1987. *Familia*. Berkeley: University of California Press.

———. 1990. The Paipai of Jamau: A test case for constitutional reform. *Cultural Survival* 14(4): 31–36.

———. 1994. Changing patterns of family and ideology among Latino cultures in the United States. In *Handbook of Hispanic cultures in the United States: Anthropology*, ed. T. Weaver. Houston: Arte Publico Press.

———. 1995. The Mexican-US border: The making of an anthropology of borderlands. *Annual Review of Anthropology* 24: 1–24.

———. 2001. Beyond the border: Nation-state encroachment, NAFTA, and offshore control in the U.S. Mexican mango industry. *Human Organization* 60: 121–127.

Alverez, J. H. 1973. A demographic profile of the Mexican immigration to the United States, 1910–1950. In *Chicano: The evolution of a people*, ed. R. Rosaldo, R. A. Calvert, and G. L. Seligmann. Minneapolis: Winston Press.

Anzaldua, G. 2007. *Borderlands/La frontera: The mew mestiza*, 3rd ed. San Francisco: Aunt Lute Books.

Arreola, D. D., and J. R. Curtis. 1993. *The Mexican border cities: Landscape anatomy and place personality*. Tucson and London: University of Arizona Press.

Arroyo, L. E. 1977. Industrial and occupational distribution of Chicana workers. In *Essays on la mujer*, ed. R. Sanchez and R. M. Cruz. Los Angeles: University of California, Chicano Studies Center.

Arvizu, S. F. 1974. Education for constructive marginality. In *The cultural drama*, ed. W. Dillon. Washington, DC: Smithsonian Institution Press.

Bacalski-Martinez, R. R. 1979. Aspects of Mexican American cultural heritage. In *The Chicanos: As we see ourselves*, ed. A. Trejo. Tucson: The University of Arizona Press.

Balderrama, F. 1995. *A decade of betrayal*. Albuquerque: University of New Mexico Press.

Barger, W. K., and E. M. Reza. 1994. *The farm labor movement in the Midwest: Social change and adaptation among migrant farmworkers*. Austin: University of Texas Press.

Barker, G. C. 1972. *Social functions of language in a Mexican-American community*. Tucson: University of Arizona Press.

Barrera, M., C. Munoz, and C. Ornelas. 1974. The barrio as an internal colony. In *La causa politico: A Chicano politics reader*, ed. F. C. Garcia. Notre Dame, IN: University of Notre Dame Press.

Barros, C. 1997. Somos indios. *La Jornada*, Dec. 28.

Bastide, R. 1968. Color, racism, and Christianity. In *Color and race*, ed. J. H. Franklin. Boston: Houghton Mifflin.

Bauman, R. 2008. *Race and war on poverty: From Watts to East L. A.* Norman: University of Oklahoma Press.

Bazant, J. 1977. *A concise history of Mexico from Hidalgo to Cardenas, 1805–1940*. New York: Cambridge University Press.

Bean, F. D., and M. Tienda. 1987. *The Hispanic population of the United States*. New York: Russell Sage.

Beezley, W., and C. MacLachlan. 2009. *Mexicans in revolution, 1910–1946: An introduction*. Lincoln: University of Nebraska Press.

Bellah, R. N., et al. 1985. *Habits of the heart*. New York: Harper and Row.

Bernal, M. E., and G. P. Knight, eds. 1993. *Ethnic identity: Formation and transmission among Hispanic and other minorities*. New York: State University of New York Press.

Bogardus, E. 1934. *The Mexican in the United States*. Los Angeles: USC Social Science Series, no. 8.

Bonilla-Silva, E. 2003. *Racism without racists: Colorblind racism and the persistence of racial inequality in the United States*. New York: Rowman & Littlefield.

Bortz, J. 2008. *Revolution within the revolution: Cotton textile workers and the Mexican labor regime, 1910–1923*. Stanford, CA: Stanford University Press.

Briggs, V. M., Jr. 1973. *Chicanos and rural poverty*. Baltimore: Johns Hopkins University Press.

Briggs, V. M., Jr., W. Fogel, and F. H. Schmidt. 1977. *The Chicano worker*. Austin: University of Texas Press.

Broyles, Y. 1990. Women in *El teatro campesino*. In *Chicana voices: Intersections of class, race, and gender*, ed. T. Cordova, N. Cantu, G. Cardenas, J. Garcia, and C. M. Sierra. Austin, TX: National Association for Chicano Studies.

Broyles-Gonzales, Y. 1994. *El teatro campesino*. Austin: University of Texas Press.

Bruns, R. 2005. *Cesar Chavez: A biography*. Westport, CT: Greenwood.

Buriel, R. 1984. Integration with traditional Mexican American culture and sociocultural adjustment. In *Chicano psychology*, ed. J. L. Martinez, Jr. and R. Mendoza. New York: Academic Press.

Bustamante, J. 1978. Commodity migrants: Structural analysis of Mexican immigration to the United States. In *Views across the border: The United States and Mexico*, ed. R. S. Ross. Albuquerque: University of New Mexico Press.

———. 1994. Racismo Mexican. *Frontera Norte*, January 24.

Cardenas, G. 1977. Mexican labor: A view to conceptualizing the effects of migration, immigration and the Chicano population in the United States. In *Cuantos somos: A demographic study of the Mexican American population*, ed. C. Teller, L. Estrada, J. Hernandez, and D. Alvirez. Austin: University of Texas Press, Center for Mexican American Studies.

Cardoso, L. A. 1980. *Mexican emigration to the United States*. Tucson: University of Arizona Press.

Castaneda, A. 1974. Melting potters vs. cultural pluralists: Implications for education. In *Mexican Americans and educational change*, ed. A. Castaneda et al. New York: Arno Press.

Cave, D. 2011. Better lives for Mexicans cut allure of going north. *New York Times*, July 6, A 1, 8–9.

Chavez, E. 1998. *Shadowed lives*, 2nd ed. Ft. Worth, TX: Harcourt Brace.

———. 2001. *Covering immigration: Popular images and the politics of the nation*. Berkeley and Los Angeles: University of California Press.

———. 2002. *My people first. I mi raza primero: Nationalism, identity, and insurgency in the Chicano movement in Los Angeles, 1966–1978*. Berkeley: University of California Press.

———. 2008. *The Latino threat: Constructing immigrants, citizens, and the nation*. Stanford, CA: Stanford University Press.

Chavez, J. R. 1984. *The lost land: The Chicano image of the Southwest*. Albuquerque: University of New Mexico Press.

Chavez-Garcia, M. 2004. *Negotiating conquest: Gender and power in California, 1770s to 1880s*. Tucson: University of Arizona Press.

Chavira, A. 1994. Latina experience and Latina identity. In *Handbook of Hispanic cultures in the United States: Anthropology*, ed. T. Weaver. Houston: Arte Publico Press.

Coatsworth, J. H. 1988. Patterns of rural rebellion in Latin America: Mexico in comparative perspective. In *Riot, rebellion, and revolution: Rural social conflict in Mexico*, ed. F. Katz. Princeton: Princeton University Press.

Cockcroft, E., and H. Barnet-Sanchez. 1993. *Signs from the heart: California Chicano murals*. Albuquerque: University of New Mexico Press.

Cockcroft, J. D. 1968. *Intellectual precursors of the Mexican Revolution, 1900–1913*. Austin: University of Texas Press.

———. 1986. *Outlaws in the promised land*. New York: Grove Press.

———. 1990. *Mexico: Class formation, capital accumulation, and the state*. New York: Monthly Review Press.

Collier, G., and E. L. Quaratiello. 1994. *Basta!: Land and the Zapatista rebellion in Chiapas*. Oakland, CA: Institute for Food and Development Policy.

Cornelius, W. A. 1978. *Mexican migration to the United States: Causes, consequences, and U.S. responses*. Cambridge: Center for International Studies.

———. 2009. Ambivalent reception: Mass public responses to the "new Latino" immigration to the United States. In *Latinos: Remaking America*, ed. M. Suarez-Orozco and M. Paez. Berkeley: University of California Press.

Cornelius, W. A., and J. A. Bustamante, eds. 1989. *Mexican migration to the United States: Origins, consequences, and policy options*. San Diego: Center for U.S.-Mexican Studies, University of California.

Cumberland, C. C. 1968. *Mexico: The struggle for modernity.* Oxford: Oxford University Press.

Daniels, C. 1991. *Chicano workers and the politics of fairness.* Austin: University of Texas Press.

De Anda, R. M., ed. 1996. *Chicanas and Chicanos in contemporary society.* Boston: Allyn & Bacon.

de la Garza, R. O. 1979. The politics of the Mexican Americans. In *The Chicanos: As we see ourselves*, ed. A. Trejo. Tucson: University of Arizona Press.

de la Garza, R., and L. DeSipio, eds. 1996. *Ethnic ironies: Latino politics in the 1992 elections.* Boulder, CO: Westview Press.

———, eds. 1999. Awash in the mainstream: Latino politics in the 1996 elections. Boulder, CO: Westview.

de la Torre, A., and B. M. Pesquera, eds. 1993. *Building with our hands: New directions in Chicana research.* Berkeley: University of California Press.

Del Castillo, A. R., ed. 1990. *Between borders: Essays on Mexicana/Chicana history.* Encino, CA: Floricanto Press.

De Leon, A., and Griswold del Castillo, R. 2006. *North to Aztlan: A history of Mexican Americans in the United States.* Wheeling, IL: Harlan Davidson.

deLeon, M. 1970. The hamburger and the taco: A cultural reality. In *Educating the Mexican American*, ed. H. S. Johnson and W. I. Hernandez. Valley Forge, PA: Judson Press.

Delgado, R., and J. Stefancic. 2000. *Critical race theory.* Philadelphia: Temple University Press.

Diaz-Guerrero, R. 1975. *Psychology of the Mexican.* Austin: University of Texas Press.

———. 1978. Mexicans and Americans: Two worlds, one border . . . and one observer. In *Views across the border: The United States and Mexico*, ed. R. S. Ross. Albuquerque: University of New Mexico Press.

Dinnerstein, L., and D. M. Reimers. 1988. *Ethnic Americans: A history of immigration.* New York: Harper & Row.

Dovidio, J. F., et al. 1992. Cognitive and motivational bases of bias: Implications of aversive racism for attitudes toward Hispanics. In *Hispanics in the workplace*, ed. S. B. Knouse et al. Newbury Park, CA: Sage Publications.

Driscoll de Alvarado, B. 1999. *The tracks north: The railroad Bracero Program of World War II.* Austin: CMAS Books, Center for Mexican American Studies, University of Texas at Austin.

Dulitzky, A. E. 2005. A region in denial: Racial discrimination and racism in Latin America. In *Neither enemies nor friends: Latinos, blacks, Afro-Latinos*, ed. A. Dzidzienyo and S. Oboler. New York: Palgrave Macmillan.

Dunbar-Ortiz, R. 2005. *Blood on the border: A memoir of the Contra War.* Cambridge: South End Press.

———. 2007. *Roots of resistance: A history of land tenure in New Mexico.* Norman: University of Oklahoma Press.

Dunne, J. G. 1967. *Delano.* New York: Ambassador Books.

El Plan Espiritual de Aztlan. 1970. In *Educating the Mexican American*, ed. H. S. Johnson and W. J. Hernandez. Valley Forge, PA: Judson Press.

Emiliano, R. 1976. Nathuatlan elements in Chicano speech. In *Grito del sol*, ed. O. I. Romano-V. Berkeley, CA: Tonatiuh International.

Ericksen, C. A. 1970. Uprising in the barrios. In *Educating the Mexican American*, ed. H. S. Johnson and W. J. Hernandez. Valley Forge, PA: Judson Press.

Escobar, E. 1999. *Race, police, and the making of a political identity: Police- Chicano relations in Los Angeles, 1900–1945*. Berkeley: University of California Press.

Esquibel, A., ed. 2001. *Message to Aztlan: Selected writings of Rodolfo "Corky" Gonzales*. Houston: Arte Publico Press.

Farnen, R. F., ed. 2004. Nationalism, ethnicity, and identity: Cross National and comparative perspectives. New Brunswick, NJ: Transaction.

Feagin, J. 2005. *Systemic racism: A theory of oppression*. New York: Routledge.

Felix-Ortiz, M., M. Newcomb, and H. Myers. 1994. A multidimensional measure of cultural identity for Latino and Latina adolescents. *Hispanic Journal of Behavioral Sciences* 16(2): 99–115.

Fernandez, R. A. 1977. *The United States-Mexico border*. Notre Dame, IN: University of Notre Dame Press.

Foley, D. E., et al. 1977. *From peones to politicos: Ethnic relations in a south Texan town, 1900 to 1977*. Austin: University of Texas Press, Center for Mexican American Studies.

Forbes, J. D. 1973. *Aztecas del norte: The Chicanos of Aztlan*. New York: Fawcett Books.

Foster, G. 1988. *Tzintzuntzan: Mexican peasants in a changing world*. Long Grove, IL: Waveland Press.

Frazier, E. F. 1957. *Race and culture contacts in the modern world*. New York: Alfred A. Knopf.

Galarza, E. 1964. *Merchants of labor*. Santa Barbara, CA: McNally & Loftin.

———. 1971. *Barrio boy*. Notre Dame, IN: University of Notre Dame Press.

Gamio, M. 1969. *Mexican immigration to the United States*. New York: Arno Press, Inc. (originally published in 1930).

Gann, L. H., and P. J. Duignan. 1986. *The Hispanics in the United States: A history*. Boulder and London: Westview Press.

Garcia, D. G. 2008. Transformations through teatro: Culture clash in a Chicano history classroom. *Radical History* 102: 111–130.

Garcia, F. C., and R. O. de la Garza. 1977. *The Chicano political experience*. North Scituate, MA: Duxbury Press.

Garcia, I. 1989. *United we win: The rise and fall of La Raza Unida Party*. Tucson: University of Arizona Press.

Garcia, J. C. 1978. Teatro Chicano and the analysis of sacred symbols: Towards a Chicano world-view in the social sciences. In *Chicano perspectives on decolonizing anthropology*, ed. S. F. Arvizu. Berkeley, CA: Tonatiuh International.

Garcia, M. T. 1989. *Mexican Americans*. New Haven: Yale University Press.

———. 1994. *Memories of Chicano history: Bert Corona*. Los Angeles: University of California Press.

———, ed. 2008. *A Delores Huerta reader*. Albuquerque: University of New Mexico Press.

Garcia, M. T., and S. Castro. 2011. *Blowout! Sal Castro & the Chicano struggle for educational justice*. Durham: University of North Carolina Press.

Gardner, R. 1970. *Grito: Reis Tijerina and the New Mexico land grant war of 1967*. New York: Harper & Row.

Gibson, M. A., P. Gándara, and J. P. Koyama, eds. 2004. *School connections: U.S. Mexican youth, peers, and school achievement*. New York: Teachers College Press.

Gibson, M., and J. Ogbu. 1991. *Minority status and schooling: A comparative study of immigrant and involuntary minorities.* New York: Garland.

Glick, L. B. 1966. The right to equal opportunity. In *La Raza: Forgotten Americans,* ed. J. Samora. Notre Dame, IN: University of Notre Dame Press.

Gomez, L. 2007. *Manifest destinies: The making of the Mexican race.* New York: New York University Press.

Gomez-Quinones, J. 1978. *Mexican students por La Raza: The Chicano student movement in southern California, 1967–1977.* Santa Barbara, CA: Editorial La Causa.

———. 1990. *Chicano politics: Reality and promise, 1940–1990.* Albuquerque: University of New Mexico Press.

———. 1994a. *Roots of Chicano politics, 1600–1940.* Albuquerque: University of New Mexico Press.

———. 1994b. *Mexican American labor: 1790–1990.* Albuquerque: University of New Mexico Press.

Gonzales, M. G. 2009. *Mexicanos: A history of Mexicans in the United States,* 2nd ed. Bloomington: Indiana University Press.

Gonzales, N. L. 1967. *The Spanish-Americans of New Mexico.* Albuquerque: University of New Mexico Press.

Gonzales, R. 1967. *I am Joaquin.* Denver: Crusade for Justice.

Gonzales, S. A. 1979. The Chicana perspective: A design for self-awareness. In *The Chicanos: As we see ourselves,* ed. A. Trejo. Tucson: University of Arizona Press.

Gonzalez, G. 1990. *Chicano education in the era of segregation.* Philadelphia: The Balch Institute Press.

———. 1994. *Labor and community: Mexican citrus worker villages in a southern California county, 1900–1950.* Urbana: University of Illinois Press.

———. 1999. *Mexican consuls and labor organizing: Imperial politics in the Southwest.* Austin: University of Texas Press.

———. 2004. *Culture of empire.* Austin: University of Texas Press.

Gonzalez, H. B. 1974. Response to Chicano militancy. In *Readings on La Raza: The twentieth century,* ed. M. S. Meier and F. Ribera. New York: Hill & Wang.

Gonzalez, J. 2000. *Harvest of empire: A history of Latinos in America.* New York: Penguin.

Gordon, M. 1964. *Assimilation in American life.* New York: Oxford University Press.

Grebler, L., J. W. Moore, and R. C. Guzman. 1970. *The Mexican-American people.* New York: The Free Press.

Griffith, B. 1948. *American me.* Boston: Houghton-Mifflin.

Griffith, D., and E. Kissan. 1995. *Working poor: Farmworkers in the United States.* Temple: Temple University Press.

Griswold del Castillo, R., ed. 2008. *World War II and Mexican American civil rights.* Austin: University of Texas Press.

Griswold del Castillo, R., and R. A. Garcia. 1995. *Cesar Chavez: A triumph of spirit.* Norman and London: University of Oklahoma Press.

Griswold del Castillo, R., T. McKenna, and Y. Yarbro-Bejarano, eds. 1991. *CARA: Chicano art: Resistance and affirmation.* Los Angeles: Wight Art Gallery, University of California, Los Angeles.

Gutierrez, D. 1995. *Walls and mirrors: Mexican Americans and the politics of ethnicity.* Berkeley: University of California Press.

Gutierrez, R. A. 2009. Chicano struggles for racial justice: The movement's contribution to social theory. In *Mexicans in California*, ed. R. Gutierrez and P. Zavella. Urbana and Chicago: University of Illinois Press.

Gutierrez, R., and P. Zavella, eds. 2009. *Mexicans in California*. Urbana and Chicago. University of Illinois Press.

Guzman, R. 1974. The function on Anglo-American racism. In *Readings on La Raza: The twentieth century*, ed. M. S. Meier and F. Ribera. New York: Hill & Wang.

Haney-Lopez, I. F. 2003. *Racism on trial: The Chicano fight for justice*. Cambridge: Harvard University Press.

Harrington, M. 1962. *The other America*. New York: The Viking Press.

Harris, C., and L. Sadler. 2004. *The Texas Rangers and the Mexican Revolution: The bloodiest decade, 1910–1920*. Albuquerque: University of New Mexico Press.

HBO Home Video. 2006. *Walkout*. Director, E. J. Olmos, Producers, E. J. Olmos, F. E. Alcalá, and G. Spence. 110 minutes.

Hernandez, G. 1991. *Chicano satire: A study in literary culture*. Austin: University of Texas Press.

Hernandez-Leon, R. 2008. *Metropolitan migrants*. Berkeley: University of California Press.

Heyman, J. 1991. *Life and labor on the border: Working people of northeastern Sonora, Mexico, 1886–1986*. Tucson: University of Arizona Press.

Hinojosa-Ojeda, R. 1994. The political economy of Latino employment and income. In *Handbook of Hispanic cultures in the United States: Anthropology*, ed. T. Weaver. Houston: Arte Publico Press.

Hoffman, A. 1974. *Unwanted Mexican Americans in the Great Depression*. Tucson: University of Arizona Press.

Hondagneu-Sotelo, P. 1994. *Gendered transitions: Mexican experiences of immigration*. Berkeley: University of California Press.

———. 2007. *Doméstica: Immigrant workers cleaning and caring in the shadows of affluence*. Berkeley: University of California Press.

Hurtado, A., and P. Gurin. 2004. *Chicana/o identity in changing U.S. society*. Tucson: University of Arizona Press.

Inkeles, A. 1977. Quoted in R. Toth. Americans' traits: Steady amid change. *Los Angeles Times*, September 20.

Katz, F., ed. 1988. *Riot, rebellion, and revolution: Rural social conflict in Mexico*. Princeton: Princeton University Press.

———. 2007. International wars, Mexico, and U.S. Hegemony. In *Cycles of conflict, centuries of change, crisis, reform, and revolution in Mexico*, ed. E. Servin, L. Reina, and J. Tutino. Durham, NC: Duke University Press.

Kearney, M. 1996. *Reconceptualizing the peasantry*. Boulder, CO: Westview Press.

Keefe, S., and A. Padilla. 1987. *Chicano ethnicity*. Albuquerque: University of New Mexico Press.

Kirk, R. C. 1979. "Honk if you're fatalistic": Chicanos and the problem of Anglo stereotypy. In *Social problems in American society*, ed. J. M. Henslin and L. T. Reynolds. Boston: Allyn & Bacon.

Kluckholm, F. R., and F. L. Strodtbeck. 1961. *Variations in value orientations*. Evanston, IL: Row, Peterson.

Knight, A. 2007. Mexico's three fin de siècle crises. In *Cycles of conflict, centuries of change: Crisis, reform, and revolution in Mexico,* ed. E. Servin, L. Reina, and J. Tutino. Durham, NC: Duke University Press.

Knouse, S. B., P. Rosenfeld, and A. L. Culbertson. 1992. *Hispanics in the workplace.* Newbury Park, CA: Sage Publications.

Knowlton, C. S. 1975. The neglected chapters in Mexican-American history. In *Mexican-Americans tomorrow,* ed. G. Tyler. Albuquerque: University of New Mexico Press.

Kristof, N. 2010. Our banana republic. *New York Times,* November 7.

Leonard, K. A. 2006. *The battle for Los Angeles: Racial ideology and World War II.* Albuquerque: University of New Mexico Press.

Lewis, O. 1959. *Five families: Mexican case studies in the culture of poverty.* New York: Harper & Row.

Linton, R. 1975. One hundred per cent American. In *Introducing anthropology,* ed. J. R. Hayes and J. M. Henslin. Boston: Holbrook Press.

Lopez, N. 2003. *Hopeful girls, troubled boys: Race and gender disparity in urban education.* New York: Routledge.

———. 2011. Racially stigmatized masculinities: Conceptualizing Latino male schooling in the United States. In *Disenfranchisement of Latino males: Contemporary perspectives on cultural and structural factors,* ed. P. Noguera, E. Fergus, and A. Hurtado. New York: Routledge.

Lux, M., and M. E. Vigil. 1979. Return to Aztlan: The Chicano rediscovers his Indian past. In *The Chicanos: As we see ourselves,* ed. A. Trejo. Tucson: University of Arizona Press.

Macias, A. 1982. *Against all odds: The feminist movement in Mexico to 1940.* Westport, CT: Greenwood Press.

———. 2008. *Mexican American mojo: Popular music, dance, and urban culture in Los Angeles, 1935–1968.* Durham, NC: Duke University Press.

Madsen, W. 1964. *The Mexican Americans of south Texas.* New York: Holt, Rinehart Winston.

Magana, L. 2005. *Mexican Americans and the politics of diversity.* Tucson: University of Arizona Press.

Marcelli, E. A., and W. A. Cornelius. 2001. The changing profile of Mexican migrants to the United States: New evidence from California and Mexico. *Latin American Research Review* 33(3): 105–131.

Marger, M. N. 1994. *Race and ethnic relations.* Belmont, CA: Wadsworth.

Marin, C. 1975. Rodolfo "Corky" Gonzales: The Mexican-American movement spokesman 1966–1972. In Early southwestern minorities, ed. M. P. Servin, *Journal of the West* 14: 4.

Mariscal, G. 1999. *Aztlan and Viet Nam.* Berkeley: University of California Press.

———. 2005. *Brown-eyed children of the sun: Lessons from the Chicano movement, 1965–1975.* Albuquerque: University of New Mexico Press.

Marquez, B. 1993. *LULAC: The evolution of a Mexican American political organization.* Austin: University of Texas Press.

Martinez, E., and E. McCaughan. 1990. Chicanas and Mexicanas within a transnational working class. In *Between borders: Essays on Mexicana/Chicana history,* ed. A. R. Del Castillo. Encino, CA: Floricanto Press.

Martinez, O. 1996. *U.S.-Mexico borderlands: Historical and contemporary perspectives.* Wilmington, DE: Scholarly Resources.

Martinez, T. 1973. Advertising and racism: The case of the Mexican American. In *Voices*, ed. O. I. Romano-V. Berkeley, CA: Quinto Sol.

Massey, D., et al. 1987. *Return to Aztlan*. Berkeley: University of California Press.

Mazon, M. 1983. *The zoot-suit riots: The psychology of symbolic annihilation*. Austin: University of Texas Press.

McWilliams, C. 1990[1968]. *North from Mexico—The Spanish-speaking people of the United States*. Westport, CT: Greenwood Press.

Meier, M. S., and F. Ribera. 1993. *Mexican Americans/American Mexicans: From conquistadores to Chicanos*. New York: Hill and Wang.

Melville, M. B. 1978. The Mexican-American and the celebration of the Fiestas Patrias: An ethnohistorical analysis. In *Chicano perspectives on de-colonizing anthropology*, ed. S. F. Arvizu. Berkeley, CA: Tonatiuh International.

———, ed. 1980. *Twice a minority: Mexican American women*. St. Louis: C. V. Mosby.

———. 1994. "Hispanic" ethnicity, race and class. In *Handbook of Hispanic cultures in the United States: Anthropology*, ed. T. Weaver. Houston: Arte Publico Press.

Menchaca, M. 1993. Chicano Indianism: A historical account of racial repression in the United States. *American Ethnologist* 20(3): 583–603.

———. 1995. *The Mexican outsiders: A community history of marginalization and discrimination in California*. Austin: University of Texas Press.

———. 2001. *Recovering history, constructing race: The Indian, black, and white roots of Mexican Americans*. Austin: University of Texas Press.

Miles, R. 1993. *Racism after "race relations."* New York: Routledge.

Miranda, M. 2003. *Homegirls in the public sphere*. Austin: University of Texas Press.

Mirande, A. 1987. *Gringo justice*. Notre Dame, IN: University of Notre Dame Press.

———. 1997. *Hombes y machos: Masculinity and Latino Culture*. Boulder, CO: Westview Press.

Mirande, A., and E. Enriquez. 1979. *La Chicana*. Chicago: University of Chicago Press.

Mitchell, S., and P. Schell, eds. 2007. *The Women's Revolution in Mexico, 1910–1953*. Lanham, MD: Rowman & Littlefield.

Monroy, D. 1993. *Thrown among strangers: The making of Mexican culture in frontier California*, 2nd ed. Berkeley: University of California Press.

———. 1999. *Rebirth: Mexican Los Angeles from the great migration to the Great Depression*. Berkeley: University of California Press.

———. 2008. *The borders within: Encounters between Mexico and the U.S.* Tucson: University of Arizona Press.

Montejano, D. 1987. *Anglos and Mexicans in the making of Texas, 1836–1986*. Austin: University of Texas Press.

———. 2010. *Quixote's soldiers: A local history of the Chicano movement, 1966–1981*. Austin: University of Texas Press.

Monto, A. 1994. *The roots of Mexican labor migration*. Westport, CT: Greenwood Press.

Moore, J. W. 1973. Colonialism: The case of the Mexican American. In *Introduction to Chicano studies*, ed. L. I. Duran and H. R. Bernard. New York: Macmillan.

———. 1978. *Homeboys*. Philadelphia: Temple University Press.

———. 1991. *Going down to the barrio: Homeboys and homegirls in change*. Philadelphia: Temple University Press.

Moore, J., and H. Pachon. 1985. *Hispanics in the United States*. Englewood Cliffs, NJ: Prentice-Hall.

Moore, J., and J. D. Vigil. 1993. Barrios in transition. In *In the barrios: Latinos and the underclass debate*, eds. J. W. Moore and R. Pinderhughes, pp. 27–49. New York: Russell Sage Foundation.

Mora, C. 2007. *Latinas in the West: The student movement and academic labor in Los Angeles*. Lanham, MD: Rowman & Littlefield.

Mora-Torres, J. 2001. *The making of the Mexican border: The state, capitalism, and society in Nuevo León, 1848–1910*. Austin: University of Texas Press.

Morales, A. 1972. *Ando sangrando*. La Puente, CA: Perspectiva Publications.

Morin, R. 1966. *Among the valiant*. Alhambra, CA: Borden Publishing Co.

Munoz, C. 1974. The politics of protest and Chicano liberation: A case study of repression and cooptation. *Aztlan*, Spring and Fall.

———. 2007. *Youth, identity, power*. New York: Verso.

Murillo, N. 1976. The Mexican American family. In *Chicanos: Social and psychological perspectives*, 2nd ed., ed. C. A. Hernandez, M. J. Haug, and N. N. Wagner. St. Louis: C. V. Mosby.

Nabokov, P. 1969. *Tijerina and the courthouse raid*. Albuquerque: University of New Mexico Press.

Najera-Ramirez, O. 1994. Fiestas Hispanicas: Dimensions of Hispanic festivals and celebrations. In *Handbook of Hispanic cultures in the United States: Anthropology*, ed. T. Weaver. Houston: Arte Publico Press.

Nelson, E. 1966. *Huelga*. Delano, CA: Farm Workers Press.

Noriega, C. 1992. *Chicanos and film: Representation and resistance*. Minneapolis: University of Minnesota Press.

Oboler, S. 1995. *Ethnic labels, Latino lives: Identity and the politics of (re)presentation in the United States*. London and Minneapolis: University of Minnesota Press.

Omi, M., and H. Winant. 1994. *Racial formation in the United States: From the 1960s to the 1980s*. New York: Routledge & Kegan Paul.

Ong, P. 1988. The Hispanization of L.A.'s poor. University of California, Los Angeles, School of Planning, photocopy.

Oropeza, L., and H. Espinoza, eds. 2006. *Enriqueta Vasquez and the Chicano movement: From El Grito de Norte*. Houston: Arte Publico Press.

Orozco, C. 1990. Sexism in Chicano studies and the community. In *Chicana voices*, ed. T. Cordova et al. Albuquerque: University of New Mexico Press

———. 2009. *No Mexicans, women, or dogs allowed*. Austin: University of Texas Press.

Ortiz Pincheti, J. A. 1998. Nuestro racism: Afrontarlo para superarlo. *La Jornada*, April 19.

Padilla, A. M., ed. 1995. *Hispanic psychology*. Thousand Oaks, CA: Sage.

Pagan, E. 2003. *Murder at the Sleepy Lagoon: Zoot suits, race, and riot in wartime L.A.* Chapel Hill: The University of North Carolina Press.

Paredes, A. 1978. The problem of identity in a changing culture: Popular expressions of culture conflict along the lower Rio Grande border. In *Views across the border: The United States and Mexico*, ed. R. S. Ross. Albuquerque: University of New Mexico Press.

———, ed. 1993. *Folklore and culture on the Texas Mexican border*. Austin: University of Texas Press.

Parsons, T. 1965. Ethnic cleavage in a California school. Palo Alto, CA: Stanford doctoral dissertation.

———. 1971. School and society: School bias toward Mexican Americans. In *Chicanos: social and psychological perspectives*, ed. N. N. Wagner and M. J. Haug. St. Louis: C. V. Mosby.

Pastor, M., Jr. 2009. Poverty, work, and public policy: Latino futures in California's new economy. In *Mexicans in California*, ed. R. Gutierrez and P. Zavella. Urbana and Chicago: University of Illinois Press.

Pawel, M. 2009. *The union of their dreams: Power, hope, and struggle in Cesar Chavez's farm worker movement*. New York: Bloomsbury Press.

Paz, O. 1961. *The labyrinth of solitude*. New York: Grove Press.

Pena, M. 1985. *The Texas-Mexican conjunto*. Austin: University of Texas Press.

Penalosa, F. 1973. The changing Mexican-American in southern California. In *Chicano: The evolution of a people*, ed. R. Rosaldo, R. A. Calvert, and G. L. Seligmann. Minneapolis: Winston Press.

Phelan, P., and A. L. Davidson, eds. 1993. *Renegotiating cultural diversity in American schools*. New York: Teachers College, Columbia University.

Phinney, J. S. 1995. Ethnic identity and self-esteem: A review and integration. In *Hispanic psychology: Critical issues in theory and research*, ed. A. Padilla. Thousand Oaks, CA: Sage.

Pizarro, M. 2005. *Chicanas and Chicanos in school: Racial profiling, identity battles and empowerment*. Austin: University of Texas Press.

Polo, A. J., and S. R. Lopez. 2009. Culture, context, and the internalizing distress of Mexican American youth. *Journal of Clinical Child and Adolescent Psychology* 38(2): 273–285.

Portes, A., and R. L. Bach. 1985. *Latin journey: Cuban and Mexican immigration in the United States*. Los Angeles: University of California Press.

Poston, D., D. Alvirez, and M. Tienda. 1977. The high cost of being Chicano. *Human Behavior*, September.

Price, J. A. 1973. *Tijuana: Urbanization in a border culture*. Notre Dame, IN: University of Notre Dame Press.

Pulido, L. 2006. *Black, brown, yellow and left: Radical activism in Los Angeles*. Berkeley: University of California Press.

Ramirez, C. S. 2009. *The woman in the zoot suit: Gender, nationalism, and the cultural politics of memory*. Durham, NC: Duke University Press.

Ramirez, M., III. 1976. Cognitive styles and cultural democracy in education. In *Chicanos: Social and psychological perspectives*, 2nd ed., eds. C. A. Hernandez, M. J. Haug, and N. N. Wagner. St. Louis: C. V. Mosby.

———. 1985. *Psychology of the Americas: Mestizo perspective on personality and mental health*. New York: Pergamon Press.

Reimers, D. M. 1992. *Still the golden door: The Third World comes to America*, 2nd ed. New York: Columbia University Press.

Reisler, M. 1976. *By the sweat of their brow*. Westport, CT: Greenwood Press.

Rendon, A. 1971. *Chicano manifesto*. New York: Macmillan.

Restall, M. 2005. *Beyond black and red: African-native relations in colonial Latin America*. Albuquerque: University of New Mexico Press.

Rios, V. 2011. *Punished: Policing the lives of black and Latino boys.* New York: New York University Press.

Robinson, W. I. 2004. *A theory of global capitalism: Production, class, and state in a transnational world.* Baltimore: Johns Hopkins University Press.

Rocco, R. A. 1974. The role of power and authenticity in the Chicano movement: Some reflections. *Aztlan,* Spring and Fall.

Rochin, R., and D. Valdes. 2000. *Voices of a new Chicana/o history.* East Lansing: Michigan State University Press.

Rodriguez, R. 1988. *Hunger of memory: The education of Richard Rodriguez: An autobiography.* New York and Toronto: Bantam Books.

Romano-V., O. I. 1968. The anthropology and sociology of the Mexican Americans: The distortion of Mexican American history. In *El grito,* ed. O. I. Romano-V. Berkeley, CA: Quinto Sol Publications.

———. 1973. *Voices.* Berkeley, CA: Quinto Sal Publications.

Romanucci-Ross, L., and G. De Vos, eds. 1995. *Ethnic identity: Creation, conflict, and accommodation.* Walnut Creek, CA: AltaMira Press.

Romero, F. 1979. *Chicano workers: Their utilization and development.* Los Angeles: University of California, Chicano Studies Center.

Romero, M., P. Hondagneu-Satelo, and V. Ortiz, eds. 1997. *Challenging fronteras: Structuring Latino and Latina lives in the U.S.* New York: Routledge.

Romo, H. 1990. *Latinos and blacks in the cities: Policies for the 1990s.* Austin: LBJ Library and the LBJ School of Public Affairs.

Romo, R. 1983. *East Los Angeles: History of a barrio.* Austin: University of Texas Press.

Rosales, F. A. 1997. *Chicano! The history of the Mexican American civil rights movement.* Houston: Arte Publico Press.

Rubel, A. 1966. *Across the tracks: Mexican Americans in a Texas city.* Austin: University of Texas Press.

Ruiz, V. 1993. "Star struck": Acculturation, adolescence, and the Mexican American woman, 1920–1950. In *Building with our hands,* ed. A. de la Torre and B. M. Pesquera. Berkeley: University of California Press.

———. 1999. The acculturation of young Mexican American women. In *Major Problems in Mexican American histories: Documents and essays,* ed. Z. Vargas. New York: Houghton Mifflin.

———. 2008. *From out of the shadows: Mexican women in twentieth-century America.* Oxford, UK, and New York: Oxford University Press.

Ruiz, V. L., and S. Tiano. 1987. *Women on the U.S.–Mexico border.* Boston: Allen & Unwin.

Rus, J., R. A. Hernandez Castillo, and S. L. Mattiace, eds. 2003. *Mayan lives, Mayan utopias: The indigenous peoples of Chiapas and the Zapatista rebellion.* Lanham, MD: Rowman & Littlefield.

Salas, E. 1990. *Soldaderas in the Mexican military: Myth and history.* Austin: University of Texas Press.

Salazar, M. T., ed. 1995. *Ruben Salazar: Border correspondent.* Berkeley: University of California Press.

Saldana, D. H. 1995. Acculturative stress: Minority status and distress. In *Hispanic psychology: Critical issues in theory and research,* ed. A. M. Padilla. Thousand Oaks, CA: Sage.

Samora, J. 1971. *Los mojados: The wetback story.* Notre Dame, IN: University of Notre Dame Press.

Samora, J., and P. V. Simon. 1977. *A history of the Mexican American people*. Notre Dame, IN: University of Notre Dame Press.

Sanchez, D. 1978. *Expedition through Aztlan*. La Puente, CA: Perspectiva Publications.

Sanchez, F. A. 1976. Raices Mexicanas. In *Grito del sol*, ed. O. I. Romano-V. Berkeley, CA: Tonatiuh International.

Sanchez, G. I. 1966. History, culture, and education. In *La Raza: Forgotten Americans*, ed. J. Samora. Notre Dame, IN: University of Notre Dame Press.

———. 1967. *Forgotten people: A study of New Mexicans*. Albuquerque: Calvin Horn Publishers (originally published in 1940).

———. 1974. Educational change in historical perspective. In *Mexican Americans and historical change*, eds. A. Castaneda et al. New York: Arno Press, Inc.

Sanchez, G. J. 1993. *Becoming Mexican American: Ethnicity, culture and identity in Chicano Los Angeles, 1900–1945*. New York: Oxford University Press.

Sanderson, S. E. 1988. *The transformation of Mexican agriculture: International structure and the politics of rural change*. Princeton: University of Princeton Press.

Sands, K. M. 1993. *Charreria Mexicana: An equestrian folk tradition*. Tucson: University of Arizona Press.

Sandstrom, A. R. 1991. *Corn is our blood*. Norman: University of Oklahoma Press.

Santana, R., and M. Esparza. 1974. East Los Angeles blowouts. In *Parameters of institutional change: Chicano experiences in education*. Hayward, CA: Southwest Network.

Segura, D. A. 1990. Chicanas and triple oppression in the labor force. In *Chicana voices*, ed. T. Cordova et al. Albuquerque: University of New Mexico Press.

———. 1992. Walking on eggshells: Chicanas in the labor force. In *Hispanics in the workplace*, ed. S. B. Knouse, P. Rosenfeld, and A. L. Culbertson, pp. 173–193. Newbury Park, CA: Sage.

Segura, D. A., and P. Zavella, eds. 2007. *Women and migration in the U.S.-Mexico borderlands: A Reader*. Durham, NC: Duke University Press.

Servin, E., L. Reina, and J. Tutino, eds. 2007. *Cycles of conflict, centuries of change, crisis, reform, and revolution in Mexico*. Durham, NC: Duke University Press.

Shaw, R. 2008. *Beyond the fields*. Berkeley: University of California Press.

Shockley, J. S. 1974. *Chicano revolt in a Texas town*. Notre Dame, IN: University of Notre Dame Press.

Shorris, E. 1992. *Latinos: A biography of the people*. New York and London: W.W. Norton.

Shweder, R., and H. R. Markus. 1995. Culture, identity, and conflict. *Social Science Research Council* 49(1): 11–13.

Simmons, O. G. 1973. The mutual images and expectations of Anglo-Americans and Mexican Americans. In *Introduction to Chicano studies*, ed. L. I. Duran and H. R. Bernard. New York: Macmillan.

———. 1974. *Anglo-Americans and change: Mexican Americans in South Texas: A study in dominant-subordinate group relations*. New York: Arno Press.

Smith, R. 2009. Gender, ethnicity, and race in school and work outcomes of second-generation Mexican Americans. In *Latinos: Remaking America*, ed. M. Suarez-Orozco and M. Paez. Berkeley: University of California Press.

Soto, S. 1979. *The Mexican woman: A study of her part in the revolution*. Palo Alto, CA: R&E Research Associates.

Spencer, M. H. 1977. *Contemporary economics*. New York: Worth Publishers.

Spindler, G., and L. Spindler. 1990. *The American cultural dialogue and its transmission.* London: The Falmer Press.

Starr, P. C. 1978. *Economics: Principles in action.* Belmont, CA: Wadsworth.

Stephen, L. 1991. *Zapotec women.* Austin: University of Texas Press.

Stonequist, E. V. 1937. *The marginal man.* New York: Russell & Russell.

Stowell, J. S. 1974. The near side of the Mexican question (1921). In *Perspectives on Mexican-American life,* ed. C. E. Cortez. New York: Arno Press.

Strum, P. 2010. Mendez v. Westminster: *School desegregation and Mexican-American rights.* Lawrence: University Press of Kansas.

Suarez-Orozco, C., and M. Suarez-Orozco. 1994. The cultural psychology of Hispanic immigrants. In *Handbook of Hispanic cultures in the United States: Anthropology,* ed. T. Weaver. Houston: Arte Publico Press.

———. 2001. *Children of immigration.* Cambridge: Harvard University Press.

Suarez-Orozco, M., and M. Paez, eds. 2009. *Latinos: Remaking America.* Berkeley: University of California Press.

Taylor, P. S. 1934. *An American Mexican frontier.* Chapel Hill: University of North Carolina Press.

Telles, E. E., and V. Ortiz. 2008. *Generations of exclusion: Mexican Americans, assimilation, and race.* New York: Russell Sage Foundation.

Thurow, L. C. 1979. Hispanics closing income gap. *Los Angeles Times,* May 5.

Trevino, J. S. 2001. *Eyewitness: A filmmaker's memoir of the Chicano movement.* Houston, TX: Arte Publica Press.

Trueba, H. T. 1991. From failure to success: The roles of culture and cultural conflict in the academic achievement of Chicano students. In *Chicano school failure and success: Research and policy agendas for the 1990s,* ed. R. Valencia. London: The Falmer Press.

Urrieta, L., Jr. 2009. *Working from within: Chicana and Chicano activist educators in whitestream schools.* Tucson: University of Arizona Press.

U.S. Commission on Civil Rights. 1970. *Mexican Americans and the administration of justice in the Southwest.* Washington, DC: U.S. Government Printing Office.

———. 1971. *Report 1: Ethnic isolation of Mexicans in the public schools of the southwest.* Washington, DC: U.S. Government Printing Office.

———. 1975. *A better chance to learn: Bilingual-bicultural education.* Washington, DC: U.S. Government Printing Office.

Valdes, D. 1991. *Al Norte: Agricultural workers in the Great Lakes region, 1917–1970.* Austin: University of Texas Press.

Valdez, L. 1992. *Zoot-suit and other plays.* Houston, TX: Arte Publico Press.

Valencia, R. R. 1991. *Chicano school failure and success: Research and policy agendas for the 1990s.* London: The Falmer Press.

———, ed. 2002. *Chicano school failure and success.* New York: Routledge.

———. 2010. *Dismantling contemporary deficit thinking: Educational thought and practice.* New York: Routledge.

Valenzuela, A. 1999. *Subtractive schooling: U.S.-Mexican youth and the politics of caring.* Albany: State University of New York.

Valle, V., and R. Torres. 2003. *Latino metropolis.* Minneapolis: University of Minnesota Press.

Vallens, V. M. 1978. *Working women in Mexico during the Porfiriato, 1880–1910.* San Francisco: R&E Research Associates.

Vargas, Z., and T. Paterson. 1999. *Major problems in Mexican American history.* London, UK: Houghton Mifflin College Division.

Varzally, A. 2008. *Making a non-white America: Californians coloring outside ethnic lines, 1925–1955.* Berkeley: University of California Press.

Vasconcelos, J. 1925[1997]. *La raza cosmica.* Trans. D. T. Jean. Baltimore: The Johns Hopkins University Press.

Vasquez, F. H., and R. Torres, eds. 2003. *Latino/a thought.* New York: Rowman & Littlefield.

Vaughn, B. 2005. Afro-Mexico: Blacks, indígenas, politics, and the greater diaspora. In *Neither enemies nor friends: Latinos, blacks, Afro-Latinos,* ed. A. Dzidzienyo and S. Oboler, pp. 117–135. New York: Palgrave Macmillan.

———. 2009. My blackness and theirs: Viewing Mexican blackness up close. In *Black Mexico: Race and society from colonial to modern times,* ed. B. Vinson and M. Restall, pp. 209–219. Albuquerque: University of New Mexico Press.

Velez-I., C. G. 1979. Ourselves through the eyes of an anthropologist. In *The Chicanos: As we see ourselves,* ed. A. Trejo. Tucson: University of Arizona Press.

———. 1983. *Bonds of mutual trust.* New Brunswick, NJ: Rutgers University Press.

———. 1996. *Border visions: Mexican cultures of the Southwest United States.* Tucson: University of Arizona Press.

———. 2010. *An impossible living in a transborder world: Culture, confianza, and economy of Mexican-origin populations.* Tucson: University of Arizona Press.

Vigil, E. 1999. *The crusade for justice: Chicano militancy and the government's war on dissent.* Madison: University of Wisconsin Press.

Vigil, J. D. 1974. *Early Chicano guerrilla fighters.* La Mirada, CA: Advanced Graphics.

———. 1978. Marx and Chicano anthropology. In *Chicano perspectives on decolonizing anthropology,* ed. S. F. Arvizu. Berkeley, CA: Tonatiuh International, Inc.

———. 1988. *Barrio gangs: Street life and identity in Southern California.* Austin: University of Texas Press.

———. 1990. Cholos and gangs: Culture change and street youth in Los Angeles. In *Gangs in America: Diffusion, diversity and public policy,* ed. R. Huff. Beverly Hills: Sage.

———. 1997. *Personas Mexicanas: Chicano high schoolers in a changing Los Angeles.* Ft. Worth, TX: Harcourt Brace.

———. 2001. Time, place, and history in the formation of Chicano identity. In *Many Americas: Critical perspectives on race, racism, ethnicity, and cultural identity,* ed. G. Campbell. Dubuque: Kendall/Hunt.

———. 2002. *Rainbow of gangs: Street cultures in the mega-city.* Austin: University of Texas Press.

———. 2003. Urban violence and street gangs. *Annual Review of Anthropology* 32: 225–242.

———. 2007. "The projects": Gang and non-gang families in East Los Angeles. Austin: University of Texas Press.

———. 2008. Barrio genealogy. *Journal of City and Community* 7(4): 366–371.

———. 2009. Community dynamics and the rise of street gangs. In *Latinos: Remaking America,* ed. M. Suarez-Orozco and M. Paez. Berkeley: University of California Press.

———. 2010. *Gang redux: A balanced anti-gang strategy.* Long Grove, IL: Waveland Press.

———. Forthcoming. Time, place, and history in the formation of Chicano identity. In *Many Americas: Perspectives on racism, ethnicity, and cultural identity,* ed. G. Campbell. Missoula: University of Montana Press.

Vigil, J. D., and G. Hanley. 2002. Chicano macrostructural identities and macrohistorical cultural forces. *Journal of Historical Sociology* 15(3): 395–426.

Vigil, J. D., and J. M. Long. 1981. Unidirectional or nativist acculturation?—Chicano
paths to school achievement. *Human Organization* 40(3): 273–277.

Vigil, J. D., and F. Lopez. 2004. Race and ethnic relations in Mexico. *Journal of Latino-
Latin American Studies* 1(2): 49–74.

Villa, R. 2000. *Barrio logos: Space and place in urban Chicano literature and culture*. Austin:
University of Texas Press.

Villarreal, A. 2010. Stratification by skin color in contemporary Mexico. *American Sociological Review* 75: 652–678.

Villarreal, J. A. 1970. *Pocho*. New York: Doubleday.

Wagley, C., and M. Harris. 1958. *Minorities in the New World*. New York: Columbia University Press.

Wallerstein, I. 1974. *The modern world-system: Capitalist agriculture and the origins of the
European world-economy in the sixteenth century*. New York: Academic Press.

Watt, A. J. 2010. *Farm workers and the churches: The movement in California and Texas*. College Station: Texas A&M University Press.

Weaver, T., ed. 1994. *Handbook of Hispanic cultures in the United States: Anthropology*.
Houston: Arte Publico Press.

Webb, W. P. 1935. *The Texas Rangers: A century of frontier defense*. Austin: University of
Texas Press.

Weber, D. J. 1973. *Foreigners in their native land*. Albuquerque: University of New Mexico Press.

———. 2009. *The Spanish frontier in North America*, the brief ed. New Haven, CT: Yale University Press.

Wolff, E. N. 1996. *Top heavy: The increasing inequality of wealth in America and what can be
done about it*. New York: Twentieth Century Fund, New Press.

Zavella, P. 1987. *Women's work & Chicano families: Cannery workers of the Santa Clara Valley*. Ithaca: University of Cornell Press.

Zeleny, C. 1974. *Relations between the Spanish-Americans and Anglo-Americans in New
Mexico*. New York: Arno Press.

Zentella, A. C. 2009. Latin@ languages and identities. In *Latinos: Remaking America*, ed. M.
Suarez-Orozco and M. Paez, pp. 321–338. Berkeley: University of California Press.

Zolov, E. 1999. *Refried Elvis: The rise of the Mexican counterculture*. Austin: University of
Texas Press.

CONCLUSION
THE CHICANO LEGACY

The Intersection of History and Culture Change

The immigrant story in America is for the most part a tale of success. Since the mid-nineteenth century one ethnic group after another has arrived in the U.S., poor and bedraggled. In addition to their initial poverty, they have confronted many barriers, some imposed by native U.S. citizens and others related to the immigrants' cultural and linguistic difficulties. With the passage of decades and one generation following another, and despite numerous obstacles, each ethnic group knocked down the barriers, persevered, and advanced. This will be no different for the Mexican people. The only difference is that it will take longer for them. Starting with a war of conquest that forced indigenous Mexicans to become incorporated into the United States, Mexican Americans, descendants of the conquest as well as those who have immigrated to the U.S. have faced challenging obstacles. Persistent racist attitudes, keyed to the more distinctive appearance of Mexicans, have been tough to overcome. But as the events of March 2006 demonstrate (discussed in chapter 10), it is a matter of time before another significant contact, conflict, and change phase is upon us. The spirit of the Chicano movement will pick up and live again (Montejano 2010).

A summary of the growth in complexity and historical development of the Chicano people leads to a discussion of the dynamics of sociocultural change. Throughout their long history, and the summary portraits for each period, various facets of culture change took center stage. Sometimes it was acculturation that characterized the period, a broad process upon initial contact between

311

two cultures in which change takes place in one or both cultures. When one of the cultures successfully dominated the interaction, the subordinate culture had little choice but to assimilate. More regularly, a syncretic amalgamation of cultures produced a new variant. In the modern period, a notion of cultural democracy or cultural pluralism came to the fore. It was a culture-change strategy that strove to incorporate various cultures and languages in a multilingual/multicultural orientation. Sometimes individuals or groups adopted this style by chance because of the nature of the culture-contact situation. More recently, government policies have attempted to help lead this democratizing effort (Beltran 2010), which, combined with large-scale immigration, continues to move Chicanos in the direction of Mexicanization.

Given the variations in change, what similarities bind the stages together? What differences separate them? How does the trajectory of Chicano culture change and history compare with that of other peoples? In short, the changes in each realm—socioeconomic (class), sociocultural (culture), and sociopsychological (color) are rooted in a world of those who have and those who have not (Gomberg-Munoz 2010; Barkin 1994). During the age of discovery and exploration, European states expanded into the lands of Third World peoples. This was the beginning of colonial rule, and the process of the expansion of some human energy systems to benefit a few at the expense of the many. Euroethnocentrism at its most extreme, malignant level ensured that indigenous populations would be subjected to a subordinate, inferior status and station. Class, cultural, and racial imperialism was practiced with impunity, and changes over the centuries never fully righted the inequity (Robinson 2004; Katzew and Deans-Smith 2009; Balandier 1966; Horowitz 1977).

When colonialism ended, neocolonialism took over, and so on with direct and indirect political control and various multitudinous forms of control. Through all these macroeconomic transformations and geopolitical realignments, the global economy emerged as the ultimate human energy system (Robinson 2004; Sassen 1991; Balibar and Wallerstein 1991; Sanderson 1995). Indigenous peoples transitioned from hunter-gatherers to sedentary farmers to peasant subjects, and in the modern period, many have entered into a mobile, migrant labor force. The world's resources and human labor became more tightly structured and regulated. Today, global networks are so connected that a change in one sector has repercussions in all sectors. One expert has even suggested that the next phase of this tightening has to involve thinking and planning for open and smoother ways of communication and cooperation in what he calls, "empathic consciousness" (Rifkin 2009).

These macrohistorical changes led to new macrostructural identities; even the resistance to these intrusions embodied a larger network, such as peasant revolts and movements or the establishment of immigrant human rights groups and the focus on related issues (Henderson 2011; Vargas 2007). The Chicano case is different from many others because it is sequential: one colonial structure was replaced by another, while a similar superordinate/subordinate relationship was retained. In each phase, a larger energy system materialized after struggles of various sorts and at different levels. Much of the ensuing ethnic conflict results from the disparity in wealth and resources. Whatever the general explanations for ethnic conflict—indeed, the condition can be traced from biblical times—it is clear that economic motives apply in this instance. In almost every major stage, colonization and native resistance to forced changes were based on economic factors. Either simultaneous to the conqueror's victory or immediately afterward, the effort to explain or rationalize the takeover occurred. This generally meant the creation and refinement of prejudicial attitudes and discriminatory behavior. The culture and race of the victor were established as superior and those of the vanquished as inferior (Ore 2010). Thus, the conqueror's feelings of guilt were averted because the natives were considered subhuman, a lower form of cultural and racial life. These beliefs and practices continue in the modern period in attenuated forms and meanings.

Structural Ideology

The social relations and cultural beliefs were the ideological glue that held these economic arrangements together (Andersen and Collins 1995). Adjustments and reactions to such oppressive systems have taken different turns. Some fought to preserve their way of life by cloaking resistance in cultural themes (Pedraza and Rumbaut 1996; Horowitz 1977). Others avoided forced change by limiting contact with the new overseers. Whatever reaction strategies were used (and there were many local adaptations), one factor stands out: accustomed to privileges and access to resources, some groups often discriminated against those less fortunate to maintain economic advantages (Telles and Ortiz 2008). Thus, discussions of *social* problems (poverty, crime, housing, education, and so on), *cultural* problems (linguistic, value, and belief barriers), *racial* problems (inferior treatment, institutional racism, prejudice, and discrimination), and *psychological* problems (inferiority and marginality based on social-cultural-racial factors) of low-income ethnic minorities are, in fact, generally about *economic-related* issues.

A historical assessment and understanding of the currents described above are necessary requisites in examining the social framework. Douglas Foley and coworkers (1977:48) write that "the notions of racial, cultural, and class superiority are so intertwined that they constitute one belief system." In many parts of the world, a "structural ideology" was created to preserve "structured inequalities." This ideology encompasses local, national, and international networks. According to Hewitt (1977), many of the world's ethnic struggles in the past were centered on these issues, causing over 10 million fatalities (in minor and major conflicts, from riots to extended wars) in the period from 1945 to 1970. The strife that presently characterizes the Middle East and some African countries clearly reflects similar underlying notions.

In the United States, as in many other countries, the ideology of oppression is in conflict with that of liberation. Southern and eastern Europeans in the past underwent a type of "structural ideological" oppression when they migrated to the United States. Their different "white" racial stock and cultural background barred them from wider opportunities. They also developed strategies similar to those used by Chicanos—cultural pluralism, assimilation, separatism, and direct action—to achieve social equality. The sociocultural life of many groups, both nationally and internationally, is affected by their powerless position and the ideological processes that keep them there. Thus, we must write "a history of the modern world in which we spell out the processes of power which created the present-day cultural systems and the linkages between them" (Wolf 1969:261).

In writing that history, we might discover that social problems revolve around the issue of "haves vs. have-nots." This macrolevel analysis provides a clearer insight into a number of conditions affecting Chicanos, including economic competition among the poor and the cumulative effects of oppression in which intragroup frictions derive from the colonial period and intergroup conflicts from the contemporary situation. However, "the study of culture change must take into account three orders of reality: the impact of the higher [dominant] culture; the substance of native life on which it is directed; and . . . change resulting from the reaction between the two cultures" (Malinowski 1945:26; see also Spicer 1962; Cockcroft 2010). A compounding factor in our macrohistorical and macrostructural analysis is how *time, place,* and *people* have varied through the centuries, adding nuances and contours to culture-change dynamics and reformulations. Both colonized and colonizer are affected by this. All the more reason for the student of change to heed Samuel Ramos's (1962) warning against over-romanticizing the native experience when there were so many extended and overlapping native experiences.

Sociocultural Change: The Sequence of Complexity

To understand the Chicano people, one must understand their history—to recognize that Chicanos have been shaped by a series of social systems. Each social system made its own imprint, adding a new and different piece to the complex mosaic that evolved under intense and strained culture change. The sequence was largely one of oppression and deprivation for the Chicano people. Thus, Chicano achievements, if they are to be fully assessed, must be measured in the context of a series of ruling elites who imposed their will on the people.

Close to five centuries of conditioned learning and relearning have inscribed certain patterns and traits into the Chicano character. It is a unique character, indeed, because of the variety of situations and changes. In some instances, no sooner were new customs learned than there was a new array of alterations. This history created a psychology of conquest, exploitation, and oppression in Mexico, and the process was repeated for the Chicanos in the United States (Cockcroft 2010; de Leon and Griswold del Castillo 2006). In addition, many ways of thinking and acting were shaped by reactions to the several types of contact-conflict-change sequences (Caso 2011; Beltran 2010). Most importantly, the people and the culture had changed, adapted, and survived. On the most culturally observable level, it was a passage of ethnic influences and linkages, from Indian to Spanish to Mexican to Anglo, each having had its impact. Changing macrostructural identities accompanied these developments. These big changes brought about overarching identities, as large groups of people were collapsed into one category (Beltran 2010; see Kearney 1996:174): Indians became peasants; peasants became immigrants.

It is also equally important that peoples learn the correct lessons from their setbacks in history (Balibar and Wallerstein 1991). In this context, some adaptive traits surfaced to aid survival, such as: (1) a strong tradition of productivity, although others have benefited from it; (2) a syncretic culture that is broad and deep and helps facilitate human interaction and understanding; (3) concern and support for family and friends in the face of adversity; (4) almost habitual striving for equality and justice; and (5) pride (recently rekindled) in the accomplishments of their indigenous forefathers. The persistence of Chicanos indicates that at least some correct answers have been learned. However, few would disagree that the Chicano community is also beset by a legacy of "wrong answers."

The Chicano community is a product of this history and broad macrostructural changes. Their original, relatively manageable local human energy system underwent a complex series of reorganizations associated with larger entities that gradually became global. This macrostructural experience is rooted in the indigenous landholding villages, which were transformed and reorganized by the Spanish into a peasantry more or less working the same land. Later descendants were uprooted completely and forced to migrate to modern service and industrial jobs. Quite a journey! The irony of indigenous peoples undergoing these changes under different European elites and mestizos and driven to reimmigrate to former ancestral lands (Aztlan) and be labelled "illegal aliens" cannot go unnoticed. As one pundit put it in his book titled, *Foreigners in their Native Land* (Weber 2003), the contradiction is obvious.

Such historical developments and macrostructural experiences have culminated in the present period, a time of heightened anti-immigrant hysteria. A people is both a product of what its forebears have undergone and a contributor to what its descendants will become, and the contemporary anti-Mexican climate in the U.S. will only make the Chicano people stronger. Not least, we have provided a framework for understanding the ways in which distinctive social and cultural patterns arose, thus clarifying the relationship between contemporary habits and their historical basis and avoiding the tendency of social scientists to assess minorities within a zero-time framework. However distant the link, the events of the past have always had an impact on the present (Caso 2011); put another way, to understand the present, one must back into the past.

Lessons from Each Stage: Continuity and Change

Something new was learned in each historical stage. Cultural revampments and the blending of traditions progressed through the centuries to create a rich cultural tapestry. The pre-Columbian period supplied the foundation for all that followed. Attachment to old lifeways, especially to certain egalitarian and familial practices, has persisted in attenuated form to the present. Foods that evolved during that period still comprise the staples of most Chicano households, and ancient motifs are prominent in the arts and folklore of the modern community. Most obvious in this indigenous heritage is the racial and physical appearance of a large portion of the Chicano people.

The arrival of the Spaniards began the colonial period. Under oppressive and exploitative conditions, the Mexican people endured 300 years of underdevelopment, with most becoming part of a macrostructural peasant category. Amassing Indians into the larger, more complicated economic system of Spanish colonial and other subsequent stages has had devastating effects. This is an inheritance that still affects many Chicanos' habits and beliefs. Overt racism and intraracial color preferences stemmed from this period and, together with a landholder–peon social relationship, continues to hinder egalitarian movements. Technological improvements were also introduced by the Spanish, as were the spiritual values of the Catholic Church (which at times ameliorated oppression), but the major legacy of the Spanish period was a social structure based on racial and class inequality. In addition, some of the most long lasting and deeply rooted cultural recombinations—e.g., the syncretic Mexican Catholic religious practices and ideology—stem from this time period.

Eventually and repeatedly there was a movement by some Mexicans to break free of this oppression. During the period of Mexican independence and nationalism, the people became more assertive and began to act on new insights. Chicanos still celebrate that independent spirit with annual Cinco de Mayo (Fifth of May) and Dieciseis de Septiembre (Sixteenth of September) parades, and the desire for control over their own destiny is reflected in the many community-action and political groups. However, old influences and habits tend to die hard. New ruling elite groups emerged, some recast from the old ones and others comprised of the new power brokers, to insist that former practices need not change so rapidly or completely. A strain between adhering to the old and adapting to the new resulted, and conflict arose between those trying to "keep the natives down" and the growing numbers of "disenfranchised workers fighting for autonomy."

While the Mexican people were in the throes of this awakening, the modern era was thrust on them. This period of time was doubly confusing; accommodating and integrating indigenous and Spanish heritages was made difficult by the imposition of a new (American) social order in the northern frontier areas, with its own set of expectations. The modern period also soon led to a reconstitution of peasants into immigrants, integrated into an even larger, denser economic system and a new macrostructural identity. The latter identity underwent permutations as it recast itself under intense and uneven cultural changes. Nevertheless, the early interactions and adjustments included experimentation with and learning of new patterns; increasing awareness of the influence of the old patterns; and a broader understanding and acceptance of a very complicated and convoluted multidimensional world. In the beginning, many were caught in the unusual dilemma of reconciling the unresolved problems of the indigenous and peasant identities and at the same time learning to integrate the new vistas of their externally imposed modern role as immigrants (Chavez 2008; Henderson 2011; Kearney 1996). With this dynamic, sometimes tumultuous mix, many experimented, learned from mistakes, and moved on in a never-ending cycle of resistance, protest, and organization. All of these activities and developments were accelerated in the United States. When more people immigrated in the aftermath of the 1910 Mexican Revolution (Slaviek 2011), bringing new ideas with them, the transition from peasant to immigrant was quickened. Eventually, a predominantly urban Chicano community flexed its political and economic muscles in the 1960s. Simultaneously, its rural component was also engaged in a militant assertion of economic rights. These developments continue today, but with the added impetus of even more immigrants clamoring for human rights (Cockcroft 2010; Caso 2011).

Contemporary Stage—Growing Awareness

As a result of events since the mid-1900s, Chicanos have reached a new plateau in which they can learn from previous stages and gain further insights into the complicated nature of a background of multiple cultural influences and macrostructural identities. However, they must not perceive each cultural antecedent or identity as separate, but rather they must incorporate all the experiences into one fabric; it is a variegated cloth of intragroup diversity (Beltran 2010). The present makeup of the population, in fact, reflects this diversity. For example, immigrants often come from Indian peasant communities as bilinguals from Mexico (i.e., speaking both a native language and Spanish) and quickly adjust to English, becoming trilinguals; this phenomenon has generally increased and expanded into various U.S cities and regions.

The Chicano population faces a hopeful, if potentially difficult, future. While past events have taken their toll, Chicanos have nonetheless gradually advanced. Because of their high birth rate and the steady flow of Mexican immigrants, they have become (with other Latinos) the nation's largest minority group; and significantly, the population now includes a critical mass of first-generation Mexicans. Moreover, the border region has taken on a life of its own, and the cultural and economic exchanges between Mexicans and Anglo-Americans in this region have increased such that many now refer to the region as MexAmerica (Alvarez 1995; Velez-I. 1996, 2010; Martinez 1996). Carlos Velez-I. (2010) points out the geopolitical significance of the region going back centuries, showing economic relations and political networks that existed before European contact.

However, the economic strains and political unrest in Mexico have begun to take center stage. NAFTA, "narcopolitics," Zapatistas in Chiapas, and the weakening of PRI (Institutional Revolutionary Party, which ruled Mexico from the 1920s until close to the early twenty-first century), and the rise of PAN (National Action Party, a conservative political group) are just a few of the crises that symbolize the turmoil and dissension of modern Mexico. Although some observers have suggested that Mexico is close to becoming a failed state, as turmoil and unrest characterize certain cities and regions where crime reigns and drug cartels have spread fear and terror, the Mexican government is struggling to maintain order. Meanwhile, the society has proven to be surprisingly resilient in the face of almost daily reports of gang-related atrocities. Even with this dire state, recent evidence has shown that jobs and education have improved, and thus the swell of immigration has subsided with more citizens selecting to stay and make a life in Mexico (Cave 2011). These developments coupled with a downturn in the American economy and the intensification of anti-immigration hysteria will continue to have a major impact on Chicanos/Mexicanos in the coming years, especially tempered by the dual citizenship that Mexican immigrants will enjoy.

The situation in Mexico and along the Mexican–U.S. border looms larger when taken alongside the continuing effort in the United States to organize other Spanish-speaking groups (Puerto Ricans, Cubans, Salvadorans, and other Latin Americans) into a Hispanic or Latino national network—especially since the current anti-immigrant (Latino) climate is helping close ranks among them. Despite historical-cultural differences among Latinos, this is considered a politically expedient goal, given some of the shared commonalities of colonized people. Moreover, the Western Hemisphere in general is becoming increasingly more vocal in pressuring the U.S. to tend to its own backyard (Raat 2010).

Geopolitical considerations and economic exchanges with Latin America will bolster the trend toward cultural democracy, even as the United States pragmatically acknowledges the importance of bilingual and multicultural

learning programs. Mexicanization has ensured the rise of ethnic consciousness, as Chicanos are becoming more accepting of and comfortable with their
racial and ethnic heritage. The prospects for participating more fully in American life are increased with this foundation of confidence and certainty, even
assertiveness. By the 2000s, for example, organizations and leaders were able
to increase naturalization rates and shepherd a higher voter turnout than in
earlier years. The 2008 election of President Obama is one indication that the
"Hispanic" vote has arrived, as Latino votes were critical to Obama's victory
in various states. To be sure, fuller participation puts Chicanos on the thresh-
old of realizing their political power and thus further strengthening their cultural rights. While such advances and inroads are significant, there is still

Poverty-stricken youth,
attracted to the illegal
drug trade, are arrested by
Mexican federal police.
Drugs are a problem on
both sides of the border.

room for improvement; for example, the educational performance of Chicanos still lags behind that of the majority population (Valencia 1991, 2008).

Beginning in the aftermath of World War II, there has been a steady increase of Chicanos in the middle-income sectors, a process that has gained even more headway since the 1980s. The accompanying mushrooming economic clout adds immeasurably to Chicanos' growing influence. Millionaires, entrepreneurs, business magnates, and national-level political leaders are more common today than at any time in the past. For many of these successful individuals and groups, it often happens that assimilation to the dominant culture goes hand-in-hand with socioeconomic mobility. This has been a choice for many, especially in earlier decades when some people equated Mexican culture with being poor. Today, however, because of the Mexicanization process, there are strong forces for culture and language retention. It appears that Chicanos/Mexicanos are increasingly opting for a bilingual/bicultural style and identity, an orientation that I have referred to as "personas mexicanas," the many faces of Mexicans (Vigil 1997). In short, feeling comfortable in drawing from multiple heritages in one's presentation of self is becoming more fashionable and practical. Some Chicano millionaires followed this strategy by establishing businesses catering to the culinary needs and cultural practices of their own ethnic group (e.g., the production of goods, hiring practices, etc.); Anglo-Americans along the border have tried to accommodate and mimic this orientation to capture the ethnic trade.

Whatever cultural route is taken, however, social mobility will undoubtedly expand, as a growing number of peasants-turned-immigrants and immigrants-turned-entrepreneurs strive to reach the American dream. Despite some activists' charges that having social aspirations translates into "selling out" your people, it is clear that Chicanos have tired of a life of scarcity and want. This is especially the case now, when the stigma of being Mexican has lessened, even in the throes of anti-immigrant hysteria. Many Chicanos feel that their time for power and influence has come. Thus, affluence is a much sought-after goal. However, affluence for many is a relative thing. Coming from an immigrant or peasant background, some families feel successful if they move out of the barrio and into a nearby tract home in a suburban area. Self-interest drives others to seek a much higher status and income. In contrast, some of these individuals have also elected to help advance the "causes" of Chicanos. Lest we forget, however, the gap between rich and poor in the United States has widened in the last 30 years, and Chicanos are still disproportionately represented in the lower-income sectors.

It is clear that when a higher income level is reached, more doors open—or are broken down. The civil-rights struggle has made a difference, even though tensions remain and few can rest on their laurels and allow the reversal of affirmative action. Many organizers and leaders of the 2006 march were old-line 1960s activists. Many race-based problems still persist. In the past, racial discrimination was blatantly practiced, and it still is in many different ways in various sections of the U.S. Relaxation of barriers has come faster in urban areas, at least in the sense that they are now subtle and covert or apply mostly to poorer people. Chicanos are slowly destroying many racial and cultural myths that have hindered their participation in mainstream America. Although they still have a long way to go, they continue to struggle—some publicly, others privately—to attain a level of parity in all areas of society.

Economic Forces and Human Expansion

The growing awareness associated with Chicano history and culture change must include the manner in which the economic sphere and its growth have dominated sociocultural features in each prior stage and the shift from one stage to the next. Each historical period has had a particular class-culture-color conformation, and each stage has terminated in a contact-conflict-change sequence. While all aspects of the sociocultural configuration are important, careful reading of Chicano history indicates clearly the priority of economic issues. This pattern appears in the current class, culture, color case.

Many Third World peoples, as well as ethnic minorities in the United States, have certain similarities with Chicanos because of the nature of the social-class system in most parts of the world (Harrison 1981). They share with Chicanos a history of exploitation of natural resources and human labor and also the propensity to fight for justice, human rights, and equality (Caso 2011). Who could argue with the fact that many indigenous peoples throughout the world have also undergone their own version of macrostructural identity transformations? Or that they will eventually join the tides of human migration presently enveloping the world (Robinson 2004; Cockcroft 2010)?

A brief review of all the historical stages reveals that certain attitudes and characteristics remain to this day. Basic human needs were thwarted at the beginning, and hopes and aspirations for improvements went unmet or only partially fulfilled. Forced labor, loss of land, and inadequate incomes still cause malnutrition and other physical suffering. Moreover, economic exploitation has resulted in a growing sense of emotional and status deprivation (Wolf 1969, 1982). Gross inequality on the basis of class and color was mitigated by the spread of Enlightenment philosophy in the late eighteenth century, but discrimination diminished only slightly (Ore 2010; Katzew and Deans-Smith 2009; Sue 2003). The struggle for independence continued into twentieth-century Mexico (Slaviek 2011; Cockcroft 1990), but for most people the sketchily conceived and unevenly implemented reforms have meant little. These people remain subject to colonial influences even as they strive to break free (Stoler and Cooper 1996); witness the Zapatista revolt of 1994 by Maya peasants. However, continued and more sophisticated resistance offers hope for the future. A question of growing concern is the volatile, almost lawless situation in Mexico where turmoil and unrest, coupled with the potential unraveling of an economic and political system, almost certainly have pushed many Mexican people to migrate back to their ancestral homeland (Aztlan), territory that was taken away from them by the U.S. government in the early- and late-nineteenth century (Henderson 2011). This migration can both aid and hinder Chicano/Mexicano advancements in the United States.

In the United States, exposure to a modern urban industrial system uncovered a host of new realities, as many of the resultant problems often matched and paralleled some of the worst features of earlier periods (Vargas 2007; Handlin 1951; Yinger 1994; Walch 1994). This involved not just unfortunate working conditions but a nearly total disenfranchisement of the worker in the economy (Gomberg-Munoz 2010). Even the increased Chicano awareness resulting from independence could not fully comprehend or integrate all these transformations in the first phases of the modern period. Nevertheless, a persistent and socially conscious method of resistance arose. Many adaptive strategies were used to ensure individual and group preservation. In a wide-ranging reaction to change, Chicanos fought, retreated, regrouped, organized, and demonstrated (Gomez-Quinones 1990; Garcia and Castro 2011). They took various paths of national integration—assimilation, acculturation, cultural pluralism, and separatism, for example (Beltran 2010). Because of the range of cultural influences and regional differences both in Mexico and the U.S. Southwest, the adjustment and adaptation could not merely be gauged on the basis of generational change (i.e., first, second, and so on), for time and place in one's background figured prominently in the tempo and style of Americanization (Telles and Ortiz 2008; Vigil 1997). For example, the contrast between rural and urban populations or the political contexts for immigrants in the 1920s as opposed to the 2000s affected the choice of cultural integration strategies. The Chicano experience in the United States is further underscored by participation in the fight for labor unions and better schools (Garcia and Castro 2011) and the dual effects of the 1910 Mexican Revolution and immigration. These effects include ongoing cultural regeneration and increased activism for ethnic and human rights and a strengthening of ideological influences for a more just society (Caso 2011).

Legacies of the Past: Patterns and Problems

Most of the social patterns outlined below evolved through several stages of change and major wars with other ethnic groups, an inheritance that compounds the problems of modern Chicanos. This complicated, interwoven experience of long duration is the backdrop for any discussion of poverty, educational attainment, social mobility, cultural marginality, social and racial inferiority, and a host of other personal and group problems. Many of these problems are compounded by persisting intragroup dynamics (e.g., Spanish racism toward Indians reflected in attitudes among Mexicans) in competition with intergroup realities (e.g., Anglo racism toward Mexicanos [both Spanish and Indians, and admixtures thereof]) that coexist side by side.

In the growth and enlargement of human energy systems, socioeconomic adaptations went hand in hand with other sociocultural changes in Chicano history. The family, education, religion, and other institutions have undergone a monumental upheaval in each stage, as the contact-conflict-change case of the twenty-first century shows. As noted previously, many surviving customs and traits were positive and beneficial. However, language and cultural values have been subjected to intense pressures. Individuals and groups either resisted accommodation to the dominant culture and fought for preservation of native traditions or synthesized a compromise. These transformations have shaped a pattern that largely reflects a lower socioeconomic lifestyle. A closer examination of this pattern will be made only to dramatize the debilitating nature of a life of scarcity, for many Chicanos have reached middle- and upper-income levels by using positive adaptation strategies.

Today, the continuing immigration of Mexicans (and other Latinos, as well as many Asian groups) is creating a critical mass in some U.S. cities and regions to threaten the once dominant Anglo population. Most of the newcomers are part of the poor or low-income sector. Importantly, it is economic concerns that drive both immigration as well as the anti-immigration hysteria. At the cultural level, intragroup variances and contrasts muddle the picture, as generational change through the decades has resulted in different cultural styles among Chicanos and Mexicanos (Telles and Ortiz 2008). No one knows where the cultural center (or amalgamation thereof!) is anymore in this constantly shifting and repeatedly redefined population. Although the fact that nearly one-half of Mexicans in the United States are first generation has made being Mexican both true and popular, economic competition and jockeying for the upper hand is nevertheless taking place at intragroup and intergroup levels in this cultural cauldron.

Historically, Chicanos have experienced a sense of inferiority and marginality. Racial and cultural imperialism supported the system of economic imperialism. Feelings of racial and cultural inferiority and marginality stem from both the Spanish and Anglo-American systems (Sue 2003). Many other examples of a similar legacy of "prejudice" are found throughout the world (Ore 2011; Brown 1995). Making people feel inferior because of how they look, speak, and/or act is clearly a mechanism to keep them socially immobile (Essed 1991). An additional handicap is the establishment of social norms that keep those who are racially and culturally different marginal to most of society's groups and institutions. They are caught between different social worlds (Andersen and Collins 1995). Therefore, the sharp and heated conflict between groups produces a marginal zone where sociopsychological ambiguities and anxieties arise (Stonequist 1937). Several human dimensions are part of this experience. Thus, a cultural identity can withstand the pressures of change up to a point but can be fractured and broken as well (Leon-Portilla 1990). Economic marginality is closely linked to this problem.

An analysis of the cultural transformations under the Spanish and, later, the Anglos offers an example of this and underscores the similarities between the colonial and modern experiences, especially when race is factored in (Katzew and Deans-Smith 2009). In short, one can view it as a nested evolution of culture and race relations. Spaniards (Anglos) neither accommodated nor appreciated Indian (Mexican) culture. Almost without exception, the subordinate culture adopted the culture of the aggressor. As a result, cultural change was largely the glorification of Spanish (Anglo) culture and the destruction of Indian (Mexican) culture. Despite this pressure to assimilate dominant ways, however, many natives took the creative approach of amalgamating their culture with that of the dominant group. Thus, they innovated a new cultural style: Mexican (Chicano), a blend of Spanish (Anglo) and Indian (Mexican) elements (Ore 2009).

Some natives came to feel inferior because of this process. Other factors added to the burden: (1) They could not adjust to the Spanish (Anglo) mode; (2) The Spanish (Anglos) did not want them anyway; and (3) They were unable to fit into the new syncretist Mexican (Chicano) culture. Lacking a definite strategy of adaptation, many became marginal to all three cultures—the dominant, subordinate, and syncretist versions.

Racism compounded these problems (Katzew and Deans-Smith 2009; van den Berghe 1967). Eventually, race became a passport to social mobility, with Indian (Mexican) features effectively barring social advancement (Brown 1995). A further complicating factor was the rise of the hybrid, mestizo race. This phenomenon created an interesting situation, particularly since Indians were considered inferior to the Spanish. Many mestizos, especially those who looked Spanish, followed the racist colonial ideology; many Indians followed this strategy by "passing" as mestizos. They attempted to change racial membership and thereby gain wider socioeconomic opportunities. Sometimes the goal included intermarriage with someone from the superior group. In the modern period, there is increasing intermarriage of Anglos and Mexicans, adding another touch to the mestizo tradition. Although feelings of inferiority or socioracial passing are still prevalent, it appears that a more confident and accepting attitude is emerging to underscore recent improvements in self-image. Notwithstanding these advances, and to reiterate, racism has generated a pronounced impact on almost every single facet of Chicano life (Menchaca 2001, 1993; Lopez 2009).

A whole series of other characteristics and habits stem from economic considerations, some firmly entrenched in the minds of observers and others bordering on speculation. For example, the "underclass" notion of William J. Wilson (1987) is in many ways an extension of Oscar Lewis's idea of the "culture of poverty" (Lewis 1959). Both of these explanations have been applied to Chicanos (and other ethnic minorities, mainly African Americans) who have experienced persistent and concentrated poverty. In large part, the explanation focuses on the customs and values that are passed from one generation to the next under situations of poverty and want. One of the main findings of Edward Telles and Vilma Ortiz's (2008) restudy of informants in the Mexican American study project of the 1960s is that "generations of exclusion" mark the lives of their descendants. Although critics have questioned the use of such an "omnibus" construct to explain the life of the poor (Moore and Pinderhughes 1993; Leacock 1971), it is a condition that must be addressed because there are segments of the Chicano population that are mired in poverty. Currently, the indices of poverty are very high among them—e.g., income, housing, education, and so on. Some writers have suggested that the "working poor" is a more apt characterization, particularly with the "self-created" jobs fashioned by many immigrants.

Poverty is often associated with other social problems, such as the high incidence of deviance and crime. Among the poor, illicit and informal economies are known to aid survival. Drug trafficking, drug use and abuse, crime, dropping out of school, and gangs, among other problems, are also clearly reflective of the current Chicano urban condition. Accordingly, if such behavior is to be eliminated, the process must begin with an economy that integrates the poor and marginal segments of our cities. Research suggests that lower-class and marginal groups often are forced to follow deviant paths to success, such as the drug market (Moore 1991; Moore et al. 1978).

Old customs were also transformed by this history of culture change. In retrospect, the somewhat more egalitarian social practices of the indigenous period were subjected to negative alternations. Two examples will suffice, one on communalism and the other on gender relations, because they seem to be regularly mentioned by modern Chicanos. Envidia (envy) is often pointed out as one of the stumbling blocks that prevents Chicanos from helping each other and getting ahead. While indigenous times were less than perfect, it is clear that cooperation and a communal spirit prevailed then; and in many instances, it still does. Obviously, an economy based on agriculture benefits from this arrangement. In the changes since, particularly during peasantization, cooperative customs were joined by a competitive orientation. This is not an exclusively Chicano quality; it affects the poor generally. George Foster (1967:305) suggests in his theory of "limited good" that "if 'Good' exists in limited amounts which cannot be expanded, and if the system is closed, it follows that an individual or a family can improve a position only at the expense of others." It appears that the process of underdevelopment has encouraged envidia in the Chicano people. During the movements of the 1960s, for example, there was great rivalry and dissension among leaders and groups, regardless of the merits of the idea or program. Perhaps it is envidia that beclouds the senses, making people call one another "Tio Taco," or traitor, without considering their worthiness or honesty.

In gender attitudes and relations, the machismo syndrome is yet another example of the corruption of a trait under conditions of poverty (Ore 2010). Machismo has a positive aspect: Males learn to protect family and home and become disciplined, responsible providers, as they once did during earlier times and still do under the supervision of mothers and sisters who value a strong, worthy person (Mirande 1997). Because of the oppressive conditions that have befallen so many Chicanos, however, there is also a negative result, especially in the context of how females lost status and were devalued in the process of these changes. Many males seek an outlet through the indiscriminate sexual conquest of females (following the lead of the Spanish, and later mestizos), with the aim of lowering females' status; escape from reality through alcohol and drug use; and fight and even kill each other for relatively minor reasons. Both Spanish and Anglo-American oppressive experiences contributed to this propensity. Indeed, it may be a way (however unfortunate) for the downtrodden to relieve negative energy and create outlets for their anxieties and frustrations.

Residue of Centuries of History

If it is true that "differences in culture—tribal, peasant, civilizational—provide different modes whereby individual personalities acquire cultural identity" (King 1974:107), then it is equally correct that a cumulative effect pertains for a culture that has undergone a relatively rapid transition. It also is the case that this transition transversed through four cultural imprints, two major wars, and three macrostructural identities. A series of identities in contrasting places and at many levels is what characterizes this complicated history. Currently, Chicanos are still thinking about and discussing what the nature of this identity would be (Beltran 2011; Hurtado and Gurin 2004). It might be wise to begin to embrace all of the influences and antecedents as a starting point. A multilingual and multicultural foundation of this sort would provide the wellspring for shifting identities or a hierarchy of identities, instead of just "one self per person" (Vigil 1997; Telles and Ortiz 2008). With the expansion of human energy systems and the incorporation of a large portion of the human population within these dense networks, the clashes and comminglings of cultures and languages are upon us (Rifkin 2009). Chicanos already have some understanding of what this entails, and they appear poised to act on it. The orientation and identity taken by those individuals and groups that feel constricted depend on these key factors: the people, the time, and the place (see Vigil 1995, 1998).

The residue of this complex cultural history remains in the Chicano people. In fact, in some ways the array of cultural styles is still with us, as literally tens of thousands of indigenous peoples today make their way from peasantry to the modern world in the United States, following old paths or charting new ones as they join older generations. Still, many suffer emotional conflict and anguish because of past and present conditions. Minimally, this book has addressed the root causes of this background to explain how the attitudes and behaviors of the people were shaped. The next step is to begin an examination of how these thoughts and habits might be revamped and reordered.

There is also a positive side to the Chicano legacy: the ability to survive by fashioning syncretic adaptive strategies to many changing conditions (Velez-I. 2010). This is the Chicano's core strength and is reminiscent of the Mexican adage, "From bad comes good." Knowing different cultures and languages, and amalgamations thereof, certainly outfits a person better for this complex, ever changing world (Ramirez 1985; Vigil 1997). The work ethic is still intact, the spirit strong, and a hope and optimism for an improved future predominates among the people. On the practical side, growing numbers and increasing political clout, fortified and motivated by a pride in ethnic awareness, will translate into a formidable force for change and empowerment.

References

Alvarez, R. R., Jr. 1995. The Mexican-US border: The making of an anthropology of the borderlands. *Annual Review of Anthropology* 24: 1–24.

Andersen, M. L., and P. H. Collins. 1995. *Race, class, and gender*. Belmont, CA: Wadsworth.

Balandier, G. 1966. The colonial situation: A theoretical approach. In *Social change: The colonial situation*, ed. I. Wallerstein. New York: John Wiley & Sons.

Balibar, E., and I. Wallerstein. 1991. *Race, nation, class: Ambiguous identities*. London: Verso.

Barkin, D. 1994. *Distorted development*. Boulder, CO: Westview Press.

Beltran, C. 2010. *The trouble with unity: Latino politics and the creation of identity*. New York: Oxford University Press.

Brown, R. 1995. *Prejudice*. Oxford: Blackwell.

Caso, M. 2011. Invisible and voiceless: The struggle of Mexican Americans for recognition, justice, and equality. Bloomington: i.Universe.com.

Cave, D. 2011. Better lives for Mexicans cut allure of going north. *New York Times*. July 6, A 1, 8–9.

Chavez, L. R. 2008. *The Latino threat: Constructing immigrants, citizens, and the nation*. Stanford, CA: Stanford University Press.

Cockcroft, J. D. 1990. *Mexico class formation, capital accumulation, and the state*. New York: Monthly Review Press.

de Leon, A., and Griswold del Castillo, R. 2006. *North to Aztlan: A history of Mexican Americans in the United States*. Wheeling, IL: Harlan Davidson.

Cockcroft, J. D. 2010. *Mexico's revolution then and now*. New York: Monthly Review Press.

Essed, P. 1991. *Understanding everyday racism*. Newbury Park, CA: Sage.

Foley, D. E., et al. 1977. *From peones to politicos: Ethnic relations in a South Texas town, 1900 to 1977*. Austin: University of Texas, Center for Mexican American Studies.

Foster, G. 1967. Peasant society and the image of limited good. In *Peasant society: A reader*, eds. J. M. Potter, M. N. Diaz, and G. M. Foster. Boston: Little, Brown.

Garcia, M. T., and S. Castro. 2011. *Blowout!: Sal Castro and the Chicano struggle for educational justice*. Chapel Hill: The University of North Carolina Press.

Gomberg-Munoz, R. 2010. *Labor and legality: An ethnography of a Mexican immigrant network*. New York: Oxford University Press.

Gomez-Quinones, J. 1990. *Chicano politics: Reality and promise, 1940–1990*. Albuquerque: University of New Mexico Press.

Handlin, O. 1951. *The uprooted*. New York: Grossett & Dunlap.

Harrison, P. 1981. *Inside the Third World: The anatomy of poverty*. New York: Penguin.

Henderson, T. J. 2011. *Beyond borders: A history of Mexican migration to the United States*. Malden: Wiley-Blackwell.

Hewitt, C. 1977. Majorities and minorities: A comparative survey of ethnic violence. In *The annals of the American academy of political and social science*, vol. 433, ed. M. O. Heisler.

Horowitz, D. L. 1977. Cultural movements and ethnic change. In *The annals of the American academy of political and social science*, vol. 433, ed. M. O. Heisler.

Hurtado, A., and P. Gurin. 2004. *Chicana/o identity in changing U.S. society*. Tucson: University of Arizona Press.

Katzew, I. and Deans-Smith, S. 2009. *Race and classification: The case of Mexican America*. Stanford: Stanford University Press.

Kearney, M. 1996. *Reconceptualizing peasantry*. Boulder, CO: Westview Press.

King, A. R. 1974. A stratification of labyrinths: The acquisition and retention of cultural identity in modern culture. In *Social and cultural identity: Problems of persistence and change*, ed. T. K. Fitzgerald. Athens: Southern Anthropological Society, University of Georgia Press.

Leacock, E. B., ed. 1971. *The culture of poverty: A critique*. New York: Simon & Schuster, Inc.

Leon-Portilla, M. 1990. *Endangered cultures*. Dallas: Southern Methodist University Press.

Lewis, O. 1959. *Five families: Mexican case studies in the culture of poverty*. New York: Basic Books.

Lopez, N. 2008. Antiracist pedagogy and empowerment in a bilingual classroom in the U.S., circa 2006. *Theory into Practice* 47(1): 43–50.

Malinowski, B. 1945. *The dynamics of culture change*. New Haven, CT: Yale University Press.

Martinez, O. 1996. *U.S.-Mexico borderlands: Historical and contemporary perspectives*. Wilmington, DE: Scholarly Resources.

Menchaca, M. 1993. Chicano Indianism: A historical account of racial repression in the United States. *American* 20(3): 583–603.

———. 2001. *Recovering history, constructing race: The Indian, black, and white roots of Mexican Americans*. Austin: University of Texas Press.

Mirande, A. 1997. *Hombes y machos: Masculinity and Latino Culture*. Boulder, CO: Westview Press.

Montejano, D. 2010. *Quixote's soldiers: A local history of the Chicano movement, 1966–1981*. Austin: University of Texas Press.

Moore, J. W. 1991. *Going down to the barrio*. Philadelphia: University of Temple Press.

Moore, J. W., et al. 1978. *Homeboys: Gangs, drugs, and prisons in the barrios of Los Angeles*. Philadelphia: Temple University Press.

Moore, J. W., and R. Pinderhughes, eds. 1993. *In the barrios: Latinos and the underclass debate.* New York: Russell Sage Foundation.

Ore, T. 2010. *The social construction of difference and inequality: Race, class, gender and sexuality.* Columbus: McGraw-Hill Humanities.

Pedraza, S., and R. Rumbaut, eds. 1996. *Origins and destinies: Immigration, race, and ethnicity in America.* Belmont, CA: Wadsworth.

Raat, W. D. 2010. *Mexico and the United States: Ambivalent vistas.* Athens: University of Georgia Press.

Ramirez, M., III. 1985. *Psychology of the Americas: Mestizo perspective on personality and mental health.* New York: Pergamon Press.

Ramos, S. 1962. *Profile of man and culture in Mexico.* Austin: University of Texas Press.

Rifkin, J. 2009. *The empathic civilization: The race to global consciousness in a world in crisis.* New York: Jeremy P. Tarcher/Penguin.

Robinson, W. I. 2004. *A Theory of global capitalism: Production, class, and state in a transnational world.* Baltimore, MD: Johns Hopkins University Press.

Sanderson, S. E. 1995. *Civilizations and world systems: Studying world- historical change.* Thousand Oaks, CA: AltaMira Press.

Sassen, S. 1991. *The global city.* Princeton: Princeton University Press.

Slaviek, L. C. 2011. *The Mexican Revolution.* New York: Chelsea House.

Spicer, E. 1962. *Cycles of conquest.* Tucson: University of Arizona Press.

Stoler, A. L., and F. Cooper, eds. 1996. *Tensions of empire: Colonial cultures in a bourgeois world.* Berkeley: University of California Press.

Stonequist, E. V. 1937. *The marginal man.* New York: Russell & Russell.

Sue, D. W. 2003. *Overcoming our racism: The journey to liberation.* San Francisco: Jossey-Bass.

Telles, E. E., and V. Ortiz. 2008. *Generations of exclusion: Mexican Americans, Assimilation, and Race.* New York: Russell Sage Foundation.

Valencia, R. R., ed. 1991. *Chicano school failure and success: Research and policy agendas for the 1990s.* London: The Falmer Press.

———. 2008. *Chicano students and the courts: The Mexican American legal struggle for educational equality.* New York: New York University Press.

van den Berghe, P. L. 1967. *Race and racism: A comparative perspective.* New York: John Wiley & Sons.

Vargas, Z. 2007. *Labor rights are civil rights: Mexican American workers in twentieth-century America.* Princeton: Princeton University Press.

Velez-I., C. G. 1996. *Border visions: Mexican cultures of the Southwest.* Tucson: University of Arizona Press.

———. 2010. *An impossible living in a transborder world: Culture, confianza, and economy of Mexican-origin populations.* Tucson: University of Arizona Press.

Vigil, J. D. 1995. Que viva la raza: The Many faces of the Chicano movement. In *Origins and Destinies: Immigration, race and ethnicity in America,* ed. S. Pedraza and R. D. Rumbaut. Belmont, CA: Wadsworth.

———. 1997. *Personas Mexicanas: Chicano high schoolers in a changing Los Angeles.* Ft. Worth, TX: Harcourt Brace.

———. 1998. Time, place, and history in the formation of Chicano identity. In *Many Americas: Critical perspectives on race, racism, and ethnicity,* ed. G. Campbell. Dubuque: Kendall/Hunt.

Walch, T., ed. 1994. *Immigrant America.* New York: Garland.

Weber, D. J., ed. 2003. *Foreigners in their native land: Historical roots of the Mexican Americans*, rev. ed. Albuquerque: University of New Mexico Press.

Wilson, W. J. 1987. The truly disadvantaged. Chicago: University of Chicago Press.

Wolf, E. 1969. *Peasant wars of the twentieth century.* New York: Harper & Row.

———. 1982. *Europe and the people without history.* Berkeley: University of California Press.

Yinger, M. 1994. *Ethnicity: Source of strength? Source of conflict?* Albany: State University of New York Press.

INDEX

PHOTO CREDITS